T0305218

IN GOLD WE TRUST

✳

In Gold We Trust

Social Capital and Economic Change

in the Italian Jewelry Towns

✱

Dario Gaggio

PRINCETON UNIVERSITY PRESS

PRINCETON AND OXFORD

Library of Congress Cataloging-in-Publication Data

Gaggio, Dario, 1966–
In gold we trust : social capital and economic change in the Italian
jewelry towns / Dario Gaggio.
p.   cm.
Includes bibliographical references and index.
ISBN-13: 978-0-691-12697-5 (hardcover : alk. paper)
ISBN-10: 0-691-12697-6 (hardcover : alk. paper)
1. Jewelry trade—Italy, Northern. 2. Gold industry—Italy, Northern. 3. Social capital
(Sociology)—Italy, Northern. 4. Valenza (Italy)—Economic conditions. 5. Vicenza (Italy)—
Economic conditions. 6. Arezzo (Italy)—Economic conditions. 7. Valenza (Italy)—Social
conditions. 8. Vicenza (Italy)—Social conditions. 9. Arezzo (Italy)—Social conditions. I. Title.
HD9747.I83N674 2007
338.4'773927—dc22
2006019002

British Library Cataloging-in-Publication Data is available

This book has been composed in Palatino

Printed on acid-free paper. ∞

pup.princeton.edu

Printed in the United States of America

1   3   5   7   9   10   8   6   4   2

"From now on, I'll describe the cities to you," the Khan had said, "in your journeys you will see if they exist."

But the cities visited by Marco Polo were always different from those thought of by the emperor.

"And yet I have constructed in my mind a model city from which all possible cities can be deducted," Kublai said. "It contains everything corresponding to the norm. Since the cities that exist diverge in varying degree from the norm, I need only foresee the exceptions to the norm and calculate the most probable combinations."

I have also thought of a model city from which I deduce all the others," Marco answered. "It is a city made only of exceptions, exclusions, incongruities, contradictions. If such a city is the most improbable, by reducing the number of abnormal elements, we increase the probability that the city really exists. So I have only to subtract exceptions from my model, and in whatever direction I proceed, I will arrive at one of the cities which, always as an exception, exist. But I cannot force my operation beyond a certain limit: I would achieve cities too probable to be real."

—Italo Calvino, *Invisible Cities*
(translation by William Weaver, 1974)

✳ *Contents* ✳

✳ *Tables* ✳

✳ Preface ✳

The status of modern Italian studies in American culture is something of a paradox. In debates about democracy, Italy simultaneously represents two distinct and seemingly incompatible "others." On the one hand, the northern and central regions of the peninsula supposedly reenact Tocquevillian scenarios of thriving social networks and grassroots democracy. Political scientist Robert Putnam has chosen the small cities of Emilia and Tuscany as the embodiment of civic virtue, and as symbols of a world of political participation that American society is on the verge of losing forever. According to Putnam, northern and central Italians make democracy work by relying on their social capital, that is, networks of associations and relations of trust and reciprocity that originated in the medieval communes.[1] To many other Americans, by contrast, Italian politics epitomize corruption and clientelism. Here the south of Italy is usually involved. But despite their historically rooted differences, the "clean hands" scandal of 1992–93 united Milan, Rome, and Naples in one overarching picture of political backwardness and decadence. By the mid-1990s, Italy arguably confirmed Mancur Olson's insights into the relationship between coalitions, democracy, and economic development.[2] Fifty years of Christian Democratic rule and the resilience of traditional local societies had led to the establishment of diffuse networks of clientelistic ties and to the transformation of politicians and entrepreneurs into rent-seeking vultures. The vitality of Italy's civil society, then, seems to explain both progress and backwardness, civic virtue and political vice, and—by way of comparison—America's loss of "social capital" and its unchallenged role as the moral paradigm of modernity.

The role of Italy in debates about industrialization is just as paradoxical. Until the 1970s, Italy was widely regarded as a minor case in the

---

[1] Robert Putnam with Robert Leonardi and Raffaella Nannetti, *Making Democracy Work: Civic Traditions in Modern Italy* (Princeton, 1993). See also Robert Putnam, "Bowling Alone: America's Declining Social Capital," *Journal of Democracy* 6 (1995): 65–78.

[2] Mancur Olson, *The Rise and Decline of Nations: Economic Growth, Stagflation, and Social Rigidities* (New Haven, 1982).

history of Western modernization—a deviation from the northern European and American model dependent on state intervention and institutional substitutive factors.[3] Then social scientists began to focus their attention on the economic wonders of towns like Modena, Prato, and Vicenza, which had grown prosperous by promoting localized networks of specialized small and medium-size firms. These northern and central Italian towns have since assumed iconic status among sociologists, organization theorists, geographers, and other social scientists. Now provincial Italy became the site of a form of capitalism with a human face, at once traditional in its reliance on family ties and the bonds of locality, and innovative in its flexibility and responsiveness to market changes. The bottom-up social construction of the market replaced top-down state intervention as the dominant explanatory mechanism for Italy's recent economic change.

But this newer emphasis on local economic change is not devoid of ambiguities. According to some scholars, Italy's clusters of small and medium-size firms epitomize a distinctive and highly efficient path to modernity. Michael Piore and Charles Sabel, among others, have pointed to these experiences as the harbingers of the post-Fordist industrial order, based on cooperation and competition between flexibly specialized producers better equipped than multidivisional corporations to take advantage of increasingly unstable and diverse global markets.[4] Other scholars, by contrast, have exposed the dark side of Italian small-scale industrialization by focusing on the practices of tax evasion, labor exploitation, and gender discrimination that give the Italian firms their competitive edge in a number of industries. Anthropologist Michael Blim, for example, views the Italian districts of small firms as instances of industrial restructuring taking place at the semi-periphery of the increasingly coercive world capitalist order, which he

---

[3] The most influential interpretation of Italy's industrialization as a "late comer" was proposed by Alexander Gerschenkron, *Economic Backwardness in Historical Perspective* (Cambridge, Mass., 1962).

[4] Michael Piore and Charles Sabel, *The Second Industrial Divide* (New York, 1984). The literature in English about the Italian flexibly specialized systems of small firms that followed Piore and Sabel's study is vast. See at least the following collections of essays: Edward Goodman and Julia Bamford, eds., *Small Firms and Industrial Districts in Italy* (London, 1989); and Frank Pyke, Giacomo Becattini, and Werner Sengenberger, eds., *Industrial Districts and Inter-Firm Cooperation in Italy* (Geneva, 1990).

calls "the global factory."[5] These clusters' flexibility seems to point both to a future of untapped possibilities for prosperity in more equal social contexts, and to a lingering past of precarious development and exploitative practices. Finally, over the last few years the drastic slowing down of economic growth and increasing competition from southern and eastern Asia in a variety of manufacturing sectors have given rise to another layer of interpretations, which point to Italy's impending decline due to the "dwarfism" of its industrial base.[6] Celebrated until very recently as the healthy backbone of the national economy, clusters of small firms are now viewed (again) as a symptom of Italy's relative backwardness in the global economy.

This study intends to bridge these seemingly incompatible interpretations of Italian modernity—both political and economic—by applying the tools of historical analysis to a case of development based on clusters of specialized small businesses, that is, gold jewelry production. In Italy this industry is concentrated in three towns: Valenza Po in Piedmont, Vicenza in the Veneto, and Arezzo in Tuscany. Each town specialized in somewhat different segments of the market, and each exhibited a different economic and political structure. In each town economic action was embedded in networks of political and social ties rooted in historical patterns of political negotiations between the local elites, their communities, and the state. But these towns also share several traits: an interweaving of formal and informal arrangements; the problematic construction of traditions of craftsmanship; and the uneasy coexistence of universalistic conceptions of democratic representation and practices of personal and discretionary power. From the early 1960s on, these towns grew into world leaders in the production and export of gold jewelry. By the early 1980s, Italy produced and exported more gold jewelry than all the other European countries combined, and in the early 1990s the jewelry industry ranked fourth in the Italian export statistics.

---

[5] Michael Blim, *Made in Italy: Small-Scale Industrialization and Its Consequences* (New York, 1990). Blim generalized his findings in "Economic Development and Decline in the Emerging Global Factory: Some Italian Lessons," *Politics and Society* 18 (1990): 143–64. For another critical view of the Italian industrial districts of small firms, viewed as largely exploitative and discriminatory structures, see Ash Amin, "Flexible Specialization and Small Firms in Italy: Myths and Reality," *Antipode* 21 (1989): 13–34.

[6] For a thoughtful review of the discourse on Italy's decline, see Gianni Toniolo and Vincenzo Visco, eds., *Il Declino Economico dell'Italia: Cause e Rimedi* (Milan, 2004).

This remarkable success was the product of contradictory, sometimes even puzzling, processes. Hierarchical relations of patronage coexisted with vibrant class mobilization; the openness of the local piazzas and bars, where information about styles and techniques flowed freely, coexisted with the secrecy of gold smuggling, illegal homework, and tax evasion; and cooperation between producers within special-purpose institutions coexisted with often ruthless competition in the marketplace. The citizens of the jewelry towns celebrated the trust they felt for one another and yet shared a passion for elaborate mutual betrayal; they engaged in forms of cooperation both along and across class lines, and yet never tired of complaining about their neighbors' irreducible individualism; they wove the ties of a thriving civil society replete with civic associations, political clubs, and local institutions, while shrouding their activities in secrecy and double-dealings.

Both the admirers and the critics of northern Italy's small-scale capitalism have often ignored these contradictions, trying instead to capture the essence of "Italian capitalism" or "Italian democracy," and forcing their evidence into neat narratives of success or failure, progress or decline, exemplary political conduct or corruption. The way out of the pitfalls of essentialism is the realization that modernity is a relational experience and that students of modernity cannot abstain from acknowledging the diverse perspectives—expressed both by actors and by observers—that make up any historical narrative, often in overt defiance of national and disciplinary boundaries. In this study I will employ some social scientific concepts—such as embeddedness, social capital, and the informal economy—that have been instrumental in the construction of narratives of progress and backwardness, but I will reinterpret them by adopting a thoroughly historicist approach sensitive to the actors' multiple meanings and by placing conflict and diversity at the center of the analysis. Both the methodology and the ambitions of this book are thoroughly interdisciplinary, but this is above all a historical study. My conviction is that history is far more than a repertoire of data and cases useful to test the theories of the social sciences. Historical analysis can not only challenge, refine, and even rethink theoretical concepts employed by other disciplines, but also develop a "way of seeing" that is every bit as theoretically relevant as the deductions of the social sciences and much closer to the concerns and perspectives of the actors who produce social change.

This book is about the power of social networks to effect long-lasting changes, but it is also the product of such power. It is a pleasure to thank the many people—in both Italy and the United States—who provided me with support and inspiration. This project began at Northwestern University, where I had the good fortune to learn from an amazing group of historians. Over the years, Ken Alder has been simultaneously a model of intellectual rigor and living proof that scholarship can be fun. I still do not know how he pulls that off. Without his prodding support I would probably have given up many times. I always felt lucky to have him as my advisor and, later on, as my friend. Joel Mokyr was the reason I decided to leave the comfortable, but also somewhat sedate, world of Italian academia and cross the ocean. He gave me what I had come for and then some. His extraordinary knowledge, generosity, and sense of fairness are known to economic historians the world over. I feel humbled that he showed those qualities to me as well. Edward Muir made me take microhistory seriously and showed me how a "historian's historian" thinks. And he did all that with unparalleled warmth and care.

So many conversations with friends and colleagues at Northwestern were crucial to the development of this project. My gratitude goes to Tessie Liu, to Charles Ragin and the participants in the seminar on International and Comparative Studies, and to Mark Granovetter, under whose supervision this project was originally conceived. Wallace Best and Sarah Fenton have been the best friends in the world. In their unique ways, they made me think, laugh, and hope for the best. And they still do. Special thanks to Karl Appuhn, Giulia Barrera, and Matthew Frankel, whose company was a consistent source of support and insight.

In Valenza Po, Lia Lenti was instrumental in making me feel less of a stranger and in introducing me to a number of charming and sharpminded informers. I am grateful to Aldo Annaratone, Ezio De Ambrogi, Franco Frascarolo, Luciano Lenti, and Ginetto Prandi for their patience and willingness to share their knowledge with me. The staff at the Biblioteca Comunale "Città di Valenza" was kind and helpful. Maria Pastore at the Archivio di Stato in Alessandria facilitated my work immensely. Roberto Botta and Giancarlo Subbrero at the Istituto per la Storia della Resistenza in Provincia di Alessandria were forthcoming with advice and support. In Vicenza, Paolo Crestanello and Luigi Fontana shared with me their knowledge of local history and their passion for the complexities of the Italian industrial districts. In Arezzo, conversations with Oscar Ceccherini and Guido Occhini at the Camera del Lavoro partially made up for the lack of openness of Uno-A-Erre. Carlo Vannucci introduced me to some of the subtleties of gold jewelry making; his intervention also opened a few doors that would otherwise have remained locked. Special thanks to my brother Ferruccio, who put me up in Arezzo and shared with me his connections with local society. I also wish to thank Renato Giannetti, my first advisor at the University of Florence and a reliable source of support over the years, David Righi, Timothy Green, and Emilio Camponovo. My Italian friends made my stay there a pleasure. A special *grazie* to Susanna Brogelli, Jacopo Di Clemente, Giacomo Piussi, and Solange Finardi. Funding for my stay in Italy was provided by a generous grant from the University of Florence and the Italian Ministry for Foreign Affairs. My stay in Providence was made possible by a Newell D. Goff fellowship at the Rhode Island Historical Society. My gratitude goes to the society's staff and archivists.

Moving from the Chicago area to Ann Arbor, Michigan, had its challenges. But I could not have hoped for better colleagues and a more rewarding intellectual environment than the University of Michigan's history department. Without the countless discussions I have had with people in Ann Arbor, and without the amazing creative energy I found there, this book and my life would be immensely poorer. Scott Spector has been a source of inspiration, support, advice, affection, and fun. Helmut Puff has brightened my life with his wit and warmth. They are living proof that intellectual community and friendship can feed on each other. Special thanks to Giorgio Bertellini, Charlie Bright, Kathleen Canning, David Cohen, Susan Crowell, Geoff Eley, Amal Fadlalla, Eric Firstenberg, Dena Goodman, Steve Gutterman, Kali Israel, Brian Porter, Sonya Rose, Peggy Somers, and Paolo Squatriti. I also wish to thank the members of the Science, Technology and Society Program at the University of Michigan, especially John Carson, Paul Edwards, and Gabrielle Hecht, and the participants in the junior faculty colloquium in the Department of History, especially Paul Anderson, Rita Chin, Martha Jones, Matt Lassiter, and Farina Mir. A final thank-you to my father, Orfeo, who fought in a war he did not believe in and lived a life he could not always enjoy. I owe him more than I am even willing to acknowledge.

The Political Economy of Small-Scale Industrialization in Twentieth-Century Italy

TRUST, NETWORKS, AND THE BOUNDARIES OF THE FIRM

EVEN though social scientists began to discuss the wonders and pitfalls of Italy's small-scale capitalism only in the late 1970s, the development of specialized clusters of firms constituted one of the basic traits of the country's heterogeneous economic "miracle" of the 1950s and 1960s, and some of these industrial and artisanal experiences dated back decades and occasionally even centuries. By the 1970s Italy's industrial sector exhibited a distinctive pattern of economic dispersion and spatial concentration. The average Italian manufacturing firm was much smaller than its French or German counterparts, but at the same time it was more likely to be a node in a local network in which actors specialized in different stages of the production and commercialization processes of specific items that were exported throughout the world.

Variably called industrial districts, clusters, or area systems, these localized networks not only proved an extremely vital component of Italy's economy but also presented scholars with the opportunity to reconsider a variety of important theoretical questions. The theoretical relevance of the industrial districts of northern Italy (but also of other parts of the world) stems primarily from the challenges they pose to two long-cherished assumptions about the direction and nature of modern capitalism. First, the persisting success of small-scale firms belies the predictions of a variety of intellectual traditions, which viewed the large integrated corporation as the inevitable outcome of economic evolution. Second, the difficulty of disentangling economic action from other kinds of pursuits that is characteristic of Italy's small-scale capitalism questions the postulated emergence of an economic sphere irreducible to other forms of action.

Of the interpretative traditions that have argued for the ultimate superiority of large-scale enterprise in modern capitalism, the most influential is associated with Alfred Chandler and Oliver Williamson. Chandler viewed the emergence of the large multidivisional corporation as a response to the challenge of reducing transaction costs in sectors where high asset specificity made firms particularly liable to contractual problems.[1] In order to solve these problems, companies extended the size and scope of their activities by internalizing transactions that had previously been carried out in the market. Among the economists, Oliver Williamson has maintained that, if we take the transaction as the analytical unit, whether it will be executed within a hierarchical setting (a firm) or in the market depends on the relative efficiency of each mode.[2] Such efficiency depends in turn on uncertainty and the likelihood of opportunistic behaviors. The higher these two variables, the more efficient hierarchical control within a firm. Finally, uncertainty and opportunism become more likely threats as investments become more transaction specific, because the assets' owners can profit from their information advantage.[3] It is worth noting that in Chandler's and Williamson's approach, political and cultural factors remain exogenous to the theory. If left unbridled, market competition selects for the institutions capable of manipulating the incentives and sanctions that make opportunism less likely, but such institutions emerge out of a strictly economic kind of rationality.

Many scholars have challenged the linear narrative proposed by transaction-cost economics. One of the most important contributions for historical studies has been Charles Sabel's and Jonathan Zeitlin's early work on the survival of communities of small independent producers in the era of mass production, an evolutionary bifurcation that proved fruitful after the crisis of Fordism and the success of "flexible

---

[1] Alfred D. Chandler Jr., *The Visible Hand: The Managerial Revolution in American Business* (Cambridge, Mass., 1977).

[2] Oliver Williamson, *Markets and Hierarchies: Analysis and Antitrust Implications* (New York, 1975).

[3] Some economists have attempted to move beyond the dichotomy between market and hierarchy by analyzing the role of coalitions and clans and by developing the notion of relational contracting. For an approach that applies the insights of transaction-cost economics to an intermediate governance mode between market and hierarchy, see William Ouchi, "Markets, Bureaucracies, and Clans," *Administrative Science Quarterly* 25 (1980): 124–41. For relational contracting, see Oliver Williamson, *The Economic Institutions of Capitalism: Firms, Markets, Relational Contracting* (New York, 1985). For a historical argument calling for the necessity to move beyond the dichotomy of markets and hierarchies, and for a reevaluation of U.S. business history in this light, see Naomi Lamoreaux, Daniel Raff, and Peter Temin, "Beyond Markets and Hierarchies: Toward a New Synthesis of American Business History," *American Historical Review* 108 (2003): 404–33.

specialization" over the last two or three decades.[4] The resistance these islands of craftsmen posed to the threats of proletarianization and mass production was predicated upon mutual trust and forms of "local corporatism," as well as on persisting diversification of market demand. Community and trust created governance structures distinct both from the atomistic world of the free market and from the hierarchical control of large corporations. Moreover, the governance site here shifts from purely economic institutions to social and cultural ties.

This conception paralleled that centered on the notion of the industrial district (ID), developed mostly by Italian economists and sociologists in the 1970s and 1980s. Building on some of Marshall's insights, Giacomo Becattini viewed the ID, rather than the industrial sector, as the primary unit of analysis of industrial economics.[5] Defined as networks of small producers in a localized area who share the benefits of external economies and solidarity ties without neglecting the efficiencies linked to competition, IDs are first of all historically rooted communities built on mutual trust among local agents. In the Italian context, IDs are characteristic of what Arnaldo Bagnasco called the Third Italy, the areas of the central and northern parts of the country that are located neither in the northwestern "industrial triangle" (Turin-Milan-Genoa) nor in the underdeveloped regions of the south.[6] Since these pioneering studies, the Italian industrial districts have come to constitute some of the most powerful counterexamples to the once-dominant expectation that small-scale firms would not withstand the competitive pressures of modern capitalism.

But large-scale corporations were expected to prevail not only on account of their higher economic efficiency but also because they epitomized one of modernity's distinctive traits—the emergence of an economic sphere endowed with its irreducible logic increasingly divorced from family ties, political affiliations, and other more traditional pursuits. The notion of homo economicus, on which the abstrac-

[4] Charles Sabel and Jonathan Zeitlin, "Historical Alternatives to Mass Production: Politics, Markets, and Technology in Nineteenth-Century Industrialization," *Past and Present* 108 (1985): 133–76.

[5] For an exhaustive theoretical and empirical survey, see Giacomo Becattini, ed., *Mercato e Forze Locali: Il Distretto Industriale* (Bologna, 1987). For a genealogy of the concept, see Sebastiano Brusco, "The Idea of the Industrial District: Its Genesis," in Pyke, Becattini, and Sengenberger, *Industrial Districts*, 10–19.

[6] Arnaldo Bagnasco, *Tre Italie: La Problematica Territoriale dello Sviluppo Italiano* (Bologna, 1977).

tions of neoclassical economics rested, would have been unthinkable without the belief in a separate economic logic. But classical sociology was also strongly implicated in the perpetuation of this narrative of separation, which sustains Ferdinand Tönnies' shift from Gemeinschaft to Gesellschaft, as well as Max Weber's theorization of "economic action" as a novel creation of modern capitalism and as the basic framework for the "iron cage," just to mention two particularly influential conceptions. Whereas traditional societies thrived in the creation of hybrid institutions encompassing different logics, such as family firms or patrimonial political power, the very hallmark of modern societies was the creation of distinct structures and realms of action, among which the economic sphere was often given a foundational role for society as a whole.

Now most of the firms that populate Italy's industrial districts are family businesses that entertain complex relationships with their environs and with political power, especially local governments. As Sylvia Yanagisako notices in her ethnographic study of Lombard silk entrepreneurial families, Italian small-scale firms are hybrid entities that combine different rationalities and dispositions—familial affection, the pursuit of profit, and political loyalties, just to mention a few.[7] Therefore, these characteristics have attracted the attention of those scholars who are committed to challenging the economic and sociological narratives of modernity founded on the divorce between the economic sphere and other forms of action. Two concepts have been particularly crucial to this agenda—embeddedness and social capital. Before examining these two notions in some detail, it is worth noting the strong link between the critique of the linear evolutionary narratives culminating with the large-scale corporation and the challenge to the narrative of separation of economic action from other pursuits. Both critiques point to a nondeterministic world of great organizational diversity, where different paths and experiences may coexist indefinitely. This conception goes well beyond the framework of modernization theories, which argued for the existence of different models of capitalism and political governance but understood societies (above all nation-states) as functionally integrated entities and placed them at different stages of development. At least potentially, the two critiques question deeply entrenched analytical foci (the nation-state, the region,

[7] Sylvia Junko Yanagisako, *Producing Culture and Capital: Family Firms in Italy* (Princeton, 2002).

4

the locality) and methodologies (the search for the nomothetic model and the primacy of economic structure, for example).

The concept that has been most influential in debunking the notion of homo economicus while rejuvenating economic sociology is "embeddedness."[8] This notion, which had already been employed by Karl Polanyi and some economic anthropologists, was refined by Mark Granovetter in the 1980s and quickly adopted by many students of the Italian industrial districts.[9] Granovetter set out to address the fundamental Hobbesian question of how social and economic order is possible in a world of self-interested individuals.[10] The answer did not lie in the magic of market mechanisms, the coercion of large-scale organizations, or in all-powerful cultural codes. Instead, Granovetter argued, economic order is possible because individuals embed their economic actions in networks of multifunctional interpersonal relations that may produce trust and cooperation.

Applied to the problem of the persisting organizational diversity of modern capitalism, Granovetter's insight leads to an explanation that is distinct from both transaction-cost economics and communitarian approaches. In Williamson's account, trust "lubricates" economic transactions by saving transaction costs. As information becomes more complex and specific, this saving strategy is carried out most efficiently *within* the boundaries of the firm. Granovetter noticed that the notion of trust proposed by transaction-cost economists is both functionalist and evolutionist. Institutions emerge in order to solve coordination and monitoring problems, and market competition selects the most efficient solution. Moreover, this conception is founded on an atomized view of economic actors, who have little choice but to relinquish control and gage the consequences of their individual actions vis-à-vis the inexorable logic of institutional change.

---

[8] For a collection of some "classics" of economic sociology, and for an introduction to the discipline, see Mark Granovetter and Richard Swedberg, eds., *The Sociology of Economic Life* (Boulder, 1992); see also Neil J. Smelser and Richard Swedberg, eds., *The Handbook of Economic Sociology* (Princeton, 1994).

[9] For a review of the concept of embeddedness and its impact, see Bernard Barber, "All Economies Are Embedded: The Career of a Concept and Beyond," *Social Research* 62 (1995): 387–98. See also Richard Swedberg, "New Economic Sociology: What Has Been Accomplished, What Is Ahead?" *Acta Sociologica* 40 (1997): 161–82.

[10] Mark Granovetter, "Economic Action and Social Structure: The Problem of Embeddedness," *American Journal of Sociology* 91 (1985): 481–510.

The early literature on industrial districts, by contrast, viewed trust as a lubricant of social relations predicated on long-lasting cultural ties.[11] In this context, communitarian norms replace hierarchical control and allow transactions *across* firms to develop smoothly. The district/community itself performs the functions of coordination typical of large organizations. As a consequence, flexible networks of small firms can achieve a high level of efficiency in unstable markets. Theories based on norms and solidarity, however, naturalize trust by taking its social and cultural determinants (the family, the ethnic group, the community, etc.) for granted. Moreover, the perfectly socialized actors who populate these scenarios behave in ways paradoxically similar to the atomized agents of transaction-cost economics: their rationality is devoid of any agency outside of the normative system of their group.

Granovetter has proposed a way out of the dichotomy between atomized and socially deterministic notions of trust ("undersocialized" and "oversocialized," in his terminology). "The embeddedness approach to the problem of trust and order in economic life," Granovetter writes, "threads its way between the oversocialized approach of generalized morality and the undersocialized one of impersonal, institutional arrangements by following and analyzing concrete patterns of social relations."[12] This approach dovetails with the evidence offered by the development of the jewelry towns in at least two ways. First, by viewing networks as governance modes, the embeddedness thesis acknowledges that actors can inhabit several networks at once and use this multiplicity of roles to challenge as well as uphold trust and social order. In other words, Granovetter incorporates in his model the notion that social ties are the locus of both trust and malfeasance schemes. If trust is fully institutionalized in predictable routines or internalized through norms of behavior, it loses its distinctiveness by turning into coercion or compulsion. Second, the embeddedness approach to eco-

---

[11] Revealingly, in his discussion of trust Putnam uses Williamson's metaphor as well, transferring it from the world of economic transactions to that of social ties: "A society that relies on generalized reciprocity is more efficient than a distrustful society, for the same reason that money is more efficient than barter. Trust lubricates social life." Robert Putnam, "The Prosperous Community: Social Capital and Private Life," *American Prospect* 13 (1993): 37. For two useful overviews of sociological and economic conceptions of trust, see at least Diego Gambetta, ed., *Trust: Making and Breaking Co-operative Relations* (Oxford, 1988); and Luis Roniger, *Towards a Comparative Sociology of Trust in Modern Societies* (Messina, 1992).

[12] Granovetter, "Economic Action," 491.

nomic action makes the boundaries of the firm dependent on conflict and historical contingency, rather than on efficiency or timeless morality. This approach predicts that, ceteris paribus, pressures towards vertical integration are stronger where an extensive network of interpersonal relations is lacking. Conversely, when economic action is strongly embedded in social relations, coordination may be achieved without creating large-scale companies.

Despite its obvious merits, however, the notion that economic action is structurally embedded in networks of relations does not address the often-contradictory meanings that actors attribute to the relations that bind them. Granovetter's networks of interpersonal relations penetrate the social body unevenly, thereby introducing a stochastic element to the central question of how order is achieved in a particular historical setting, but these networks function almost as mechanical devices—albeit flexible and occasionally faulty ones. They process inputs (the actors' strategic behaviors and their information about each other and their activities) and produce an output (trust and social order). In other words, not unlike the approaches it challenges, structural embeddedness treats trust as a homogenous and relatively unproblematic "substance" and does not acknowledge that order is an inherently normative notion that is embedded in the perspective of a "center," be it the power structure of the state or a set of privileged institutions in civil society.

My contention here is that there is no order and trust in the abstract—that is, outside the actors' multiple and conflicting perspectives. In fact, evidence from the jewelry towns challenges the very dichotomy of order and disorder. One of the distinctive traits of these experiences is the impossibility of identifying a moral center, a privileged pivot from which to spin the actors' stories. Order and disorder coexisted within the same social world, and their meanings changed with the actors' shifting perspectives. Was gold smuggling, for example, a sign of anomie and disorder or an indication of the resilience of delicate—and therefore all the more precious—social ties? The towns' key traders embraced both interpretations of their actions, telling one version of the story to the state authorities and quite a different one to their subcontractors.

Granovetter's original focus on social structure and structural embeddedness needs to be expanded and refined in order to increase its analytical usefulness to social and economic historians. In particular, we need to bring into the picture political action and cultural conflict in order to explore the historical development of social networks as well as the origins of trust and its contested meanings. In sum, as Paul DiMaggio and others have argued, structural embeddedness needs to be complemented by political and cultural embeddedness.[13] One of the limitations of structural embeddedness is its difficulty in explaining how the networks of interpersonal relations in which economic action is embedded originate and develop. What are these relations made of? What do "trust" and "mistrust" mean and to whom?

An answer to these questions has been proposed by sociologists committed to pluralizing the meaning of embeddedness. Paul DiMaggio and Sharon Zukin view structural embeddedness as only one of several processes through which economic action is socially constructed.[14] To Granovetter's original form, they add "political embeddedness," or the realization that economic action is inseparable from struggles over power, resources, and opportunities; "cultural embeddedness," or the fact that ideologies, beliefs, and symbolic constructs inflect economic life and set limits to narrow interpretations of economic rationality; and "cognitive embeddedness," or the psychological underpinnings of economic behaviors as they emerge at the subjective and collective levels. One of the implications of this plural understanding of embeddedness is that trust ceases to be a homogenous substance without a history and becomes a contested set of practices embedded in the actors' multiple perspectives.

Many of the problems associated with the notion of embeddedness stem from the distinction, borrowed from Weberian thought and classical sociology more generally, between economic action and social structure. Even though Granovetter explicitly criticizes social determinism, the distinction between economic choice on the one hand and social (but also political or cultural) constraints and opportunities on the other remains an underdeveloped and problematic assumption of the embeddedness approach. It is at this theoretical juncture that the notion of social capital may be useful. This concept has been used in a wide variety of ways, not all productive. Therefore, I will briefly re-

---

[13] Paul DiMaggio, "Cultural Aspects of Economic Action and Organization," in Roger Friedland and A. F. Robertson, eds., *Beyond the Marketplace: Rethinking Economy and Society* (New York, 1990), 113–36.

[14] Sharon Zukin and Paul DiMaggio, eds., *Structures of Capital: The Social Organization of the Economy* (New York, 1990), introduction, 1–36. See also David Dequech, "Cognitive and Cultural Embeddedness: Combining Institutional Economics and Economic Sociology," *Journal of Economic Issues* 37 (2003): 461–70.

view some of the most influential approaches in light of the particular definition that I will employ in this study.[15]

The current history of the notion of social capital started in the 1970s, when Pierre Bourdieu discussed it alongside economic, cultural, and symbolic capital without, however, giving it much prominence. Bourdieu defined social capital as "the aggregate of the actual or potential resources that are linked to possession of a durable network of more or less institutionalized relationships of mutual acquaintance and recognition . . . which provide each of its members with the backing of collectively owned capital."[16] Bourdieu's explanandum here is above all social inequality, and he stressed the ways in which the fungibility of different kinds of capital reinforces and legitimizes patterns of accumulation, with the explicit assumption that economic capital must be given a primary and foundational role.

We can contrast this definition with that adopted around the same time by James Coleman. Like Bourdieu, Coleman was interested in relating different kinds of capital, but his approach lay squarely within the confines of rational choice theory. He presented social capital as a crucial factor in the attainment of human capital, defined as the kinds of educational credentials in which individuals and families are willing to invest in their rational expectation of future rates of return.[17] Coleman argued that the excessive individualism of human capital theory (introduced in the 1960s by economists Theodore Schultz and Gary Becker) needed to be tempered by the realization that motivations and opportunities for learning are always embedded in a social context. In a highly controversial example, Coleman maintained that kids in Catholic schools perform better than those in public schools because of the networks that link parents, teachers, and students to each other and to larger organizations in religious institutions. By investing in the creation and nurturing of social networks (for example informal ties

[15] For a more complete critique and literature review, see Dario Gaggio, "Do Historians Need Social Capital?" Social History 29 (2004): 499–513.

[16] Pierre Bourdieu, "Forms of Capital," in John Richardson, ed., Handbook of Theory and Research in the Sociology of Education (New York, 1985), 249. In French, see Pierre Bourdieu, "Le Capital Social: Notes Provisoires," Actes de la Recherche en Sciences Sociales 31 (1980): 2–3.

[17] James Coleman, "Social Capital in the Creation of Human Capital," American Journal of Sociology, 94/Supplement (1988): S95–S120. Coleman and Bourdieu collaborated in the 1980s. The fruit of this collaboration was Pierre Bourdieu and James Coleman, Social Theory for a Changing Society (Oxford, 1991), which, however, does not discuss social capital.

among parents in a school setting), families and individuals may enhance their probability of future success. Whereas Bourdieu was mostly interested in relating different forms of capital to the perpetuation of social distinction and inequality, Coleman stressed the potential benefits that social actors—qua individuals choosing under conditions of bounded rationality—can reap from the fungibility of human and social capital.[18]

Much of the recent popularity of social capital, however, dates to the descent on Italy of Robert Putnam, who spent most the 1980s in Italy studying the outcome of the devolution of several government functions to the country's twenty regions at the beginning of the previous decade.[19] There he gathered an impressive array of quantitative and qualitative evidence on the relationships between political performance, grassroots participation in voluntary associations, and economic performance. In the northern regions of the country Putnam found confirmation of the idea that a strong civil society is good both for democracy and for the economy. By contrast, in the south he was confronted with citizens' passivity and isolation, accompanied by political ineffectiveness and economic backwardness. Northerners seemed to have access to social assets (trust, norms of reciprocity, and networks of interpersonal relations) that were sorely lacking in the south. With what has proved to be a stroke of academic genius, Putnam chose to call these assets *social capital*. Thus, a classic political science project (the cross-sectional assessment of participation in voluntary associations and political performance in the wake of an institutional reform) managed to connect the traditional concerns of sociology (the origins and consequences of sociability) to some of the hottest research agendas in economics (the production of public goods and its relationships with economic development).

Not content with this ambitious argument, Putnam proceeded to trace the historical roots of Italy's north-south divide, finding them in the Middle Ages, when the communal institutions of the northern city-states contrasted with the centralizing monarchy of the southern Norman kingdom. Thus, Putnam not only challenged established disciplinary boundaries; he also broke new methodological ground by combining cross-sectional and historical analysis. Famously, Putnam

---

[18] For a systematic treatment of social capital within Coleman's version of rational choice theory, see James Coleman, *Foundations of Social Theory* (Cambridge, Mass., 1994).

[19] Putnam, *Making Democracy Work*.

went on to argue that many of the problems with U.S. democracy in recent years could be encapsulated by the fact that U.S. citizens now bowled alone, instead of joining clubs and leagues.[20] The increasing poverty of associational life in what Tocqueville had called a country of joiners seemed to presage a near future of social isolation, political cynicism, and declining economic prosperity. Glued to their television sets and oblivious to the pleasures and challenges of sociability, Americans were unwittingly choosing the southern Italian route.

Putnam's ideas (and the notion of social capital more generally) have been widely debated over the last ten years, and not only in academic circles. Without any claim to exhaustiveness, it might be useful to reconstruct this broad and often confusing debate around three main questions: (1) who possesses social capital; (2) how social capital is created (and destroyed); and (3) what kinds of consequences social capital (or its lack) produces.[21]

The main divide over the issue of who owns social capital lies between those who claim that collectivities can have social capital and those who regard it primarily as the property of networks of individuals. Putnam clearly belongs to the former group: In northern Italy, trust and norms of reciprocity permeate public life and make cooperation for shared goals possible. In the south, by contrast, citizens are stuck in a low-trust equilibrium that hinders or even precludes cooperation. In these scenarios, social capital is a public good that enables or constrains action by individuals and groups. It is worth noting, however, that Putnam does not break with methodological individualism, even though he does not openly embrace it either. High- and low-trust equi-

[20] Putnam first published his application of social capital to the U.S. context in a series of articles, starting with "Bowling Alone: America's Declining Social Capital," *Journal of Democracy* 61 (1995): 65–78. Five years later he proposed his thesis in book format with massive qualitative and quantitative documentation. See Robert Putnam, *Bowling Alone: Collapse and Revival of American Community* (New York, 2000).

[21] This way of framing the debate excludes the scholars who deny any role for social capital and invoke its erasure from the conceptual repertoire of the social sciences. For some influential examples of this line of argument, see Ben Fine, *Social Capital Versus Social Theory: Political Economy and Social Science at the Turn of the Millennium* (London, 2001). For a synthetic version, see Ben Fine and Francis Green, "Economics, Social Capital, and the Colonization of the Social Sciences," in Tom Schuller, Stephen Baron, and John Field, eds., *Social Capital: Critical Perspectives* (Oxford, 2000), 78–93. For a similar perspective see Stephen Smith and Jessica Kulynych, "Liberty, Equality, and . . . Social Capital?" in Scott McLean, David Schultz, and Manfred Steger, eds., *Social Capital: Critical Perspectives on Community and "Bowling Alone"* (New York, 2002), 127–46.

libriums are explained in terms of individual choices to join voluntary associations or to retreat to private life.[22] Therefore, the cumulative effect of individual choices ends up forging structures (dare I say cultures) of participation or isolation, which in turn shape actors' behaviors. Somewhat paradoxically, this is a choice-based thesis that is quite skeptical of actors' agency.

The most vocal opponent of this approach is sociologist Alejandro Portes, who prefers to view social capital as the property of individuals and networks. According to Portes, the main problem with Putnam's conception is logical circularity: "As a property of communities and nations rather than individuals, social capital is simultaneously a cause and an effect. It leads to positive outcomes, such as economic development and less crime, and its existence is inferred from the same outcomes."[23] Only by viewing social capital as the property of individuals, Portes argues, does it become possible to distinguish between social relations and the resources actors gain through them—a distinction that was present in Bourdieu's original conception. Paradoxically, in both Bourdieu's and Portes's research, this focus on individuals' resources steers clear of methodological individualism much more explicitly than Putnam's collective approach. In his study of immigrants' entrepreneurship, for example, Portes shows how actors' opportunities for the mobilization of social networks are shaped by powerful structural constraints emerging both from the entrepreneur's community of origin and from society at large.[24]

Another controversial dimension of social capital concerns its origins and sources. By conceptualizing it as a public good, Coleman and Putnam view social capital primarily as an unintentional process—as the by-product of actions pursued for goals other than its creation and nurturing. Families do not send their children to religious schools in

---

[22] For a very useful discussion of methodological individualism in economics and other social sciences, see Malcolm Rutherford, *Institutions in Economics: The Old and New Institutionalism* (Cambridge, 1994). From a methodological standpoint, Putnam's approach is more compatible with the new institutional economics pioneered by Oliver Williamson than with the older approach to institutional change and economic action exemplified by Thorstein Veblen, Wesley Mitchell, and John Commons.

[23] Alejandro Portes, "Social Capital: Its Origins and Applications in Modern Sociology," *Annual Review of Sociology* 24 (1998): 16.

[24] Alejandro Portes, "Economic Sociology and the Sociology of Immigration: A Conceptual Overview," in Alejandro Portes, ed., *The Economic Sociology of Immigration* (New York, 1995), 1–41.

order to weave informal networks of solidarity and reciprocity among parents and teachers, even though such networks prove crucial to educational success. By the same token, citizens do not join the Lions Club or labor unions to create the networks of participation that make democracy work, even though democratic control relies on these associations to function effectively.[25] From this perspective, social capital is the product of the invisible hand of civic interaction—an unintended consequence of countless individual actions carried out for heterogeneous reasons. The unintentional nature of social capital means that actors routinely underinvest in it, as in any other public good. In other words, this approach configures the production of social capital as something of a market failure.[26] The paradox here is that the state could not directly intervene in this realm (as it does, say, in the production of basic scientific research or other public goods) without killing the goose that lays the golden eggs—that is, an unbridled civil society. The solution proposed by Coleman was a return to primordial forms of sociability, above all the traditional nuclear family. Putnam is arguably more progressive than that, although his stress on the importance of community is not incompatible with problematic calls for cultural regeneration. A more palatable option, to which Putnam has given his blessing, is for societies to reduce economic inequality, which has been shown to correlate with the decline of trust and participation.[27]

Many scholars have criticized the conception of social capital as an unintentional process. Some commentators have argued that "unintentional social capital" is something of an oxymoron at the micro level

[25] Coleman explicitly theorized the unintentional character of social capital: "A major use of the concept of social capital depends on its being a by-product of activities engaged in for other purposes." See *Foundations of Social Theory*, 312. This emphasis on unintentionality is crucial to viewing social capital as a public good in a rational choice framework.

[26] Another way of making this point in the language of economics is by arguing that social capital is productive of externalities—that is, economic effects that are not reflected in market prices and therefore escape the rational decisions of each individual agent. For this kind of conceptualization of social capital, see Paul Collier, *Social Capital and Poverty* (Washington, D.C., 1998).

[27] For such correlation, see Eric Uslaner, *The Moral Foundations of Trust* (Cambridge, Mass., 2001). Neither Putnam nor Uslaner, however, resolves the ambiguity inherent in this correlation. Is inequality a cause or a consequence of lack of trust and social capital? Uslaner laments the effects of inequality but is also quite skeptical of state intervention. Furthermore, on the basis of this line of argument, equalizing efforts would not be carried out in the name of justice or citizenship rights but as the result of a utilitarian calculus.

of intersubjective networks. By focusing on individual strategies of accumulation and by linking social capital to patterns of mutual acquaintance and recognition, Bourdieu stressed the instrumental character that social networks assume when deployed as forms of capital. Likewise, Portes and Sensenbrenner emphasize the deliberative dimension of social capital when applied to economic behavior by defining it as "Those expectations for action within a collectivity that affect the economic goals and goal-seeking behavior of its members, even if these expectations are not oriented towards the economic sphere."[28] In other words, for these authors social relations assume a multiplicity of meanings and functions for individuals and collectivities; actors can only turn these relations into "capital" through an act of instrumental deliberation. Several scholars have also exposed the limitations of the unintentional conception of social capital at the macro level of institutional change. Coleman's and Putnam's focus on the unintentional consequences of sociability discounts the role that state agencies, the legal system, and political movements play in shaping the desirable traits of civil society.[29] In other words, Putnam's approach tends to reify the distinction between civil and political society.

As for the third broad theme, the consequences of social capital, there has been a general trend in the literature towards an increasingly nuanced assessment. In his early work Putnam, much like Coleman, focused almost exclusively on the positive effects that tight social networks have on political and economic performance, both at the micro level of interpersonal relations and at the level of the polity as a whole. In his pioneering work of the 1970s and 1980s, Mark Granovetter introduced the distinction between strong and weak ties, arguing that weak ties reveal their strength by providing actors with nonredundant information and that excessive redundancy and social closure may have

[28] Alejandro Portes and Julia Sensenbrenner, "Embeddedness and Immigration: Notes on the Social Determinants of Economic Action," *American Journal of Sociology* 98 (1993): 1321.

[29] Theda Skocpol, for example, has noticed that many of the associations extolled by Putnam in the U.S. context, such as the Parents' and Teachers' Association and the American Legion, not only emerged with the support of the federal government but also built their success on political campaigning efforts that led to the expansion of the welfare state (respectively through the Sheppard-Towner program to promote maternal and child health and the GI Bill). See Theda Skocpol, "Unravelling from Above," *American Prospect* 25 (1996): 20–25.

negative consequences.[30] Many social scientists, ranging from Mancur Olson and Ronald Burt to Alejandro Portes, have elaborated on these insights and applied them to social capital theory. The result has been to expose the "dark side" of social capital.[31] The vibrancy of social networks in civil society is as essential to economic predation by Mafia-like organizations as it is to economic cooperation among civic-minded entrepreneurs. Moreover, social cohesion can lead to the exclusion of outsiders and to the burdening of individuals and groups with conflicting and escalating expectations, with stifling implications for innovation and personal freedom. Putnam himself has recently acknowledged the negative potentialities of sociability, while trying to reserve the notion of social capital for its positive and productive dimensions.[32]

In light of this admittedly selective review, I would like to distinguish two major currents in the literature on social capital. The first current, inaugurated by Coleman and championed by Putnam, views social capital as a public good that is unintentionally produced and functionally deployed. I will criticize Putnam's arguments in more detail in the next chapter, but, in short, I believe that his understanding of social capital is of little use to historians. The second current, started by Bourdieu and exemplified by Portes among others,[33] views

[30] See Mark Granovetter, "The Strength of Weak Ties," *American Journal of Sociology* 78 (1973): 1350–80.

[31] Within a rational choice framework, the costs of sociability have been explored by Olson, *Rise and Decline*, who, however, does not employ the notion of social capital. Within network theory, much of the pioneering work has been done by Ronald Burt. See "The Contingent Value of Social Capital," *Administrative Science Quarterly* 42 (1997): 339–65, for a synthetic overview. See also Alejandro Portes and Patricia Landolt, "The Downside of Social Capital," *American Prospect* 26 (1996): 18–21.

[32] For a useful synthesis, see Michael Woolcock, "Social Capital and Economic Development: Towards a Theoretical Synthesis and Policy Framework," *Theory and Society* 27 (1998): 151–8l. According to Woolcock, there are different kinds of social capital, namely the ties that bind actors together in networks (which can be grouped under the category of embeddedness) and the ties that bridge actors across different networks and with government institutions (which endow actors with autonomy). On the basis of this distinction, Woolcock devises two matrixes, one for the micro level and the other for the macro level, which demonstrate that successful societies need high levels of both embeddedness and autonomy. Southern Italy is an example of a society that has too much embeddedness and too little autonomy.

[33] For examples of historical studies that use a notion of social capital similar to the one I recommend here, see Marjorie McIntosh, "The Diversity of Social Capital in English Communities, 1300–1640 (with a Glance at Modern Nigeria)," *Journal of Interdisciplinary History* 19 (1999): 459–90. See also Sheilagh Ogilvie, "How Does Social Capital

social capital as the property of individuals and networks, as a resource that is constructed in the arena of political deliberation, and therefore as a relational practice that can be as productive of conflict and inequalities as of order and harmony.[34] I believe that this second understanding of social capital is potentially fruitful and should be taken seriously by historians. I would argue that social capital as defined above draws attention to the need to incorporate economic action in any understanding of historical change. The notion of social capital does not necessarily reduce the social to instrumental calculation by rational agents, much as the notion of identity does not necessarily reduce cultural interaction to naturalized interpretations of gender and race.[35] From this perspective, the conceptual core of social capital is that relational networks are productive of value for their participants, but that does not mean that networks can be reduced to value-producing assets or that such value can be assessed in isolation from its historical context.[36]

This understanding of social capital as a deliberative project builds and improves on basic notions of embeddedness by restoring agency

---

Affect Women? Guilds and Communities in Early Modern Germany," *American Historical Review* 109 (2004): 325–59. For a full-length treatment of these issues, see also Ogilvie's book *A Bitter Living: Women, Markets, and Social Capital in Early Modern Germany* (Oxford, 2003). For other examples of the ways historians have employed this concept, see Robert Rotberg, ed., *Patterns of Social Capital: Stability and Change in Historical Perspective* (Cambridge, 2001).

[34] My reading of the social capital literature is somewhat similar to the one proposed by Edwards and Foley, who distinguish within social capital theory a useful structural and relational core identified by Coleman and Bourdieu from a fruitless normative and sociopsychological layer added by Putnam. However, they conveniently downplay the fact that Coleman developed his approach from an explicit rational choice perspective. See Bob Edwards and Michael Foley, "Civil Society and Social Capital Beyond Putnam," *American Behavioral Scientist* 42 (1998): 124–39.

[35] See Margaret Somers, "The Narrative Constitution of Identity: A Relational and Network Approach," *Theory and Society* 23 (1994): 605–49. In a recent contribution to the debate, Somers denies the possibility of interpreting social capital from a relational and network perspective. See "Beware Trojan Horses Bearing Social Capital: How Privatization Turned *Solidarity* into a Bowling Team," in George Steinmetz, ed., *The Politics of Method in the Human Sciences: Positivism and Its Epistemological Others* (Durham, N.C., 2005), 346–411.

[36] For a similar conceptualization, see Nan Lin, *Social Capital: A Theory of Social Structure and Action* (Cambridge, 2001). Lin defines his agenda as follows: "The theory of social capital focuses on the resources embedded in one's social network and how access to and use of such resources benefits the individual's action" (55).

16

to historical actors and steering clear of social determinism. Networks of interpersonal relations assume complex and diverse meanings for actors, who can capitalize on family ties, the bonds of friendship, or the complicity of political affiliation to gain access to resources and opportunities. In so doing, however, they may change the context in which they move and create conflicts and sources of inequality that may be challenged by others. Furthermore, actors rarely manage to fully solve the problems posed by the hybridity of social relations, even though they may devise institutions to limit these challenges. A family business may choose to incorporate and change its legal status, for example, but this does not necessarily squeeze the affective dimension out of the enterprise. It may even draw attention to it, and with messy consequences.

This understanding of networks also challenges linear conceptions of historical change. But it is not enough to move from linear narratives to an ontology of networks, if networks remain disembedded structures that shape action in a linear fashion. In other words, networks should not be conceptualized as structures, but as processes that include firms, families, politicians, commercial agents, as well as technical routines and materials. As Michel Callon and Bruno Latour have argued, networks are hybrids of heterogeneous relations in which "actors define one another in interaction."[37] This process of definition is inherently political, in the sense that success is based on a network's ability to enroll "actors" (in the broadest sense of the term, which includes other networks) and make them speak and work for the network itself. The material underpinnings of what we traditionally call "structure" have themselves agency, while the deliberating actor of traditional narratives would go nowhere without engaging, enrolling, and translating people and materials. In this vein, I intend to follow gold and other materials around and map the ways in which these materials were transformed into a variety of local and extralocal "currencies"—money and promissory notes; trust and malfeasance; familial affection, class solidarity, and clientelistic loyalty—all of which built vulnerable and shifting relations.

If we are to take the notions of embeddedness and social capital seriously, Ronald Coase's famous question ("why do firms exist at all and

---

[37] Michel Callon, "Techno-economic Networks and Irreversibility," in John Law, ed., *A Sociology of Monsters* (London, 1991), 135. See also Bruno Latour, *We Have Never Been Modern* (Hemel Hempstead, 1993). For a similar perspective applied to business prac-

how are their boundaries set?") needs to be replaced with a broader focus on the boundary of the economic. If firms are themselves hybrids of heterogeneous relations endowed with different logics (as the practices of the "family firms" detailed in this book clearly show), the challenge for the historian becomes to understand how historical actors at different junctures and in different contexts distinguish what is economic from what is not, or conversely how they deliberately blur the boundaries between potentially distinct realms of action. Thanks to its heterogeneous nature and functions, trust is heavily implicated in this process of boundary making (and unmaking), but it is overly simplistic to posit a linear relationship between trust and a specific kind of economic structuring: Different *kinds* of trust have different kinds of consequences.

This conception of trust and social capital dovetails with a variety of innovative approaches that have drawn attention to the actors' ability to reflect on their individual and collective conditions in ways that are themselves productive of economic change. Geographer Michael Storper, for example, has pointed out that economic action, which must be viewed in its spatialized dimensions, often relies on interdependencies that are themselves not traded—that is, on localized conventions that frame the boundaries of what constitutes the economic realm.[38] These interdependencies are the product of processes of mutual recognition among actors who become aware of their interconnectedness as they produce, exchange, and consume in a spatial setting. In a similar vein, Sabel and Zeitlin have revised their earlier evolutionary approach to mass production and its historical alternatives by challenging the very distinction between actors and their context. Rather than viewing the actors' identities and their context as preformed categories engaged in a game of action and reaction, they advance "a conception of the actors as defining themselves strategically in the very act of constituting their context."[39] Reflexivity is crucial to this process of mutual construction, and it assumes the modes of narration: "The present is connected to the future by the possibility of imagining alternatives; the present is connected to the past because of the necessity of

---

tices, see Walter Powell, "Hybrid Organizational Arrangements: New Form or Transitional Development?" *California Management Review* 30 (1987): 67–88.

[38] Michael Storper, *The Regional World: Territorial Development in a Global Economy* (New York, 1997).

[39] See "Stories, Strategies, Structures: Rethinking Historical Alternatives to Mass Production," in Charles Sabel and Jonathan Zeitlin, eds., *Worlds of Possibilities: Flexibility and Mass Production in Western Industrialization* (Cambridge, 1997), 1–33.

imagining the future as a re-elaboration, however fanciful, of what has gone before."[40]

Reflexivity as boundary making and reflexivity as narration come together in Callon's revision of the notion of externality, the unintended (or deliberately ignored) consequences of economic calculation. The particular economic arrangement that we call the market derives simultaneously from the actors' ability to embed economic action in a variety of norms and institutions (including theoretical understandings of the economy), and in their ongoing attempts at disentangling other actors and objects from their multiple ties in such a way that calculative exchange can take place. The particular features of this balancing act of framing and deframing vary over time and across locations, so that an "anthropology of markets" becomes necessary to capture the diversity of economic action arising in different social settings.[41]

The main advantage to viewing economic action as a reflexive and deliberative process lies in the possibility of redefining the old dichotomies of structure and agency, actor and context, and materiality and meaning. But these conceptions are not devoid of risks, the most damaging of which is the potential construction of an ideal agent in charge of her future and capable of conjuring up alternative worlds simply by virtue of her social interconnectedness and imaginative skills. In other words, the risk lies in ignoring the role of power and conflict in deciding whose imagination and connections will carry the day. In order to avoid this risk, we need to move from economic to political action and investigate how power differentials were produced and reproduced in rapidly changing social settings.

PATRONAGE, POLITICS, AND THE PARADOXES OF INFORMALITY

In the jewelry towns, the boundaries of economic action were negotiated within networks of social and political relations that were constantly redefined. In the previous section, I have attempted to move beyond structural understandings of social networks so as to make them a suitable subject for historical analysis. In this section I will do the same for political culture. My goal is to pluralize and decenter po-

---

[40] Ibid., 11.

[41] Michel Callon, "Introduction: The Embeddedness of Economic Markets in Economics," in Michel Callon, ed., *The Laws of the Markets* (Oxford, 1998), 1–56.

litical culture as an analytical category in such a way that it might become sensitive to the historical actors' multiple and often conflicting perspectives. Instead of viewing socialism, Catholicism, or ideologies of self-help as fixed repertoires of meanings with specific and uncontroversial economic functions (for example the production of trust), I will emphasize their flexibility and the conflicts surrounding their interpretations.

A good place to begin this discussion is the distinction between the public and the private spheres—another narrative of separation crucial to the construction of Western modernity. For Hegel, modernity emerged from a series of fractures within an original whole (the Spirit). These fractures were epitomized by the distinction between state and civil society and dialectically resolved in the organic conception of the state.[42] Weberian modernization was predicated on the distinction between private interests and public roles assumed by actors within rational-legal bureaucracies bound to objective rules and procedures.[43] More recently, Habermas's theory of the origins of the public sphere in Western liberal polities has emphasized the social and economic autonomy of citizens from state relations as a prerequisite for rational-critical debate.[44] Common to these conceptions of modernity is the assumption that political legitimacy is predicated on the establishment of universalistic rules of conduct and on the promotion of a common and unambiguous language for the articulation of aspirations and the regulation of conflict.

Although modernity and democracy are conceptually and historically distinct processes, debates over democracy have been informed by the same dichotomies. For Habermas, for example, the tension between the instrumental rationality of market competition and the values of democratic control was worked out in the open arenas of civil society, where voluntary associations, a free press, and a variety of interest groups negotiated the rights and entitlements of democratic rep-

[42] Hegel developed these concepts in the *Philosophy of Right*, published in 1821. See also Jean Cohen and Andrew Arato, *Civil Society and Political Theory* (Cambridge, Mass., 1992).

[43] Weber outlined the relationship between capitalism and state formation in part 1 of *Economy and Society*, written in 1918–20. See also Randall Collins, "Weber's Last Theory of Capitalism," *American Sociological Review* 45 (1980): 925–42.

[44] Jürgen Habermas, *The Structural Transformation of the Public Sphere* (Cambridge, Mass., 1989). See also Craig Calhoun, ed., *Habermas and the Public Sphere* (Cambridge, Mass., 1992).

resentation. In this scenario, the conceptual and institutional distinction between public and private spheres is key to political legitimacy and to the incorporation of new claims and differences into the polity.

The path to modernity taken by the Italian jewelry towns challenges these theoretical accounts by presenting the puzzling paradox of modern polities in which the distinction between the public and private spheres is blurred at best. The three most influential mayors in the modern history of Valenza Po, for example, were a socialist accountant specializing in bankruptcy law, who put his career on the line to save the local jewelry industry from a crisis in the 1910s; a Fascist accountant specializing in extrajudicial agreements between creditors and debtors, who during the commercial crisis of the 1930s played a similar—albeit more controversial—role; and a communist gold recycler who led the town during the economic boom of the late 1950s and 1960s by combining his credit services for the local left-wing artisans with his political activity. Public roles and private interests in the jewelry towns were inextricably linked and deliberately blurred.

This interweaving of public and private roles was the product of the embeddedness of economic action in political relations. Such embeddedness challenges the distinction, so evident in Putnam's understanding of social capital, between civil and political society. Far from acting as an impartial arbiter or as an extraneous agent, the state actively constructed the social as much as it was constructed by it. In particular, in the social spaces discussed in this book the politics of patronage built bridges between local societies, public authorities, and global markets. If taking the notion of embeddedness seriously leads to a conception of economic change founded on hybridity and heterogeneity, patronage ceases to be a synonym of corruption—a degenerative pattern to be contrasted with putatively healthy and rational scenarios. By denoting a certain kind of compenetration of political and economic action, patronage (or clientelism) ceases to be regarded as exceptional. Much like *parentela*, its cousin in many stereotypical depictions of backwardness, *clientela* can be fruitfully viewed as one of the main venues through which the market is constructed. This is not to argue that familial and political loyalties were always compatible with the calculative action typical of market relations. As we will see throughout this book, embeddedness and hybridity did not always act as lubricants of social relations. Instead, some actors' desire to disembed economic action from political loyalties and familial affection created tensions and conflicts that proved quite hard to resolve. This tension between embeddedness and disembeddedness or, to put it in Callon's terms, between framing and deframing is key to understanding the political economy of the local societies I explore in this book.

Scholars have long acknowledged the "survival" of patronage relations as one of the distinctive traits of Italian modernity.[45] Italy provides critics of modernization theories with a powerful counterexample. Most observers, however, have regarded patronage as one of the causal factors of the relative underdevelopment of southern Italy.[46] Despite the rejection of evolutionary and deterministic models of modernization, the link between patronage and backwardness remains strong.[47] Students of the Third Italy, concerned with extolling the liberal virtues of the industrial districts of small firms, have emphasized the differences between the central and northeastern regions of the peninsula and the south. For these scholars, clientelism is a distinctively southern phenomenon. This excision of patronage from the study of northern Italy's development is puzzling. The very scholars who ignore patronage also argue for strong continuity between rural relations and small-scale industrialization.[48] The transition of the Third Italy to industrial modernity—these scholars argue—was not only permeated with civic virtues, it was also smooth and painless. In this scenario, the entrepreneurial spirit and cooperative dispositions of the sharecroppers (*mezzadri*) of central and northern Italy paved the way for the development of the industrial districts. The irony is that Italian sharecropping (*mezzadria*) has provided generations of anthropologists and sociologists with one of the archetypal models of patronage in

[45] See, for example, Luciano Graziano, *Clientelismo e Sistema Politico: Il caso dell'Italia* (Milan, 1980); and Maria Pitrone, *Il Clientelismo tra Teoria e Pratica* (Acireale, 1994).

[46] Luciano Graziano, "Patron-Client Relations in Southern Italy," *European Journal of Political Research* 1 (1973): 3–34. Putnam's contrast between southern and northern Italy is a particularly influential version of this argument.

[47] See Robin Theobald, "The Decline of Patron-Client Relation in Developed Societies," *Archives Européennes de Sociologie* 24 (1983): 136–47; Michael Korovkin's critique of Theobald's argument, "Exploitation, Cooperation, Collusion: An Inquiry into Patronage," *Archives Européennes de Sociologie* 29 (1988): 105–26; and Theobald's rejoinder, "On the Survival of Patronage in Developed Society," *Archives Européennes de Sociologie* 33 (1992): 183–91.

[48] The most influential scholars who have stressed these continuities can be found in Giorgio Fuà and Carlo Zacchia, eds., *Industrializzazione Senza Fratture* (Bologna, 1983); and Massimo Paci, ed., *Famiglia e Mercato del Lavoro in un'Economia Periferica* (Milan, 1980).

Mediterranean societies.[49] The relationship between landowner and the head of the sharecropping family exhibited all the traits usually attributed to patronage ties, including a distinctive combination of loyalty and antagonism, and of trust and malfeasance.

The uncritical acceptance of universalistic models of liberal democracy has shaped an ideological agenda aimed at replacing detached analysis with palatable myths of origin. This study corrects this approach by mapping the interaction between the politics of patronage and economic action at the micro level of local change. As I will show in chapter 4, the elements of continuity between *mezzadria* and small-scale industrialization did not lie in vague notions of entrepreneurship and cooperation, but in the new patrons' ability to build on a long-standing political culture dominated by clientage, and in the clients' ability to carry the multiplicity of roles and the political flexibility of *mezzadria* over to industrial and artisanal relations.

Patronage is—quite appropriately—a hybrid category of social and political practice that blurs the distinction between private interests and public good. Patrons use their clout and resources to grant favors and protection to their clients, who reciprocate with loyalty and support. In addition to combining seemingly contradictory social categories, such as trust and coercion as well as instrumentality and sentiments of loyalty, patronage challenges notions of political legitimacy that do not allow for the coexistence of a multiplicity of perspectives.[50] Patronage ties are legitimate within specific social boundaries defined by networks of personal relations, which often include state officials. Yet modern patronage usually lacks the positive sanction of a formal state authority. Therefore, patronage can weave the web of relations necessary for the development of viable informal economies.

[49] See especially Sydel Silverman, "'Exploitation' in Rural Central Italy: Structure and Ideology in Stratification Study," *Comparative Studies in Society and History* 12 (1970): 327–39 on Umbria; Carlo Poni, *Fossi e Cavedagne Benedicon le Campagne* (Bologna, 1982) and David Kertzer, *Family Life in Central Italy, 1880–1910* (New Brunswick, 1984) on Emilia-Romagna; and Desmond Gill, "Tuscan Sharecropping in United Italy: The Myth of Class Collaboration Destroyed," *Journal of Peasant Studies* 10 (1984): 146–69 on Tuscany.

[50] Reuven Kahane, "Hypotheses on Patronage and Social Change," *Ethnology* 23 (1984): 13. The sociological literature on patronage is vast. The conception of patronage as a multifunctional and ambiguous relation is developed by S. N. Eisenstadt and Louis Roniger, "Patron-Client Relations as a Model of Structuring Social Exchange," *Comparative Studies in Society and History* 22 (1980): 42–77. For a more traditional conception of patronage within a modernization-theory framework, see Ernest Gellner and John Waterbury, eds., *Patrons and Clients* (London, 1977).

This emphasis on the politics of patronage leads to a reinterpretation of the kinds of political cultures (usually of either socialist or Catholic orientation) that were until recently characteristic of many areas of northern and central Italy. According to Carlo Trigilia, these "subcultures" represented "a form of defense of local societies against the changes brought about by the market and the national state."[51] Trigilia maintains that the development of these cultural identities at the end of the nineteenth century went hand in hand with a particular process of class formation. Proletarianization in the Third Italy was not as fast and advanced as in the metropolitan areas of the industrial triangle. Persistent ties to the land and the survival of family networks as a general resource contributed to the creation of a scarcely polarized class structure. Cross-class policies, based on the mobilizing force of territorial subcultures, were remarkably successful, thereby mitigating individualistic tendencies and mediating between diverging interests. In other words, the vertical ties created by local identities and loyalties have been stronger than the horizontal ones of class politics.

The evidence from the jewelry towns suggests that Trigilia's contrasts between the national and the local, and between the capitalist and the premodern, as well as his emphasis on the homogenizing qualities of political culture, need to be refined. To a large extent, local political cultures articulated the meanings of the relations of patronage (but also of class) that constructed both political authority and the market. Rather than the language of confrontation and defense, I will be employing notions of translation and negotiation between local societies, the state, and powerful economic actors. Furthermore, socialism and Catholicism did not always produce cohesion and cooperation among local actors. On the contrary, the meanings to be assigned to these ideologies and their relations with social and economic practices were never uncontroversial, and these ideologies were by no means shared by all members of local society. In Valenza Po after World War II, for example, artisans tended to profess socialist or communist ideals, while the traders embraced the principles of political Catholicism. In this case political cultures fueled conflict rather than defusing it.

This understanding of local political cultures makes sense of the coexistence of patronage ties and class mobilization in the jewelry towns. Disproving the predictions of modernization theories, class mobilization failed to uproot patronage ties even during the globalization of

---

[51] Carlo Trigilia, *Grandi Partiti e Piccole Imprese* (Bologna, 1986), 26.

local industries after World War II. State authority was negotiated at the local level through multifunctional political relations linking the local and the national. During the "economic miracle" of the 1950s and 1960s, Arezzo's society developed into a hierarchical structure in which subcontracting relations were embedded in clientelistic ties devoted to negotiating the position of the thriving informal economy vis-à-vis the state. Widespread gold smuggling and tax evasion, two closely related practices in the Italian jewelry towns, prompted a chain of alliances and compromises between unionized workers, small-scale manufacturers, larger companies, local politicians, and state officials. Forged in secrecy, these alliances were multifunctional. They channeled local tensions into the semilegitimate arena of clientage, thereby simultaneously regulating market competition and political conflict. In other words, patronage may provide a highly flexible venue for political integration even in "modern" societies. As sociologist Luis Roniger has pointed out, "sometimes patronage can be seen to reconcile public and private authority and formal and informal rules of the game."[52] One of the main thrusts of this book is to treat the state and the market with a degree of symmetry: patronage can provide not only a venue for political integration but also a mode through which market relations can be effectively constructed.

In sum, patronage should be regarded as a set of distinctive modes of economic and political governance, rather than as a relic from premodern times. This approach is also instrumental in understanding the development of local informal economies in the Third Italy. Recent studies have challenged simplistic interpretations of the informal economy as the outcome of large companies' decentralization strategies in periods of crisis,[53] or as a reaction to the increasingly "predatory" policies of the welfare state.[54] Both empirical research and theoretical studies have shown that viable informal economies rely on historically specific networks of interpersonal relations at the local and global levels, and on elaborate patterns of negotiation between local societies and

---

[52] Luis Roniger, "Civil Society, Patronage, and Democracy," *International Journal of Comparative Sociology* 35 (1994): 214.

[53] See, for example, Philip Mattera, *Off the Books: The Rise of the Underground Economy* (New York, 1985), who remarks, "Operating off the books . . . represents the ultimate goal of the profit-maximizing entrepreneur: proverbial free enterprise" (38).

[54] See, for example, Bruno Contini, "The Italian Second Economy," in Vito Tanzi, ed., *The Underground Economy in the United States and Abroad* (Lexington, 1982), 199–208, who calls the informal economy "the revenge of the market."

the state.[55] Clientage fulfills both requirements: it weaves ties of trust and complicity in local societies, and it provides informal relations with a degree of protection from state authorities.

The strong conceptual and historical link between patronage and the informal economy helps to explain why many students of the Italian industrial districts have neglected both phenomena or treated them as exceptions.[56] Yet the level of informality in the areas of small-scale manufacturing was (and is) exceptionally high, and it increased in the crucial years of the economic boom of the 1950s and 1960s.[57] Informality in the gold jewelry industry was particularly pronounced, since most of the gold and virtually all the precious and semiprecious stones processed by the Italian manufacturers were smuggled into the country. The use of smuggled materials made tax evasion rampant. Moreover, undocumented homework and the violation of labor standards became widespread. In the jewelry towns, as in other Italian districts, international success and informality reinforced one another. Internationalization was not a disembodied process led by abstract principles of rationality, but the outcome of particular interpersonal relations between the towns' commercial elites and a growing number of international traders. These traders actively promoted and supported the local informal economies because of their advantages in terms of taxes and labor costs. And the clientelistic ties between the local elites and state authorities made sure that Rome turned a blind eye to these practices.

[55] See the essays collected in Alejandro Portes, Manuel Castells, and Lauren Benton, eds., *The Informal Economy: Studies in Advanced and Less Developed Countries* (Baltimore, 1989); for a synthetic survey, see Alejandro Portes, "The Informal Economy and Its Paradoxes," in Smelser and Swedberg, *Handbook of Economic Sociology*, 426–49.

[56] A partial exception is Vittorio Capecchi, "The Informal Economy and the Development of Flexible Specialization in Emilia-Romagna," in Portes, Castells, and Benton, *The Informal Economy*, 189–215, who acknowledges the role of the informal economy in the Third Italy but sees it as simply functional to models of development based on small scale. More representative of the general attitude of Italian scholars is A. Saba, *Il Modello Italiano: La "Specializzazione Flessibile" e i Distretti Industriali* (Milan, 1995), who argues that "from the point of view of economic development, it does not matter whether the new firm will develop underground and for how long it will remain underground. . . . What matters is that a new entrepreneurial group has decided to organize the factors of production and is willing to take the risk to launch a product in the market. The only and true judge is the market" (40–41).

[57] Mattera, *Off the Books*, estimates that between 25 and 35 percent of the Italian workforce was clandestine in the late 1970s. Contini, "The Italian Second Economy," reports that the Italian participation rate declined from 44 percent in 1959 to 34 percent in 1977, in the presence of a low and fairly constant unemployment rate. Regional variation of this phenomenon is far lower than other indicators of economic development. Formality and prosperity are weakly correlated in the Italian context.

This focus on the relationships between patronage and informality also sets the development of the Italian industrial districts in the context of specific patterns of state formation and legitimation. In her controversial studies, Linda Weiss has developed a state-centered approach to the analysis of the informal economy, with a particular emphasis on Italy.[58] According to Weiss, the informal economy is a political creation whose conditions of existence are shaped by the state. Because of their ideological commitments, the Christian Democratic governments of post–World War II Italy crafted an extensive body of laws devoted to promoting and protecting small businesses, thereby establishing strong incentives for firms to limit their official size. For many companies, the only way of reaching this goal was to go underground and develop clientelistic ties of protection with state officials.

Although Weiss's approach provides a valuable corrective to the mystifying optimism of the literature on the Italian industrial districts, her dismissal of the impact of local conditions is problematic. The differences between the informal economies of Modena and Naples, for example, are too wide to be ignored.[59] Informality in the Third Italy was not a measure of last resort adopted by small elites to gain additional competitiveness, as was the case in parts of the south. Rather, the informal economy of the northern districts of small firms developed historically from the negotiations between a variety of local and extralocal actors. Therefore, the "benefits" of informality were widely shared in local society. In the jewelry towns, skilled workers received generous payments under the counter; tax evasion was key to attaining and preserving small-scale proprietorship; and, of course, the leading companies used the informal economies to spread both risks and business opportunities among their client-subcontractors. The clientelistic manipulation of state regulation played a major role in consolidating these practices, but state policies did not initiate them. Most developed countries, after all, grant a degree of preferential treatment to small firms without thereby developing the kinds of extensive and competitive networks we find in northern and central Italy.

[58] Laura Weiss, "Explaining the Underground Economy: State and Social Structure," *British Journal of Sociology* 38 (1987): 216–34; Weiss, *Creating Capitalism: The State and Small Businesses Since 1945* (Oxford, 1988).

[59] See Mark Warren, "Exploitation or Cooperation? The Political Basis of Regional Variation in the Italian Informal Economy," *Politics and Society* 22 (1994): 89–115. Warren distinguishes between egalitarian and exploitative informal economies. The informal economies of the northern industrial districts are egalitarian, whereas the southern ones are exploitative. But the world of the industrial districts is not consistently egalitarian, as Warren readily admits in his discussion on gender discrimination and clientelism.

These examples challenge simplistic notions of formality and informality as distinct and separate modes of social and economic interaction. Evidence from the jewelry towns corroborates a conception of the informal economy as a pole in a continuum of shifting and overlapping social relations. After drawing attention to the distinction between work and employment, engendered by the development of capitalist relations and state bureaucracies, Philip Harding and Richard Jenkins have pointed to small businesses as paradigmatic cases of the coexistence of formal and informal relations in many modern societies:

> First, for the self-employed the relationship and distinction between work and employment is in many circumstances unclear. This is most obviously the case with respect to family labour. Second, many small enterprises straddle, with greater or lesser degrees of comfort, the gray area . . . between the formal and informal.[60]

In the jewelry towns actors tended to organize most of their relations in the gray area linking the formal and informal. At least two processes informed this pattern. First, the informal economy depended on the formal sector to thrive. Many workers, for example, combined a regular job with undocumented work in their own basements, and the contacts and skills developed in their official workplace were key to the success of their parallel activities. Second, the more vulnerable actors resorted to formal relations whenever their position in the informal economy threatened to deteriorate. Valenza Po's small-scale artisans, for example, promoted rule-bound institutions to bypass the role of local traders in their dealings with export markets. These institutions simultaneously enhanced the flexibility of the local economies while diffusing social tensions. In other words, they struck a balance between competition and cooperation.

The Structure of the Book

The structure of this book reflects the diversity of local conditions and the need for detailed historical accounts. This diversity, however, will also allow me to foreground in each chapter different theoretical and methodological issues. The next two chapters are devoted to Valenza

---

[60] Philip Harding and Richard Jenkins, *The Myth of the Informal Economy* (Milton Keynes, 1989), 111.

Po, a town located on the Po River halfway between Turin and Milan in northwestern Italy. Valenza Po was an unlikely candidate for a position of leadership in the gold jewelry industry, since it lacked an industrial and artisanal tradition before the late nineteenth century. The town's development can only be explained by reconstructing the interweaving of political and economic relations that turned this previously rural outpost into a major center for jewelry production and a hotbed of socialist activism. Valenza Po's economic structure was dispersed and polycentric from the start and led by an emerging elite of socialist proprietors. The problematic and yet powerful tie between socialism and craftsmanship in the local political culture, as well as the establishment of diffuse networks of patronage relations, was key to Valenza Po's specialization in artisanal jewelry. In chapter 1, I adopt a microhistorical methodology and contrast it with Putnam's macrosocial approach. In so doing, I reinterpret the relation between social networks, political culture, and economic change by crafting a narrative sensitive to the specificity of place and yet informed by theoretical considerations. In particular, I recast social capital as a deliberative process by which certain ties are put to value by actors in perennial conflict over disparate and often contradictory expectations that defy a clear distinction between trust and opportunism.

As chapter 2 will show, Fascism transformed local economic life by creating an ideological fracture between producers and traders. Such fracture also constituted the leitmotif of Valenza Po's political economy after World War II. The commercial agents and larger manufacturers gravitated towards the Christian Democratic Party, while the small-scale producers kept the local leftist tradition alive. This ideological divide made the politics of patronage more problematic, since potential patrons and clients no longer shared the same political views. The outcome of this tension was a distinction between the domestic market, for which hierarchical and informal ties remained crucial, and the international markets, where the left-wing artisans managed to carve a sphere of relative autonomy buttressed by a series of rule-bound institutions. This compromise was key to perpetuating the town's dispersed economic structure and specialization in the upper segments of the market. On a theoretical level, this chapter addresses the relationships between institutional and economic change, with a special emphasis on the distinction between formal and informal relations. In particular, I will show that this distinction was crucial to both drawing and blurring the boundaries between economic action and other spheres of activity, such as political affiliation, the ties of locality, and familial affection. The Coasian issue of the boundary of the firm should be seen as a subset of this broader process of (dis)embedding calculative action in (or from) the fabric of social life.

Whereas the rise of commercial agents in Valenza Po led to an ideological fracture with important social and economic consequences, in Vicenza, the subject of chapter 3, ideological divides originated in the late nineteenth century along class lines, pitting socialist and anarchist workers against their largely Catholic employers. Located in the core of the Veneto, a deeply Catholic region of northeastern Italy, Vicenza had a tradition of artisanal jewelry making dating back to the Middle Ages. Ironically, though, it was there that mechanization made its Italian debut as early as the 1890s, triggering massive resistance from the workers. These tensions exploded in the 1900s, when a series of strikes culminated in the foundation of a cooperative that ended up employing nearly half of the city's jewelry workers. Paradoxically the competition between the cooperative and the local "capitalist" firms accelerated the mechanization and standardization of production and led to the defeat of the workers' movement on the eve of World War I. This defeat led to the creation of a hegemonic group of manufacturers who manipulated access to credit and commercial opportunities for the next fifty years, as Vicenza's jewelry industry boomed into an export-oriented industrial district of small and medium-size firms. This complex trajectory warns us of the difficulties in drawing clear-cut distinctions between horizontal and vertical ties and illustrates the unintended economic consequences of social and political action. Social networks can be promoted for one goal (say, the promotion of utopian change) and effect quite different results (the entrenchment of hierarchical ties of patronage).

A strike was also key to shaping the structure of Arezzo's jewelry industry—the subject of chapter 4. Jewelry making was introduced to Arezzo, a Tuscan town halfway between Florence and Perugia, by Gori & Zucchi in the 1920s. This firm specialized in relatively standardized jewelry produced by highly mechanized processes and hired growing numbers of former sharecroppers, many of whom were women. In the 1950s and early 1960s the company grew into the largest producer and exporter of gold jewelry in the world. Plans for further growth were disrupted by a strike in 1962, after which the company began to farm out an increasing portion of its activity. This process of decentralization was facilitated by two emerging social networks: the hierarchy of subcontractors and home workers that the company had fostered in order to cut on costs and protect itself from state regulation; and the alliance between organized labor and local public authorities, eager to stem what they perceived as the impending feminization of the workforce. This combined effort promoted male entrepreneurship as the solution to the city's problems, and Arezzo's jewelry industry began to approach the model of the Marshallian district of small firms. This chapter will give me the opportunity to discuss the impact of rural relations, especially sharecropping, on Italy's small-scale industrialization, and the importance of gender to the construction of local economies.

In the decades following World War II, Italy carved out a niche in the international division of labor founded on the production and export of "style." Most of the activities falling in this broad category were organized in networks of localized heterogeneous agents, including small and medium-size firms. What is the relationship between local networks and the production of style? I address this question in chapter 5, where I focus on the reinvention of craftsmanship after centuries of "decline"; on the patterns of taste formation that connected the jewelry towns to the international centers of jewelry (above all Paris and the German town of Pforzheim) on the one hand and to the final markets on the other; and on the troubled coexistence of systems of apprenticeship and public schooling as means to transmit knowledge across generations. These cognitive patterns qualify the jewelry towns as sites of a kind of tacit knowledge that was strongly embedded in social and political relations. The goal of this chapter is to investigate the political construction of tacit knowledge, viewed as a collective (rather than public) process that draws boundaries between insiders and outsiders and is constantly negotiated at the local level by actors eager to expand or restrict access to knowledge and redefine its meanings.

Whereas the analysis of the jewelry towns as cognitive spaces draws attention to their boundedness, a discussion of their relations with the international markets and the Italian state reminds us that the ties of locality are constructed, rather than natural. In chapter 6 I situate the Italian jewelry towns in a global map that includes the international trade centers from which gold was imported (above all the Swiss banks), and examine the negotiations between the towns' elites and the state about taxation and the enactment and enforcement of standards. These processes allow me to demonstrate how the local, the national, and the global interacted and constructed each other at different scales. The survival of a global market for gold, for example, required the strong localization of several production and commercialization phases, of which jewelry making was only one part. In a similar vein, local identities were often articulated to the state by resorting to the global languages of science and political justice. In other words, I will treat localization and globalization as symmetrical and interactive processes.

The last chapter of the book situates the jewelry towns in a larger Italian and international context. For all its peculiarities, the Italian jewelry industry was paradigmatic of the country's diverse small-scale capitalism, even though in other sectors certain tensions and contradictions were more subdued. This chapter will also give me the opportunity to compare the Italian jewelry towns with similar experiences around the world. Special attention will be paid to the jewelry industry of Providence, Rhode Island, where I have conducted some archival research. In this section, I intend to defamiliarize a certain kind of American industrial experience by showing how many similarities Providence shared with the Italian towns in terms of organization, labor practices, and political concerns. As in Italy, jewelry making in Providence was strongly embedded in networks of local and extralocal social relations. In the course of the twentieth century, these ties came to be increasingly ethnicized (due to the link between jewelry making and the local immigrant communities) and gendered (due to the extensive use of homework). As Providence deindustrialized and shed much of its population after World War II, jewelry making became simultaneously the city's largest manufacturing industry and a "residual" activity employing thousands of workers in an expanding informal economy buttressed by a strongly rooted political machine. Even though structurally very similar, the Providence jewelry district differed from the Italian cases in the historical context in which it developed and in the culturally situated meanings attached to it. The case of Providence shows the importance of narratives and understandings of the economy to economic change itself.

The Socialists' "City of Gold":
Valenza Po's Jewelry Industry from the 1890s
to the Fascist Era

Even in Italy, few people know that a remarkable portion of the fine jewelry sold at stores in Milan, Venice, and Rome, as well as in New York and Frankfurt, is manufactured in Valenza Po, a small city perched on the misty hills that overlook the Po River a few miles before Piedmont gives way to Lombardy. With a population of less than twenty-five thousand, Valenza Po today boasts more than twelve hundred gold jewelry firms with over seven thousand employees, not to mention the undocumented workers who toil at home in the few months before the Christmas rush. There is hardly a family in town not involved with the jewelry business. Yet the uninformed visitor would probably never realize that this is one of the leading jewelry centers in the world, one of the very few places in which the daring designs of a Cartier or a Bulgari can be turned into objects of exquisite craftsmanship. Aside from the inconspicuous plates by the doors of some small factories in the city center, very few signs advertise the town's most prestigious activity. Even the factory plates are relatively recent: until the 1940s, locals had to give strangers directions to the shops by referring to the color of their building or their proximity to public sites.

Several international companies specializing in the trade of gold and precious stones opened branches in town after. World War II. But one need not be a Dutch diamond trader to feel like a stranger in Valenza Po. Carlo Fuoco, the editor of a trade journal based in Milan, took a day trip to the Piedmontese town at the height of its postwar economic boom in the late 1950s. Upon his return, he rhetorically addressed Valenza Po's inhabitants in his magazine and complained about their notorious unfriendliness and diffidence:

> Valenza Po has always been a strange town. Maybe you who live there don't realize it, but the visitor is shocked into a state of frustration and mortification. To start with . . . the town is very badly

connected by railway. The visitor finds it extremely hard to get directions to a street or even to a very well known firm. Everyone stares at you with an inexplicable sense of mistrust. When you ring the bell of an office or factory, people take their time to open the door, and then an intimidated face or a couple of inquisitive eyes show up, as though people in Valenza never received any visits except from the tax police or the finance minister![1]

The treatment reserved for nosy journalists from the big city might have been particularly harsh, but overall Fuoco's assessment resonates with my own experience as a researcher forty years later. The glamour of Valenza Po's production still contrasts with the atmosphere of secrecy that envelops its activities.

Secrecy and mistrust appear all the more paradoxical in light of the town's political history. Between 1890 and 1920, Valenza Po developed a double identity as an entrepreneurial center and a hotbed of socialist politics. Small-scale jewelry entrepreneurs were at the forefront of political change, and Valenza Po's prosperity relied on political connections whose common bond was socialist ideology. This link between socialism and proprietary capitalism survived the onslaught of Fascism and the war. Until very recently, despite the success of separatist Lega Nord (Northern League) in much of small-town Piedmont, Valenza Po remained a "red" island in an expanding sea of xenophobia and parochialism.[2] Signs of the recent left-wing past still dot the urban landscape. A monument at the edge of town commemorates the Lenti gang, a group of local partisans executed by the Nazi-Fascists in 1944. The link between the partisans' struggle and the town's self-image as a socialist manufacturing center is vividly rendered in the decorations of the public swimming pool by Mirko Gualerzi. In his bas-reliefs, representations of agriculture, jewelry making, and shoe manufacturing fuse with images of popular struggle against fascism to suggest a coherent identity forged in work and progressive politics.[3] The main piazza and the surrounding streets buzz every evening with the whispers and shouts of political debate. The Valenzani, even many of those

---

[1] Carlo Fuoco, "Lettera aperta al Comm. Luigi Illario di Valenza Po," *L'Industria Orafa Italiana*, 15 May 1959, 3.

[2] A Right-of-center coalition led by Berlusconi's party, Forza Italia, and including the post-Fascists (but not the Northern League) captured the city government by winning the municipal elections in April 2000.

[3] Franco Castelli, *Le Storie d'Acqua di Mirko Gualerzi* (Genoa, 1991).

who no longer vote for the parties of the Left, are proud of this political heritage and never tire of celebrating their town's vibrant associational life. The web site of the city government lists fifty-seven associations, ranging from the Lions Club and two blood and organ donors' groups to a boxing club and no less than ten business and union organizations.[4] This image of social and political vibrancy is reinforced by Valenza Po's economic success. The town's prosperity is almost legendary in the province of Alessandria, where Valenza Po is located, and is well known in northern italy as a whole.

On the one hand, thus, Valenza Po's economic and political development seems to confirm Putnam's model of social capital. The vitality of the town's civil society was key to both economic success and political participation. On the other hand, however, mistrust and diffidence are distinctive traits of the town's social and economic life. Nor is this contradiction easily mapped onto the distinction between locals and strangers. As I will show in this chapter, the coexistence of trust and diffidence, of cooperation and guile, and of inclusive and exclusive practices informed relations both among locals and between the town and the larger world. In addition to the problems I have outlined in the introduction, Putnam's notion of social capital postulates the existence of an autonomous structure of resilient relations of trust and participation, which makes it hard to explain abrupt historical changes. Putnam's social networks are firmly anchored in the *longue durée* of deep continuities to which historical actors might even be completely oblivious. It is the task of the omniscient social scientist to distinguish the ephemeral and contingent (and therefore irrelevant) event from the long-term structural patterns that inform the actors' response to each other and the world beyond them. Only through this problematic process of selection does it become possible to ignore the fact that networks of social relations embedded in the life forms of civil society generate a broad range of contradictory phenomena, some of which have little to do with trust and prosperity. The rise of fascism in 1920s northern Italy and the success of the Lega Nord in the 1990s are cases in point. In sum, Putnam's model fetishizes civil society and associational life, which come to stand for precisely the kinds of "positive" traits (trust, democratic participation, economic prosperity) that are supposedly related to social capital itself. The ultimate irony is that the circularity of the argument makes the theory of the omniscient scientist

[4] See http://www.valenza.it/comune/associazioni.php, accessed on 29 January 2006.

and the perspective of the interested participant coincide: both Putnam and many of Valenza Po's citizens link civic virtues and economic prosperity through palatable myths of origin.

My goal in this chapter is not to unmask these myths and retrieve an authentic dimension of historical change and social action. Rather, I will take these myths of civic virtue seriously, as powerful cultural practices promoted and shared by historical actors themselves. I will show that socialist politics in turn-of-the-century Valenza Po should be interpreted as problematic practices meant to construct civic virtue and thereby mediate the challenges of economic competition and political conflict. But I will also show how socialist politics coexisted uneasily with clientelistic ties, familial loyalties, class antagonism, and gender inequalities. This richness of social life was the venue for diverse and contradictory choices, which can only be appreciated in their interaction. In other words, I will reinterpret social capital not as an explanatory model rooted in the long-term structural traits of local society, but as a set of social resources unequally distributed in local society. To do this means to challenge the distinction between the actors' choices and the social networks they help define. Instead of focusing on the resilience of social networks, I chart the flow of multiple local and extralocal "currencies"—gold, money, and promissory notes; trust and malfeasance; familial affection, class solidarity, and clientelistic loyalty— that built vulnerable and shifting relations. Instead of taking community and the institutions of economic cooperation as my starting point, I view them as problematic and provisional projects.

The methodology adopted in this chapter is primarily microhistorical: I offer a thick description of exchanges taking place among specific actors, rather than propose a model based on the interpretation of aggregate data.[5] The rationale for this methodological choice is not merely suggested by the relatively small size of Valenza Po, a town of little more than ten thousand people at the turn of the twentieth century. Rather, I intend to explicitly contrast the microhistorical approach with the statistical treatment of long-term quantitative variables collected at the regional and national levels. Putnam's

[5] This is only one of the possible interpretations of microhistory. Many scholars have remarked that there is no uncontroversial definition of the microhistorical method, and some would deny that such a thing even exists. For an overview of this debate, see Edward Muir, "Observing trifles," In Edward Muir and Guido Ruggiero, eds., *Microhistory and the Lost Peoples of Europe* (Baltimore, 1991), vii–xxviii; and Florike Egmond and Peter Mason, *The Mammoth and the Mouse: Microhistory and Morphology* (Baltimore, 1997).

methodology aims at calculating disembedded indicators of political participation, which convey average or normative characteristics (say, membership in voluntary associations relative to the total population) amenable to producing social scientific generalizations. This chapter aims instead at providing a narrative sensitive to the complexities and ambiguities of local meaning. From the perspective of the omniscient social scientist intent on mapping large-scale and long-term disparities, membership in an association assumes a homogenous and unproblematic meaning (namely, receptivity to democratic participation), which can be easily aggregated. But viewed "from below," from the perspective of the historical actors themselves, membership in an association appears as a vastly more heterogeneous and contradictory form of action, which combines diverse motivations and consequences, at both the individual and the collective levels. A single act of membership in a local association might simultaneously represent an altruistic choice, a calculating decision, an emotional response, and an attempt at devising a scheme to cheat others. In sum, as many microhistorians have argued, choices of scale have powerful epistemological and political implications.

Even though the microhistorical approach resists the generalizing impulse associated with the "top-down" gaze of the omniscient social scientist, microhistorians are not necessarily bound to simply celebrate the uniqueness of the unrepeatable event. Rather, they investigate the historical record with a keen eye ready to detect the "normal exception," in Edoardo Grendi's famous and whimsical expression.[6] Two possible interpretations of this oxymoron are central to the argument of this chapter. First, the practices of trust and community are always predicated on the constant potential presence of their opposites: guile and defection. Even in a putatively trust-conducive social environment, the possibility and plausibility of betrayal give meaning to the actors' choices. Therefore, the norm and the exception are ontologically linked, and only a methodology sensitive to such ambiguity can move beyond the truisms of circular reasoning ("in a trust-informed context people trust each other") and do justice to the contingencies and unpredictability that make historical change an interesting subject of inquiry ("what does trust mean to whom, and when

---

[6] Edoardo Grendi, "Microanalisi e storia sociale," *Quaderni Storici* 35 (1977): 506–20. For a more recent reformulation of Grendi's expression, see Edoardo Grendi, "Ripensare la microstoria?" *Quaderni Storici* 86 (1994): 539–49.

and why is such trust broken?"). Second, historians are themselves potential victims of a very specific kind of cheating scheme: not only is the past rewritten by the victors, but the very memory of conflict is often erased as well. If presentism is a constant danger, the historian must treat the past as thoroughly dead in order to revive it, to paraphrase Carlo Ginzburg.[7] Conflict (the norm) can be retrieved by focusing on the (exceptional) moments in which the vulnerability of normality becomes apparent. The meanings of trust and community reveal their politically charged dimensions when they cease to be taken for granted. This is my rationale for concentrating on the sources of mistrust (bankruptcy records, petty criminal trials, anonymous allegations, etc.), which illuminate the transactions through which community is built and challenged. In so doing, it is necessary to move from an ontology of structured networks to a topology of flows in which normality and exception are mutually constitutive.

A Sense of Place

To move from nodes to flows—and from positions in resilient networks to transactions between shifting and overlapping social spaces—does not mean to lose sight of the materiality of social interaction. We need to resist the temptation (so pervasive in contemporary economic theory) to interpret transactions in terms of disembodied information, subject to the iron laws of rational action and therefore impermeable to the inflections of time and space. The topology of flows that I propose is firmly anchored in the specificity of place. Sensitivity to place is indeed crucial to the historical study of economic action and dovetails with the attention to the politics of scale characteristic of the microhistorical approach. Attention to the spatial dimension of historical change is a powerful antidote both to the totalizing ambitions of ppnomothetic social science à la Putnam and to the disembodied self-referentiality of discourse analysis. Above all, to view place as recursively linked to social action (both as an actor in its own right and as a product of historical change) simultaneously restores and contextualizes

---

[7] Carlo Ginzburg, "Paradigma indiziario e conoscenza storica," *Quaderni Storici* 12 (1980): 3–54. See also Jacques Revel, "Microanalisi e costruzione del sociale," *Quaderni Storici* 86 (1994): 549–75.

agency.[8] In other words, economic action is not only embedded in social networks of interpersonal relations, but also enacted and en-placed in malleable spatial contexts.

Valenza Po's debut as the "socialist city of gold" at the beginning of the twentieth century was not simply an example of localized socioeconomic change or the local incarnation of a disembodied path to modernity appropriate to provincial Italy. These formulas take locality for granted, and in so doing they naturalize community, trust, and prosperity, viewed as unproblematic products of geographical and social proximity. I intend to invert this equation and investigate first the production of locality as a contested and provisional practice and then the multiple meanings that locality assumed for various actors at different times—meanings themselves productive of social and spatial change.

So what kind of place was Valenza Po in the late nineteenth century? In more than one sense, it was a non-place. Located at the intersection of the spheres of influence of Turin and Milan, Valenza Po was too far from both cities (approximately ninety kilometers) to be regarded as a satellite of either. In the early modern period, it had profited from this liminal position to become a fortress town and a minor commercial center presiding over the trade flowing along the Po River between the territory of the Savoy dynasty and Lombardy. The course of the river shifted a few hundred meters to the north and its former bank ended up hosting a meandering little tributary, the Grana. Moreover, the unification of Italy in 1859–60, which erased the border between the Kingdom of Piedmont-Sardinia and Austrian Lombardy—together with the development of railways and a more extensive road network linking Turin, Milan, and Genoa—made the formerly strategic location of Valenza Po more of a hindrance than an advantage. The creation of an integrated national market threatened to push Valenza Po into oblivion. Squeezed between the hills of Monferrato to the south and west, and the hazardous alluvial banks of the Po to the north and east, the town looked more like a space bypassed by modernity than a promising locale for industrial activity. Nor was Valenza Po blessed with fertile agricultural land. Neither the plain nor the hills yielded particularly valuable produce. If anything, the surrounding vineyards stood

[8] For the methodological and epistemological consequences of taking spatiality seriously, and not simply as a neutral background to social processes, see Thomas Gieryn, "A Space for Place in Sociology," *Annual Review of Sociology* 26 (2000): 463–96. For a valuable collection of essays foregrounding spatiality in the Italian context, see John Agnew, *Place and Politics in Modern Italy* (Chicago, 2002).

out for their mediocrity, nested as they were between the renowned Piedmontese hills to the west and Pavia's Oltrepo to the east.

The town layout was not particularly distinctive either, at least until the very end of the nineteenth century. The growth of the town had been stunted by its position, since no construction was allowed (or advisable) on the alluvial banks to the north and east, towards the river. In this constrained urban environment, population density was very high and publicly lamented by the local notables. Cholera and other infectious diseases were distressingly recurrent. What constitutes today the town center (and was until the 1890s the whole town) still preserves its medieval character almost intact, though it is no longer surrounded by walls. Two relatively broad and almost straight streets, probably of Roman origin, divide the town into three sections, called *sorti* in the local dialect, each with its name (Bedoglio, Astigliano, and Monasso) and putatively distinctive identity. Superimposed on this simple pattern lies a maze of narrow alleys and cul-de-sacs interrupted only by the relatively small piazza, where a homely duomo faces an equally unimpressive city hall. The broader streets and the piazza are the only truly public spaces in the town center. Many of the alleys lead to minuscule blind courtyards, hybrid spaces that are simultaneously private and public and are therefore overlooked by the map drafters. Only the people who live in the surrounding buildings are fully entitled to frequent these courtyards. A stranger would be immediately spotted. It was primarily in the garrets and basements facing these cul-de-sacs that gold jewelry making spread at the turn of the twentieth century.

How did this unimpressive town develop its distinctive identity? How did it shift from a non-place to a unique locality? This transformation took place relatively rapidly at the end of the century, and it bore the signs of modernity. First of all, of course, there was gold jewelry production. This activity arrived in Valenza Po in quite an accidental way in the mid–nineteenth century. At this time, the only major industry in town was a silk-spinning mill founded by an entrepreneur from Turin and employing young rural women willing to put in eleven hours of work a day to come up with a respectable dowry. Local historians have painstakingly reconstructed the "genealogy" of the earliest jewelry makers. The "patriarch" seems to have been Vincenzo Morosetti, who was born in the provincial capital of Alessandria and established a small factory in Valenza Po in the early 1840s. Thirty years later, in 1872, there were 5 firms employing 110 workers.

All these entrepreneurs had been trained in Morosetti's factory, and were also related to each other through marriages.[9] Growth was very gradual but steady. In 1889, there were 25 firms with 222 workers, and by 1911 there were 43 firms with 613 workers. At the same time, the population had not increased much, from roughly 9,500 in the early 1860s to approximately 10,500 fifty years later. This data shows that both jewelry production and shoe making, the other industry that developed after 1890,[10] were locally based activities that did not attract much immigration.

These economic changes were partly reflected in the town's layout. In the 1890s a modern addition of a couple dozen blocks was built directly south of the old section—a prelude to the much larger expansion to the south and west that took place in the 1950s and 1960s. The rational layout of the neighborhood, with its perfectly perpendicular streets arranged around an ample square, now named after Antonio Gramsci, contrasted with the seeming chaos of traditional Valenza. The most important jewelry entrepreneurs chose the modern section for their plants, even though they often brought their wares to the family businesses in the old part of town to be polished and finished.

The rationally planned neighborhood was not the only physical sign announcing the dawn of a new era. On the other side of town, pitted against the northern slope of the hill hosting old Valenza, a plant for the production of gas began its activity in 1893. The construction of this plant, chartered as a cooperative, signaled the debut of a new kind of politics in town. The old elite of wealthy professionals and landowners, who had dominated public life for generations, had to come to terms with a dynamic group of progressive entrepreneurs determined to fight paternalism and stagnation. After much debate the city government, led by a conservative coalition, granted the cooperative the authority to manage the town's first modern system of public lighting.[11] Faced with the choice between gas lighting and electricity, the cooperative chose the former, even though electricity was widely seen as technically superior. The rationale for this decision was the need to foster gold jewelry production, gas being a fuel much more suitable to goldsmithing than the coke and charcoal used by the first Valenza Po

[9] Lia Lenti, *Gioielli e Gioiellieri di Valenza: Arte e Storia Orafa 1825–1975* (Turin, 1994), 118–36.

[10] In 1911, there were twenty shoe-making firms with 560 workers. See Archivio Storico della Città di Valenza, vol. 1126, Censimento industriale 1911.

[11] "L'illuminazione di Valenza," *Avanti*, 11 December 1892.

artisans in the 1870s and 1880s. The fact that the leaders of the cooperative included several jewelry manufacturers was barely remarked
upon. In one bold stroke, public good and private benefits were made
to coincide. The local debate over this program revealed the progressive character of the initiative. The foundation of the gas cooperative
paralleled a number of changes that affected local public life at the end
of the century, for example novel public health measures against cholera.[12] To respond to public health concerns, another cooperative was
established for the distribution of drinking water and the restructuring
of the sewage system.

Municipal socialism, then at the height of its expansion in many
parts of Europe, saw the city government itself as a glorified cooperative providing public services and mediating local conflicts.[13] But in
Valenza Po municipal socialism was not merely a strategy to offer public goods in the sectors in which market relations threatened to fail. As
the example of the gas cooperative shows, these collective initiatives
created spaces for public debate in which competing private interests
and the common good meshed to create hybrid political creatures. The
link between the physical networks for the distribution of gas or run-
ning water and the social networks of locality was more than meta-
phorical. A renewed sense of place, now tied to visions of progress
rather than to the shackles of tradition, was being forged at the intersection of market relations and political ties. Valenza Po's citizens—at
least those who were endowed with a political voice—felt that they
were in charge of shaping their future. They were conquering darkness
and cholera, and when a different kind of disease, phylloxera, began
to wreak havoc in the local vineyards in the late 1890s, it became clear
that a clean break with the past was called for.[14]

However mediocre, Valenza Po's wine had been the town's only export for generations. Now the phylloxera epidemic, which threatened
to expel small-scale farmers from the land, signaled the end of an era.
Jewelry making and shoe manufacturing would provide the solution
to hunger and unemployment. A new class of entrepreneurs was

---

[12] In the face of the severe cholera epidemic that struck the town in 1893, the socialist
journal *Avanti* insisted on the need to organize a distribution system of drinking water.
See "Socialismo municipale," *Avanti*, 9 February 1895.

[13] About municipal socialism, see at least Patrizia Dogliani, *Un Laboratorio di Socialismo
Municipale: La Francia (1870–1920)* (Milan, 1992); and Maurizio degl'Innocenti, *Le Sinistre
e il Governo Locale in Europa: Dalla Fine dell'800 alla Seconda Guerra Mondiale* (Pisa, 1984).

[14] Archivio Storico della Città di Valenza, vol. 1115, Agricoltura, folder 2.

ready to rise to the challenge. In a sense, gold and leather were not different from gas and water: they could be fruitfully used to forge alliances in the face of uncertainty. Of course gas and water were public goods, while gold and leather were—at least at first sight—undeniably private. But as they began to circulate in local society, these raw materials assumed public meanings and functions. For the endangered farmers, they represented an opportunity to diversify the household economy and partake of the promises of industrial modernity. For the entrepreneurs, gold and leather were more than materials to be processed at a profit: they built obligations and conferred prestige, which could in turn be transformed into political clout. The flow of local materials tended to blur the boundaries between private interest and public good.

To many of Valenza Po's emerging economic and political entrepreneurs, progress was inseparable from socialist ideals. Socialism provided the ideological and emotional cement with which the ties of locality could be created and enforced. At the same time, socialism linked the town's fortunes to broader—even universal—discourses. The founder of the local socialist movement, Giusto Calvi, was a journalist with a literary background who crossed the Atlantic Ocean twice in the 1880s and 1890s, first to go to Buenos Aires—the destination of choice for Valenza Po's emigrants—and then to the United States. It was probably in Argentina that he moved from the radical-republican ideas of his youth to socialism, which he then proceeded to import to his hometown. Upon his return, Calvi simultaneously founded Valenza Po's first local paper and the town's first political club, named after Giuseppe Garibaldi. The popularity of these initiatives was remarkable. Though the suffrage was restricted to less than 20 percent of the population, in 1893 Calvi and two of his comrades (one of whom was a gold jewelry producer) won seats in the city council, where they began to fight for "modernization." The gas cooperative, the new water supply system, and the struggle against cholera were the tangible signs of this political change.

But cholera, according to the local socialists, was not the only disease to disrupt Valenza Po's social body. The expansion of gold jewelry and shoe making raised the specters of capitalism and mechanization. In the eyes of the local socialist press, these were monstrous forces: "The machine . . . will continue its leveling action, equalizing men, women, and children."[15] Capitalism meant above all competition, which would have led first to the general qualitative deterioration of production, and then to the widespread barbarization of social relations, increasingly permeated with opportunism and diffidence.[16] In fact, the local socialists' political culture was rife with ambiguities. Despite their attacks on the dangers of mechanization, they attributed the backwardness of the local and national jewelry industry vis-à-vis Germany precisely to the resistance of local producers against mechanized division of labor. Moreover, the determinism of the Second International viewed any struggle against the advancing forces of capitalist production as hopeless.[17]

The local socialists' official solution to these threats was the formation of production cooperatives, which constituted both an alternative to capitalist competition and the basis of the future society, founded on the collectivizing power of the machines. In this scheme, small independent firms were ruled out as relics of a preindustrial past. Yet, while the only production cooperative, founded in 1902, never played a major role in local economic and political life, the emerging elite of socialist entrepreneurs in fact fostered the development of networks of small firms. Why were Valenza Po's socialists railing against the dangers of capitalism, and at the same time promoting the very changes they were stigmatizing? What was the actual role of socialist ideology in the development of jewelry production and small businesses in general?

Valenza Po's socialists were not simply reacting to changes imposed by the state or the market. Instead, they were actively promoting and interpreting "modernization" on their own terms. The socialist political culture was key to the local construction of market relations. As an emerging elite, local entrepreneurs could not resort to tradition as a source of legitimization. Vulnerable as it was, Valenza Po's entrepreneurial elite relied on a distinctive and locally based political culture as a way of charging unstable social and economic ties with moral connotations. This political culture provided uncertain economic relations with a language of solidarity and expectations of reciprocity. In other words, socialist politics reshaped the meanings and functions of locality, without, however, erasing the possibility of conflict. This process

---

[15] "La nostra produzione economica," *Avanti*, 18 February 1893.

[16] "Siamo un popolo di furfanti?" *Avanti*, 14 May 1893.

[17] See, for example, James Joll, *The Second International, 1889–1914* (London, 1975).

was so successful that by the 1910s the interweaving of political and economic ties made "this small and industrious town, so high and clear against its splendid sky, all feverish with Bolshevik insanity," as a Fascist pundit remembered in the 1930s.[18] How was the construction of this paradoxical community of socialist proprietors achieved?

SERVING GOD AND MAMMON

The socialists' obsession with trust, betrayal, and the threat of social barbarization can be viewed as a commentary on the consequences of market volatility. Their faith in the virtues of cooperation stemmed from the belief that in a Smithian scenario of self-serving actors freely competing in the marketplace, uncertainty and instability would escalate out of control, dissolving the social fabric from within. Despite some of their rhetoric, however, the local socialists did not want to replace a world of calculating agents with a utopian community in which complete forbearance would become the norm. Rather, they hoped that the ties forged in political activity would lay the foundations of an "enlightened" form of calculativeness, in which both profits and losses would be widely shared in local society in such a way as to smooth over the peaks and valleys of business cycles. This desire for stability was not a carryover from a traditional rural past, for the Valenzani knew all too well that the ups and downs of agriculture could be brutal. Instead, the local socialists were responding to a need widely felt among the emerging entrepreneurs themselves.

The volatility of the jewelry business was (and is) extreme. Market demand had a seasonal component, with a major peak in the fall (in preparation for the Christmas festivities) and a smaller one in the early spring (in preparation for the late-spring and early-summer wedding season). Superimposed on this seasonal rhythm was the long-term economic trend, which alternated phases of expansion and contraction, the demand for gold jewelry being very sensitive to a wide variety of national and international circumstances. By the end of the nineteenth century, Valenza Po's citizens were so aware of market fluctuations that they had devised special words in their dialect for market boom (*la bón-na*) and crisis (*la móla*). As a common adage warned, crisis always followed boom (*dop la bón-na la móla*). As we will see, local leaders de-

[18] "Martirologio fascista: Vincenzo Alferano," *Il Piccolo*, 13 June 1931.

vised ways of coping with short-term seasonal fluctuations, mostly by promoting an informal sector populated by married women and children. But long-term volatility posed more serious challenges, which could not be addressed only at the local level.

Socialist ideology was crucial to the construction of locality and community precisely because it promised to forge bonds strong enough to weather market crises and resist opportunistic behaviors. But it is important to steer clear of functionalist reasoning: socialist ideology did not simply serve as a solution to a problem of coordination between economic agents by promoting commitment and trust. First of all, socialist ideology spoke the language of promises and projects; it did not offer ready-made solutions to economic challenges. Socialism warned that people might have to serve Mammon (the lures of commerce), but they must keep in mind that faith in God (the promise of justice and equality) was what gave their life meaning. However, such meaning was highly contested: socialism in Valenza Po did not emanate from a clearly defined center. Giusto Calvi refused to merge the local clubs into the national party (founded in Genoa in 1892) for as long as he could. Socialism had to be coextensive with the tensions and hopes of *local* society. In a very material sense, socialism was a local God that spoke a language of universal values. Ideology was not superimposed on social and economic relations in order to lubricate and facilitate them. Rather, ideology was enacted in the shops and in the streets as a matter of everyday life. Much like gold itself, socialism was a universal currency with contested and shifting local meanings.

Two economic downturns tested the resilience of locality and the relatively young link between socialism and entrepreneurship. The first crisis took place in 1905–6, and the second in 1911–12. In both cases, the downturns led to chains of bankruptcies whose records are preserved at the Archivio di Stato in Alessandria. These bankruptcies did not affect only marginal firms; they hit the very core of the local social and economic system, thereby reconfiguring the pathways through which flowed promises, commitments, betrayals, and their material embodiments (money, promissory notes, precious metals, etc.). By focusing on these episodes of crisis, it becomes possible to map local interpersonal relations precisely when such relations became simultaneously most vulnerable and most critical to actors' survival.

The first link in the chain of bankruptcies was that of Carlo Balzano, tried for fraudulent bankruptcy, fraud, and embezzlement in 1905–6.[19] Balzano was a well-known member of the local socialist movement and former city councilor. The socialist journal *La Scure* defined him as both a "loser" and "one of our most fervent comrades, . . . forthcoming with all kinds of initiatives, highly esteemed even by his enemies."[20] Balzano embodied many of the opportunities and contradictions of a town like Valenza Po, where economic and political action were intertwined in fruitful and yet unpredictable ways. Political ties had turned this thirty-two-year-old plebeian (*popolano*) into an entrepreneur "capable" of piling up debts for over 300,000 lire.[21] Born to an extremely poor family, even at political meetings he expressed himself "in his distinctive Valenzan dialect, barely Italianized in its terminations."[22] Balzano started his political career and his economic venture in his early twenties, when Carlo Visconti, an established goldsmith of socialist faith, offered him a loan of 8,050 lire. Carlo Visconti and his partner Gaudino ran one of the largest jewelry firms in town, with thirty-seven workers in 1899.[23] Visconti was also one of the founders, with Giusto Calvi, of the Circolo Garibaldi, the precursor of Valenza Po's first socialist club.[24] The contiguity between Balzano and the local socialists did not stop there. The trial records reveal that both Balzano's house and the premises of his factory belonged to Carlotta Garrone, Giusto Calvi's mother and a socialist activist herself. Balzano really was a creature of Valenza Po's socialist movement.

Defending her "fallen" comrade, Carlotta Garrone argued before the court that Balzano's "ambition was to demonstrate that it [was] possible to make a fortune, and yet scrupulously preserve one's honesty in

---

[19] Archivio di Stato di Alessandria, Tribunale di Alessandria, processi penali, vol. 3407.

[20] "Un vinto: Carlo Balzano," *La Scure*, 3 May 1906.

[21] To give a sense of the size of this debt, it is worth mentioning that at the time, one gram of 18-carat gold was worth 2.5 lire. Balzano's debt corresponded to some 120 kilograms of precious metal.

[22] "Un vinto: Carlo Balzano," *La Scure*, cit.

[23] Archivio Storico della Città di Valenza, vol. 846, Industrie Diverse, folder 451.

[24] Francesco Bove, "Diffondere il veleno: Giusto Calvi e gli inizi del socialismo a Valenza," *Quaderno 15 dell'Istituto per la Storia della Resistenza in provincia di Alessandria e Asti* 8 (Spring 1985): 17–48.

business relationships."[25] Garrone's remarks echoed those in the local socialist press, which, in presenting Balzano's case as paradigmatic, used a well-traveled biblical image: he had tried to serve God and Mammon at the same time. Carlo Visconti, on the other hand, stigmatized Balzano for "financing generously his political friends,"[26] forgetting that he had done precisely the same thing ten years before in Balzano's favor.

Within an emerging elite like the jewelry entrepreneurs of Valenza Po, social and political status was crucially dependent on economic success. Consequently, some of the most vulnerable members of this elite tended to make up for their handicaps by outdoing their rivals through economic achievement. Balzano's case is paradigmatic of this tendency. In 1899, his firm included a partner, a polisher, and an apprentice. Thus, it began as the smallest technically viable size. Six years later, right before declaring bankruptcy, the firm employed between thirty and thirty-five workers. The inventory of the factory included over sixty-six thousand lire's worth of jewelry. Balzano had even opened a branch for precious stone trade in Milan, activity that during the trial was repeatedly defined as an overly ambitious step for a small provincial entrepreneur, and as one of the main causes of the bankruptcy.

What is rather surprising is that Balzano inaugurated his Milanese activity in 1901, when his firm started to show the first signs of financial stress. These connections in the big city allowed Balzano to start building his network of clients by involving many of his fellow citizens in audacious speculations. He tried to become a well-connected middleman specializing in diamond trading and convinced several small entrepreneurs from his hometown to join him in his ventures. As his jewelry business started to go down because of the bankruptcy of several of his customers, Balzano concentrated all his efforts in the trade of precious stones. Many of the stones and of the other items commissioned to him ended up in Milan's main pawn agency. As he grew more and more desperate for money, Balzano started to sell even the pawn bills for a small percentage of their value, in a spiral of ruinous operations. It was Balzano's stone suppliers in Milan that tracked him down in Switzerland, where he had fled after the bankruptcy. Re-

---

[25] Archivio di Stato di Alessandria, Tribunale di Alessandria, processi penali, vol. 3407, 70.

[26] Ibid., 67.

vealingly, the person who convinced Balzano to surrender was the Republican lawyer Alberto Merlani, a native of Valenza Po, member of Parliament, and foremost patron of the town's emerging entrepreneurial elite.

Balzano was found guilty of several counts of fraud and embezzlement, but he only spent a few months in jail during and after the trial. The court judgment stated that his downfall was due "not so much to the despicable sake of gain . . . as to his thoughtlessness and desire to avoid, more than his own, other people's ruin."[27] He had acted on the desperate attempt to preserve his loyalty and reputation before his comrades and employees. In other words, in taking advantage of other people's trust, he had tried to fulfill his obligations. His fellow townspeople, however, were less lenient. Balzano was effectively banned from Valenza Po's political and economic life. Since the Ministry of the Interior had a file about him, we know that he moved to Milan, where he became a pearl salesman.[28] Without strong connections, there he was tempted to take advantage once again of his customers' trust, and in 1915 was sentenced in Rome to a year and a half of imprisonment for embezzlement. During the Fascist era he openly repudiated his old socialist ideals and was consequently canceled from the list of the subversives in 1930.

Balzano's vicissitudes show social capital at work. He built an extensive social network by exchanging a variety of connected currencies, both material and immaterial. Gold, promissory notes, pearls, pawn bills, and of course political loyalty were all implicated in constructing "the market." Economic credit and political loyalty were coextensive in Valenza Po, in the sense that one could be easily translated into the other and both worked as hedges against an uncertain future. This political economy of localized flows, however, did not operate in a vacuum; connections to the larger world had to be established, nurtured, and carefully monitored. The ties of locality could work their magic only by reaching out into the unknown. And though local actors admired economic prowess as a sign of progress and defiance of tradition, it mattered a great deal who raised his head above the crowd and built bridges with Milan, Antwerp, and other centers of economic power. Valenza Po's hierarchy was predicated on the degree of access

[27] Ibid., 235.

[28] Archivio Centrale dello Stato, Ministero dell'Interno, Casellario Politico Centrale, vol. 298, folder Balzano Carlo.

of local actors to external connections. To climb the social ladder meant to preside over the flows of goods and relations entering and exiting the town, and the ties of locality were protected above all by monitoring who got to serve this all-important function. Balzano had exceeded his rightful place in the local hierarchy by dealing directly with the diamond suppliers in Milan, and in so doing he had upset the unstable balance between local cohesion and individualistic action. Balzano's conduct might have ruined the reputation of Valenza Po's producers vis-à-vis the Milanese suppliers, and his fellow citizens were generally happy to show the Milanese that they could enforce local discipline. The gap between the court's sentence and the community's attitude towards Balzano shows how complex the interplay of individual honor and collective morality was in Valenza Po. No one doubted that Balzano had tried to fulfill his obligations towards customers, friends, and employees; the court and his former allies concurred that his zeal in so doing had been a central factor in his ruin. But sometimes one had to lose face for the sake of a greater good. Balzano was expected to let a few down to save the many. His fellow citizens interpreted his insistence on protecting his individual honor as hubris and never forgave him for that.

If Balzano's case represents the archetypal story of an individual's rise and fall, in which economic, social, and political ties are inextricably intertwined, the bankruptcy of the local bank of Lorenzo Visconti in 1910–11 brought the contradictions of the local industrial and political development to the surface. The three volumes of trial records, containing more than two thousand pages of testimony, represent a veritable mine of information on the social and economic relationships among Valenza Po's jewelry producers before World War I.[29] Roughly nine-tenths of local goldsmiths resorted to the bank's services, and therefore almost all the local jewelry firms were affected by its downfall.[30] Visconti's bankruptcy signaled the apex of a cumulative process of market crisis and financial difficulties that began in 1904–5, peaked during Italy's conflict in Libya in 1911–12, and only ended after the Great War. The relationships between the bank and local producers show once again the interconnectedness of local currencies, adding clientelistic loyalty to the mix. The bank provided not only credit and

[29] Archivio di Stato di Alessandria, Tribunale di Alessandria, processi penali, vol. 3573.

[30] "Il fallimento della Banca Lorenzo Visconti," *La Scure*, 23 July 1910.

raw gold, but also protection and personal connections to those who were regarded as trustworthy. Lorenzo Visconti himself was much more than a professional banker: he was a powerful patron who could determine one's success or failure at the drop of his hat.

The establishment of the Visconti Bank represented yet another sign of the political changes shaking Valenza Po at the end of the nineteenth century. The old elite of landowners had pooled its resources to take over a bank in a nearby town, the Banca Popolare della Lomellina, and moved it to Valenza Po under the leadership of a much-discussed Milanese director. But this operation proved ill fated. After a few years the bank closed its doors, and many in town immediately blamed the debacle on the absenteeism of the old elite and the greed and incompetence of the "foreign" director. Now it was time for the emerging progressive entrepreneurs to give it a shot. In 1897 Carlo Visconti, Balzano's original supporter, contacted a former employee of the Banca Popolare della Lomellina, Lorenzo Visconti (no family connection, as far as I can tell) about founding a new financial institution with the resources of the local entrepreneurs.

From the very beginning, the bank catered to the local jewelry producers by offering two crucial services: the supply of precious metals and the discount of long-term promissory notes. Quite often the producers gave the bank the promissory notes and received gold in return. It is easy to see why trust and reputation were central to these operations. In accepting the notes, the bank had to rely on the producer's reputation, since it had very little information on their customers (jewelry retailers or wholesalers were scattered throughout northern and central Italy). On the other hand, the power achieved by Visconti vis-à-vis local producers is highlighted by the bank's ability to unilaterally exploit this trust. As far as gold was concerned, for example, during the bankruptcy trial several goldsmiths accused Visconti of cheating on measures of fineness, selling 970- or 980-millesimal metal as pure gold.[31] The most serious problem, however, concerned credit practices. Because of the intense competition among producers and the market crisis that accompanied the war in Libya in 1911, many jewelry producers were forced to accept long-term promissory notes (for over six months) from their customers. The terms of these promissory notes were too long to be immediately bankable. Therefore, Visconti's bank

---

[31] Archivio di Stato di Alessandria, Tribunale di Alessandria, processi penali, vol. 3573, folder 1, 89.

asked the producers to sign shorter-term promissory notes in its favor for the amount corresponding to the original long-term promissory note. This way the bank could give the producers money (or gold) and wait for the original promissory notes to become bankable. In practice, Visconti's customers saw their debts double, even if only temporarily. The mechanism could work only if the bank did not put the long-term promissory notes into circulation. Struck by the bankruptcy of several of its customers, the bank started to do precisely that, obviously behind the producers' backs, for a total deficit of more than half a million lire.

In order to understand the social and political implications that lay behind banking techniques, it is useful to examine the specific case of Arturo Antonioli, a small gold chain producer who declared bankruptcy together with Visconti's bank.[32] Antonioli's experience is paradigmatic of the class of producers constantly hovering between dependent employment and self-employment. In fact, the liquidator himself defined Antonioli's relationship with Visconti as a case of "vassalage," thereby implying that self-employment was no shelter from the demands of patronage. Born in Verona, Antonioli settled in Valenza Po in 1906 and worked as a jobber for a local jewelry firm. After a few months, despite his increasing income, he decided to open his own business under Visconti's protection and with the direct involvement of Luigi Repossi, a powerful jewelry trader who promised Antonioli to buy his whole production of chains. Despite Antonioli's alleged incompetence and dubious morality, Visconti's bank opened its coffers. This decision, however, was hardly an act of altruism. According to the trustee of Antonioli's case, the bank's bill circulation mechanism represented an operation of "exploitation" whose victims were small producers like Antonioli. These producers became docile debtors who increased the bank's portfolio and were forced to pay very high discount rates. Thus, credit mechanisms reveal a complex hierarchy of economic and social actors behind Valenza Po's communitarian facade.

Public authorities played an active role in this phase of crisis. The main trustee of Visconti's bankruptcy was Luciano Oliva, an accountant and first socialist mayor of Valenza Po. By this time, he had been in office for a few months. The president of the tribunal of Alessandria appointed him, assuming that "it would be easier for him to mitigate the trauma which the town was to experience on account of Visconti's

---

[32] Ibid., 134–41.

bankruptcy."[33] Given the local links between socialist politics and jewelry production, and between political and economic action, it is hard not to agree. However, whereas the president of the tribunal hoped that the mayor would simply mediate conflicting interests by means of his office, Visconti expected Oliva to acknowledge him as one of the town's key patrons. In the event, Oliva barely saved himself.

The latent contradictions inherent in these multiple roles exploded when the court examined the fate of a missing thirty-thousand-lire jewelry lot produced by the firm of Visconti's nephew, Dante Ceriana, who also was one of the main debtors of the bank. It turned out that Visconti had tried to embezzle the lot by taking advantage of family complicity and had contacted higher-ranking patrons, namely member of Parliament Merlani.[34] The court suspected that Visconti had sold the jewelry lot and tried to bribe both Mayor Oliva and Representative Merlani. However, the news somehow leaked, maybe through Merlani himself. The consequence was to get other people, including the mayor, directly involved as defendants, charged with corruption and complicity in fraud. Of course this was not good news for a young politician at the beginning of his career. The suspicion of attempted bribery was not proved, and Mayor Oliva was acquitted. Visconti, on the other hand, was sentenced to more than three years of imprisonment.

Visconti did not succeed in tying his destiny to that of the "community" as a whole. According to him, if the paramount task was to save Valenza Po, this could not be accomplished without supporting the man and the institution that had been central to its cohesion and development. The problem was that the community's cohesion was actually quite fragile. On the one hand, some of the most prominent jewelry producers, on whom Visconti had bestowed considerable resources, argued before the court that the banker "had actually sacrificed himself in supporting many industrialists, who owed him their economic success."[35] On the other hand, however, other witnesses, such as Antonioli, were far more critical of the banker's behavior. Moreover, local agents had to come to terms with external pressures, especially with

[33] Archivio di Stato di Alessandria, Tribunale di Alessandria, processi penali, vol. 3573, folder 3, 2.

[34] Archivio di Stato di Alessandria, Tribunale di Alessandria, processi penali, vol. 3573, folder 1, 147–232.

[35] Archivio di Stato di Alessandria, Tribunale di Alessandria, processi penali, vol. 3573, folder 3, 78.

the Milanese gold and stone suppliers who proved relentless in shedding light on Visconti's activities.

The rise and fall of the Visconti Bank is emblematic of the complexities and ambiguities of civil society institutions when observed from the perspective of the historical actors themselves. Much like the gas cooperative, the bank was a hybrid creature straddling private interest and public functions. At the bank, the connections acquired in preaching the values of socialism could be transformed into credit for one's private venture; and while Lorenzo Visconti turned to his family ties to salvage whatever was left of the bank's assets, the court appointed Mayor Oliva (Valenza Po's most visible public figure) as a trustee in the bankruptcy trial. Like Balzano, Visconti was no simple crook; he clearly realized the impact of his actions on the collectivity and desperately tried to fulfill his obligations in the face of mounting adversities. He was a patron whose main function was the exchange of favors and protection for loyalty. Therefore, he simultaneously promoted trust and created opportunities for the exploitation of trust. The chains of obligations forged by socialist politics and the ties of locality were implicated simultaneously in the production of trust and in its demise. Faced with the inability to pay their workers and fulfill their commitments, Valenza Po's entrepreneurs felt compelled to extend credit and promises even further, thereby ending up cheating the people they meant to protect. The production of social capital was a vulnerable and contradictory project, ever straddling private and public ties as well as past, present, and future commitments.

WAR, EXPANSION, AND DEPRESSION

World War I led to the virtual paralysis of the jewelry industry, already severely hit by the consequences of the Libyan conflict and the collapse of Visconti's bank. As market demand shrank and skilled workers were mobilized, unemployment became rampant among those left behind. In late 1915, the city government pointed out that thirty-four of the forty-one jewelry factories were closed, while the others worked only two or three days a week.[36] The shoe-making sector did not fare much better. As an example of local solidarity, the city government

[36] Archivio Storico della Città di Valenza, vol. 1126, folder 2, Collocamento, disoccupazione, riposo settimanale.

chartered a relief organization to support the unemployed. With the contribution of private agents and public organizations (the consumers' cooperative and the Società Artisti e Operai), the local government raised more than 5,500 lire to be distributed among eighty families, twenty-three of which were "headed" by jewelry workers.[37] As an uncommon example of classic artistic patronage, one of the most elaborate buildings in the town center, Palazzo Lora Moretto (better known locally as the goldsmiths' palace), was built during the war by unemployed jewelry workers with the support of a wealthy townsman who had emigrated to Brazil.[38] Quite appropriately, this building now hosts the town's library and archive.

Public relief and private patronage were temporary solutions to the market crisis, but the collapse of Visconti's bank and the consequences of the war threatened to destroy the vulnerable ties of locality that had been established at the turn of the century. Once again, socialist politics came to the rescue. In this period of crisis, however, the contradictory meanings of socialism for local actors became all the more evident. Political culture acted at two uneasily coexisting levels. On one level, the socialist press used the orthodox language of the social sciences, integrating positivism and Marxism. Citing Herbert Spencer, the local socialist paper defined modern commerce as a form of cannibalism and declared that "the capitalists without capital are now legion, and have begun to devour each other to the detriment of production quality and commercial honesty."[39] The practice of selling jewelry by weight instead of by item, and the general price reduction to the limit of barely recovering the cost of raw gold, triggered a spiraling process whose outcome was all too often bankruptcy.[40] At the same time, credit tended to become more indiscriminate, because Visconti's bank found it more difficult to fulfill its obligations and needed any kind of liquidity. The war-related crisis compounded these contradictions. As we have seen, this diagnosis closely mirrored court sentences.

The solution proposed by the socialist press was based on a pact among entrepreneurs, workers, and public authorities. The government would oblige producers to place an official mark on jewelry items (a measure that was taken only in the mid-1930s) and enact strict forms

---

[37] Ibid.

[38] Lenti, *Gioielli e Gioiellieri*, 150.

[39] A. Biscaldi, "La crisi orafa: Cause e rimedi," *La Scure*, 18 February 1911.

[40] A. Biscaldi, "La crisi orafa," *La Scure*, 1 April 1911.

of control over production and commerce, so as to enhance quality and support prices. This decision would drive the weaker agents out of the market, so that only a few large companies would survive. This would in turn lead to a profound change in the political consciousness of the local classes. The hope was that the formation of strong production cooperatives would stem unfair and destructive competition. The final outcome was to be "true socialism, the class-based one," which needed "an advanced industrial bourgeoisie and a proletariat rooted in its organizations, vigilant, audacious, and combative."[41] Paradoxically, the local socialists did not doubt the necessity of competition and selection, which Spencer extolled as the basis for the survival of the fittest. But they pitted the undisciplined competition of the market against a transition to modern large-scale capitalism guided by state regulation.

The orthodoxy of this position contrasted with the role of socialist ideology in weaving the fabric of everyday life. At this second level, socialism promised, above all, solidarity against an uncertain future, rather than an abstract mechanism for progress. The events of the 1917 May Day provide a clear illustration of this second dimension of socialist politics.[42] At the height of the conflict, a few months before the debacle of Caporetto, the celebration of May Day turned immediately into a demonstration against the war. Even though the carabinieri had given permission for a meeting at the socialist club, they had banned all forms of public demonstration. Nevertheless, after the end of the meeting, a select group of participants enacted a march along one of the town's main streets. The carabinieri intervened immediately to disperse the crowd, most of whom were women and children. In the meantime, groups of kids scattered in the town streets "armed" with stones, which they proceeded to throw at the windows of the traditional landed elite's houses, targeting the most vocal supporters of the war. By the afternoon the protesters calmed down and the day ended without arrests or major disorders. Two days later, however, another demonstration took place, this time without any permission from the authorities. In the afternoon, after the lunch break, a group of women and children began to march in the streets of the modern addition to the south of the town center, where the largest jewelry and shoe factories were located, chanting antiwar slogans and inviting the workers

---

[41] Biscaldi, "La crisi orafa: Cause e rimedi."

[42] Archivio di Stato di Alessandria, Pretura di Valenza, processi penali, year 1917, trial 22.

inside to quit work and join them. The invitation was successful and the demonstration turned into a "spontaneous" strike. This time the carabinieri intervened more decisively and arrested twenty-seven women and children, reporting them to the lower criminal court (Pretura Penale) for seditious behavior and obstruction. When the trial opened several weeks later, it became clear that the strike had been planned with the tacit approval of the entrepreneurs. The carabinieri testified against the defendants, whom they had arrested and identified. But one after another, the local jewelry and shoe manufacturers testified in favor of the defendants, many of whom they employed, and argued that the arrested women were at work as the demonstration was taking place and that work had to be interrupted in order to avoid violence. Unconvinced that the manufacturers had been forced to give in by a bunch of women and children, the judge chose to believe the police officers and fined the majority of the defendants.

Socialist ideology acted both as an indictment of unbridled competition under capitalism (the orthodox position assumed by the local press) and as a practice that promised to bridge class, gender, and generational divisions and thus build and preserve the ties of locality, as the 1917 May Day protest demonstrated. In Trigilia's scheme, the first meaning of socialism was directed at the potentially disruptive consequences of the market, while the second pitted locality against the demands of the state. Or, to use Putnam's language, socialism defined a participatory public sphere in which actors could negotiate conflicts, build trust, and articulate novel identities. However, the meanings of socialism were not simple epiphenomena of a preexisting social structure, as both Trigilia and Putnam assume. Socialism was not the ideological translation of resilient and unproblematic patterns of cooperation and local solidarity. Competition, class divisions, and gender tensions were as much part of the social fabric as their opposites. Instead, we should view socialism as a cultural practice that allowed local actors to imagine possible futures and alternative moralities. In a sense, socialist ideology resembled the promissory notes exchanged by economic agents; it allowed the articulation of promises and commitments that could be kept or broken. The postwar years demonstrated the vulnerability of these projects in painful and largely unexpected ways.

The reconstruction of the jewelry industry after World War I did not develop through the concentration and selection of companies, as the local socialist intellectuals preached, but through the further differentiation and proliferation of local firms. By the same token, the kind of inclusive public sphere envisaged during the 1917 May Day demonstrations gave way to the increasing informalization of female labor and the rise of Fascism. On the level of economic relations, the two main organizational innovations were the general implementation of cottage labor and the internalization within the "community" of some commercial functions previously fulfilled by external (above all Milanese) agents. These innovations in turn promoted a gradual specialization in higher-quality jewelry made with precious stones and pearls.

The fragmentation of production units, highlighted by table 1, went hand in hand with the expulsion of female labor from officially registered firms. Until the end of World War I, Valenza Po's jewelry firms hired unmarried women, who were, however, expected to quit their jobs in their late twenties, soon after getting married.[43] Of the 134 women working in the jewelry industry at the beginning of the century, only 6 were over thirty years of age, and only 11 were married.[44] The absence of married women in the factories remained a long-term characteristic of the industry.[45] After World War I, as local industry shifted from mechanized production (especially gold chains) to custom-made jewelry, increasing numbers of younger women became undocumented home workers. Between 1911 and 1927, the average firm size declined from 15.0 employees (owners included) to 5.2. At the same time, the percentage of women hired by the official jewelry businesses declined from 31 percent in 1915 to 21 percent in 1927. This process is only partly revealed by the census data, because censuses failed to include undocumented workers, but it signaled the expansion of an increasingly gendered informal sector. Younger women no longer enjoyed the political visibility they had showed during the antiwar demonstration of 1917.

Underlying these changes was a remarkable boom in demand, due to the war-related postponement of purchases, the postwar inflation

[43] This was the case, for example, of the most prestigious company in town, Vincenzo Melchiorre & Co., in the 1900s. See Archivio Storico della Città di Valenza, vol. 1127, Lavoro donne e fanciulli.

[44] Archivio Storico della Città di Valenza, vol. 846, folder 444, Dati statistici sul commercio e industria locali.

[45] In the twenty families headed by jewelry workers who received unemployment aid in 1915, fourteen wives had no official occupation, and the others worked in the shoe or textile industries. The latter were all below thirty years of age. Archivio Storico della Città di Valenza, vol. 1126, folder 2, Comitato per i sussidi agli operai disoccupati.

TABLE 1

Jewelry Firms in Valenza Po by Size, and Distribution of Employees by Firm Size, 1911 and 1927

No. of Employees in Firm	1911		1927	
	% of Firms (N = 47)	% of All Employees (N = 674)	% of Firms (N = 152)	% of All Employees (N = 796)
>40	11.1	39.0	0.7	5.4
30–39	6.7	15.9		
20–29	13.3	20.3	2.6	11.6
10–19	11.1	11.0	12.5	30.3
1–9	57.8	13.8	84.2	52.7

Source: For 1911, Archivio Storico della Città di Valenza, vol. 1126, Censimento Industriale 1911; for 1927, Archivio del Comune di Valenza Po, vol. 11–3–4A, Statistiche Commerciali.

crisis (which made gold jewelry an appealing hedge against loss of money value), and the rising marriage rate. The political and economic ties established at the turn of the century became at the same time more diffuse and deep, thereby creating a hierarchy of agents made up of a restricted number of commercially oriented agents on the top level, a larger group of official subcontracting firms on the middle level, and on the third level an even larger number of individual, and sometimes undocumented, cottage workers who were generally active only a few months a year.

The analysis of the "bottom" of the hierarchy, that is, the workers who performed their activity at home, highlights the increasing flexibility of firm boundaries. This category included approximately nine hundred workers in the mid-1920s. Of these, approximately three hundred worked as stone mounters or engravers either alone or in very small, officially registered firms (with two or three members). The other six hundred were totally undocumented workers, half of whom were women.[46] The factory workers at this date were approximately

[46] This calculation is based on the comparison between Donato Debenedetti's estimate of 900 "lavoratori a domicilio" and 476 factory workers and employers in 1926, and the official census data for 1927, which reports a total of 795 "official" employers and employees. See Donato Debenedetti, "L'Oreficeria nella Città di Valenza Po," laurea thesis,

five hundred, a fifth of whom were women. Thus, two-thirds of the workers carried out their activities at home, but these workers were actually a very heterogeneous group. Officially registered and highly skilled artisans who provided larger firms and commercial agents with specialized services usually worked at home, as did the undocumented jewelry polishers (mostly women) who were active only a few months a year, during the demand peaks preceding Christmas and the spring marriages. What these two groups had in common was their dependence on networks led by commercially oriented agents that distributed and supervised production. Even in the case of the stone setters and other highly skilled cottage workers, direct access to the market was viewed as a form of unfair competition. Generally, subcontracting agents allowed their subcontractors to work only for them and a few other local agents of their choice, because if cottage workers were to sell their production (e.g., jewelry parts) directly to the retailers, nobody could have exerted control over quality and styles, with dire consequences for the whole local industry. In fact, these recommendations were not always followed.[47]

Why did many of these workers set up their "independent" businesses after the end of the postwar depression, instead of being hired by a few leading companies, as some local socialists had hoped? Valenza Po's leading entrepreneurs, with over thirty years of experience in the vicissitudes of market cycles and the dangers of small-scale industrialization, decided after the war to specialize in custom-made jewelry. Part of this calculation included the rise of the other Italian jewelry-producing center, Vicenza, which was successfully specializing in more standardized and mechanized production lines (see chapter 4). This decision was in turn related to the wealthier entrepreneurs' gradual shift from production to commerce. The impact of the war enabled some local key actors, already active in the industry, to bypass the role of outside wholesalers (mostly from Milan) and sell directly to the jewelry stores across the country through their traveling salesmen. Fragmentation of production served the interests of these commercially oriented agents. The reservoir of undocumented labor, for example, could shrink or expand in sync with the seasonal nature of jewelry demand. Fragmentation also reduced the risks of bankruptcy for the

---

Università L. Bocconi, 1926, chap. 1. See also *Guida Generale alla Provincia di Alessandria, Alessandria* (Alessandria, 1925), vol. 1.

[47] Debenedetti, "L'Oreficeria," 48–49.

top agents. Finally, there were fiscal advantages, as the labor inspectors soon realized. Questioned about the emergence of cottage labor in 1923, Valenza Po's mayor replied that, in the case of the jewelry sector, there was no dodging of taxes and workers' benefits, because the cottage workers in this industry were all "highly skilled and independent entrepreneurs who work[ed] for the local wholesalers, generally on a piecework basis."[48] Therefore, the mayor concluded disingenuously, they had nothing to do with wage labor. The mayor's reply testifies to a partly new social and political consensus that viewed (male) small-scale entrepreneurship as a solution to conflict and governance problems. The mayor's attitude also signals the emergence of a local informal economy that needed to be kept hidden from the demands of the state. The invisibility of the largely female home-workers was enforced by redrawing the boundaries between family, locality, and the public sphere of political negotiations.

This process of informalization, however, did not stop at the threshold of the household. Relations between official firms also became increasingly informal during the postwar boom. After the war, the practice of subcontracting became so widespread that jewelry production came to assume the features of a putting-out system. Even many official firms had no direct contact with the market and depended on commercial agents for raw materials and stylistic directions. At the same time, the coordinating role fulfilled by Visconti's bank before the conflict was left vacant. Several regional banks opened their branches in Valenza Po, and the supply of raw gold was partly separated from other forms of credit, as companies specialized in gold supply flocked to the town. Thus, the local system became at the same time more differentiated and flexible. Fragmentation and the rise of undocumented labor made informal ties even more important, thereby posing problems of coordination and supervision of which other actors could take advantage. For instance, a particularly skilled and adventurous subcontractor could in fact try to gain direct access to the market and build his own independent network. At the same time, this meant that "unfair" competition between official and "unofficial" firms was a constant threat. In other words, the ties of locality became even more contradictory and vulnerable than before the war.

---

[48] Archivio Storico della Città di Valenza, vol. 1126, Disoccupazione, folder 2, Commissione Comunale di Avviamento al Lavoro.

Once again, we can unravel the complexities of local economic life by focusing on a period of crisis. The postwar boom proved to be short lived. In late 1926, Mussolini announced the beginning of a drastic deflationary policy, meant to restore the value of the lira vis-à-vis the British pound and the other major international currencies. Since Valenza Po's jewelry producers imported all of their raw materials, they saw their stock of gold and precious stones devalued almost overnight. Moreover, their dependence on long-term credit made them particularly sensitive to the consequences of rising interest rates. The onset of the Great Depression a few years later compounded these difficulties and sent many local firms over the edge. Again, the crisis hit the very core of the local economy and forced even several of the leading companies to declare bankruptcy. Within this group, the case of the Vecchio brothers is particularly illustrative. The Vecchios filed bankruptcy in September 1930.[49] Theirs was one of the oldest firms in town, founded by Paolo Vecchio in the 1870s. Paolo's sons, Vincenzo, Pietro, and Giovanni, had taken over from their father in 1899. Under the leadership of Pietro, the firm became extremely successful by combining jewelry production with the recycling of gold ashes and powder, thereby becoming the first gold recycler and supplier in town. This activity proved to be very profitable until the early 1920s, when other agents, including the Milan-based S. A. Metalli Preziosi started to offer the same service. Competition became harsher and profits went down. The firm, however, had diversified its activities even further during the war by opening up a branch in nearby San Salvatore Monferrato for the manufacturing of silver and gold links for ladies' handbags. The branch employed forty workers, all women. Even this activity proved to be ill-fated. Workers went repeatedly on strike demanding higher wages and forcing the Vecchios to close down the factory in 1919.

Within this family firm, the brothers pursued a degree of specialization. Pietro specialized in gold refinement and trade, Vincenzo in jewelry production, and Giovanni in jewelry commerce. All these activities were coordinated by the factory and office in Valenza Po, which employed only nine workers, two of which were assigned administrative tasks. Production was carried out by subcontractors, all of whom collapsed with the Vecchios. Pietro, the firm's leader, used family and patronage ties to bridge the gap between formal and informal transactions. For instance, Pietro's younger brother, Giovanni, had a small

---

[49] Archivio di Stato di Alessandria, Tribunale di Alessandria, fallimenti, vol. 2101.

firm of his own, specialized in jewelry commerce, which filed bankruptcy in September 1930. Raw gold was purchased from the Milanese bankers and regularly invoiced. It was first transformed into alloys (especially white gold, then very fashionable) in Pietro's factory. At that point, the metal followed a tortuous path through the Vecchios' subcontractors (chain producers, stone setters, engravers, polishers, etc.) who manufactured the jewelry. Most of these transactions were undocumented and informal. Gold, so to speak, went back underground. Finally, when the jewelry was finished, Giovanni took the wares, put them in a case, and traveled throughout the country visiting the family's customers. Jewelry retailers were all too happy to accept items whose purchase could be invoiced for a small percentage of their value or not invoiced at all. They usually paid with medium- to long-term promissory notes, depending on the level of market demand. At this point Giovanni and Pietro went to a local bank in Valenza Po and presented the promissory notes to receive credit and buy new gold. If their credit situation happened to be in bad shape and the bank raised objections, the brothers could resort to their subcontractors and have them sign pro forma (accommodation) promissory notes in their favor. These notes turned the subcontractors into debtors of the Vecchio brothers. Clients signed these notes to prove their "loyalty" to their patrons and to assure themselves of further contracts in the future. The firm's clients/subcontractors were both beneficiaries and victims of these mechanisms. When the Vecchios' financial situation became unbearable, their network of subcontractors fell with them.[50]

The Vecchio brothers' organization shows that a provisional solution to the threat of cutthroat competition (Spencerian "cannibalism") was achieved not through economic concentration and class polarization, but through market expansion and the further differentiation of local agents. The demand boom of the early 1920s partly shifted competition from prices to commercialization. Whereas before the war Valenza Po's jewelry was mostly sold to sales representatives and wholesalers based in northwestern Italy, after the conflict the traveling salesmen who worked for the local key agents left Valenza Po to reach the retailers in the most remote corners of the peninsula. As a conse-

---

[50] See the following trials for bankruptcy dating to 1930–31: Mario Sassetti, Archivio di Stato di Alessandria, Tribunale di Alessandria, vol. 2101; Romolo Provera, ibid.; and Teresio Terzano and Ricci Lorenzina, Archivio di Stato di Alessandria, Tribunale di Alessandria, vol. 2090.

quence, competition shifted to the search for the most secure commercialization channels and reliable retailers. The vicissitudes of Vecchio's firms also show how the assumption of commercial competencies by the local top agents brought them to respond very quickly to changes in fashion and to diversify their activities further than in the prewar period. At the same time, their growing specialization in custommade jewelry made them more dependent on subcontracting relations with minor local firms.

The new commercial opportunities, however, also entailed new risks. The outcome of the search for reliable retailers, for example, depended on the level of prestige and power achieved at the local level. The weaker agents had to be content with higher-risk commercial opportunities or give up on establishing their own commercial network altogether. At the same time, a strong norm developed according to which traveling salesmen had to establish their own clientele without trying to undercut the potential competitors from their hometown. In practice, if a customer was already "taken," salesmen were supposed to move on to the next one.[51] This solution to governance problems worked only as long as market demand was high. In the late 1920s, when retailers started to find it increasingly difficult to meet their obligations, the repercussions on Valenza Po's economy and sociopolitical balance were severe.

On the one hand, it is reasonable to argue that the fragmentation of the 1920s, together with the increasing assumption of commercial activities by local firms, made risk more diffuse, thereby reducing the likelihood of a general collapse of the local economy. The experience of Visconti's bank, for example, could never have repeated itself under the new conditions. On the other hand, low-ranking agents saw their personal risk increase enormously. Trust and reputations were no longer a local affair. Now it was necessary to assess the trustworthiness of agents who lived hundreds of miles from Valenza Po, and this task was left to the traveling salesmen and their informal network. It is hard to tell to what degree they shared information about their customers, but this kind of informal cooperation certainly played a role. Even so, only the major British companies were willing to insure Valenza Po's jewelry producers. As a consequence of reduced bank credit and in-

[51] Debenedetti, "L'Oreficeria," 75–77.

creasing insurance costs, informal ties between producers and traders became even more crucial.[52]

The case of Ettore Varona's firm, which filed bankruptcy at the end of 1931, highlights the risks attached to the new commercial organization.[53] In 1920, Varona used his savings of 5,000 lire accumulated while working in a local factory, plus another 40,000 lire from his partner and brother-in-law, Oreste Sereno, to establish a factory and a commercial office specialized in customized jewelry. Ettore worked in the factory, while Oreste traveled throughout southern Italy. The firm never employed directly more than three or four workers, but the trial records reveal that production was subcontracted to several stone setters and engravers in Valenza Po. The first year was prosperous, but in 1921 Sereno was robbed as he was traveling near Naples. Although the loss was severe, over 50,000 lire, the firm recovered by resorting to its insurance company, Eagle Star & British Dominions. In January 1926, however, as Sereno was in Sicily, he was killed in an ambush by one of his customers, who had invited him to his house. This time, the financial loss was remarkable, over half a million lire. The insurance company paid only half that amount, and over 150,000 lire had to be given back to several customers both in Valenza and in the south. Unsurprisingly, the banks did not open their coffers. The surviving business partner, Varona, had to borrow more money from Sereno's parents, who were entitled to a share of the company as heirs of their son, and from the main private gold bank in Alessandria, Ivaldi & Ferrari. The killers were caught and sentenced to life imprisonment in July 1930, but it turned out that all their possessions were heavily burdened with liens. At least in this case, the local information network about prospective customers had badly failed.

The more established firms were exposed to less lethal kinds of risk. Nevertheless, external shocks such as the deflation and the market depression of the late 1920s and early 1930s did not spare them. In order to build their commercial networks, the top agents had to deal with the international market on a daily basis, especially after their specialization in customized jewelry. Precious stones were only available in a few international centers such as Paris and Antwerp, and it was in the

---

[52] According to one observer, the level of credit that local banks were willing to give jewelry firms in 1926 was the same as in 1914. Taking inflation into account, this meant that banks regarded local agents as one-fifth to one-sixth as "trustworthy" as before the war. Data from ibid., 85.

[53] Archivio di Stato di Alessandria, Tribunale di Alessandria, fallimenti, vol. 2099.

interest of Valenza Po's jewelry producers to bypass all intermediaries and deal directly with the suppliers. The relationships between Valenza Po's jewelers and these international agents were rather problematic. On the one hand, the precious stone dealers trusted the Piedmontese traders enough to adopt them as brokers for the local market and consign wares to them on the basis of promissory notes. On the other hand, they were not willing to rely too heavily on informal ties. Typically, they were prone to bring insolvent debtors to court at the first difficulty. In short, these ties exposed Valenza Po's jewelry traders to new risks, and to rules and procedures quite different from those of locally based patronage.

These problems are revealed in the case of one of the top firms and networks of Valenza Po, led by the brothers Mario and Ugo De Rossi, who filed bankruptcy in December 1930.[54] Even before the war, Mario had become an expert in precious stones, and his firm specialized in this field in the late 1910s. Mario traveled abroad, bought the stones, and acted as an intermediary agent for many of Valenza Po's producers. Ugo remained in town and supervised the firm's production of jewelry. The brothers also hired two traveling salesmen, one for northern Italy and the other for Rome and the south. These activities were very prosperous for a few years. When Mussolini announced the beginning of the regime's deflationary policy in 1926, Mario De Rossi had just bought a considerable amount of diamonds in Antwerp. The sudden deflation decreased the value of the stones almost overnight. At the same time, the craze for white gold began. Since most of the De Rossis' production consisted of platinum and yellow gold, much of their jewelry had to be melted down. These major blows signified the beginning of the firm's downfall. When the depression hit, the De Rossis had to confront their international creditors, above all London-based Ullman & Son and Antwerp-based Bonnard & Pressel. They first reached an informal agreement for the payment of 50 percent of their debt, but at their first delay Ullman & Son brought the brothers to court.

In reconstructing the causes of the bankruptcy, the trustee focused on two interesting practices. First, he pointed out that external factors and market difficulties were only partly responsible for the company's financial stress. During the years of prosperity, the brothers had led an expensive lifestyle, buying property and luxury items for almost a

---

[54] Archivio di Stato di Alessandria, Tribunale di Alessandria, fallimenti, vol. 2095.

million lire, instead of reinvesting their profits. In particular, the two villas where the brothers lived were defined as "extravagant" for a town like Valenza Po. The entrepreneurs had even bought one of the best boxes in the local theater for their families' soirées. This was a recurrent theme in the trials of high-ranking agents. Extravagance was common practice and was seen by the courts as a sign of social over-reaching and bad economic conduct. Pietro Vecchio, for example, was openly rebuked for his lifestyle, and the trustee pointed out that in the garden of his villa, built by his workers during the slack season, he even raised peacocks and ornamental pheasants. It would be a mistake to dismiss these attacks on conspicuous consumption as trivial. As we shall see in the next section, after the war conspicuous consumption was reinterpreted as a form of defiance against the authorities and a way for ex-socialist patrons to advertise their status.

The second practice denounced by the trustee during the trial shows that local status, achieved and displayed by Valenza Po's top agents, was key to reproducing patterns of diffuse patronage. As a consequence of banks' reluctance to provide loans, the De Rossis became "generous" moneylenders to the lower-ranking jewelry producers. Revealingly, they reenacted the credit mechanisms that had brought the Visconti Bank to its ruin in the early 1910s. In addition to providing loans, the De Rossis replaced long-term promissory notes with shorter-term and bankable ones. In practice, they acted as an unofficial bank that was willing to take higher risks in exchange for economic influence and social prestige. The De Rossis were at the same time the patrons of many "smaller" jewelry producers and their brokers with respect to the official banks. Given their local reputation and status, the brothers could guarantee the shorter-term promissory notes, which were thus discounted by the local banks. When the news of their worsening financial situation spread in 1929 and discounting became more difficult for the brothers, their international creditors offered to play the same game in their favor: the brothers would accept long-term notes from their clients, but the De Rossis' creditors rather than the brothers themselves would guarantee them. When the crisis proved to be anything but temporary, the whole mechanism collapsed.

The development of these complex hierarchies of social actors straddling private and public roles demonstrates that the contradictory promises of socialist politics went largely unfulfilled. The postwar economic boom led neither to the selection of the fittest companies and to class polarization, as the orthodox position recommended, nor to the creation of communitarian ties capable of equally distributing risks and opportunities within a participatory public sphere, as the rituals of the antiwar movement envisaged. The spread of small-scale proprietorship took place instead in a regime of increasing informalization, affecting male and female workers as well as unofficial and official firms. The rise of the informal economy made the ongoing production of locality even more crucial to economic and social survival. Informality was not merely a reaction to the demands of the state; it was a central element in the construction of market relations themselves. Family ties and the bonds of clientage shaped behaviors that can hardly be explained in terms of disembedded economic rationality. Valenza Po's citizens confronted the demands of disparate loyalties and obligations, which claimed their imagination as well as their resources. The demands of patronage were particularly implicated in perpetuating the ties of locality in periods of potentially disruptive market crisis. Valenza Po's economic agents clearly understood that long-term success depended on the protection of sociability from short-term calculations. Clients exchanged their "loyalty" and their absence from the market for protection from the high instability and volatility of the market itself, while patrons exchanged the shouldering of higher risks for local prestige and status. During the depression of the 1930s, as in the crisis of the early 1910s, the line between loyalty and betrayal became increasingly blurred. The demands of patronage, paradoxically the most enduring legacy of socialist politics, built chains of expectations that simultaneously enforced trust and made it vulnerable to betrayal.

FAMILY, CLASS, AND HONOR

Valenza Po's contemporary citizens, much like the local socialists a century ago, are wont to unfavorably compare their town's social and economic life to largely imaginary models of virtuous modernity. Until quite recently, one of the most widespread discourses in the local press pitted Valenza Po's unreconstructed individualism against the examples of collective discipline and personal restraint supposedly exhibited by actors in the industrial districts of Emilia and Tuscany.[55] According to this trope, whereas Tuscan leather tanners and Emilian tile

[55] See, for example, Pier Giovanni Barbano, "L'Associazionismo Imprenditoriale nel Settore Orafo: Il Caso di Valenza Po," laurea thesis, University of Pavia, 1985–86, 70–74.

producers—just to take two possible examples—are organized in unions and cooperatives, Valenza Po's jewelry makers tend to think for themselves and dismiss the importance of class-based organizations, both among manufacturers and among workers. Most of my local informers presented me with a version of this contrast between Valenza Po's individualism and the collective virtues that could be found "elsewhere."

This language has a long lineage in Valenza Po, as we have seen. In the early twentieth century the local socialist press explicitly condemned all that local economic life seemed to stand for: "We declare our strong opposition to small industry and craftsmanship, which are sources of competition and ruin, and we hope that production will fall into a few industrialists' hands on the one side, and to cooperatives on the other."[56] The fact that the local socialists did indeed foster the development of small-scale industry should not be interpreted as an unproblematic contrast between theory (or ideology) and practice. The contrast between an uncivilized present and a mythical future (or an equally mythical "elsewhere") embodying the values of modernity and civic virtue constituted a crucial element of social capital, interpreted as cultural practice. This dichotomy shaped ideology as common sense and informed everyday practice.

The contrast between local vice and "foreign" virtue translated into a subtle sense of inadequacy, which came to the surface both in the public sphere of political confrontation and in more private, supposedly "business-oriented," relations. Against the traditional moderate and monarchical coalition, which presented itself as a showcase for the "educated" members of the local elite, the socialist electoral lists included members of all the "productive" classes, workers as well as entrepreneurs. For example, the list that in 1910 brought the first socialist mayor to Valenza Po, Luciano Oliva, included among others two jewelry industrialists and two jewelry workers. Their political rivals, knowing all too well how to strike a raw nerve, called them "virtually illiterate gang leaders" (*capoccia semianalfabeta*), to which the socialists responded quite feebly that "true, our lists include mostly workers and small manufacturers, but that is just right, since they represent our town's most numerous and industrious classes."[57] At least they had numbers on their side!

---

[56] "Il fallimento della Banca Visconti Lorenzo," *La Scure*, 23 July 1910.

[57] "Avvisaglie elettorali,"*La Scure*, 30 June 1907.

In more private realms, the same feeling of inadequacy appeared almost as a slip of the tongue. One of the most serious insults that local economic agents could exchange in business relations was *paesano*, which through its associations with the backwardness of rural life was interpreted to mean uncultivated, narrowly individualistic like a peasant, and therefore unreliable. Of course *paesano* is also a potentially harmless term meaning fellow townsman. Moreover, its links to rurality could have made it an appropriate descriptor for the majority of Valenza Po's citizens, who after all lived in a small center and were at most one generation removed from the land. The offense, nonetheless, was so serious as to call for legal redress, as some libel suits demonstrate.[58] By calling each other *paesano*, Valenza Po's citizens measured the distance between, on the one hand, the perceived backwardness and incivility of local life and, on the other, the sophistication and reliability that supposedly could be found in more modern contexts. But in constructing this dichotomy, they also held each other to shared standards of conduct that allegedly had been violated.

The discursive contrast between individualism, perceived as the legacy of backwardness, and class solidarity, viewed as a modern form of collective action, provides a fruitful background for the analysis of social relations in Valenza Po. In contrast with Vicenza, the other jewelry-producing center in the country (see chapter 3), Valenza Po's formal working-class institutions, namely unions and production cooperatives, did not play a major role. A cooperative for the production of jewelry was founded in 1902 with the high ambition of contributing to the general improvement of the trade's "morality" and the workers' conditions. In fact, the cooperative simply acted like any other low-ranking firm in town, working for some of the larger firms and gradually increasing its size from seven members in 1902 to twenty-six in 1913.[59] The union played a more visible role in the years of socialist administration (1910–21), even though the local socialists still complained about the lack of combativeness and consciousness of the jewelry workers. In 1909, the local union became part of the national Federazione degli Orefici (Goldsmiths' Federation), affiliated with the socialist Confederazione Generale del Lavoro. Still, union members in

[58] See, for example, Archivio di Stato di Alessandria, Pretura di Alessandria, processi penali, year 1923, trial 77 against Sassetti Felice, in which the exchange of the insult resulted in a suit and in a countersuit.

[59] Luigi Ratti, "Origini ed evoluzione storica di Valenza Orafa," *Rassegna Economica della Provincia di Alessandria* 22 (July–August 1969): 32–34.

Valenza Po were less than a hundred, a small number when compared with the over five hundred (out of approximately two thousand) organized by the socialist union in Vicenza.[60] Valenza Po's socialist leaders attributed the union's limited appeal to the fact that younger people were becoming ever more individualistic, as well as to the decreasing size of local firms.[61] This reductive obsession with the degeneration of local mores, however, contrasted with the subtleties of local negotiations between workers and manufacturers.

In pre-Fascist Valenza Po, agreements on wages and working hours carried the weight of norms embedded in comprehensive patterns of personal relationships. For example, the eight-hour working day became widespread in 1907 without overt instances of conflict.[62] Entrepreneurs were persuaded of the "fairness" of the workers' claim, and their informal networking did the rest. Even though working hours fluctuated wildly in sync with demand, it was in the workers' interest to differentiate clearly between overtime and regular hours, since overtime was paid more. The strength of these kinds of agreements stands out in one of the few instances of overt industrial conflict before W.W.II, the strike at Leopoldo Bissone's firm in March 1910.[63] At the time, Bissone's firm was one of the largest in town, with ninety workers, forty-nine of whom were women. In some ways, this was an anomalous company, specializing in gold chains and relatively standardized items. This partly explains the high percentage of female laborers, who linked and polished the chains. In 1910, Bissone had unilaterally decided to raise the working hours to nine, thereby breaking the agreement reached a few years before. The irony was that Bissone was a prominent local socialist himself. The workers responded by going on strike on 15 March 1910, and the struggle soon took on the tones of a local feud. Bissone appealed to personal loyalties and convinced twenty-two workers to go back to work. The union started to collect money to support the strikers, while the socialist periodical published the names of the strikebreakers.[64] While it would be inappropriate to define Bissone as a "gang leader," the struggle assumed quite shady overtones when two of his "loyal" workers threatened an ex-colleague

[60] "Dopo il congresso degli orefici," *La Scure*, 16 May 1909.

[61] "Agli operai orefici," *La Scure*, 5 April 1907. It is worth noting that at this time firms in Vicenza were not any bigger than in Valenza Po.

[62] *La Scure*, 22 September 1907.

[63] "Sciopero alla ditta Bissone," *La Scure*, 19 March 1910.

[64] "Lo sciopero degli orefici," *La Scure*, 2 April 1910.

with a gun in the town center. Apparently the victim was going around town revealing the firm's secrets and disparaging the "scabs." Fortunately, no shot was fired.[65] This highly charged atmosphere made it clear that Bissone had crossed a very sensitive boundary. Consequently, he had to give in to workers' demand a few weeks later.

This episode shows that the union's small following was not due to the powerlessness of the workers. To the contrary, class confrontation was one of the main options open to the workers when contractual obligations (formal or informal) were not met and personal arrangements proved unsatisfactory. In practice, workers were able to combine patronage ties and class solidarity in flexible and creative ways. Once cross-class loyalty ties were broken, the consequences for manufacturers could be severe. The fate of Leopoldo Bissone clearly proves this point. Just a few months after the end of the strike, Bissone's firm was hit by the crisis of Visconti's bank, and filed bankruptcy in December 1911. Suspicion of embezzlement and fraud was strong from the very beginning, as the shady practices of the bankrupts became the talk of the day in the local bars. In short order, Bissone and his partner, Oreste Gervaso, had to withstand a criminal trial.[66] The court determined that the defendants had encouraged their wives and daughters to embezzle tens of kilograms of gold jewelry and silverware, which they hid in coal baskets and took to several relatives' houses. The weight of the baskets had inspired the bad idea of asking two of their employees for help. But the two manufacturers' poor reputation and scarce loyalty meant that the workers were willing to turn them in and become decisive witnesses for the prosecution. Bissone and Gervaso were sentenced to over two years of imprisonment, and as late as April 1914 the carabinieri advised against granting them pardon, arguing that such a decision would have been ill-received in town and created some turmoil.[67]

Despite political and economic instability, the latent tensions between patronage relations and class solidarity did not increase in the period that followed the end of the conflict. The balance worked out at the beginning of the century proved to be quite resilient, at least until the advent of Fascism. As we have seen, the years after World

[65] "Lo sciopero della ditta Bissone," *La Scure*, 16 April 1910.

[66] Archivio di Stato di Alessandria, Tribunale di Alessandria, processi penali, vol. 3611.

[67] Ibid., folder 3, 3.

War I were a phase of great economic opportunities, as demand for jewelry increased to unprecedented levels. In this period of growth, the well-traveled paths to conflict resolution still proved quite effective. In May 1919, for example, an agreement between jewelry manufacturers and the union was signed without strikes or lockouts.[68] In addition to pay raises for all the categories, the agreement disciplined overtime work, which could not exceed six hours per week and was ruled out in case of general unemployment. Moreover, piecework practices were completely abolished. The only major concession to the manufacturers was the union's commitment to stop workers from performing overtime work for firms other than their official one. What is particularly interesting about this agreement is its focus on factory relations. Fragmentation and cottage labor were still uncommon practices, and Valenza Po's workers and proprietors intended to deal with the impending market expansion through the network of small to medium-size firms that had developed before the war. The generally consensual character of conflict resolution was confirmed by the results of the municipal elections of September 1920, in which all adult males could participate.[69] The socialist list, which included the usual sample from all the "productive classes," obtained a remarkable victory, totaling almost three-fourths of the vote.

At the same time, however, widespread political conflict all over Piedmont and beyond troubled Valenza Po's prosperity. The rise of Fascism in the Po valley, together with the local feuds between the Blackshirts and the "reds," threatened to upset the balance reached in the socialists' gold town. Socialist politics had played such a crucial role in the town's achievement of economic prosperity and in shaping local ties, that the Fascist challenge was seen as an external enemy that would have brought local society to its ruin. Political violence reached an apex in June 1921, when a Blackshirt was shot dead and the local Chamber of Labor was ransacked in reprisal. In the wake of this incident, the Fascists obtained the resignation of the socialist mayor, Giuseppe Marchese, a prominent local jewelry manufacturer, and his replacement with an external commissioner appointed by the prefect of Alessandria. Eleven years of socialist government came to a sudden end. Before resigning, the mayor wrote to the prefect that the Fascists were individuals alien to Valenza Po's social body, and that the social-

[68] "Movimento operaio," *La Scure*, 24 May 1919.
[69] *La Scure*, 2 October 1920.

ist government had been the guarantor of the local community's "unity, civility, and industriousness."[70] In other words, his resignation spelled ruin for the whole town. Although the mayor's perception of Fascism as an alien disease was something of an overstatement, the collapse of the local political coalition and the Fascist takeover of the local government a few months later were widely perceived as an unexpected and almost unexplainable coup.

And yet the mayor's dire predictions of impending ruin did not materialize. From a political point of view, the new national regime brought to the fore the local conservative elite that had been marginalized by the rise of socialist politics in the 1910s. Most of the *podestà*, the prefect-appointed mayors who governed Valenza Po in the late 1920s and throughout the 1930s, had been previously active in the minority conservative coalition. In fact, some of them belonged to the "productive classes" as well, in the sense that they were shoe-making entrepreneurs or local professionals. Under their rule, the preexisting socialist practice of cross-class solidarity within a "community of producers" was recast in the new regime's pompous language of corporatism. Some of Valenza Po's older political and economic practices proved surprisingly compatible with the new climate. In particular, the intermingling of private and public functions continued unabated. The activities of the mayors provide a clear illustration of this continuity. The longest-governing *podestà*, Mario Soave, who remained in office from 1923 to 1934, was an accountant who worked both as an insurance agent and as a bankruptcy trustee. The analogies with the town's first socialist mayor, Luciano Oliva, are remarkable. Soave played a key role in some major bankruptcy trials of the early 1930s, including the De Rossi case. Moreover, he specialized in extrajudiciary agreements, to which he brought the weight of his political clout. Yet, despite these similarities, Soave's activities were more controversial and contested than Oliva's. The Archivio di Stato of Alessandria holds several anonymous complaints about Soave's government and professional activities, and he was eventually forced to resign.[71] During the Fascist era, political patronage could no longer enjoy the moral justification offered by socialist politics and democratic consensus. Socialist and anti-

---

[70] Archivio Storico della Città di Valenza, vol. 1157, folder 1, Comizi, serrate, scioperi e disordini.

[71] Archivio di Stato di Alessandria, Prefettura di Alessandria, Ufficio di Gabinetto, vol. 147, folder 153, Comune di Valenza.

Fascist feelings, on the other hand, proved quite resilient in Valenza Po. When Oliva died in 1939, the carabinieri had to intervene in order to prevent his funeral from turning into a political demonstration.[72]

Despite these continuities, however, Fascism brought about some important changes. Workers' organizations were silenced, and class mobilization ceased to represent a viable strategy of defense and social promotion. The repression of independent workers' organizations probably favored the increasing informalization of economic relations, even though there are few indications that the workers resented the fragmentation of production units and the spread of micro-entrepreneurship. The manufacturers, and especially the jewelry entrepreneurs, who had been most active in turning Valenza Po into a socialist "hotbed," were obliged to retreat from public life. Excluded from the arena of local politics, many manufacturers turned to other venues in order to preserve their local prestige. An interesting myth developed after the fall of the regime, according to which the entrepreneurs used their prosperity to resist the dictates of Fascism. Their rising income supposedly allowed them to resort to conspicuous consumption, which was perceived by the authorities as an act of resistance and defiance. As a communist observer remarked in his memoirs, "Any pretext was good to show nonconformity. Any show, conference, or film screening could turn into an act of protest."[73] In this somewhat mythical scenario, sport and hunting clubs, which threw raucous parties, became the patrons' new public arenas. The local elders still revel in telling the stories of several jewelry manufacturers, each with his nickname, who allegedly enraged the local authorities by sporting their expensive cars and clothes in the town center.

There are some indications that the Fascist authorities took some of these episodes seriously, and occasionally brought the organizers of parties to court for unruly behavior and obscenity.[74] Especially in the late 1930s and early 1940s, the soccer team, the society in charge of the opera theater, the municipal music band, and so on, became terrain of contention, as Fascism tried to win over the workers' support by implementing politically more compatible institutions such as the *do-*

[72] Archivio Centrale dello Stato, Ministero dell'Interno, Casellario Politico Centrale, vol. 3585, folder Oliva Luciano.

[73] E. C. Guidi, "Note sulla fondazione del PCI a Valenza." Undated typed document held by the Municipal Library of Valenza Po.

[74] See, for example, Archivio di Stato di Alessandria, Pretura di Valenza, processi penali, year 1924, trial 4 against Mario Marchese.

polavoro.[75] Even as late as 1944, the local Fascists complained about the "sectarian and unfavorable local partisanship, which has profound roots not only in the working class but also, and even more, among the rich manufacturers racing for money."[76] Despite these sporadic indications of tension and defiance, the notion that civil society resisted the mobilization efforts of the regime should also be viewed as a rationalization through which the former socialists tried to come to terms with their defeat. The construction of these myths of resistance offers further evidence of the ability of cultural projects to affect social and economic life. This is one of the main reasons why social capital cannot be interpreted as a reified property of social structure: political culture is directly implicated in the practices that put social networks to value for their participants.

While workers' mobilization in formal organizations became virtually impossible after the Fascist takeover, family ties remained crucial to social promotion. As we have seen in several examples, the low barriers to entry typical of jewelry manufacturing often enabled families to rely on their savings to open up a business. Moreover, division of labor within the family lay at the basis of economic organization in both official and unofficial firms. Even these strategies, however, varied within the complex local hierarchy. There is some evidence that Valenza Po's least privileged families adopted a strategy of diversification by distributing their members among the local industrial occupations, especially jewelry and shoe making. Given the high wages paid by jewelry firms, many peasants and unskilled workers saw placing their sons and daughters in jewelry work as a means of family survival or even social promotion.[77] Due to the extreme volatility of this industry, however, it was safer not to concentrate all family energies in this sector. As a rule it was the oldest son who was initiated into the jewelry trade as a shopboy in his early teens, whereas at least some of the other children were directed to other occupations. As for the

---

[75] For a history of this enormous institution, see Victoria De Grazia, *The Culture of Consent: Mass Organization of Leisure in Fascist Italy* (Cambridge, 1981).

[76] Archivio di Stato di Alessandria, Prefettura di Alessandria, Ufficio di Gabinetto, vol. 147, folder 153, Comune di Valenza.

[77] The daily wage of an adult man (over twenty-one years of age) in 1905, for example, was 30 percent higher in the jewelry industry than in shoe making. Women were paid roughly the same. As a consequence, wage differentials in the jewelry sector were correspondingly higher. Archivio Storico della Città di Valenza, vol. 1127, Lavoro donne e fanciulli.

women, as we have seen, the town's shift from mechanized production (especially gold chains) to custom-made jewelry reduced radically the demand for female factory labor, while the number of undocumented female home workers increased accordingly.

Whereas in the workers' families women's labor represented a crucial source of income, especially in the early periods of their life cycle, for the upwardly mobile entrepreneurs it was women' leisure that provided social prestige within local society, since the "goldsmith's wife did not need to work."[78] Usually this also applied to the skilled workers, who wavered between the condition of employees and self-employed clients/subcontractors. These higher-income families adopted different strategies to cope with the uncertainty and volatility of the market. By far the most common one was the purchase of land. Almost all the manufacturers tried for bankruptcy had at least a vineyard run by a sharecropping family. One of the most difficult tasks for the trustees was to assess whether the land plots could be regarded as part of the bankruptcy assets, since they were often registered in a family member's name, usually the wife's. Typically, in these cases the family was seen as a de facto business unit (società di fatto), and the property was sold after some inquiries.[79] As we have seen, the role of family property went beyond precautionary strategies. Despite socialist politics, high-ranking patrons were expected to lead a somewhat conspicuous lifestyle. They usually built small villas that were given their family names, and some owned a second house in nearby Fogliabella, on a hill overlooking the Po and its valley, where they spent their summer vacations.

This evidence shows that at both ends of the social hierarchy the household economy was not merely a holdover from the rural past. Among the lower ranks of local society, it was enforced through the rise of the informal economy and the increasing adoption of undocumented homework. For the higher-income strata, the conflation of family relations and business initiatives was even sanctioned in court sentences. In other words, the seemingly unproblematic practices associated with "family businesses" relied on a whole political and cultural apparatus of norms and expectations, which simultaneously rei-

---

[78] Debenedetti, "L'Oreficeria," 56.

[79] See, for instance, the trial of Teresio Terzano and Lorenzina Ricci, who filed bankruptcy in November 1930. Archivio di Stato di Alessandria, Tribunale di Alessandria, fallimenti, vol. 2090.

fied the household economy and exposed its contradictions. Both the power and the vulnerability inherent in the conflation of family bonds and business relations are best explored at the level of ideological practices, defined as the strategies that gave meaning to everyday experience. Consider, for example, the widespread notion that Valenza Po's jewelry making reproduced itself "by filiation" (*per figliolanza*). This expression denoted the practice by which the most gifted local kids were taught the secrets of the trade within a firm so that they would one day be able to found a firm of their own. This kind of rhetorical move drawing an explicit analogical link between economic reproduction and social reproduction *tout court* reinforced the notion that the firm was a family, and that the family could be conceived as a firm, despite the potential (and obvious) tension between the unconditional love of familial affection and the instrumental rationality of business calculation.

This tension was particularly evident in the early phases of socialization, when the young worker/child could not yet be trusted to behave as expected by his or her employer/parent. The normality of trust was defined through the ever-present possibility of (exceptional) betrayal. In his brief description of Valenza Po's jewelry industry for a local magazine, a manufacturer felt compelled to mention in one breath filial devotion and the constant threat of the ultimate betrayal—the pilfering of precious metals by young employees:

> The kid will never, even for a minute, think about stealing. He might well continue to steal grapes and cherries in the fields, but from the factory he will not take anything. I believe that in the many decades of existence of the jewelry industry, dishonesty has been very rare, and the few (usually immigrants) who did behave dishonestly had to leave immediately or change profession, since no firm would hire them. Thus, [this is] a traditional system based on great, boundless trust, but also on harsh severity.[80]

In fact, the pilfering of small quantities of gold or jewelry parts must have been a constant temptation for factory workers.[81] At a time when metal detectors were still unheard of, industrialists had to rely on hear-

---

[80] Luigi Visconti, "L'oreficeria valenzana," *Alexandria* 3–4 (November–December 1951): 82.

[81] Paradoxically, home workers were less exposed to this kind of temptation, since the jobber carefully inventoried all the items entrusted to them, and of course the home worker could not blame eventual losses on his or her colleagues.

say assessments of workers' honesty, that highly valued and yet intangible entity. Conversely, the workers who yielded to the temptation to pilfer and were caught in the act faced an uphill battle to explain their motives and restore their reputation.

Even though it is impossible to verify the statement that pilfering was very rare (most of these incidents were dealt with in an informal way), the analysis of the few cases that left a paper trail in court proceedings opens a window onto the tensions raised by the interplay of personal loyalties, family bonds, class solidarity, and gender relations. The case of Zenisia Cavallero is particularly revealing.[82] Interestingly, it was the alleged pilferer who filed a libel suit against her boss. Giovanni Canepa had fired Zenisia in December 1921 on the pretext of a lack of orders. A few days later, however, someone told Zenisia that the real reason was quite different: some of her colleagues had seen her steal. At age seventeen, she was at a loss, and she turned to her mother in tears. Since her father had emigrated to Argentina, her mother sent for Uncle Stefano, who lived in a town nearby. Uncle and niece decided to confront Canepa about his accusations, and the following Sunday they went to his place. Canepa confirmed that two of Zenisia's colleagues had seen her slip some gold into her pockets. During the trial, he reported that, after the first rumors, he had searched Zenisia's smock after she had left, finding some pieces of gold alloy.[83] Instead of confronting her directly, the next day he had addressed all the workers about his discovery. It was only after he found more gold in her pockets a few days later that he had decided to act. When confronted by Zenisia and her uncle, the manufacturer told them that he was willing to turn a blind eye and give her severance pay, if she gave up on the threat of a lawsuit for having been fired without notice. She refused the offer and decided to sue. Fortunately for Canepa, a friend and fellow jewelry manufacturer, Giuseppe Soro, had attended the meeting between him and the accuser. Soro confirmed Canepa's story before the judge, and the girl had to give in without being able to restore her honor.

Even in this seemingly trivial incident, it is possible to see how class relations and family ties interacted with individual strategies in mo-

---

[82] Archivio di Stato di Alessandria, Pretura di Valenza, processi penali, year 1922, trial 50.

[83] As is still the case, workers' overalls must remain on the factory premises and be processed every few days in order to recycle the gold particles that might have stuck to the fabric.

ments of difficulty and uncertainty. If the wealthier entrepreneurs, especially before the advent of Fascism, could establish reputations in the arena of politics and public events, the workers, and especially women, had to resort to their kin. Throughout the period, for example, the recommendation of a well-known relative was necessary for prospective employees and low-ranking subcontractors. This constraint partly explains the absence of massive immigration, despite the high wages paid in the jewelry sector and the relatively depressed economy of the towns near Valenza Po.[84] The most interesting aspect of this story, however, is that both contenders resorted to an external party. While Canepa summoned another manufacturer, Zenisia had to resort to family relations in her desperate attempt to defend her reputation. Revealingly, she did not turn to her mother. In a world of personal and informal agreements, the weight carried by one's word was strongly gender-specific. Unfortunately for her, Uncle Stefano, who did not even live in Valenza Po, was not influential enough. Thus, despite the doubts that class solidarity among manufacturers might have played a role in discounting the testimony of Canepa's proprietor friend, his word proved to be decisive. The judge reasoned that his words were more objective than Uncle Stefano's.

Other instances of pilfering show that socialization was a problematic and contradictory process that did not take place only within the confines of real and imagined "familial" relations. Stealing was indeed taken seriously by the manufacturers as a form of disloyalty, but in the social world of young workers pilfering could also be viewed as an act of defiance and bravery—something one could even boast of. Thus, Flippo Mensi, aged eighteen, showed up at the Bar Sport with a piece of gold wire, which he proceeded to show to his friends, who later testified in court against him.[85] In another instance, Dionigi Conti was confronted by the carabinieri, summoned by his employer.[86] To the officers the boy confessed that he had stolen some gold in imitation of one his colleagues, who had made a ring with the metal he had taken from the factory; Dionigi had stolen some gold from his neighbor's

[84] "Even the workers who were only good at putting up a few brooches received daily wages higher than two elementary teachers and a lower court judge." *La Scure*, 17 May 1919.

[85] Archivio di Stato di Alessandria, Pretura di Valenza, processi penali, year 1920, trial 45.

[86] Archivio di Stato di Alessandria, Pretura di Valenza, processi penali, year 1925, trial 161.

counter, thinking that he could make a ring just as beautiful, but his boss had caught him in the act. In these cases, the same social networks that motivated the boys to break the rules ended up turning them in to the employers and ultimately to the authorities. We can surmise that these boys were not all that exceptional in their attempt to reconcile conflicting impulses and expectations. Maybe they simply commanded less loyalty in their workplace than many of their peers, but they surely were not alone in navigating a world in which loyalty and trust depended on the constant threat of defiance and betrayal.

Clientage, class, and kinship (the three kinds of networks that informed Valenza Po's social life) built market relations and political participation in flexible and generally successful ways, despite the erratic swings of market demand. Their resilience in the first decades of the twentieth century, however, should not be taken as evidence of centuries-old continuities. This chapter has demonstrated that the pillars of the local social order had been laid quite recently, at the end of the nineteenth century. There is no need to turn back to the age of the medieval communes, as Putnam does, to explain the differences between northern and southern Italy. Valenza Po's diffuse clientage networks were a far cry from the exclusive ties of dependence linking the southern landlords to their peasants. By the same token, class mobilization was a key (and relatively recent) feature of northern Italian society, and it acted as a bulwark against the potential abuse of patrons—once again in stark contrast with parts of the south. As to kinship ties, they were as crucial to social survival and promotion in Piedmont as they were in Calabria. But the economic opportunities enjoyed and seized by northern family networks were unknown in much of the south. In sum, actors in Valenza Po were embedded in multiple social networks, and they resorted to some of them to preserve or increase their economic resources. In other words, they produced and accumulated social capital. Nevertheless, it would be inaccurate to say that Valenza Po had more social capital than, say, Montegrano, the archetypal locus of southern backwardness studied by Edward Banfield in the 1950s.[87] Like any other form of capital, social capital in Valenza Po produced inequalities as well as opportunities. The difference between Valenza

[87] Edward Banfield, *The Moral Basis of a Backward Society* (Chicago, 1958). Montegrano was the pseudonym Banfield chose for the town of Chiaromonte, in the province of Matera.

Po and Montegrano was that more citizens of the former had access to a larger number of more profitable networks, which provided them with a degree of power and allowed them to understand political struggle as a viable strategy for change.

Within this plurality of networks, trust was certainly one of the main "currencies" exchanged by Valenza Po's citizens. But the evidence I have examined in this chapter leads to an understanding of trust that differs from both transaction-cost economics and communitarian arguments. Trust was not a homogenous substance. Like any other currency, it was inflected in a variety of ways and assumed disparate meanings in local society. The kind of trust that existed between socialist proprietors and business partners was qualitatively different from the loyalty that was expected of a recently hired shopgirl. In addition, the extension of trust often paved the way for acts of betrayal, for example by creating conflicting expectations that could not be fulfilled. Trust generates vulnerabilities that may lead to tensions and conflicts. Finally, trust was neither the product of rational calculation nor the automatic by-product of primary relationships of kin and community. The evidence presented in this chapter is consistent with Yanagisako's conception of trust and betrayal as complex sentiments that act as forces of production, bridging the boundaries between economic rationality, familial affection, and political loyalty.[88]

[88] Yanagisako, *Producing Culture and Capital*, especially chapter 4, in which the author shows that trust and betrayal in the Como's silk district are "integral aspects of the recurring process through which new family firms are generated and the industry regenerated" (144).

Negotiating the Economic Miracle:
Valenza Po's Jewelry Industry in the Decades
after World War II

O<small>N</small> 15 JULY 1959, a century after the first jewelry shop was opened in Valenza Po, the Piedmontese town finally began receiving some recognition from the state authorities. Giovanni Gronchi, the president of the Italian republic, paid Valenza Po an official visit and led the inauguration of the "Home of the Goldsmith," a nineteenth-century villa that housed a permanent exhibition of local jewelry open exclusively to foreign buyers. The visit was a personal success of Luigi Illario, the president of the local jewelers' association, who had devoted more than ten years of his life to the promotion of Valenza Po's production in the domestic and international markets. After negotiating for months with secretaries and prominent Roman members of his own (and the president's) party, Christian Democracy, Illario could finally reap the benefits of his efforts. But Illario was not among the select few who walked with the president in the spacious rooms where the very best of Valenza Po's jewelry was being shown. Like all other local producers, Illario was not even allowed to cross the threshold of the show. The regulations of the exhibition, whose paramount goal was to discourage plagiarism, had no exceptions. Thus, one of the most prominent local patrons, a man who lobbied in Rome for tax concessions and in the international markets for deals on gold batches, was simply kept out the room. Illario abode by the rule willingly, demonstrating to the president and to his fellow citizens the rectitude of the institution he had promoted.

During his brief visit in Valenza Po, the president was given an extremely elaborate gold casket crafted by a local artisan and was appointed honorary citizen. The speech delivered on this occasion by the Communist mayor, Luciano Lenti, reconstructed the history of Valenza Po in the previous century, beginning with the partisans' struggle against Fascism and the Nazi occupation, and moving backwards to the town's contribution to Italy's unification in the nineteenth century.

In his words, political rebirth and economic achievement came together in the passionate defense of craftsmanship and the celebration of political debate:

> Valenza is a highly industrialized and modern city. Its citizens are profoundly permeated with—and strenuous defenders of—a more humane and modern civilization that originates from work, the foundation of everything. Lively is the associational life of these people, fast and passionate is the circulation of ideas. Valenza readily participates in the political and civic events of national life. Fiercely vital, Valenza's citizens follow with enthusiasm the life of the state and that of their town alike.[1]

The mayor's words reveal an emotional dimension that goes well beyond the strategic manipulation of a powerful outsider. Far from emerging spontaneously from the invisible hands of market competition or civic sociability, cooperation and civility were imagined and deliberated upon in ceremonies like the president's visit and the jewelry exhibit itself, and for the benefit of both local actors and the greater world. But I will show that the same stories of progress and civility were also privately contested, criticized, and even torn apart. No simple mechanism could smooth over the contradictions between the consequences of economic competition and the claims of political participation, however intertwined the two had grown to be. The final outcome, as we will see, was the waning role of the institutions that had presided over the economic miracle and their replacement with more hierarchical (but no less informal) relations in the marketplace.

At the very beginning of his influential ethnographic account of social life in a southern Italian village in the late 1950s, Edward Banfield measured the distance between North American prosperity and Mediterranean backwardness by pointing to the southern Italians' inability to establish reliable institutions of cooperation: "Except as people can create and maintain corporate organization, they cannot have a modern economy. To put the matter more positively: the higher the level of living to be attained, the greater the need for organization."[2] Like generations of social scientists before and after him, Banfield drew an unequivocal connection between the institutions of sociability, the production of trust, the unleashing of economic growth, and

---

[1] Franco Cantamessa, *AOV: 30 Anni di Vita Associativa* (Villanova Monferrato, 1976), 81.
[2] Banfield, *Moral Basis*, 7.

modernity at large. While their fellow citizens hundreds of miles to the south remained mired in generalized distrust beyond the boundaries of the family, the people of Valenza Po were seemingly busy living Banfield's dream. They founded institutions and gave themselves an increasingly "corporate organization." The jewelry show was only one of a series of institutional innovations that the town's residents promoted in the years of the economic miracle, when Valenza Po became almost overnight one of the most important jewelry centers in the world. But this chapter will show that the connection between institution building, trust, and economic growth is not as straightforward as Banfield argued, and that the difference between the open and progressive north and the secretive and regressive south is above all an essentialist construction.

In the last few decades social scientists have emphasized the role of institutions in economic development, criticizing the simplistic tenets of neoclassical economics. Their argument contends that economic growth needs clear rules of the game, and that societies with different rules tend to have different levels of economic performance.[3] In the case of the Italian industrial districts of small firms, however, the importance of institutions has only recently been acknowledged.[4] The relative decline experienced by many industrial districts in recent years has led to a general revision of the early literature on the Third Italy, which viewed cooperation as the automatic outcome of family and community ties, and of the cohesion offered by local political cultures. Some scholars have raised doubts about the long-term viability of communitarian ties and on the resilience of the relations constituting what Coleman called "primordial social capital."[5] This revisionist narrative maintains that in the immediate postwar decades the ties of

---

[3] Douglass North, arguably the most influential among the economists interested in institutional change, defines institutions as "humanly devised constraints that structure political, economic, and social interaction. They consist of both informal constraints (sanctions, customs, traditions, and codes of conduct), and formal rules (constitutions, laws, property rights). Throughout history, institutions have been devised by human beings to create order and reduce uncertainty in exchange." "Institutions," *Journal of Economic Perspectives* 5 (Winter 1991): 97.

[4] For a recent and influential assessment of the importance of institutions in the Third Italy, see Alessandro Arrighetti and Gilberto Serravalli, eds., *Istituzioni Intermedie e Sviluppo Locale* (Rome, 1999), especially the editors' introduction.

[5] See, for example, Carlo Marco Belfanti and Sergio Onger, "Mercato e istituzioni nella storia dei distretti industriali," in Giancarlo Provasi, ed., *Le Istituzioni dello Sviluppo: I Distretti Industriali tra Storia, Sociologia ed Economia* (Rome, 2002), 245–68.

family and community led to cooperation through spontaneous and unintentional processes, but the erosion of these traditional ties in the wake of economic prosperity, coupled with the consequent rise of individualism, has made it necessary to construct institutions capable of coordinating economic activities, discouraging acts of free riding, and reshaping the cognitive maps of firms and individuals in ways conducive to collectively shared innovation.[6] In this Weberian scenario, institutions emerge to replace the waning role of primordial values, eroded by modernization.

The case of Valenza Po only partially fits this narrative. Formal institutions like the jewelry show were crucial to the economic boom itself, as they were to the construction of those values of cooperation and forbearance that, as we have seen, had not constituted primordial traits of local society before the war either. As in the prewar period, such values had to be imagined, fought over, and negotiated. In other words, they had to be constructed in the political arena. The fruits of the postwar institutional activity were plentiful. Valenza Po's jewelry industry grew at an unprecedented rate until the early 1970s. The number of firms and employees increased by a factor of five between the end of the war and the oil shock. Much of this growth was led by exports, which in a period of relatively stable prices increased from less than 100 million lire in the late 1950s to a stunning 11 billion lire in the mid-1960s.

The most remarkable feature of this growth is that it did not disrupt the local economic structure. An indication of the resilience of Valenza Po's productive networks over a period of forty years is conveyed by table 2, which charts the distribution of workers by firm size. The stability of this structure is striking. After the decentralization of the early 1920s and the spread of outwork practices, the local economic structure tended to "reproduce" itself at larger scales. Both the demographic expansion of the 1950s and 1960s, when Valenza Po's population almost doubled, and the export boom failed to disrupt this pattern. In sum, we are confronted with a fundamental continuity at the level of economic structure in the face of important institutional innovations.

---

[6] The cognitive, rather than merely regulative, dimension of institutions is emphasized by many recent studies on the Italian industrial districts. See, for example, Leonardo Parri, "Le istituzioni dello sviluppo economico: I distretti italiani a confronto con il modello tedesco e il sistema giapponese," in Provasi, *Le Istituzioni dello Sviluppo*, 3–39, who also argues that "because of their social embeddedness, institutions inevitably have dimensions that are symbolic, ethical, and related to identity" (7).

This chapter argues that this complex mix of continuity and rapid growth was predicated on delicate political compromises among contentious parties—compromises that were worked out in painstakingly crafted institutional arenas. The distinction between formal and informal arrangements was particularly instrumental in steering Valenza Po's economy towards a collectively desirable path. Since much of the story I am about to tell hinges on this distinction between formal and informal relations, it is necessary to reintroduce the concept of the informal economy, already discussed in the introduction. One of the most influential sociological definitions of this phenomenon is provided by Manuel Castells and Alejandro Portes: "The informal economy is . . . a process of income generation characterized by one central feature: it is unregulated by the institutions of society, in a legal and social environment in which similar activities are regulated."[7] The main advantage of this definition is that it does not rely on an unproblematic distinction between the state (the legal environment) and civil society. In fact, rule-bound institutions do not necessarily enjoy legal standing from the point of view of the state authorities (Valenza Po's jewelry show is a case in point), while informal arrangements can be embedded in the multiple rationalities of state regulation, as we will see in chapter 6. The main problem with Castells and Portes's definition is that it posits the informal economy as an exception developing outside of a society's institutional framework, thereby reintroducing a privileged perspective (arguably the one of state regulators), to which they ascribe the task of setting the boundaries of normality. In fact, the distinction between formal and informal regulation, between written and oral norms, between impersonal and personal relations, and so on, should be examined as one of the main political and discursive processes through which actors construct society, the market, and political legitimacy. In other words, we should treat formality and informality in a symmetrical way, as devices that define each other through their interaction.[8]

In this chapter I will focus on the shifting boundaries between formal and informal relations to map the construction of the market *and* social relations at the local level. My thesis is that historical actors draw

---

[7] Manuel Castells and Alejandro Portes, "World Underneath: The Origins, Dynamics, and Effects of the Informal Economy," in Portes, Castells, and Benton, *The Informal Economy,* 12.

[8] This is one of the main methodological points made by Barbara Misztal, *Informality: Social Theory and Contemporary Practice* (London, 2000).

TABLE 2

Jewelry Firms in Valenza Po by Size, and Distribution of Employees by Firm Size, 1927–81

No. of Employees in Firm	1927		1951		1968		1981[a]	
	% of Firms (N = 152)	% of All Employees (N = 796)	% of Firms (N = 296)	% of All Employees (N = 1809)	% of Firms (N = 1,021)	% of All Employees (N = 5,562)	% of Firms (N = 1,491)	% of All Employees (N = 7,162)
>50			0.3	3.0	0.2	2.5	0.4	7.4
20–49	3.3	16.9	3.1	12.6	3.5	16.2	2.5	14.3
10–19	12.5	30.3	15.9	34.3	13.0	32.0	8.7	23.5
1–9	84.2	52.8	80.7	50.1	83.3	49.3	88.4	54.8

Source: For 1927, Archivio del Comune di Valenza Po, vol. 11–3–4A, Statistiche Commerciali. For 1951 and 1968, Archivio del Comune di Valenza Po, vol. 11–2–1B, Censimento Industriale e Commerciale 1951. The 1968 data were collected for the Regional Institute for Economic Studies (IRES). For 1981, elaboration from Dario Velo and Carla Cattaneo, "L'area orafa valenzana," in *L'Economia Alessandrina dal Secondo Dopoguerra a Oggi* (Alessandria, 1993), 59–70.

[a] Data refer to the entire province of Alessandria.

and redraw the boundaries between formality and informality to change the distribution of power and resources in society and to make sense of the ever-shifting combination of strategic (instrumental) behavior and other kinds of commitments, such as affection and emotional attachment. We saw in the previous chapter how economic action in prewar Valenza Po was inextricably linked to the making of projects and deliberations that constructed the Piedmontese town as a unique place where socialism and commerce (God and Mammon) defined one another. This deliberative process continued after the war, but it also became increasingly delicate and vulnerable, as the town opened up to the rest of the world in both economic and cultural terms.

Consistent with the Weberian scenario, rule-bound institutions like the jewelry show were the consequence of the town's increasing vulnerability to strategic instrumentality, which threatened to wipe out Valenza Po's identity and distinctiveness. The jewelry show, for example, was simultaneously the product of strategic/instrumental trust (each individual artisan put his confidence in the rules of the institution as a bulwark against the temptation of plagiarism) and affective/sentimental trust (the show turned a collection of individual producers into a collective whole, and individuals trusted this collectivity to provide meaning and venues for participation).[9] For affective trust to be cultivated, informal agreements were no longer enough: clear rules of the game needed to be declared.

These negotiations over institution building originated from the transformation of the local political relations after the war. Now economic agents no longer shared the same socialist ideology. While most commercially oriented entrepreneurs, who made up the town's economic elite, gravitated towards the Christian Democratic Party, a growing number of independent artisans carried on the local tradi-

[9] I prefer to talk about emotional trust, rather than moral trust (which is the concept influentially employed by Uslaner in *Moral Foundations of Trust*), because I doubt that trust can ever be completely generalized and viewed as an ethical attitude. Uslaner links trust to optimism and confidence in one's ability to make the world a better place. As he puts it, "The central idea distinguishing generalized from particularized trust is how inclusive your moral community is" (26–27). One of the problems with this approach is that historical actors usually inhabit a plurality of moral communities at once, and that the observer can find a moral center to historical processes only at the risk of privileging one perspective at the expense of others. The shift from the "I" of strategic trust to the "we" of emotional trust, on the other hand, does not presuppose the existence of a paramount commitment (by social actors or by the observer) to a particular understanding of community.

tion of leftist politics. Production and commerce came to be politically connoted in different ways. In this context, patron-client relations became more problematic and contested than before the war. Moreover, immigration and the crisis of the shoe-making industry, by reconfiguring the local labor market, made social relations increasingly volatile and contentious.

The growing divide between artisans and traders threatened to dissolve local trust, and Valenza Po's citizens set out to craft institutions capable of bridging this gap and restoring "community." By exposing old tensions and shaping new conflicts, the opening up of the international market weakened the roots of patronage and personal relations, and promoted rule-bound practices of conflict resolution. However, at least two processes hindered the formalization of economic relations. First, personal and informal (sometimes even extralegal) relations remained crucial in the domestic market and in the supply of raw materials (gold and precious stones). Second, weaker agents actively negotiated their relations with the state and its demands for prestige and revenue. Paradoxically, the agents who were pushing for a higher degree of formalization in their contacts with the final markets, that is, the left-wing artisans, were also those who profited more from "gray-market" relations in other realms (e.g., raw-material supply and fiscal policy). These contradictions called for flexible and largely informal solutions, which, however, could easily degenerate into exploitative practices that only clear rules and the external authority of state regulation could keep in check. By navigating the shifting balance between formality and informality, Valenza Po's citizens negotiated their "miracle." In sum, institutions like the jewelry show should be seen as complex arenas for action and participation, rather than as mere functions of sociability or as ways of regulating market competition.

POLITICAL CONFLICTS AND ECONOMIC RECONSTRUCTION (1945–56)

Like the Great War, World War II and the Nazi occupation of 1943–45 disrupted Valenza Po's economy. A few firms in the shoe-making industry managed to secure military procurements, but most of the local companies had to face almost insurmountable problems in the supply of raw materials. In particular, the jewelry industry was hard hit by the 1941 law that banned gold trade and gold jewelry manufac-

turing in order to concentrate gold reserves on the importation of war-
related materials. For those who did not comply and kept producing
and selling gold jewelry, punishment could be severe, especially during the Nazi occupation.[10] Unlike what happened during the Great
War, however, many local jewelry manufacturers did not remain idle.
They rather replaced gold with silver and nonprecious metal alloys.
The temporary replacement of gold with other metals had interesting
consequences. If producers wanted to make a reasonable profit by
working nonprecious alloys with their equipment, they had to manu-
facture very elaborate jewelry that required manual skills and long
working hours. Moreover, as a jewelry craftsman pointed out in his
memoirs, "The large capital stock for gold purchases was no longer
necessary. All the artisans were in a state of ferment. Labor was scarce,
as many mama's boys (figli di papà) with a little money were looking
for a worker partner to be dragged along."[11] Many postwar entrepreneurs laid the foundations of their activities in these difficult years.

The foregoing quotation hints at the formation of the divide between
producers and traders, which remained a salient trait of postwar Valenza Po's social and political life. At a first level, this divide stemmed
from potential conflicts of interests, in the sense that no matter how
proficient individual artisans might have been at their workbenches,
they needed intermediaries capable of working the market, both on
the side of the supply of raw materials and on the side of the final
buyers. The autonomy that many of Valenza Po's artisans had
achieved in their work practices did not necessarily extend to their relations with the market, and they resented these ties of dependency.
As it had before the war, this dependency also originated from the artisans' ongoing need for credit. The traders were more than willing to
extend such credit, but in periods of crisis they often took advantage
of informal relations, pulled out of their relationship with the artisans,
and let the producers fend for themselves. Trust, vulnerability, and
even coercion were still inextricably intertwined. In the words of Aldo
Annaratone, one of the most active and successful left-wing artisans,

---

[10] In the fall of 1944, for example, Romolo Provera was deported to Germany with
several "Communists, rebels, and subversives" for selling gold jewelry. See Archivio del
Comune di Valenza, XI-3–4D, Frodi, Contravvenzioni, Diffide, letter dated 9 November
1944.

[11] Fernando Dabene, "Frammenti per il romanzo autobiografico 'L'Orefice di Valenza,' " Valensa d'na Vota 6 (1991): 110.

Here in Valenza traders could run debts for millions of lire without going bankrupt. Why? Because Valenza has always relied on production. ... Then, [the artisan reasoned,] someone willing to sell would come by. Here it's always been normal to sell other people's production. ... When the crash comes, who's to pay? The trader certainly isn't. Those who supplied him with merchandise are supposed to pay. ... Risk is widely shared. ... [Yet] producers ultimately pay. That's Valenza's problem.[12]

But this divide between producers and traders should also be examined at the level of the local political culture. Craftsmanship was ultimately about beauty and skill, not about money. And none of my interview partners expressed any doubt as to what their town was really about: "Valenza Po's citizens have been given a natural gift, that of knowing how to produce, and a great disgrace, that of not knowing how to sell."[13] Valenza Po's uniqueness lay in its labor and its skills—something whose value could not be reduced to costs, prices, and profit margins. Instrumental calculations were for the traders—the artisans worked for a higher order of motivations. It goes without saying that these roles and motivations often coexisted within the same firm and even the same person, but their dichotomous meanings did a lot of political and social work. God and Mammon kept vying for the loyalty of Valenza Po's citizens.

Despite these burgeoning tensions, the experience of the war and the resistance against Fascism and the Nazi occupation represented a phase of temporary unity. As in many other parts of northern Italy, the Resistance in Valenza Po was a cross-class experience. The Piedmontese town was the stage of two brutal executions of partisans in 1944–45, and participation in the liberation struggle, though hardly quantifiable, was remarkable. It is hard to overestimate the legacy of the Resistance in the local political culture. This experience offered a repertoire of widely shared myths that brought about a general reinterpretation of local history. The partisans' struggle was closely related to Valenza Po's identity as a socialist manufacturing center, which Fascism had failed to tame. Much like socialist politics at the beginning of the century, the Resistance created a language of solidarity and community to be pitted against the practices of economic competition. Even though Valenza Po's identity was increasingly shaped

---

[12] Aldo Annaratone, interview by author, October 1996.
[13] Ibid.

by its commercial and industrial vocation, the instrumentality of the market never became all-encompassing. Both formal and informal institutions were called on to frame market relations and draw the boundaries between instrumental and affective action.

The drawing of these boundaries, however, also exposed the vulnerabilities of both instrumentality and affection. The spirit of unity created by the Resistance was immediately translated into institutional activity, with a veritable barrage of rules and regulations. In June 1945, two months after the town's liberation, a group of manufacturers and workers met to form the local jewelers' association (Associazione Orafa Valenzana, hereafter AOV), which was to play a crucial role of coordination and promotion of local activities during the economic boom of the late 1950s and early 1960s. Significantly, the president of the association, Dante Fontani, was a former skilled worker in one of the town's most prestigious firms, owned by the Illario brothers, and a prominent member of the local National Liberation Committee, the partisans' provisional government. He also was a Florentine, and therefore thought to be "super partes."[14] A month after the first meeting, the association already organized 156 firms out of 250 and seemed to be on the verge of becoming a forum in which all the components of the local economy could participate on an equal footing.

In the early months of its activity, AOV tried to become a governance institution capable of mediating conflicting interests. For example, a committee was founded in the summer of 1945 to discipline competition by exposing unlicensed or fraudulent goldsmiths.[15] A few months later, representatives of the left-wing union and of the industrialists were invited to join the meetings and discuss minimum wage rates and paid vacations.[16] At the same time, the city government gave AOV the task of distributing coal and other raw materials among the jewelry manufacturers. These measures testify to the participatory character of the association and to the desire to establish unequivocal rules of the game. AOV's goal, however, was not merely the regulation of competition, but also the radical restructuring of economic relations through potentially compulsory political deliberation. In due time, all firms in town were to become members of the association, contribute to its ac-

[14] Cantamessa, *AOV*, 43–45.

[15] Archivio AOV, Verbali Riunioni Consiglio Amministrativo, 1945–49, 7 August 1945, 3.

[16] Ibid., 5 December 1945, 6.

tivities, and accept its collective authority. Nevertheless, AOV's attempts to assume a truly collective role proved short-lived. As early as March 1946, the council started to denounce the fact that many new entrepreneurs were refusing to apply for membership.[17]

The latent conflicts between artisans-producers and industrialists-traders came to the fore a few months later, when the municipal tax agent asked AOV to propose a list of the local jewelry firms divided by category (artisans, jewelry producers, jewelry traders, etc.).[18] Since commercially oriented agents were subject to the highest tax rate, it was in their interest to be listed as simple producers. This led to ongoing conflicts and negotiations that exposed the fragility of local consensus. At this stage, the commercially oriented companies staged a little coup by raising the yearly membership fee to a thousand lire, much more than artisans were willing to pay. The AOV's transformation was completed at the beginning of 1948, when Fontani was replaced by an accountant and business consultant, Mario Genovese, as president of the association. Significantly, one of Fontani's former bosses, Gino Illario, was elected vice president.[19] Gino was Luigi Illario's brother, a prominent jewelry industrialist and trader, and—like his brother—one the leaders of the local Christian Democrats. Several left-wing members resigned in reprisal. The conflict between artisans and traders, and between leftists and Catholics, brought AOV to a standstill that lasted almost ten years.

As AOV's attempts to create an effective governance institution foundered, demand for gold jewelry increased to unprecedented levels. The causes of this increase were similar to those that had led to the post–World War I "boom": the growth of the marriage rate; the fear of inflation; and the pent-up demand for consumer goods. The "gold town" was in a state of ferment. The number of hallmarks released by the Chamber of Commerce of Alessandria to Valenza Po's goldsmiths increased from 129 in 1945 to 316 in 1951, and to more than 500 in the mid-1950s (see table 3).[20] The 1951 industrial census reported 335 jewelry firms in Valenza Po, which means that almost all the local jewelry producers possessed a hallmark, and thus were entitled to sell their

[17] Ibid., 6 March 1946, 8.

[18] Ibid., 7 November 1946, 13.

[19] Ibid., 8 February 1948, 22.

[20] After 1934, all the official gold-jewelry manufacturers had to stamp their production with a hallmark bearing the acronym of their province of residence and their identification number.

TABLE 3
Active Hallmarks in Valenza Po

Year	Hallmarks	Year	Hallmarks	Year	Hallmarks
1935	109	1951	316	1967	960
1936	128	1952	349	1968	786
1937	126	1953	406	1969	810
1938	134	1954	428	1970	794
1939	143	1955	462	1971	815
1940	143	1956	490	1972	840
1941	148	1957	505	1973	821
1942	132	1958	534	1974	826
1943	129	1959	564	1975	803
1944	128	1960	598	1976	859
1945	129	1961	651	1977	913
1946	151	1962	708	1978	966
1947	184	1963	776	1979	982
1948	228	1964	821	1980	1001
1949	259	1965	850		
1950	297	1966	920		

Source: Data obtained from the Chamber of Commerce of Alessandria.

production directly in the national market. The network structure that had developed in the 1920s, based on the existence of a limited number of commercially oriented agents, was put under severe strain. In the new conditions, every firm could, at least potentially, bypass the commercial agents.

This possibility raised again the specter of cutthroat competition. Within AOV and in the town as a whole, two solutions to this threat were prospected. The traders' solution was based on hierarchy and coercion. Each trader was to create and monitor his network of producers, and develop his market niche among the retailers. On the political level, this scenario was embraced by the local Christian Democratic Party, many of whose leaders were commercially oriented

entrepreneurs. The left-leaning artisans' solution to governance problems was no longer based on production cooperatives, as in the first
two decades of the century, but on the creation of institutional arrangements like AOV, which could enforce trust and monitor local
manufacturers without restricting market opportunities for weaker
agents. When some of the left-wing members of the local Comitato di
Liberazione Nazionale founded AOV in 1945, their main intention
had been to challenge the traders' role. As we have seen, the traders
took over the association in the late 1940s, reshaping its agenda and
eventually causing its temporary paralysis. As we will see shortly, an
effective solution to this conflict was worked out within the association in the late 1950s, but only as far as exports were concerned. No
definitive governance mechanisms developed to monitor local producers' access to the domestic market.

The character of the conflict between artisans and traders highlights
the transformation of the patronage relations that had permeated Valenza Po's economic and political life in the first decades of the century.
This transformation had first of all a political dimension. The experience of the Resistance and the opportunity to produce silver and custom jewelry during the war had given rise to a new class of left-wing
small manufacturers who used political activity to enhance their position and gain direct access to the market. The depression of the 1930s
and the impact of Fascism on local society had driven out of the market
most socialist traders and former political patrons. The majority of the
surviving industrialists/traders, such as Illario, did not share their potential clients' ideology, while the new commercially oriented agents
gravitated towards the Christian Democratic Party (DC). The local political and economic divide was soon translated into electoral politics,
and the parties of the left commanded a clear lead over the Catholics
through the postwar decades. The municipal elections of March 1946,
for example, gave the leftist coalition, composed of the Partito Communists Italiano (PCI) and the Partito Socialista Italiano (PSI), almost
three-quarters of the votes. The support for the Christian Democrats
increased somewhat in the 1950s, but it rarely reached 30 percent.[21]
Under these new conditions, political patronage could no longer work
as the main governance mechanism, but local actors struggled to find
viable alternatives through the 1950s. Consequently, Valenza Po's jew-

---

[21] Pier Giorgio Maggiora, "Il Movimento Operaio a Valenza dal 1945 al 1968," laurea
thesis, preserved at the Municipal Library, Valenza Po.

elry industry developed in the late 1940s and early 1950s in ways that many observers regarded as "chaotic" and potentially disruptive.[22]

In the middle to late 1950s, when the domestic market started to slow down and exports were still uncommon and difficult, an increasing number of Valenza Po's small producers were victims of frauds perpetrated by nonlocal commercial agents, a clear consequence of the growing conflict between local artisans and traders. Typically, fraudulent agents gained the artisans' trust by dealing with them correctly for a few months, after which they simply vanished with a large amount of jewelry.[23] Since many of these transactions were highly informal, producers found it hard to turn to the police for help. Moreover, since these small producers had challenged the role of local traders, they could not rely on the informal help of more established agents either. Together with runaway firm proliferation, these incidents threatened to bring the recently reconstructed jewelry trade to an irreversible crisis.

The general perception of "chaos" was not just caused by the startling number of new start-ups in the jewelry industry, but also by the massive immigration that Valenza Po was experiencing for the first time in its history. Between 1951 and 1955, for example, 1,257 families moved to the Piedmontese town. Almost three-quarters of these immigrants came from neighboring areas in Piedmont, Lombardy, and Emilia, 17 percent from the Veneto, and 10 percent from the south.[24] Immigration was largely responsible for population increase: The town grew from less than fourteen thousand in 1951 to almost twenty-four thousand twenty years later. As I noted in the previous chapter, Valenza Po's relative prosperity had failed to attract immigration in the first decades of the century. This was largely a consequence of the existence of underutilized local labor and of the patronage-based hiring practices followed by the local jewelry and shoe-making firms. Personal connections and recommendations were necessary for prospective workers. These practices also reinforced patronage ties and the system of informal obligations on which patronage was predicated.

Postwar immigration put these personalistic practices under strain. Upon their arrival, most immigrants took over farms left behind by

[22] See, for example, Luigi Illario's ongoing complaints about firms' "splintering" (*polverizzazione*) and incorrect behaviors in AOV, Verbali Riunioni Consiglio, 1957–59.

[23] See, for example, *Il Piccolo*, Cronaca di Valenza, 19 April 1958, 14 June 1958, 22 August 1958, and 24 January 1959.

[24] Archivio del Comune di Valenza, XI-1-D, Agricoltura, Dati Statistici.

recently urbanized workers, but their ambition was to work in (or for) the local factories, and the jewelry industry, with its high wages, was their ultimate goal.[25] This availability of unskilled or semiskilled labor radically changed the character of the local labor market. Whereas local artisans became more politicized and autonomous from commercial agents, traders' outwork was taken up by the recent immigrants, eager to learn new skills and integrate themselves in local society.

In addition to political fractures and immigration, a third element tended to upset social relations in postwar Valenza Po. As the jewelry industry was experiencing its unprecedented expansion, shoe making entered into a prolonged period of crisis which in the late 1960s turned Valenza Po into a one-industry town. In short, Valenza Po's shoe industry before World War II offered a wide range of products and was technically innovative.[26] Its structure differed from that of the jewelry industry. In 1927, for example, 50.5 percent of the labor force worked in factories with more than fifty employees, and 56.5 percent of the workers were women. Start-ups and failures were less common than in jewelry making, as was outwork. Moreover, given the larger scale of the shoe-making firms, workers and proprietors were more differentiated. As I mentioned in the previous chapter, the relative stability of the shoe industry affected family decisions, as parents adopted hedging strategies and directed their children to occupations in both local sectors.

This situation changed radically after the war. Valenza Po's specialization in high-quality shoes no longer represented a competitive advantage, as neighboring centers like Vigevano occupied increasing shares of the market. Moreover, the coexistence of shoe making with gold jewelry became gradually more uneasy. The high wages paid by jewelry firms and the prospect of attaining proprietorship attracted young workers, including those born to immigrant families. High wages in the jewelry industry produced upward pressures on labor costs in shoe making. As a consequence, Valenza Po's production became less and less competitive vis-à-vis other less "prosperous" centers.

[25] See the letter of the mayor, Luciano Lenti, to the Chamber of Commerce of Alessandria on 22 February 1962 in Archivio del Comune di Valenza, XI-I-1A, Agricoltura, Studi e Problemi.

[26] In the early 1920s, for example, Carlo Lenti built the first Italian factory for the production of rubber-soled shoes in Valenza Po. See Paolo De Michelis, "L'industria Calzaturiera di Valenza," La Provincia di Alessandria, June 1959.

Layoffs and labor conflicts were the outcomes of this volatile economic situation. Whereas jewelry workers were scarcely unionized,[27] and labor controversies were uncommon until the 1960s, in shoe making strikes and social unrest became ongoing problems. Three waves of strikes in 1946, in 1951–52, and in 1956 failed to stem layoffs, which affected especially the larger firms.[28] In 1951, the percentage of the labor force working in factories with more than fifty workers had decreased to 35.8 percent, and ten years later it was down to 32 percent. Overall employment, however, decreased in a rather sluggish way. The 1951 census reported 1,522 workers, a level close to that reached in the 1920s. Ten years later employment had risen to 2,036. Only in the 1960s did the shoe industry collapse. The 1971 census reported only 1,040 workers. A wave of start-ups and the proliferation of small firms account for the discrepancy between total employment and the fate of large firms in the shoe-making sector. Whereas young workers moved to the jewelry industry, some older workers, who had accumulated technical skills for decades, reacted to the threat of unemployment by trying to take the path to proprietorship. This was a somewhat tragic mockery of what was occurring in the jewelry industry: it was the entrepreneurship of desperation. Without stable connections within a network of suppliers and traders, these firms were usually short-lived.

In this context, local authorities were at a loss. Once again, the two main local parties (PCI and DC) diverged not only about the possible solutions to the shoe industry's problems, but also about the diagnosis. The local communists argued that the crisis was the outcome of local producers' obsession with quality and diversity—the very qualities of the local jewelry industry that they strenuously defended. In 1966, a communist city councilor argued that "only now do we see the introduction of some new machines. However, [local manufacturers] hold on to their propensity to put too many models on the market and never compromise on quality."[29] According to him, the city government had to promote technical education and investments in mechanization. Luigi Illario, who at this time was president of AOV, city councilor, and president of the Chamber of Commerce of Alessandria, replied that "shoe manufacturers cannot pay the wages of the jewelry industry.

[27] Only three hundred of the approximately two thousand members of Valenza Po's Chamber of Labor (Camera del Lavoro) were jewelry workers.

[28] Archivio del Comune di Valenza, XI-6–2, Associazione Calzaturieri.

[29] Archivio del Comune di Valenza, XI-2–1D, Sviluppo Economico e Sociale, Verbale di Deliberazione del Consiglio Comunale no. 107, 2 June 1966.

Valenza Po's shoe-making factories are full of old workers. As they retire, few young workers replace them." The other problem, Illario argued, was the unions' resistance to outwork. In the most competitive areas of Italy, such as the Marche, "They make shoes at home too, and therefore costs are four times as low as here in Valenza Po."[30] According to him, it was pointless to struggle against this process, and in fact homework was already pervasive in the local jewelry industry. In due time, according to Illario, the jewelry sector was bound to absorb shoe making's labor surplus. Indeed, Illario's prediction proved to be correct. In the early 1970s, jewelry workers outnumbered shoe workers five to one, even without taking undocumented labor into account.

Even in a small center like Valenza Po, dispersed entrepreneurship and proprietary capitalism had a variety of economic and social causes, and a variety of political implications for different agents. Whereas in shoe making, proprietorship often represented a measure of last resort against unemployment, in the jewelry industry it represented a sign of vitality. Even in jewelry making, however, proprietorship was a complex phenomenon with a variety of meanings. Whereas before the war political allegiances presided over the formation of networks led by local commercial agents, in the postwar period the conflict between artisans and traders challenged the established social and economic relations. While outwork was the traders' preferred strategy for reducing labor costs and preserving a high degree of control over production practices, for many home workers, often recent immigrants, it represented the first step towards proprietorship and social promotion. The traders' strategy was challenged by a group of highly politicized small proprietors who assumed an artisanal identity that, we have seen, the local Left had criticized for decades before the rise of Fascism.

For much of the 1950s, the future of Valenza Po as an industrial center hung in the balance between formality and informality. On the one hand, institutions like AOV tried to establish open arenas in which most components of society could participate and in which political deliberation could replace competition. On the other hand, political fractures, immigration, and the crisis of the shoe industry fueled the proliferation of loosely connected start-up firms that entertained highly informal (even disorderly) relations with each other and the larger world. At this stage, these two modes of integration seemed to

[30] Ibid.

be more incompatibly juxtaposed than effectively integrated. But the export boom was about to change all that.

THE ASSOCIATIONAL REVIVAL (1951–57)

The divide between Valenza Po's jewelry producers and traders needs to be set in the context of the shifting relationships between local and extralocal agents. Although the sources concerning this important subject are not abundant, it is possible to outline the trajectory followed by the suppliers of gold and precious stones in their relationships with Valenza Po's manufacturers. Before the crisis of 1910–11, as I have shown in the previous chapter, Visconti's bank was the privileged local gold supplier for the majority of the local jewelry producers. Visconti mostly bought gold from a few specialized banks in Milan. Larger firms also dealt directly with the Milanese suppliers. After Visconti's bankruptcy and the Great War, Valenza Po's jewelers could count on an ever-increasing variety of suppliers: several regional and national banks, which opened their branches in the Piedmontese town; specialized gold "banks" (*banchi metalli*), which catered to minor firms;[31] and commercially oriented agents, who provided producers with gold via personal and informal transactions. This trend towards the diversification of gold supply channels continued after World War II, especially through the proliferation of specialized firms that sold gold in limited batches (the gold banks). Small producers profited from this process of diversification, that reduced their dependency on local commercial agents. Though hardly quantifiable, gold smuggling also increased throughout the 1950s, both in Valenza Po and in the other jewelry districts in the country. The available evidence suggests that suppliers dealt with both legal and smuggled (or even stolen) gold.[32]

[31] These were not banks in the traditional sense, but firms specialized in the supply of raw gold, which they obtained (at least in theory) from the state. I chose to call these institutions "banks," which translates the Italian *banco*, to underline their multifunctional character. These companies combined sale of gold with several forms of credit supply: It was customary for manufacturers, for instance, not to pay for gold right away and wait for the customer's (usually a retailer's) payment for manufactured jewelry, a process that could take several months to complete. I discuss another form of credit granted by the *banchi metalli*, which was related to wear-and-tear losses of gold, later in this chapter.

[32] In the fall of 1959, for example, a jewelry maker complained that one of his workers routinely stole small amounts of gold from his factory, which he then sold to a small

The functions of the gold banks were not limited to the supply of small quantities of precious metal. These companies also fulfilled important credit functions for the local producers. The recycling of gold residues, which was one of the gold banks' main activities, allowed the small producers to reduce their dependence on gold suppliers. Moreover, the services offered by the gold banks partially made up for the regular banks' reluctance to give "improvised" entrepreneurs credit. Luciano Lenti, the founder of one the main postwar gold banks and longtime mayor, described these mechanisms in an interview. As is still the case, the jewelry factories were carefully monitored to ensure that no gold left the premises. All residues, including trash, were kept on the premises and then processed to retrieve the minutest particle of precious metal. Whereas before the war several larger companies had owned their own furnace for melting these residues (as was the case with the De Rossis in the previous chapter), in the postwar period this activity was increasingly carried out by the gold banks. The local norms regulating the transactions between gold banks, producers, and buyers lay at the crossroads between formality and informality. One of these norms concerned the wear-and-tear that gold underwent during the various phases of jewelry manufacturing. In the 1950s and 1960s, wear-and-tear varied between 2.5 and 3.5 percent of total input, and it was taken into account in the costing and pricing practices. However, producers were allowed to overcharge the buyers, selling 750-millesimal jewelry as if it had sustained a loss of 7.5 percent. The 4 to 5 percent differential was an important source of self-financing, especially for small-scale producers. The gold bank refined the residues, withheld a 1.5 percent fee, and gave the rest of the gold back to the producer.

In order for this practice to work smoothly, a procedure was established to assess gold fineness and reduce the likelihood of controversies. The gold bank took three different samples from the batch of refined gold, which could be pure or, more often, already transformed into 750-millesimal alloy. One of the samples was kept on the bank's premises and assayed; the second sample was given to the producer; and the third sample was sealed and preserved for settling eventual controversies. The producer could get a second opinion by having his sample assayed elsewhere. According to Lenti, "This is a procedure

---

local "bank" specialized in gold refinement and trade. See *L'Orafo Valenzano*, November 1959, 3.

that forced both parties to be as careful as possible."[33] However, controversies seldom arose. The personal nature of the transaction and the desirability for a long-term relationship between the agents discouraged malfeasance. The difference between this arrangement and the centralized practices that existed before the Great War, when Visconti was the only gold bank in town, is evident: small producers could turn to a different gold bank in case their trust was abused. It is worth noting that—however elaborate and strictly defined—the procedures regulating the wear-and-tear standards were not sanctioned by the state, at least until the mid-1960s. Rather, these were local norms to which practitioners were expected to adhere if they wanted to preserve their reputation and rightful place in the community. On the one hand, these kinds of procedures had the potential to weaken patronage ties, for they made access to credit more routinized. On the other hand, however, the hybrid nature of the norms themselves—straddling personal and impersonal, formal and informal, and written and oral relations—called for a higher layer of control that only the interweaving of private and public roles could offer.

It was no coincidence that Valenza Po's longest-serving mayor after World War II was the owner of a gold bank. The importance of these firms in local society is revealed by the ties between these activities and local politics. Whereas the most influential mayors in the pre-Fascist and Fascist eras (Luciano Oliva and Mario Soave) were accountants specializing in judicial and extrajudicial agreements, Luciano Lenti, the mayor who led Valenza Po in the years of the "economic miracle," was the founder of one of the largest gold banks in town. Since gold banks fulfilled several crucial functions for the small artisanal firms, this change epitomizes the increasing political influence of the independent artisans in local society.

The career of Luciano Lenti, a member of the Communist Party since the Resistance years, is another example of the close ties between political and economic action—and between public and private roles—in Valenza Po's society. Born in 1921 to a family of local professionals, Lenti joined the Resistance movement in 1943 as a member of the local Group of Partisan Action (GAP). After the end of the war, he completed his studies by taking a degree in chemistry at the University of Turin. Back in Valenza Po in the late 1940s, he soon realized that local job opportunities for a chemist were very limited. Thus, in 1951 he de-

---

[33] Luciano Lenti, interview by author, October 1996.

cided to open up a lab for the analysis and refinement of precious metals. Thanks to his local connections, this activity proved quite successful, and Lenti soon became an intermediary agent between the Milanese gold dealers and Valenza Po's jewelry producers. In the early 1950s, when his gold bank had only three local competitors, Lenti was able to build a reputation as a reliable economic agent and a defender of the artisans' interests. Thus, after winning the local elections of 1955, the Communist Party chose him as Valenza Po's mayor. Lenti remained in office until 1963, when he was elected member of Parliament. In Rome, he continued to protect the interests of Valenza Po's small-scale artisans until 1973. As we will see in chapter 6, in the late 1960s he used his training as a chemist to win his lifetime political battle for a new law regulating jewelry production and commerce. He retired in 1973 from both his political and economic careers, and sold his gold bank to his former employees, thereby living up to his socialist ideals. When I met him in 1996, Lenti told me in no uncertain terms that the "golden age" of Valenza Po was over. His generation had tried to navigate the conflicting impulses of instrumentality and emotional attachment, of gain and beauty. But the younger generations flaunted a kind of materialism and individualism that belied their town's history. They probably also resented his benevolent paternalism: his interpretation of the town's history and identity admitted few ambiguities.

The same complex mix of formal and informal relations was also in full evidence in the case of precious stones, the other major "raw material" for Valenza Po's jewelry industry. After the Great War, many local firms found a profitable market niche in the production of custommade jewelry that combined gold and precious stones. This trend towards specialization accelerated after World War II, when Vicenza and Arezzo saturated the national market with their relatively more standardized jewelry (see chapters 3 and 4). The market for precious stones was even less formally organized than the one for gold, and risks were correspondingly higher. Local producers had two main options. They could rely on middlemen who bought precious stones in Antwerp, London, or Paris, or they could try to bypass all intermediaries and travel to these international trade centers themselves. There is some evidence that the role of middlemen was crucial in the early period of Valenza Po's industrialization. Writing about the beginning of the twentieth century, Ugo Melchiorre, the son of one of the leading entrepreneurs specializing in high-quality jewelry, gave the following vivid account:

Every day diamond dealers rushed to Valenza Po. Most of them were Jews and Armenians. Expert businessmen as they were, they kept prices up and gave credit especially to the new small firms that were proliferating like mushrooms in autumn. . . . As if this wasn't enough, here came the Milanese "con artists," who bought their stock of diamonds abroad and came down to Valenza to feed on manna in the promised land. They granted limitless loans to close deals (by means of promissory notes, of course). The Jews . . . soon retreated, leaving to the Milanese the privilege of exchanging precious stones with doubtful promissory notes.[34]

The crisis of 1910–11 brought this volatile situation to an end. After the Jewish traders retreated, the Milanese agents left as well. Unlike the local gold market, the market for precious stones became more concentrated in the interwar years because few local industrialists had the reputation and the resources necessary to travel to the northern European centers and deal directly with the international dealers. We saw some examples of these practices in the previous chapter. It was at this juncture that Valenza Po's jewelry firms laid the foundations of their long-term specialization in medium- to high-quality jewelry. It was also in this period that Valenza Po's commercial agents reached the apex of their power at the local level.

Until the 1950s, Valenza Po's jewelry was only sold in the national market, except for a limited trade with South America, where some of the town's jewelers had migrated at the beginning of the century. In the post–World War II period new opportunities for export emerged. Once again, the role of the precious stone dealers was crucial. The Jewish traders, who had deserted Valenza Po in the early 1910s, started to show a renewed interest in the activities and potentialities of the Piedmontese town. Their connections at the international and local levels enabled them to assess the overall reliability and technical proficiency of Valenza Po's jewelry makers. Their assessment turned out to be positive. Here is how Franco Frascarolo, a local accountant who played an extremely important role in the "internationalization" of Valenza Po's jewelry industry, reconstructed these early contacts between the international stone dealers and the local manufacturers:

It all started with occasional exports. Foreign agents who came from abroad and placed orders. Back then, foreign meant interna-

[34] Ugo Melchiorre, "Valenza nel passato," *Valensa d'na Vota* 2 (1987): 63.

tional Jews. Why? Because Jews are connected to this market, to the stones. ... These gentlemen assessed the possibility of exporting through my activity [as an accountant and economic consultant], and started to say that we might make it in the larger world.[35]

It was at this juncture that the jewelers' association (AOV) was revived by becoming a coordination and governance institution devoted to promoting Valenza Po's jewelry in the international market. Two main factors informed this change. First of all, international agents, including the dealers in precious stone, needed a local point of reference capable of coordinating the activities of Valenza Po's specialized artisans. Revealingly, the first local agents who profited from exports were not the industrialist-traders, who held solid positions in the national market, but the independent artisans, who were struggling to carve out a niche for their high-quality production. These artisans were not bound by any exclusive sales agreements with commercial agents. Second, exports posed daunting technical and economic problems to Valenza Po's agents. Standards of quality and commercial reliability were significantly higher than in the domestic market, while information concerning styles, costs, and prices was hard to obtain and, if spread locally, might lead to ruinous competition.

Most important from a social and political point of view, exports tended to impose more formal transactions, at least as far as the final buyers were concerned (as we have seen, relations with the suppliers of raw materials became increasingly informal), and shorter terms of payment. This in turn increased liquidity and made credit more accessible. Since the difficulty of obtaining credit was one of the main underpinnings of patronage relations, artisans saw exports as an opportunity to enhance their autonomy from local agents. However, direct contact between local artisans and international traders could also have disruptive consequences, since traders could easily play one local producer against another. Collective institutions allowed the artisans to fulfill their aims without leading to cutthroat competition. If they presented themselves as a collectivity bound to mutual respect, local artisans could negotiate from a much stronger position than they

---

[35] Franco Frascarolo, interview by author, October 1996.

would as isolated agents. At least in this case, instrumentality and affectivity reinforced each other.

AOV became once again an arena where local agents could work out different agendas and diverging interests. In short, exports succeeded in achieving the provisional unity among the diverse range of local actors, a task that only the Resistance had fulfilled before, however briefly. The institutional dimension of this change was once again crucial. In 1957, AOV's executive council admitted several left-leaning artisans as full-time members. Luigi Illario, the Christian Democratic president of the association, understood that only by opening up to the Left could the association solve the problems posed by the internationalization of the local jewelry production.[36]

In 1957, AOV prepared the international debut of Valenza Po's jewelry step by step. First of all, the association tried to monitor the relationships between the artisans and the dealers in precious stones. In January, twelve local traders who acted as middlemen between the international stone traders and Valenza Po's artisans were summoned by the executive council. The official purpose of the meeting was to urge the middlemen to act within the law and abstain from dealing with unauthorized stone traders "for the sake of the whole jewelry class."[37] However, since the vast majority of the stone dealers were in fact "unauthorized," in the sense that they smuggled their goods into the country, the real purpose of the meeting was to create and enforce personal connections between the association and a select group of stone suppliers.[38]

The second step was to choose the appropriate stage for Valenza Po's debut as an international jewelry center. Through informal contacts between Frascarolo, the dealers in precious stones, and the association, the 1957 New York World's Fair was chosen as the ideal arena. This fair, which was to begin in April at the Coliseum, would attract wholesalers and commercial agents from all of the Americas and western Europe. AOV's participation had three main purposes: to make Valenza Po known among the international agents; to gather information about the American markets; and to establish contacts for further com-

---

[36] Barbano, L'Associazionismo Imprenditoriale, 103.
[37] AOV, Verbali Riunioni Consiglio, 1957–59, 18 January 1957, 2.
[38] Franco Frascarolo, interview by author, October 1996.

mercial developments.[39] The final step was to select a group of manufacturers who could represent the whole range of Valenza Po's jewelry production. AOV chose thirty-seven firms with a collection of nineteen hundred items. The potential tensions between the participants were avoided "by selecting items that were not in direct competition, and by setting price ranges in advance, a solution extremely favorable to all participants."[40]

The fair was a resounding success. As Frascarolo recalled, "We could have sold the entire collection, but it was not in our best interest to do so because of the gap between wholesale and retail prices in America (almost 50 percent), and the extremely high sales taxes."[41] Valenza Po's agents in New York decided instead to take orders, send the jewelry back to Italy, gather information about the prospective foreign buyers, and ship the requested goods to America. This was also a way of collectivizing the connections made in New York. It had to be clear that the jewelry exhibited in New York was indeed "made in Valenza"—in some sense it belonged to the town as a whole. The message got across. Despite the general lack of organization and know-how that plagued the early years of Valenza Po's export activity, foreign buyers began to flock to the Piedmontese town soon after the end of the world's fair. This sudden success posed coordination problems that AOV could not tackle within its institutional framework. Therefore AOV's leaders devised three distinct but interrelated organizational innovations: a private export company for local jewelry production; a permanent show to be housed in town; and several export consortiums between specialized firms.

Organizational Innovations and the Export "Boom" (1957–61)

Valenza Po's export company (Export-Orafi s.r.l., hereafter E-O) was chartered in January 1958 after a discussion that touched on several important governance issues. The firms that had participated in the world's fair had only been able to ship their production to the U.S. buyers after applying for state export licenses on an individual basis,

[39] AOV, Verbali Riunioni Consiglio, 1957–59, 10 May 1957, 14.
[40] Ibid., 11 March 1957, 9.
[41] Ibid., 10 May 1957, 14.

a costly process that took several months. Moreover, foreign buyers found it distressing to deal with an array of specialized producers in order to put together the assortment of jewelry they needed. E-O was supposed to solve these problems by acting as an intermediary agent between the buyers and the manufacturers, and between the latter and the state bureaucracy. By relying on E-O's services, small producers could bypass the state bureaucracy altogether and spare themselves the costly process of acquiring the know-how necessary to become exporters.

The members of E-O's board of directors largely coincided with AOV's executive council, and most of the issues concerning export practices were discussed within AOV. Revealingly, E-O's initial capital of 2.4 million lire was split equally among the twenty-four founders, even though their private resources and social status varied widely. Unsurprisingly, Luigi Illario was elected president of E-O as well.[42] At least in the founders' intentions, and not unlike AOV itself in the aftermath of the war, the company was supposed to take on an egalitarian and almost compulsory character. All Valenza Po's exporters were to become in due time partners of the new company.[43] However, once again tensions lurked beyond this facade of unanimity. The left-wing artisans in AOV's executive council wanted firms to deal with foreign buyers exclusively through the export company. According to them, all manufacturers had to pool their customers in order to strengthen E-O's collective functions. The Catholic wing of the council saw this measure as an infringement on free enterprise. A compromise was reached by making exclusive sales "desirable" but not compulsory.[44]

Similar tensions arose when the council proceeded to tackle the delicate issue of how and when to punish violations of the association's rules.[45] The communist wing argued that competition over prices was to be regarded as a violation of the institution's spirit. The rest of the council, including the socialists, rejected this view. Cheating on gold fineness was unanimously regarded as a serious infraction that automatically led to the expulsion of the culprit, but the council did not devise any clear control mechanism. Arguably, assays were simply delegated to the buyers. The most delicate issue was plagiarism. As Illario

[42] Archivio AOV, Export-Orafi s.r.l. Valenza, Libro Verbale delle Assemblee dei Soci, 8.

[43] AOV, Verbali Riunioni Consiglio, 1957–59, 29 October 1957, 32.

[44] Ibid., 31 May 1957, 22–23.

[45] Ibid., 29 October 1957, 30–33.

argued, E-O had to refrain from promoting any form of standardization of production. Every firm ought to preserve its individuality, since diversity was key to Valenza Po's success.[46] On the other hand, it was virtually impossible to prevent producers from following the styles in vogue, which of course was just as crucial to local manufacturers' success. Caught in this quandary, the council limited itself to giving the president the task to work out ad hoc compromises whenever conflicts over imitation arose. These debates illustrate first of all the uneasy co-existence between competition and cooperation: E-O was simultaneously a commercial venture among self-interested partners and a political association among subjects willing to find common ground through open deliberation and argumentation. But E-O also exposed disagreements over different meanings of cooperation. While the Catholic traders espoused an instrumental conception of cooperation, which stopped short of questioning the sanctity of individual property, the leftist artisans embraced the institution as a collective response to the threat of instrumental action. Cooperation was not a means to an end, but a good in itself—a way of increasing participation and equality. Despite (or maybe because of) these tensions, E-O was quite successful in the long term. The company started in 1958 by dealing with twelve local firms, and by the early 1970s it supervised more than eight thousand transactions a year between hundreds of local producers and almost six hundred foreign buyers for a total value of more than 4 billion lire.[47]

Another organizational innovation was instrumental in achieving this success, that is, the permanent exhibition of local jewelry. This exhibition was to be held in the villa that AOV had recently bought, humbly called "the home of the goldsmith." The need for a permanent show was widely recognized. In Europe, only Pforzheim, in south-western Germany, had a permanent exhibition of local jewelry. Valenza Po's production was even more diverse than Pforzheim's, and the utility of a show was correspondingly higher. Soon after the world's fair, it became apparent that foreign buyers needed to have ready access to Valenza Po's production without having to shop around the town's numerous small factories. Moreover, artisans, electrified by their recent successes, demanded an institutional arrangement that could put them in touch directly with the international markets. Artisans wanted to

[46] Ibid., 7 January 1958, 42.
[47] Cantamessa, *AOV*, 135–36.

make sure that the intermediation of powerful local agents, which was the rule in the domestic market, did not extend to exports as well.

Local agents differed as to the exact meaning and long-term potentialities of the exhibition. The main issue was access to the show. This was a two-pronged problem. First, exhibitors needed to be protected from the risk of plagiarism. As we saw at the opening of this chapter, this risk was avoided by prohibiting access to the show to all local agents, including the exhibitors themselves. Second, AOV's executive council had to decide if the exhibition was to be open to national as well as international buyers. The two issues were closely interrelated, because some national buyers could use their networks of producers in Valenza Po or elsewhere to copy particularly promising or innovative styles with short delays. On the other hand, the national wholesalers' access to the show was seen by some left-wing artisans as a long-awaited opportunity to bypass the role of the local commercial agents in the internal market as well. After a long and heated debate, this quandary was solved through a compromise. As a rule, only foreign buyers could visit the show, but exceptions could be made for national agents.[48]

The permanent exhibition was established in the spring of 1959, but the official inauguration took place on July 16 with the participation of Giovanni Gronchi, the president of the republic. This was the first time in Valenza Po's history that the head of the state visited the town, and the initiative had great symbolic value for many of the town's residents. As we saw in the opening of the chapter, the visit was another personal success of Luigi Illario, who had met Gronchi in Florence a few months before. In his speech, delivered before the president at the "home of the goldsmith," Illario focused on the democratic and egalitarian character of the exhibition. Even though all exhibitors had to pay a fee in order to rent a showcase, one of the clauses of the exhibition's regulations allowed any artisan who employed not more than five workers to share a showcase (hence saving on costs). Thanks to this possibility, Illario argued, "All jewelry manufacturers, from the modest artisan to the big industrialist, are placed on the same starting line before the foreign customers, all with the same opportunities to bring out the refinement, ingeniousness, and technical proficiency of their production."[49] When Valenza Po's jewelers defined exports as a "safety

[48] AOV, Verbali Riunioni Consiglio, 1957–59, 19 February 1959, 68–73.
[49] Cantamessa, AOV, 79.

valve,"[50] they did not refer only to the economic opportunities that international markets offered. Exports also relieved political tensions that could disrupt the delicate solidarity achieved at the local level. It is also worth emphasizing that the painstakingly detailed rules of the exhibit, with their obsession with formal control, were meant to equalize power and participation. This projected public sphere of symmetrical ties, however fictitious, was very much the product of political deliberation and institution building, rather than the unintended consequence of associational life.

Partly by virtue of the carefully crafted compromises on which it was based, the exhibition was an immediate success. The number of foreign buyers who visited the show increased by 73 percent in the first year, and by 154 percent in the second year. Over the same period, the number of countries from which the buyers came from increased from 38 to 51. Approximately half of the buyers came from the United States (18 percent), West Germany (13 percent), Switzerland (12 percent), and France (8 percent).[51] Some countries, such as Venezuela, imported Valenza Po's jewelry for a short period, before raising high tariffs in order to promote domestic production. Other destinations, however, made up for the loss, as was the case with many Arab countries throughout the 1960s. AOV built on the permanent exhibition's success by organizing a long series of shows around the world, from Australia to the United States.

The role of Illario as president of the institution was subjected to ongoing scrutiny. Despite his well-defined political affiliation as a Christian Democrat, Illario was a charismatic leader capable of promoting changes and solving controversies across the political spectrum. As I will show in chapter 6, he also acted as Valenza Po's foremost political patron in Rome, where he could boast many fruitful connections. At the local level, he ran Export-Orafi in personalistic ways that resembled the patronage-based practices of the prewar period. As Aldo Annaratone recalled,

> Export-Orafi experienced [in the early 1960s] such a profitable phase that it became possible to accumulate some savings ... a remarkable amount of money. Therefore, some desperate artisans begged: "Could you give us a little money in advance?" Export-Orafi found a way of meeting the needs of many who had not seen

---

[50] AOV, Verbali Riunioni Consiglio, 1957–59, 20 March 1959, 76.
[51] G. Andreone, "L'Anno Secondo," *L'Orafo Valenzano*, May 1961, 21–27.

a lira from their customers. This way [the organization] became an aid on the economic level as well.[52]

And yet, when Illario asked the city government to grant AOV the permit to build a street through the public park in front of the "home of the goldsmith," Luciano Lenti, the Communist mayor, firmly rejected the request. Used to equating Valenza Po's prosperity and the interests of the jewelry industry, Illario openly challenged the city government's decision. He went as far as to write to Palmiro Togliatti, the national leader of the Communist Party, to ask for his intercession with the mayor. The problem was that Illario's house was located across from the public park, and his political rivals suspected him (probably unjustly) of having a personal stake in the matter. A compromise was finally reached, but many in Valenza Po took pride in protecting the law and the public park against the "goldsmith's greed."[53] In another incident that took place in 1961, Illario was even fined by the communist-led city government for allowing alcohol consumption after hours in the House of the Goldsmith, while he was entertaining foreign visitors.[54] Especially when it came to policing a political rival, it had to be clear to all that life in Valenza Po was not just about moneymaking!

The contradiction between personalistic and rule-bound practices was never fully resolved. AOV challenged traditional patronage relations by fulfilling functions that had been characteristic of the prewar patron-client networks. During a speech in January 1961, Illario proclaimed before a large audience of local jewelry manufacturers that AOV had obtained from a powerful Turin-based bank "the *verbal* promise to grant Valenza Po's artisans . . . a loan of half a million lire without collateral, on condition that they become members of the association, and that they present a letter from the association itself."[55] The verbal nature of this agreement and the association's discretionary power reveal an attitude towards personalistic relations that was quite ambiguous. On the one hand, the association undermined patronage by introducing a series of rules of conduct that were supposed to be completely impartial. On the other hand, also because of the political

[52] Aldo Annaratone, interview by author, October 1996.
[53] AOV, Verbali Riunioni Consiglio, 1957–59, June 1959, 88–95; and Cantamessa, *AOV*, 74–75.
[54] *L'Industria Orafa Italiana*, 11 November 1961, 5–8.
[55] AOV, Verbali Riunioni Consiglio, 1959–61, 10 January 1961, 96; emphasis added.

feuds between its members, AOV acted as a collective patron for Valenza Po's numerous artisans.

Even though many small firms relied on the services of Export-Orafi, the "collective" export company, many others reaped the benefits of the permanent exhibition without resorting to any intermediary agents. These firms tried to establish privileged personal contacts with foreign buyers. The tension between personalistic and rule-bound practices was only one of the contradictions that informed Valenza Po's economic and social life in the years of the economic "miracle." The tension between local solidarity within collective institutions and more individualistic ventures was at least as important. In theory, the exhibitors were supposed to allow (and even encourage) their prospective buyers to visit as many other local producers as the foreigners pleased. But as early as July 1959, AOV's council denounced the way some exhibitors prevented the foreign buyers who had contacted them from visiting the other producers on their list. The council chastised these artisans for forcing the buyers into dealing exclusively with their "friends" and "allies."[56] It is highly doubtful that these kinds of reprimands rooted out individualistic "greed," but they certainly sent a signal.

It must also be said that, for all their achievements, E-O and the permanent exhibition were bureaucratic structures that tended to be somewhat sluggish in reacting to the changes in the international markets. Moreover, some local agents soon accumulated enough know-how and personal connections to capitalize on the export expansion on an individual basis, bypassing the intervention of collective institutions. These agents introduced another organizational innovation: the export consortiums between specialized firms. These initiatives were innovative on two counts. First, they represented the first joint-stock companies in Valenza Po's history: whereas all other local firms were partnerships, consortiums were organized as limited liability companies. Second, consortiums had the opportunity to register their own trademarks and implement independent marketing strategies.

One of the largest and longest-lived consortiums, GAM, was founded in 1957 by Franco Frascarolo, the accountant and business consultant who was simultaneously helping the jewelers' association organize the New York exhibition. After returning from the world's fair, Frascarolo realized that specialization had both advantages and

---

[56] AOV, Verbali Riunioni Consiglio, 1957–59, 29 July 1959, 115.

disadvantages. Whereas the small scale and artisanal proficiency of Valenza Po's firms were proving remarkably successful in the world market, foreign agents needed full assortments of jewelry to be delivered with punctuality, services that small specialized firms could hardly provide. Most important, Frascarolo also realized that it was becoming possible for local manufacturers to go on the international market with their own trademarks, instead of relying on internationally based and more established names. Whereas E-O sold jewelry to foreign wholesalers who imposed their trademarks on Valenza Po's production, the consortiums intended to establish their own marks.

As usual, personal connections proved crucial in launching the new venture. Frascarolo approached three jewelry manufacturers who had been his clients for years:

> I told them: "Let's put together this consortium." They replied: "Yes, we accept, but you must take care of it. We don't know how to do it." So I said: "Yes, I'll make it work." I knew that my professional activity [as an accountant] would be jeopardized. . . . Here people are jealous of each other, as in other places. . . . But I made a commitment, and I said to myself: "I'll keep my professional studio, but I'll also be a manager."[57]

GAM collected the production of three firms with more than one hundred workers in three distinct factories. Each firm preserved its specialization, as the consortium took orders from the international agents (mostly American retail chains), coordinated production, organized sales, and took care of redistributing the profits among the participants. Frascarolo also supervised the publication of a catalogue of GAM's production displaying almost two thousand items. He sent hundreds of copies to consulates and chambers of commerce around the world. The activity was very successful for more than a decade. GAM opened two branches in Milan and one in New York, thereby becoming an example of commercial and managerial inventiveness for other local producers.

Consortiums could be seen either as examples of cooperation or as individualistic threats to more collective-minded institutions such as E-O and the permanent exhibition. On the one hand, a Danish observer went as far as to argue that cooperation, epitomized by the export consortiums, represented Valenza Po's "gold mine." According to him,

---

[57] Franco Frascarolo, interview by author, 17 October 1996.

consortiums were "the secret" of the town's international success.[58] On the other hand, observers from the far left of the political spectrum maintained that these organizations represented instances of potentially disruptive competition, which weakened the role of governance institutions.[59] Whatever the case, consortiums did not survive the international market crisis of the early 1970s. Despite its earlier success, GAM, for instance, closed in 1974. The slump made it harder to coordinate production and distribute the profits among the participating firms, mostly because every firm wanted to produce the most profitable items. Of the more than thirty consortiums founded in the late 1950s and early 1960s, only a handful survived into the 1990s.

THE CHALLENGES OF THE LEFT-WING ARTISANS AND ORGANIZED LABOR TO THE INFORMAL ECONOMY (1961–71)

The causes of the left-wing artisans' defeat in their struggle to preserve their autonomy in the international market are related to their failed attempts at bypassing the local commercial agents in the domestic market. Throughout the 1960s, a combative group of small-scale producers tried to set up institutions and initiatives that might enable them to reach the Italian wholesalers and retailers directly. The local collective institutions, such as the permanent exhibition and Export-Orafi, had established a dichotomy in the way Valenza Po's agents dealt with the domestic and international markets. Artisans had achieved a degree of autonomy vis-à-vis the foreign buyers, but still had to rely on local traders to place their production in the domestic market. This was a highly unstable compromise because of the ties between the two markets, especially as far as raw materials were concerned. It soon became apparent to local agents that this balance was untenable in the long run. Control over the domestic market came to be seen as the crucial factor in the long-term balance of power between Valenza Po's factions.

Within AOV, the debate began at the end of 1959, soon after the inauguration of the permanent exhibition. The left-wing artisans understood that they had an opportunity to capitalize on their recent interna-

---

[58] Torsten Hjern, "La collaborazione costituisce la forza di Valenza . . . e le sue miniere auree," *L'Orafo Valenzano*, January 1964, 22.

[59] AOV, Verbali Riunioni Consiglio, 1957–59, 26 August 1958, 56–57.

tional success, and launched the proposal of organizing a separate annual exhibition of local jewelry for the Italian wholesalers and retailers. In the words of Elio Provera, this was "the only way of dealing directly with the wholesalers, without the intervention of any intermediary agent."[60] In order to make the proposal more palatable to the local traders, the artisans promised that only their surplus, if any, would be sold to the Italian wholesalers, so that the interests of the local commercial agents would not be damaged. Moreover, the artisans claimed, direct selling would have increased their liquidity and made the artisans more reliable in their transactions with the traders. In other words, everyone would profit from the innovation.

The local traders, however, immediately realized that the artisans were trying to challenge the unequal credit mechanisms that linked local small producers and commercial agents in a hierarchical way. Therefore, they called for strict rules in order to thwart any possible transformation. One of the traders' counterproposals was that the list of the wholesalers invited to the exhibition be subjected to the veto of "a good many local commercial agents." Moreover, the traders argued, in Valenza Po "there are artisans who do not work in conformity with the law, and therefore can set prices which are much lower [than those of the official firms]." To offer these artisans the opportunity to deal directly with the national buyers in a formal setting was tantamount to encouraging unfair competition.[61] By drawing attention to gray market artisans in this way, traders conveyed the message that informality was built into the local system, and that both small producers and commercial agents reaped the benefits of informal relations. Implicit in the local traders' argument was the consideration that they sheltered and monitored gray market artisans, so that an element of potential disruption (extralegal transactions) was turned into a competitive advantage (lower prices). Without their control, local economic relations would degenerate into a free-for-all scrambling for buyers.

Other considerations concerned the threat of plagiarism. One of the traders' strongest arguments against the exhibition for Italian wholesalers maintained that information about styles had to be protected from external agents. The network of local commercial agents worked as a buffer preventing external wholesalers from spreading and imitating successful styles before Valenza Po's production reached its final

[60] AOV, Verbali Riunioni Consiglio, 1957–59, 25 September 1959, 143.
[61] Ibid., 139–44.

markets. As a consequence, local traders were key to Valenza Po's co-hesion and competitiveness. After a long and heated debate, it became apparent that the establishment of the annual exhibition for the domes-tic market would have disrupted the local balance of power. The initia-tive did not materialize until the 1980s, after the left-wing artisans had been defeated both ideologically and on the ground. One of the conse-quences of this impasse was the leftists' retreat from the activities of AOV in 1961. The balance of power within the council shifted again towards the Catholic commercial agents, as the left-wing artisans fo-cused their energies on more pliant (but also less inclusive) venues, such as the local sections of the Socialist and Communist parties.

Despite their institutional defeat, the left-wing artisans tried two more times in the 1960s to enhance their autonomy in the domestic market. In 1965 and 1966, after the celebration of the twentieth anniver-sary of AOV's foundation, the artisans used their connections with other cities' producers to set up two exhibitions in Reggio Emilia and Turin. The traders' resistance and the ensuing debate led to the estab-lishment of very complicated regulations. The exhibitions were open to the public, since their principal aim was to promote Valenza Po's production. However, in order to avoid direct contacts between the public and the exhibitors, the names of the artisans and the prices of their jewelry did not appear in the showcases. They were replaced by numbers, so that AOV's representatives could decide whether to dis-close this information to prospective buyers or to keep it secret.[62] Al-though the exhibitions were quite successful in terms of public re-sponse, the regulations prevented artisans from carving out their own networks of commercial agents.

A second initiative with potentially more radical implications was proposed after the first signs of the market crisis of 1969, which hit the internal market sooner and harder than the international one. The politically active artisans proposed the establishment of a Center for the Defense of Valenza Po's Jewelry, a collective institution devoted to the promotion and coordination of local production—an ersatz AOV that would represent their interests and aspirations. According to Elio Provera, the chief organizer of the initiative, the center had five princi-pal aims: (1) to improve the quality of Valenza Po's production; (2) to defend the artisans' intellectual property from plagiarism; (3) to moni-tor prices both in the production and in the commercialization phases;

---

[62] AOV, Verbali Consiglio di Amministrazione, 1962–67, 102–35.

(4) to make credit more accessible; and (5) to promote local production through advertisement campaigns.[63] In order to achieve these goals, local jewelers had to bind themselves to a detailed series of norms of conduct (the "Jeweler's Charter"). The members of the center could then sell their production under a collective name and take advantage of the ensuing shared reputation.

This was an ambitious plan that aimed at curtailing the importance of gray market and extralegal practices in local society. Such practices represented one of the main venues for the traders' control over production and the domestic market, for while engaged in these transactions artisans needed protection from the vagaries of the market and the watchful eye of the state. But the informal economy had also made the fortunes of many an artisan. As a trader pointed out within AOV, the new project was predicated on a degree of cooperation that was very difficult to attain and preserve.[64] First, the establishment of the center was an expensive endeavor that had to be paid for by the artisans themselves. Even more important, the artisans who decided to join the center would suffer from a short-term competitive disadvantage, since they would not enjoy the benefits of informal (and extralegal) practices—such as avoiding taxes and buying smuggled raw materials. In the long run, perhaps, the promotion of their craft and the establishment of a reputation for high quality and reliability might have made up for these short-term losses, but this was undoubtedly a risky undertaking.

The artisans hoped that the deterioration of the market conditions would play in their favor by weakening the local traders. The center's promoters gained the provisional consensus of two hundred artisan-entrepreneurs out of a total of nine hundred, which was regarded as a good start.[65] The artisans' calculations, however, had not included the state's reaction to the general market crisis. The government threatened to raise taxes on luxury goods, including jewelry, to a staggering 15 percent for gold work and 30 percent for precious stones. The tax that was eventually levied did not reach those levels, but it became clear to Valenza Po's agents that the times were not ripe for a general "moralization" of the industry. Consequently, the proposal for the es-

[63] "Verso la costituzione di un centro di sviluppo del prodotto orafo valenzano," *L'Orafo Valenzano*, May 1969, 39–40.

[64] AOV, Verbali Consiglio di Amministrazione, 1969–70, 15–17.

[65] "CEDIS: Un passo in avanti," *L'Orafo Valenzano*, April 1970, 27–28.

tablishment of the center was not taken up again until the 1990s. In 1990 AOV made an almost identical proposal for the creation of a collective institution with the joint goal of promoting Valenza Po's production and ensuring its quality. To signify the paramount importance of artisanal quality, the institution was named the Consortium among Valenza's Master Jewelers (Consorzio Maestri Gioiellieri Valenzani). This time only a dozen companies decided to participate in the initiative, and the proposal was quietly called off again.[66]

Another group that tried to curtail the flexibility of production practices in Valenza Po was organized labor. Throughout the 1960s, the left-wing unions organized membership drives and strikes whose success usually fell short of their expectations. Unlike other Italian industrial districts, Valenza Po's jewelry workers showed a low propensity to unionize. One of the main reasons for this lack of mobilization was the relatively easy access to proprietorship. At least in the workers' expectations, wage labor was part of a career path that started with apprenticeship and led to an independent productive or (more rarely) commercial activity, rather than a permanent condition. Moreover, the extremely small scale of most factories made informal agreements between entrepreneurs and workers easy to achieve and enforce. However, a few episodes of labor conflict did take place, almost always in connection with national controversies.

One such episode of labor strife concerned the 1960 national contract for jewelry workers. This contract laid out rules on such sensitive issues as overtime pay and piecework, and it granted the workers significant wage increases.[67] The problem was that the contract did not bind the "artisanal" firms, defined as those that employed less than twenty workers and did not adopt completely mechanized processes.[68] Artisanal firms remained under the 1949 regulations, which were very

[66] Rodolfo Bosio, "Non Teme Concorrenti la Valenza dei Gioielli," in Marco Moussant and Luca Paolazzi, eds., *Gioielli Bambole Coltelli: Viaggio de "Il Sole 24 Ore" nei Distretti Produttivi Italiani* (Milan, 1992), 279–85.

[67] "Il nuovo contratto nazionale collettivo di lavoro per gli orafi," *L'Orafo Valenzano,* September 1960, 19.

[68] The distinction between industrial and artisanal firms was disciplined by law number 860 issued on 25 July 1956. No exam was necessary to be listed as an artisan. The discriminating variables were the quality of the work process, which could not be entirely mechanized, and firm size. Artisans could not employ more than ten apprentices and ten workers (five and five in the case of partly mechanized production processes). In the case of artistic occupations (*mestieri artistici tradizionali*), there was no size con-

flexible as far as working hours and piecework practices were concerned. All but a handful of Valenza Po's firms were officially "artisanal" enterprises and therefore could ignore the terms of the new contract.[69] Even though in 1960 the representatives of Valenza Po's artisans vowed to apply the contract anyway, practices changed very little.[70] When demand peaked in the fall, workers were asked to toil for up to sixty hours a week, and sometimes even on Sundays. Skilled workers were compensated for this extreme flexibility by receiving very high wages in the form of under-the-counter payments, which employers handed out on a discretionary basis. In the fall of 1961 the Chamber of Labor threatened to organize a strike in the few industrial establishments if working conditions in the town as a whole did not change. The unionists' strategy was to make standards for industrial firms even stricter, thereby forcing the industrialists to crack down on the informal practices of their subcontractors for fear of unfair competition. The threat was taken quite seriously, and the mayor himself, Luciano Lenti, decided to turn to AOV in order to settle the controversy.[71] Although labor disputes did not fall under AOV's competence, the association debated the union's requests before the mayor. A handful of left-wing artisans saw this as an opportunity to challenge the Catholic industrialists and signed a petition proposed by the mayor and calling for negotiations between industrialists and union representatives. However, 92 members out of 125 rejected the proposal. The union's threat turned out to be a bluff, since the strike was never called, among the relative indifference of local jewelry workers.

This episode shows that in periods of booming demand and increasing wages like the early 1960s, most workers in Valenza Po consented to flexible and informal labor relations. What about periods of market crisis? As the politically active artisans were trying in vain to implement novel institutions to cope with the impending crisis of the late 1960s (for example, through the Center for the Development of

---

straint. Gold jewelry production was included in this category at the end of the 1950s. Most of these clauses are still valid. See, for instance, Corrado Barberis, *La Società Italiana* (Bologna, 1994), chap. 2.

[69] In the 1960s, only Illario's firm employed more than fifty workers (eighty-five in 1968). A few other industrial firms produced chains and jewelry parts via mechanized processes. The number of workers directly employed by Valenza Po's jewelry firms never reached two hundred.

[70] AOV, Verbali Riunioni Consiglio, 1959–61, 14 October 1960, 65.

[71] AOV, Consiglio di Ammministrazione, 1961–62, 6 October 1961, 65–71.

Valenza Po's Jewelry), the town was hit by the wave of strikes that swept through the country in the fall of 1969, the so-called "hot autumn." Students of the Italian industrial districts have paid considerable attention to this phase of labor unrest. In many areas of northern and central Italy the strict regulations that were imposed on large firms in the aftermath of the strikes (above all the Statuto dei Lavoratori) promoted outwork and the development of small firms as a managerial strategy to cut on labor costs.[72] By contrast, in Valenza Po, where informal transactions and outwork had been widespread traits of the local economy for decades, labor unrest had the opposite results, at least on paper. The strikes led to more formal standards of conduct for the artisanal firms.

In December 1969, a large portion of Valenza Po's workers (between 30 and 40 percent) went on strike demanding higher wages, the end of under-the-counter payments, fringe benefits, the radical revision of piecework, and higher standards of work safety.[73] Many of the workers' requests were not satisfied, but the nationwide strike succeeded in promoting the first national contract regulating specifically the artisanal (as opposed to industrial) jewelry firms. By setting limits to working hours and regulating piecework, the contract aimed to reduce the gap between the work practices of industrial and of artisanal firms. The first consequence of the 1970 contract was to increase labor costs for Valenza Po's small firms. At the same time, gold prices increased after a long period of stability.[74] Therefore, barriers to entry in the jewelry industry rose to unprecedented levels. Whereas the yearly average difference between the number of start-ups and bankruptcies in the 1960s was seventy, with peaks of more than one hundred in 1961 and 1966, in 1970 and 1971 the difference was down to twenty.[75] For the

[72] See, for instance, Piore and Sabel, *The Second Industrial Divide*, 228. For the most famous regional case, Emilia-Romagna, see Sebastiano Brusco, "The Emilian Model: Productive Decentralization and Social Integration," *Cambridge Journal of Economics* 6 (1982): 167–84.

[73] Maggiora, "Il Movimento Operaio," 210.

[74] The Bretton Woods agreement set the price of gold at thirty-five dollars an ounce. In March 1968, the members of the "gold pool" met in Washington to declare the inconvertibility of the dollar for all transactions except the ones between the central banks. In 1971, even this exception was dropped. As a consequence, the price of gold for industrial uses quadrupled between 1968 and 1972, and kept increasing throughout the 1970s. For an overview of these issues, see A. Quadri-Curzio, *The Gold Problem: Economic Perspectives* (Oxford, 1982).

[75] "Rallenta l'espansione delle aziende orafe in provincia di Alessandria," *L'Orafo Valenzano*, February 1971, 47.

first time since the end of the war, it was becoming almost as easy to go bankrupt as to start a company. The slump of the late 1960s and early 1970s brought the latent contradictions between community-based regulation and informality to the fore. As soon as the skilled workers realized that wages, job security, and—most important—the prospect of attaining proprietorship were jeopardized by the crisis, informal agreements lost much of their appeal.

To sum up, the 1960s saw two main challenges to Valenza Po's informal economy. The first challenge was promoted by the left-wing artisans, who attempted to curtail gray market transactions as a way of enhancing their autonomy from the local commercial agents. This attempt foundered in the face of the state's increasing fiscal pressure. The second challenge was that of organized labor, which in 1970 succeeded in enacting stricter standards of conduct for the artisanal firms. Even this attempt, however, was not successful in the long run. Later in the 1970s and throughout the 1980s, the economic recovery encouraged the formation of a new alliance between skilled workers and small entrepreneurs, as proprietorship became once again a realistic prospect for a large portion of the male labor force. By that time, the stricter labor regulations of the early 1970s actually served to increase the level of informality even further. These processes illustrate what Alejandro Portes has identified as one of the main paradoxes of the informal economy: efforts to curtail the degree of informality in an economic system can effect the opposite results.[76] The resilience of the social and economic networks that made up Valenza Po's jewelry industry allowed the informal economy to perpetuate itself. The socially acceptable degree of informality, however, was historically contingent and predicated on the political negotiations between a variety of local and extralocal agents.

The left-wing artisans failed to sustain their momentum into the late 1970s and early 1980s, when the price of gold fluctuated wildly, putting a premium on the availability of considerable financial resources. The effects of the instability of the gold market were compounded through the 1970s and 1980s by the definitive crisis of Valenza Po's shoe industry, which reshaped the local labor market, allowing the town's traders to rebuild extensive networks of subcontracting relations that escaped the control of the combative left-wing artisans. Overall, these social and economic trends increased the power of the local commercial

[76] Portes, "Informal Economy and its Paradoxes," 433.

agents, who developed extensive contacts with a variety of international actors, largely bypassing the collective institutions that had been founded in the years of the economic miracle. This tendency was particularly evident in the organization of exports. Both the consortiums and the permanent jewelry show lost much of their importance in the local economy. The vulnerability of these cooperative institutions in times of crisis shows that trust among local actors was far from automatic in Valenza Po, and that more individualistic behaviors could come to the surface whenever opportunities shrank and political mobilization subsided.

As these institutions waned, two private commercial companies rose to prominence in the local economy. Casa Damiani, by far the town's most successful exporter and one of the world's twenty-five most successful small firms of the 1990s, became the first company in Valenza Po to organize an internationally successful marketing campaign.[77] Thanks to testimonials by people of the caliber of Isabella Rossellini, Damiani is today the only locally based company with an internationally recognized brand name. By the early 1990s, Damiani directly employed two hundred people and supervised the work of more than fifty other firms with approximately five hundred workers.[78] The other prominent company in town, Crova, was founded in 1977 by a former worker at Luigi Illario's company. This also became a networked company, supervising the work of approximately one hundred firms around town. Unlike Damiani, however, Crova carried on the local tradition of organizing production for the internationally recognized maisons, above all Bulgari.[79] Unlike the older export consortiums, there-

[77] Damiani 's sales increased by 1,119 percent between 1991 and 1996, totaling almost eighty million dollars in 1996. See *Business Week*, 23 March 1998, 52. Damiani fancies itself the heir of the town's most genuine artisanal tradition, on account of the fact that the current owners' grandfather established a small workshop in 1924. But my interview partners presented me with a very different picture. The founder's son, the person directly responsible for building up the company in the 1970s and 1980s, was no artisan at all. Instead, according to my informants, he was an exceptionally gifted *commerciante* (a word that they uttered with a smirk on their faces).

[78] For an overview of Valenza Po's jewelry districts in the 1980s and early 1990s, see Anna Maria Falzoni, "Il Distretto Orafo di Valenza Po," in Fabrizio Onida, Gianfranco Viesti, and Anna Maria Falzoni, eds., *I Distretti Industriali: Crisi o Evoluzione?* (Milan, 1992): 357–72.

[79] Bulgari has recently purchased 50 percent of Crova's capital, amidst fears by local actors of loss of control over the town's economy to the top international players. See "Il Distretto Risente della Crisi Internazionale del Lusso," *Il Mondo*, 7 July 2003.

fore, these companies promoted hierarchically organized networks in which control was relatively concentrated. These hierarchical networks are more similar to Benetton, for example, than to the consortiums founded in the 1960s. Following the example of Damiani and Crova, other leading commercial agents managed to reproduce internationally the marketing structure they had established in the domestic market since the 1920s—a structure in which small-scale producers gave up direct contact with the market in exchange for financial and commercial stability. Therefore, the development of Valenza Po after the 1970s is consistent with a pattern detected in other industrial districts, where collective institutions have given way to hierarchies of private (and largely informal) networked relations linking a leading firm and its subcontractors.[80] It is too soon to tell whether this institutional arrangement will be able to weather the current crisis.[81]

The emergence of these networked companies with strong ties to the international markets, however, did not go unchallenged. AOV tried repeatedly to provide smaller producers with venues where direct market contacts could develop. The most successful of these venues was a jewelry fair, called "Valenza Gioielli," established in 1978 and held every year since then in the spring and fall. Although the fair was to be open to all of Valenza Po's producers, the association's goal was to increase the opportunities available to the small artisanal firms, many of which felt betrayed by the waning fortunes of the permanent show. The number of visitors, all accredited Italian and foreign buyers, rose from 450 in 1978 to 2,500 in 1984.[82] In the meantime, the initial reluctance of the larger commercial companies gave way to their enthusiastic support of the institution. Even this venue, therefore, did not completely placate some of the smaller artisans' concerns.

In response to the agitation of its leftist members, AOV also promoted a much smaller fair, significantly called Review of the Jewelry Maker (Rassegna del Fabbricante Orafo—or RAFO), to be held twice a year, in which only a select group of local firms without commercial

[80] See especially Giancarlo Corò and Roberto Grandinetti, "Strategie di Delocalizzazione e Processi Evolutivi nei Distretti Industriali Italiani," *L'Industria* 20 (April 1999): 897–924.

[81] For a recent overview of the challenges facing Valenza Po today, see Gioacchino Garofoli, ed., *Il Distretto Orafo di Valenza: Tendenze Evolutive e Prospettive Future* (Milan, 2004).

[82] Data released by AOV. See www.gruppoitalia.it/aov/aov_press98/autunno/storia.htm.

offices could participate and to which only reputable wholesalers were invited. Painstakingly detailed rules regulated transactions at this fair. In order to create a truly level field for all participants, in this venue as well the names of the artisans did not appear in the showcases. They were replaced by numbers, so that AOV's representatives could check the prospective buyers' credentials. This rule shows how threatening the development of personal ties could be to some of the weaker producers, who prized enforced anonymity over branding and even privileged relations between particular sellers and buyers. In this case, it was disembeddedness that created trust among economic actors. Whereas Valenza Gioielli bloomed into one of Europe's most important jewelry shows, especially for the medium-high segments of the market, RAFO remained a primarily experimental venue where more daring designers could test their ideas. Nevertheless, it was also thanks to initiatives like RAFO that local actors managed to preserve the extreme fragmentation of the local economic structure and a degree of independence for the smaller artisans.

Indeed, the resilience of Valenza Po's network structure shown in table 3 should be understood as the outcome of the interaction between conflicting strategies pursued by different actors. Centralization and concentration of production, for example, failed to develop because specific actors in Valenza Po (the left-wing artisans) actively and continuously opposed this scenario. On the other hand, the high level of flexibility built into the local economic system did not lead to cutthroat competition because specific agents (the traders) used their strategic location, which enabled them to connect local and extralocal networks, as a way of monitoring local society.[83] This power enabled them to maintain a degree of control over production practices. The interaction between these strategies prevented the proliferation of firms from either escalating into a scenario of ruinous competition or degenerating into an increasingly centralized structure. The origin and location of the traders were important. Valenza Po's economic system internalized some crucial commercial functions as early as the 1920s. This process of internalization was largely the consequence of the crisis of the 1910s, which discontinued many of the ties that had linked Valenza Po's pro-

---

[83] The relationship between actors' power and their position within and among social networks is widely debated in the sociological literature about networks. See, for example, Ronald Burt, *Structural Holes: The Social Structure of Competition* (Cambridge, Mass., 1992).

ducers to the extralocal wholesalers and suppliers. After the crisis, networks of *local* intermediary and commercial agents in the raw-material and final markets monitored production resisting the temptation to play one manufacturer against another in order to reduce prices. The traders' embeddedness in local society was key to the development of trust-informed relations.[84]

This shifting balance of power between producers and traders was largely predicated on subtle negotiations over the boundaries between formal and informal relations. Clearly Valenza Po's actors cared a great deal about whether formal or informal institutions carried the day in any specific context. Most of the negotiations I examined in this chapter focused on moving the boundaries between formal and informal relations in one direction or the other. Informality had two distinct meanings in local society. It could function as a signal of affectivity and participation, shaping a collective identity that did not need detailed rules to function, but it could also signal profound asymmetries of power that some actors tried to present as inevitable or traditional, as was the case with local traders in their dealings with the artisans. Formality had multiple meanings as well. Formal relations signaled a breach of trust and the possibility of exploitation of the weak by the strong: local actors (especially the most vulnerable ones) resorted to formal rules to protect themselves from potential abuse. But formal rules could also establish a framework for the construction of trust-based relations and arenas for more equal participation, as was the case with AOV and its subsidiary organizations (the jewelry show and Export-Orafi) in the late 1950s and early 1960s. Both formal and informal relations could enhance trust, but the two modes were mutually constitutive and contingent on political struggle over economic opportunities and venues for participation. In sum, it was the political and cultural embeddedness of formal and informal institutions—rather than their seemingly unproblematic functions—that proved crucial to the preservation of workable levels of trust and cooperation. To put it another way, negotiations over (in)formality were crucial to negotiating the shifting boundaries between instrumental action and affectivity.

---

[84] This scenario can be contrasted with the plight of Providence, R.I., where the local jewelry industry floundered in the face of ruinous competition openly encouraged by New York—based jobbers. See Philip Scranton, *Endless Novelty: Specialty Production and American Industrialization, 1865–1925* (Princeton, 1997), chaps. 10 and 12.

From Craftsmen to Craftsmen: The Development
of Vicenza's Jewelry Industry

In 1536, Valerio Belli, also known as Valerio Vicentino, decided to leave Rome and return to Vicenza, his home town in the Venetian terra ferma.[1] For his mastery of the art of engraving metals and stones, he could already boast the title of "prince of engravers." His fellow citizens greeted him with great pomp, and the goldsmiths' guild, founded almost two centuries before, appointed him *gastaldo*, the highest office in the local artisanal hierarchy. Belli accepted the office as an honor, although the duties of the *gastaldo* consisted above all of arguably tedious inspections of the goldsmiths' workshops. During these visits, the *gastaldo* was supposed to check on his colleagues' hallmarks and measuring instruments. In case of suspected fraud, the guild could count on two *toccadori*, men who specialized in assaying precious metal objects. As a self-regulating institution, the guild discouraged defection (the fee for emigration was steep) and guarded its secrets. Moreover, in order to protect its members—masters and journeymen alike—from potential abuse of power, no office could be held for longer than a year. The guild made no exception for Belli, who served his time and left again for Venice.

Centuries later, in the 1900s, a new rule, adopted by several of Vicenza's jewelry firms, precipitated a wave of strikes. The rule stated that the weight of objects had to be assessed before and after they were given to the workers, who were held responsible for the weight differentials and eventual errors.[2] The workers, organized in a socialist union, saw this measure as the last move in a process that was dismantling the last vestiges of the artisanal economy. The function of the *gastaldo*, supposed to be *super partes*, was now carried out by the employer, an innovation that outraged the workers because of its obvious partiality.

---

[1] Franco Brunello and Nevio Furegon, *L'Artigianato Vicentino nella Storia* (Bassano del Grappa, 1985).

[2] "I crumiri della ditta Girardello," *El Giornale Visentin*, 5 December 1903.

Vicenza's jewelry reached the apex of its prestige in the fifteenth and sixteenth centuries. The following centuries were a protracted period of crisis. Nevertheless, the local tradition of jewelry making was never completely discontinued. Even when other industries, namely engineering and textiles, developed in the town in the latter part of the nineteenth century, gold jewelry remained the symbol of the artisanal proficiency of Vicenza's citizens. Ironically, however, Vicenza was the Italian center that in the first quarter of the twentieth century pioneered many of the techniques that transformed gold jewelry into an industrial activity. During the same period in which Valenza Po, a town with no tradition of craftsmanship, emerged as Italy's artisanal jewelry district, Vicenza gained the title of national capital of mass-produced jewelry. The first section of this chapter will propose a historical explanation of this paradox.

In the previous chapters I showed how a tradition of craftsmanship was invented in Valenza Po as part of the local culture of socialist patronage, and how this "tradition" was defended by a militant group of left-wing artisans during the years of the economic boom. In Vicenza, social and political conflict had the opposite outcome. Work practices changed in the 1890s and 1900s in response to the increasing demand for low-quality gold jewelry. The first moves towards mechanization and standardization date back to this period, and the evolution towards industrial practices gained steam after the Great War. Social and political conflict shaped the form of industrialization in Vicenza. By the end of the nineteenth century, Vicenza already had a well-organized labor movement of socialist orientation. This movement was just at the time breaking with the tradition of Catholic paternalism typical of the local friendly societies, and in particular with the jewelers' Friendly Society, named after Valerio Belli, which had been founded in 1880. In the heart of Catholic Veneto, the jewelry workers became the aristocracy of the city's socialist movement, and their political influence was stronger than their number might suggest (there were approximately two hundred jewelry workers at the beginning of the 1890s).

For a few years, organized labor resisted the transformation of work practices with a degree of success. However, the contradictions in the local socialist culture led to outcomes that the labor movement had not anticipated. The foundation of a production cooperative, which was supposed to provide a long-term alternative to private firms, hastened the industrialization process. The cooperative soon became the largest "firm" in town, while its competition with private companies concentrated on quantity and prices rather than on quality and styles. Rather than upholding craftsmanship, the labor movement ended up contributing to its demise through the promotion of this cooperative. This story shows that the existence of an artisanal tradition can have unexpected outcomes, and that the specific pattern of small-scale industrialization depends on the complex and often unpredictable interaction between competing strategies.

The other turning point in the history of Vicenza's jewelry industry took place in the late 1950s and early 1960s, when an export-led expansion triggered a veritable entrepreneurial boom. The local leading manufacturers promoted the development of a plethora of small businesses, organized in hierarchical networks linked by subcontracting relations. The new "artisanal" firms, however, strengthened Vicenza's specialization in mechanized and relatively standardized gold jewelry. In stark contrast with Valenza Po, Vicenza's economic structure became more fragmented as the economic and political influence of the larger firms increased. Moreover, unlike Valenza Po, Vicenza's export boom did not challenge the informal relations between larger- and smaller-scale entrepreneurs and traders. The importance of the informal economy probably increased between the end of World War II and the oil shock. Informality was both the product of hierarchical relations (larger firms profited from gray-market activities) and a resource for weaker actors, who often pushed its limits well beyond the leading firms' strategic goals. In sum, Vicenza's case illustrates the many faces of sociability and its complex and often unpredictable economic consequences. In the early twentieth century, the social capital invested and accumulated by jewelry workers in the establishment of their cooperative led to the creation of more hierarchical relations. After World War II, the development of patronage relations coordinated by the Christian Democratic political machine guaranteed the survival of the informal economy in the face of the internationalization of the local production.

The Rise and Fall of a Labor Aristocracy: Vicenza's Jewelry Workers in the Early Twentieth Century

The last decade of the nineteenth century was a period of rapid social and economic change in Vicenza. The city of Palladio was home to a group of gold jewelry producers who uneasily straddled the traditional world of craftsmanship and the new opportunities offered by an increasingly integrated national market. The town's jewelry manufacturers responded to the increase of the national demand for low-quality gold jewelry in two main ways, both of which challenged the "moral economy" of artisanal tradition. First, they introduced a degree of mechanization, especially by adopting drawing and chain-making machines imported from Germany. Second and more important, the manufacturers started to employ young workers in order to break the control traditionally enjoyed by skilled male labor over the work process.[3] Piecework became widespread, as employers grew more impatient to enforce factory discipline with unprecedented severity.

These changes made cross-class collaboration unpalatable for the skilled workers, who founded in 1897 a local union (Lega di Miglioramento). The union broke with the tradition of paternalism typical of the goldsmiths' Friendly Society, to which it was formally affiliated. The union's statute openly admitted striking as a weapon in the mounting class conflict and excluded the employers from membership. Moreover, it made the regulation of production and skill formation its paramount goal.[4] The union was an immediate success. By the end of the year it organized 115 members, approximately three-quarters of all jewelry workers. The example of Vicenza's skilled workers was soon followed by their colleagues in nearby Bassano, where a smaller Lega was founded in 1897. The female polishers had to wait six more years before chartering their own union, which remained little more than an offshoot of its male counterpart. By statute, almost half of the organizational council was made up of representatives of the male union.[5]

This burst of organizational activity preceded the first wave of strikes in the long history of Vicenza's jewelry industry. In December 1899, the employees of one of the leading firms in town, Girardello-Corradini, went on strike demanding higher wages and the radical re-

<hr>

[3] Luciano Chilese, "Vicenza operaia: Le origini del socialismo urbano tra mutualità, cooperazione e resistenza," in Emilio Franzina, ed., *La Classe, gli Uomini e i Partiti: Storia del Movimento Operaio e Socialista in una Provincia Bianca: Il Vicentino (1873–1948)* (Vicenza, 1982), 311–44.

[4] *Statuto della Lega di Miglioramento fra i Lavoranti Orefici, Argentieri, Gioiellieri, Bigiottieri, Incisori, Pulitrici* (Vicenza, 1897). Preserved at the Biblioteca Nazionale Centrale in Florence.

[5] *Statuto della Lega di Miglioramento tra Pulitrici in Oro* (Vicenza, 1903). Preserved at the Biblioteca Nazionale Centrale in Florence.

vision of work practices.[6] In a typical instance of solidarity between manufacturers, the employers reacted by subcontracting their production to Vallotto, another local firm. This decision triggered a chain reaction that extended the strike to five other firms, including Vallotto itself. More than one hundred workers joined the strike, relying on the financial support provided by the local union. A few weeks after the beginning of the strike, the manufacturers had to yield to the workers' requests, which included shorter working hours, higher overtime wages, the abolition of piecework, and the reduction of disciplinary fines within the factories. The workers' victory, however, was not achieved painlessly. The two leaders of the strike at Girardello, Biscaldi and De Moro, were fired in reprisal a month later on the pretext that they were less productive than average. When the procedure for reemployment failed, Biscaldi had to move to Genoa, since no local entrepreneur would hire him without the authorization of his former employer.[7] The traditional ties of loyalty that bound manufacturers and workers had been severed and replaced by class solidarity.

From his "exile," Biscaldi kept following the vicissitudes of Vicenza's jewelry workers. A skilled stone mounter, he soon understood that the employers' next move was to try to break workers' solidarity by offering select skilled workers partnerships in their firms.[8] This was a long-established practice, adopted, for instance, throughout the 1880s and 1890s by the pioneering firm Navarotto, in which many of Vicenza's entrepreneurs had acquired their technical and managerial skills. However, Biscaldi argued, the meaning of extended partnerships had changed after the debut of class confrontation. Partnerships were part of a deliberate strategy to get around the abolition of piecework and enforce factory discipline.

Less than two years after the strike of 1899, four skilled workers at Navarotto were offered a share in the firm's profits.[9] Despite the union's warnings, the workers accepted the offer. The immediate result of the agreement was new factory regulations of unprecedented severity, especially as far as late fines were concerned (the fine for drunkenness was applied regardless of the specific circumstances). Moreover, the new directors raised the daily production goals from sixty to sev-

---

[6] *El Giornale Visentin*, 16 December 1900. See also Luca Romano, "Tra partito e CdL: I riformisti, i sindacalisti rivoluzionari e le lotte operaie," in Franzina, *La Classe*, 467–508.

[7] "Il soverchio rompe il coperchio," *El Giornale Visentin*, 27 January 1901.

[8] A. Biscaldi, "Agli orefici visentini," *El Giornale Visentin*, 28 July 1901.

[9] "La questione orefici: Carte in Tavola," *El Giornale Visentin*, 26 January 1902.

enty-five grams of jewelry per worker. The socialists denounced the requirement that workers sign the regulations, under the threat of unemployment. For the first time in Vicenza's history, the socialist press compared the jewelry factories to jailhouses.[10] The socialists also complained about the deterioration of production quality that the new disciplinary practices entailed and tried to expose the traitorous ex-workers' actual motives: "Now . . . their dreams will be fulfilled, and their opportunism and subservience will be compensated by master Navarotto, who will provide them with the equipment and the gold necessary to open up their own firm."[11]

Extended partnerships were also part of a strategy that allowed Vicenza's leading employers to concentrate on commercialization and grant a few "loyal" workers control over production. Sometimes this goal was achieved simply by hiring a foreman, another unprecedented organizational solution. In October 1903, the workers at Girardello went on a new strike in reaction to the dismissal of Crestana, the union's secretary. The tension within the factory had risen because of the new foreman's "excessive rigor."[12] At first, forty of the forty-three workers joined the strike, but in the following weeks the number who failed to honor the strike increased. As a consequence, in December the strike was transformed into a boycott. If one of the strikebreaking workers was hired by another firm, all the workers in that firm would stop production immediately. Despite the boycott, new regulations were enacted at Girardello as well. "It is forbidden to smoke, eat, drink, speak . . . as if workers were life convicts." One of the most hated rules stated that the weight of objects had to be assessed before and after they were given to workers, who were held responsible for the weight differences. The socialist press commented dryly, "This show[s] the level of trust Girardello ha[s] in his workers."[13]

The tension built to a climax in 1904, when the jewelry workers became the most "advanced" section of Vicenza's labor movement. One of the main consequences of the strikes of 1900–1903 was the foundation of the local Chamber of Labor, an institution devoted to the coordination of the unions' activities.[14] Within a few years the chamber came

[10] "Ai gerenti della fabbrica Navarotto," *El Giornale Visentin*, 5 January 1902.

[11] "La questione degli orefici: Carte in tavola," *El Giornale Visentin*, 2 February 1902.

[12] "Lo sciopero degli orefici," *El Giornale Visentin*, 11 October 1903.

[13] "I crumiri della ditta Girardello," *El Giornale Visentin*, 5 December 1903.

[14] Emilio Franzina, "La Camera del Lavoro di Vicenza," in Franzina, ed., *Operai e Sindacato a Vicenza* (Vicenza, 1984), chap. 1.

to represent more than three thousand workers in the province. Whereas the organizers were mostly goldsmiths, printers, and weavers, the chamber managed to mobilize the increasing number of women who worked in the textile mills. In the city of Vicenza alone, more than a thousand women worked in two textile plants, Rossi and Schroeder. The interaction between the city-based labor aristocracy of the "artisans" and these recently urbanized workers shaped Vicenza's labor movement in the following years.[15] The Catholic city government saw this alliance as an ominous threat to social order, especially because it threatened the church's grip on the countryside. The much-feared movement of socialist ideas from the city to the rest of the province did not materialize. Nonetheless, the city government decided to set up an institution alternative to the Chamber of Labor, the Ufficio del Lavoro (Labor Office), which was supposed to work as a public, and yet patronage-based, employment agency. The unions' resistance prevented the office from playing a significant role in the city's social and economic life, but the socialists began to see the lack of support from the municipal authorities as a major constraint on the future of the labor movement.

The jewelry manufacturers' response to the creation of the Chamber of Labor was more direct and aggressive. In July 1904, the proprietors of Vallotto fired four workers, two of whom were prominent members of the jewelry workers' union.[16] The labor movement immediately showed its newly acquired strength by calling a strike at Vallotto and raising a citywide subscription in support of the dismissed workers. Although the proprietors refused to yield to the workers' requests, they offered to grant the dismissed workers the right to suggest the names of their successors.[17] When the workers rejected the offer, Vallotto's proprietors proceeded to hire two lower-skilled workers who were not union members. At this point, the confrontation took on a symbolic dimension. At stake was no longer the fate of a few workers, but the long-term viability of labor organization, which the socialists saw as the only way to defend the threatened world of artisanal practices. After seventy days of strike at Vallotto, the union proclaimed a

---

[15] The trajectory of Santa Beordo is paradigmatic of this interaction. After leading several strikes at the Vicenza's leading silk-spinning company, Schroeder, she was fired in reprisal in 1901. Consequently, Santa became a jewelry polisher and the city's most prominent female activist.

[16] "Agitazione orefici," *El Giornale Visentin*, 27 August 1904.

[17] "Agitazione orefici," *El Giornale Visentin*, 10 September 1904.

citywide strike of all jewelry workers. The strikers' platform called for a series of measures borrowed from the artisanal tradition. The second article of the platform, for example, mandated that only members of the union and of the Chamber of Labor could be hired as jewelry workers; the eighth article set the number of apprentices to a proportion of one to eight workers; the tenth article called for the repeal of most disciplinary fines; finally, promotions were to be decided jointly by the proprietors and the union representatives within each firm.

These "corporative" and artisanal aspirations represented only one side of the socialists' complex and somewhat contradictory ideology. As in Valenza Po, their attention to production standards and their reliance on personal agreements between proprietors and the narrow labor aristocracy of highly skilled workers were at odds with their official doctrine, which argued for the inevitability of mechanization and collectivization. Within this gap, an array of ideological positions competed in the local political arena. During the long strike of 1904, one of these positions seemed to gain sufficient clout to overshadow its rivals. An engineer of socialist faith, Domenico Piccoli, started to propagandize his own version of social cooperativism as a third way between revolutionary "massimalism" and "bourgeois" reformism. According to Piccoli, production cooperatives represented a major step towards socialism, for they transformed private capital into collective wealth: "Once it has become public, private capital will remain collective for eternity."[18] In order to achieve this goal, cooperatives had to establish very close relationships with the corresponding unions, to the point that the cooperatives' partners had to be union members as well. From this perspective, cooperatives were at the same time effective tools in the social struggle between workers and capitalists and the keystones of the future society of the "free and equal."

Especially in the jewelry industry, cooperatives were also seen as a response to extended partnerships, "the antithesis of true cooperation," and as a challenge to market competition and its rules: "One day we'll find ourselves in one factory, built and managed by us. By defying capitalist exploitation, we'll lead our industry, now disrupted by competition, along the path of true art."[19] As was bound to become painfully clear in the next few years, however, this program was marred by a fundamental paradox. In order to succeed and become a

---

[18] D. Piccoli, "Cooperazione," *El Giornale Visentin*, 7 January 1905.
[19] "Ai colleghi orefici," *El Giornale Visentin*, 5 August 1905.

viable alternative to private firms, cooperatives had to be competitive and carve out a profitable share of the market, and this goal could not be achieved without coming to constraining compromises with capitalist institutions and rules.

Two events precipitated the decision to implement Piccoli's program in the jewelry industry. The first was the workers' partial victory after eighteen weeks of strike. The agreement reduced the working hours from ten to nine and a half, regulated apprenticeship more strictly, ruled out dismissals in case of temporary crises, and increased wages. On the other hand, the employers refused to recognize the union's exclusive right as the only official bargaining agent, and rejected the union's proposal of shared management.[20] Overall, however, the labor movement had proven its strength, and the moment seemed ripe for raising the stakes of the confrontation. Even more important, some union members were contacted by a prominent Milan-based company, Oreficerie Italiane, which showed considerable interest in supporting the formation of a production cooperative of Vicenza's jewelry workers. In particular, the Milanese company guaranteed the commercialization of the cooperative's production in the entire country. This was enough for a group of skilled workers to move from theoretical pronouncements to the practical implementation of their ideals.

In January 1905, the jewelry workers' union proceeded to found a production cooperative, which was named after Valerio Belli, the famous engraver who had led the goldsmiths' guild in the sixteenth century.[21] This name choice is revealing of the worker's ideology. By claiming the name of the Friendly Society, the workers intended to convey the message that their organization was the embodiment of "true" solidarity among producers. Moreover, Belli's name suggested continuity with artisanal practices. Aside from ideological issues, however, it was the co-op's agreement with Oreficerie Italiane that made the workers' organization a potentially strong competitor to private firms. The compulsory character of the initiative also was a source of tension with the manufacturers. All the cooperative's members had to belong to the union, and all union members had to make a yearly financial contribution to the cooperative. This rule set the cooperative apart from capitalist enterprises, but it also created expectations and obligations in terms of employment. If a union member was fired, he or she expected to be

<hr />

[20] "La vittoria degli orefici," *El Giornale Visentin*, 12 November 1904.

[21] "Sulla cooperativa orafa di produzione," *El Giornale Visentin*, 7 January 1905.

hired by the cooperative as compensation for his or her disinterested support over the years. Moreover, the private employers were particularly concerned about the prospect of training a generation of apprentices who could leave their jobs at any moment and join the cooperative, a practice that the informal agreements among local entrepreneurs traditionally ruled out.[22] As a trust-informed institution and a product of collective action, the cooperative wove extensive webs of complex obligations and expectations, thereby sowing the seeds of potential betrayal—a pattern typical of many of Valenza Po's institutions as well.

These threats tended to upset the local labor market and prompted Vicenza's jewelry manufacturers to form a coalition led by the three largest firms, Vallotto, Trevisan, and Dal Corno, which the socialist press immediately scorned as the "triumvirate."[23] Not coincidentally, the secretary of the employers' association, Arturo Marzari, was an ex-worker who had been the workers' union's secretary in the late 1890s, before being offered a partnership at Navarotto. But despite the manufacturers' unified opposition, the cooperative achieved a high degree of control over Vicenza's jewelry industry. When one of Vallotto's engravers (who were the highest-skilled and best-paid workers in the industry) resigned and joined the cooperative, four other workers were fired in reprisal. Trevisan threatened to do the same if one of "its" engravers did not refrain from working for the cooperative at night and during the holidays. The cooperative dismissed the request, and the firm proceeded to fire the workers.[24] All these workers ended up in the co-op's payroll.

The presence of the cooperative also affected discipline within the factories. In December 1905, for example, an apprentice polisher at Pressanto accidentally ruined an earring and was subjected to a one-lira fine. Antonio Cibien, a skilled worker and union representative at Pressanto who was also a relative of the employer, contested the fine. Pressanto repealed the fine but imposed two days of suspension. The polisher simply resigned and joined the cooperative. Frustrated, the manufacturer held Cibien responsible for the incident and fired him and his wife. Apparently, this move was part of a strategy to convince Cibien to become a partner of the firm and eventually run a separate branch. Needless to say, however, both Cibien and his wife joined the

---

[22] "La tracotanza dei padroni orefici," *El Giornale Visentin*, 27 May 1905.

[23] "Licenziamenti e sistema moderno," *El Giornale Visentin*, 7 April 1906.

[24] "Gli orefici e la cooperative," *El Giornale Visentin*, 2 September 1905.

cooperative.[25] Through such episodes, the cooperative came to hire more than forty workers within a year from its foundation.[26] By the beginning of 1906, the cooperative was already one of the largest jewelry firms in town.

The sources do not allow us to examine the actual differences between the work practices adopted by the cooperative and by the private firms. All we have are the boasts of the socialists who took pride in pointing out that within the cooperative, discipline was no longer an issue: "Who doesn't remember the jewelry workers' brawls? . . . Who doesn't remember that for them it was always carnival time? The union has provided quite different models of conduct . . . and the cooperative proves this point."[27] Maybe because they had implemented their own version of work discipline, the socialists dropped the jailhouse metaphor and started to compare private factories to nursery schools. "Factories are turning into kindergartens. Proprietors don't even abide by the rules and employ children younger than eleven and 'apprentices' in their twenties."[28] Apparently, the co-op's success had created a shortage of skilled labor, which the manufacturers tried to solve by hiring unskilled workers. It is easy to imagine the effect of this practice on the quality of production. The confrontation between the cooperative and the private firms was already producing consequences that neither contender had anticipated. Whereas private firms increasingly resorted to unskilled labor, some Neapolitan traders praised the co-op's production with words of which Valerio Belli would hardly have approved: "The largest quantity of jewelry was purchased at the lowest possible price."[29]

In 1906, the cooperative's growing commercial success prompted a new wave of strikes. The workers' union put forward a platform that was even more radical than the one presented in 1904. In particular, the union asked the proprietors to recognize the Chamber of Labor, to reduce working hours to nine, and to enforce regulations of apprenticeship that were even stricter and more detailed than those agreed upon (but never fully implemented) two years before.[30] The manufacturers' response was unexpected and unprecedented. In November,

[25] "Vergogne padronali," *El Giornale Visentin*, 23 December 1905.

[26] *El Giornale Visentin*, 17 March 1906.

[27] "La potenza dell'organizzazione," *El Giornale Visentin*, 7 October 1905.

[28] "I proprietari d'oreficeria e l'asilo infantile," *El Giornale Visentin*, 5 May 1906.

[29] *El Giornale Visentin*, 27 July 1906.

[30] "Il nuovo memoriale degli orefici," *El Giornale Visentin*, 22 September 1906.

seven of the twelve firms, including the largest ones, decided to lock the workers out.[31] In short order, the workers called another citywide strike and reorganized the cooperative's activity so as to offer the strikers temporary employment. Approximately 150 workers were organized in three shifts. At the same time, the cooperative started to build a new plant that was supposed to make room for more than 500 workers. Throughout the strike, Oreficerie Italiane, the Milanese company, was forthcoming with orders and raw materials, thereby enabling the strikers to resist.

Faced with the union's successful strategy, the manufacturers had to accept many of the workers' requests, including the nine-hour working day and stricter age limitations for apprentices.[32] Even so, many of the cooperative's newest recruits did not return to their former jobs. In March 1907, the cooperative still employed approximately 100 workers, and it was by far the largest jewelry firm in town. Defeated on the terrain of direct confrontation, the manufacturers adopted more subtle strategies. Partnerships were still established whenever possible, while Vicenza's employers opened new branches in the city's outskirts, where the union's influence was negligible.[33] Moreover, the manufacturers' informal solidarity was reinforced by the creation of a consortium, Fabbriche Riunite Oreficerie Vicentine (FROV), which the socialists immediately called a "trust."

The reformist wing of the socialist movement, to which the majority of the cooperative's organizers belonged, argued that the establishment of the manufacturers' consortium, which epitomized the concentration of capital, and the success of the cooperative, which embodied the concentration of labor, jointly fulfilled Marxist predictions.[34] The reformists maintained that the cooperative would win the competition with private firms, and that this accomplishment would be a major step towards socialism. The revolutionary wing of the movement, led by a group of anarchists who were tightening their control over the Chamber of Labor and the goldsmiths' union, disagreed strongly. According to the anarcho-syndicalists, "The cooperative [was] only useful to the Milanese traders, who realized that they could raise a fortune by providing the workers with capital and reserving the right to exclusive

---

[31] "Lo sciopero degli orefici," *El Giornale Visentin*, 17 November 1906.

[32] *El Giornale Visentin*, 29 December 1906.

[33] "Tentacoli," *El Giornale Visentin*, 30 March 1907.

[34] "Tra l'oro," *El Giornale Visentin*, 20 April 1907.

selling."[35] In order to overcome capitalism, the workers' movement had to concentrate on its class organizations, namely the unions and the Chamber of Labor, and turn them into revolutionary forces. The jewelry cooperative, led and organized by former skilled workers turned bourgeois and managers like Piccoli, no longer qualified as a genuine working-class organization.

The rivalry between reformists and revolutionaries went so far as to lead to the expulsion of all the "intellectuals" from the Chamber of Labor.[36] The anarchists, led by the engraver Vasco Vezzana, shrouded the confrontation in the language of artisanal relations. For instance, they had the union repeal the clause according to which all union members had to be members of the cooperative. The reason was that, as craftsmen, the jewelry workers' aim was to reach the market directly with their production, without the intervention of intermediary agents. For the revolutionaries craftsmanship and socialism were perfectly compatible, since they were both founded on the superiority of manual labor. The reformists replied that "Craftsmanship . . . is the most pernicious and dangerous form of work, since it gives free rein to capitalist exploitation. In a socialist society . . . there will be no room for the past."[37] Paradoxically, the defenders of small-scale industrialization and artisanal practices in this phase were the revolutionary anarchists. The moderate socialists, who had emerged as a local force ten years before by protecting craftsmanship and its social implications, had tied their destinies to the cooperative, and thus saw artisanal relations as a thing of the past.

At the same time, in the elections of May 1909, the reformist socialists forged an alliance with the Republicans and the bourgeois Radical groups, and managed to ousted the Catholics from the city government and elect a Radical lawyer, Alfredo Dalle Mole, as Vicenza's mayor. The reformists' victory at the polls, combined with a failed citywide strike called in response to the czar's visit to Italy, led the anarcho-syndicalists to a standstill. Their political influence declined rapidly, and their periodical, *Le Lotte del Lavoro*, closed down a few months later.

The moderate socialists, however, could not reap the benefits of their political victory. In October 1909, the jewelry cooperative entered into

---

[35] "Proprio tutti imbecilli?" *El Giornale Visentin*, 20 March 1909.

[36] *El Giornale Visentin*, 20 April 1907.

[37] "Artigianato e socialismo," *El Giornale Visentin*, 13 February 1909.

a period of crisis from which it never fully recovered. The cooperative's workers saw their wages and working hours reduced by half,[38] while a group of engravers of anarchist faith threatened to leave and found their own cooperative, which they eventually did in March 1910.[39] The contradictions that had marred the cooperative's activities since its foundation came to a head shortly thereafter. Oreficerie Italiane, the Milanese subcontracting company, advised the cooperative to reduce its employees, while some of the stockholders called for its dissolution.[40] At the same time, the cooperative's leaders found out that the Milanese company was on the verge of bankruptcy. In the next few months, the cooperative dismissed a large portion of its workers, who decreased from almost two hundred in 1909 to only sixty at the end of 1910.[41] Many of the dismissed workers were young and therefore able to find alternative employment. The remaining workers faced a series of very difficult years, starting with the Libyan war of 1911–12 and culminating with the Great War.[42] Nevertheless, the cooperative did not dissolve. It survived the war and even the advent of Fascism. In 1926, the cooperative still had forty-two workers but—bitter irony—its exclusive client was FROV, the once-hated consortium that the manufacturers had founded in response to the cooperative's success.[43]

Two data can fruitfully summarize the final outcome of the most serious class confrontation Vicenza was to experience for a long time. In the 1880s, the yearly amount of gold processed per worker in the province of Vicenza was approximately 500 grams. In 1910, the average jewelry worker processed 7,500 grams of gold—a fifteen-fold increase.[44] In the meantime, the workforce only approximately doubled, increasing from less than two hundred to almost four hundred, one-third of whom were women. This trend towards concentration and increasing productivity continued throughout the 1920s and 1930s. The average number of employees per firm increased from 15.8 in 1926 to 28.0 in

---

[38] "Alla coop orefici," *El Giornale Visentin*, 24 October 1909.

[39] "Sempre contro gli odiati capitalisti," *El Giornale Visentin*, 20 March 1910.

[40] "Nella classe orafa," *El Giornale Visentin*, 6 February 1910.

[41] *El Giornale Visentin*, 11 December 1910.

[42] Camera di Commercio di Vicenza, *Le Industrie e i Traffici della Provincia di Vicenza negli Anni 1914–1922* (Vicenza, 1923), 94–98.

[43] Archivio Camera di Commercio di Vicenza, Archivio Storico, Anno 1926, Faldone 13, Relazioni Statistiche ed Economiche. At this date, FROV employed fifty-two workers.

[44] Brunello and Furegon, *L'Artigianato Vicentino nella Storia*, 80.

1937.[45] The defeat of the labor movement had triggered a process of increasing mechanization and standardization of production that transformed Vicenza from an artisanal city into the main Italian center for the industrial production of jewelry. Most of the jewelry manufactured in the province of Vicenza before World War II was sold in the domestic market, but a small portion of it was already exported to Latin America and the eastern Mediterranean. Despite a tendency towards decentralization, no entrepreneurial boom occurred in Vicenza before World War II. Unlike Valenza Po, the Venetian city preserved a clear-cut distinction between proprietors and workers. This trend, however, changed radically during the economic "miracle."

THE RETURN OF THE CRAFTSMEN AND VICENZA'S ENTREPRENEURIAL BOOM OF THE 1950S AND 1960S

The process of economic concentration that had affected Vicenza's jewelry industry before World War II was radically discontinued after the war. "Craftsmanship," which social conflict and mechanization had brought to the verge of extinction in the first decades of the century, was resurrected during the economic boom of the 1950s and 1960s. The average size of Vicenza's jewelry firms decreased from 28 employees in 1937 to 20 in 1951, 15.9 in 1961, and 12.6 in 1971. At the same time, the firms legally recognized as artisanal increased from 60 percent of the total in 1951 to 89 percent twenty years later. It is worth noting that decentralization went hand in hand with rapid growth. The number of jewelry firms in the province increased from 40 in 1951 to 395 in 1971. In the same period, the number of employees increased from almost 800 to approximately 5,000. Much of this expansion (between 60 and 70 percent of the firms) occurred in the city of Vicenza or its immediate environs. The rest of the growth took place in two other towns, that is, Bassano del Grappa, where the production of gold jewelry had long-standing tradition, and Trissino, a small town west of the provincial capital where a group of entrepreneurs from Vicenza founded several firms in the 1950s.[46]

---

[45] Archivio Camera di Commercio di Vicenza, Archivio Storico, Anno 1937, Faldone 169, Censimento Industriale 1937.

[46] Tommasina Andrighetto, *L'Artigianato Orafo in Vicenza: Analisi del Settore* (Vicenza, 1986), chap. 3.

TABLE 4

Jewelry Firms in the Province of Vicenza

Year	Firms	Employees	Employees per Firm	Concentration Index[a]
1926	21	331	15.8	36.8
1937	15	420	28.0	33.3
1951	40	794	20.0	30.5
1961	220	3,353	15.9	38.9
1971	395	4,990	12.6	43.7
1981	654	6,237	9.5	50.0

Source: Elaboration from Tommasina Andrighetto, L'Artigianato Orafo in Vicenza. Analisi del Settore (Vicenza, 1986).

Note: The correlation between the third and fourth columns is $-.873$; $R^2 = .762$.

[a] Percentage of workers employed by the 10-percent largest firms.

To be sure, the new artisans had little in common with the preindustrial craftsmen who had led the labor movement in the 1900s. Mechanization became pervasive in the postwar decades, as Vicenza strengthened its specialization in relatively standardized jewelry. Small businesses flourished in these years, but their productive practices relied on the use of automatic machines and complemented the activities of the larger firms. Some of the technology adopted in Vicenza, for example, the chain-making machines and the machines for the polishing processes, could be used as effectively by very small firms as by larger ones.

As we have seen, extended partnerships and subcontracting relations had a long-standing tradition in Vicenza. Nevertheless, it was only in the 1950s and 1960s that the conditions developed for a veritable entrepreneurial boom. As was the case in Valenza Po, many of the new entrepreneurs were ex-workers who maintained close ties with their former bosses. Unlike Valenza Po's left-wing proprietors, however, Vicenza's "artisans" did not fight openly for their independence from larger firms and commercial agents. Instead, an intricate network of subcontracting relations developed almost without overt conflict.

The jewelry industry shared this feature with other sectors in northeastern Italy. In much of the Veneto, the postwar decades saw a clearcut political hegemony of the Christian Democrats. Both workers and entrepreneurs usually belonged to the Christian Democratic Party and to the fast-growing Catholic associations. The tradition of leftist politics that had informed Vicenza's political life at the beginning of the century was never completely forgotten, and some jewelry artisans in the urban center of Vicenza remained faithful to the local tradition of leftist and anarchist politics.[47] These urban artisans, however, were overwhelmed by the success of the Catholic political machine in the countryside and in the city's outskirts, where much of the postwar expansion took place. This Catholic hegemony was conducive to small-scale industrialization, but this was a distinctly more "market driven" process than the more openly negotiated industrialization of the leftist areas, such as Valenza Po. The leading companies were not challenged by potentially hostile city governments and labor organizations. Soon after the end of the war, these leading companies began to promote start-ups in order to keep up with the increasing demand for mass-produced gold jewelry. The leading firms could thus reap the benefits of flexibility and retain a high degree of control over production and commercialization.

In terms of economic structure, the outcome of this process was increasing polarization. Between 1951 and 1971, the workers employed by the top 10 percent of firms (measured by number of workers employed) increased sharply from 30.5 percent of the total number of jewelry workers in the province to 43.7 percent (see table 4). The workers employed by very small firms (from one to five employees) also increased from 6 percent to 14 percent of the total between 1961 and 1971. Thus, it was mostly the midsize firms that decreased in importance. As table 4 shows, the proliferation of small firms (whence the reduction in the average firm size) and the increasing importance of larger firms were highly correlated. The correlation coefficient is $-.87$ and R^2 is .76. This hints at the existence of a development pattern that can be contrasted with that of Valenza Po, where the local economic structure remained remarkably stable in the face of rapid growth. In Vicenza, demand increased enormously in the late 1950s and early 1960s, and much of this growth was led by exports. The absence of an organized challenge to the leading firms' role in local society resulted in the increasing polarization of the local economic structure. The larger firms

[47] Leopoldo Magliaretta, "Gli orafi," in Giovanni Luigi Fontana and Ulderico Bernardi, eds., *Mestieri e Saperi fra Città e Territorio* (Vicenza, 1999), 391–412.

carried out part of the production process in their plants and farmed out the rest. The boundary between internal and subcontracted activities could shift in sync with demand changes. Subcontracting proprietors, the new "artisans," rarely voiced their complaints, and they never reached a level of organization comparable to that achieved by their colleagues in Valenza Po.

Coercion, however, was only one aspect of this process of fragmentation and polarization. The local system was flexible enough to allow a degree of social mobility, which reached its apex during the economic "miracle." In absolute terms, the number of entrepreneurs belonging to the local elite increased throughout the postwar era. Since Vicenza's leading firms were far from holding a monopoly over trade channels, it was possible for smaller firms to turn to extralocal traders and play one subcontractor against another, so as to carve out a profitable market niche. The career of Romeo Salin is a clear example of the opportunities that opened up in the 1950s for some skilled jewelry workers. After a career at FROV, Romeo decided to establish his own business in 1950, when he was forty-six years old. His family provided the first nucleus of workers: Romeo, his wife Alice, his brother Gianni, and his sister Gianna all worked at the same table. From the very beginning the firm's production was placed with wholesalers who came from Milan and several southern cities such as Naples, Catania, and Palermo. These agents also provided the Salin family with gold and other raw materials. After a few years, the southern wholesalers suggested that Romeo specialize in the production of gold watch straps for the international markets: "Without the southern wholesalers . . . we would never have sold anything abroad. We had no knowledge of the markets. To be honest, without some help from a priest relative, we didn't even know how to get to America!"[48] In short order, Salin's production did get to America, Switzerland, Germany, Belgium, and many other countries. In 1968, Salin produced 1,200 kilograms of gold watch straps per year, 80 percent of which were exported.[49]

This example also shows the importance of family mobilization in the years of the economic boom. Family members were often the first

[48] Stefano Tendini, *La Fabbrica delle Idee: Imprenditori Vicentini si Raccontano* (Vicenza, 1992), 150.
[49] Archivio Camera di Commercio di Vicenza, 1965/68-XIX, Lavoro e Previdenza Sociale, Premiazione ditte operatrici con l'estero, folder 1968.

employees of newly founded firms. This was another sign of the flexibility of the local economy. The reliance on family labor and the role of the "paterfamilias" also introduced an additional element of hierarchy, and contributed greatly to the reproduction of the informal economy. For all its success, moreover, Salin's firm was an exception within the plethora of start-ups that dotted the 1950s and 1960s. Most of these businesses were never able to reach the final markets directly, and remained subordinate to their subcontractors. Only two of the ten artisanal jewelry firms sampled in 1966 by the Chamber of Commerce as part of a general survey of local small companies entertained any independent relationship with the final buyers (wholesalers or retailers). Consistent with the pattern revealed by table 4, all the other businesses only worked for very few subcontractors (and often only one).[50] This remained a resilient trait of local industry. As late as the mid-1980s, approximately 60 percent of Vicenza's firms worked mostly for local subcontractors.[51]

One institution had the potential to overcome the limitations of this hierarchical structure of subcontracting relations. As early as 1946, the Chamber of Commerce and the city government, after reaching an agreement with the local industrialists' association, inaugurated a trade fair that was destined to become the most important jewelry fair in Italy, and one of the largest in Europe.[52] Although at first all the industrial activities of the province were represented in the fair, in 1957 the organizers decided to specialize in the three sectors that were proving more dynamic, that is, ceramics, marble, and gold jewelry. The jewelry show turned out to be the most successful. The number of participants doubled between 1958 and 1966, while the value of the transactions carried out at the fair quadrupled in the same period. Consequently, starting in 1966, three distinct fairs for each industry took place at different times of the year. In 1969, finally, two yearly jewelry shows, one in the spring and one in the fall, had to be organized to cater to the increasing number of participants and visitors. The success of the fair boosted Vicenza's jewelry exports. For example, the export of local jewelry doubled between 1966 and 1970, when it

[50] Archivio Camera di Commercio di Vicenza, 1966-XXI–4, Indagine campionaria sulle aziende artigiane.

[51] Andrighetto, L'Artigianato Orafo, chap. 6.

[52] Archivio Camera di Commercio di Vicenza, 1964/68-XVIII–4, Pratiche Varie, Ente Fiera.

exceeded 33 million dollars.[53] The fair, however, soon became a national event in which Vicenza's firms played an important but by no means exclusive role. Moreover, at least until the mid-1970s, more than half of Vicenza's exports were directed to West Germany, and most of these transactions eluded the fair entirely. The local leading firms were periodically contacted by a small number of powerful German wholesalers who, according to some sources, tended to squeeze high profits out of Vicenza's manufacturers.[54] The German wholesalers reexported some of Vicenza's jewelry to France and Britain. Overall, therefore, the trade fair failed to provide the bulk of Vicenza's small businesses with an opportunity to reach the market directly.

Salin's career might suggest too rosy a picture of Vicenza's jewelry production during the economic boom. Many smaller firms did not have the connections and the skills necessary to carve out a profitable share of the market for their production. If these firms wanted to challenge the role of the more established local companies and reach the market directly, they had to take high risks. In Hirschman's terminology, if "voice" was not a viable strategy for the smaller artisans, "exit" could become the rule.[55] Throughout this period, Vicenza's jewelry industry was plagued by illegal practices carried out by the weaker local agents, some of which were totally undocumented. These practices were already widespread in the 1950s. At the end of the decade, the Chamber of Commerce conducted a report on the problems of Vicenza's artisans. In the section concerning the jewelry industry, the artisans' situation was defined as "pitiful."[56] Unfair competition between industrial, artisanal, and undocumented firms was rampant. According to the report, the typical pattern was the following. A leading industrial entrepreneur sponsored one or more start-ups in a period of booming demand, "in order to avoid an excessive burden on his company." When demand subsided, the leading firm stopped providing the new proprietors with gold and orders. At this point, if the new

---

[53] Archivio Camera di Commercio di Vicenza, 1965/71-XXI, folder 5, Statistiche Economiche.

[54] Archivio Camera di Commercio di Vicenza, 1968/70, Industria, folder Industria Orafa, dated 9 September 1965.

[55] The notion of "exit" is developed by Albert Hirschman, *Exit, Voice, and Loyalty: Responses to Decline in Firms, Organizations, and States* (Cambridge, Mass., 1970).

[56] Archivio Camera di Commercio di Vicenza, Sezione Archivio del Centro Produttività Veneto, folder Relazioni Artigianato, Relazione no. 5, 25 February 1959. Unfortunately, this section of the archive is neither inventoried nor ordered.

entrepreneurs wanted to survive and pay off their debts, they had to turn to a wholesaler, who had a vested interest in fueling unfair competition even further. The report commented that "many of these firms ... cheat on gold fineness [so as] not to renounce all profit margins. Sometimes even the hallmarks are forged." The reporters called for stricter controls over production quality, which had reached a dismally low level. These controls had to be carried out by public authorities, but the report was vague as to precisely what institutions were supposed to step in.

These problems became endemic to the development of Vicenza's jewelry industry. In the late 1960s, the president of the national association of jewelry producers and traders (Confedorafi) wrote to the president of Vicenza's Chamber of Commerce complaining that "in Vicenza, like in other centers specializing in the mass production of jewelry, some manufacturers sell their production at prices that do not even take manufacturing costs into account. Low prices are compensated for by low and illegal degrees of gold fineness. Production bears the 750-millesimal mark, but the identification mark is hard or even impossible to decipher."[57] Since some of this production found its way to the international markets, and therefore threatened to ruin the reputation of all Italian manufacturers, something needed to be done with urgency. The problem, however, was made more delicate by the informal agreements between these local producers and some extralocal wholesalers, who encouraged illegal practices and helped place the fraudulent jewelry with its final buyers. Local authorities had very little control over these commercial agents. The president of Confedorafi limited himself to calling for a higher degree of collaboration between economic agents and local authorities.

The match between the two reports, penned ten years apart from each other, is remarkable. As I have noted in the case of Valenza Po, these instances of illegal or highly informal activity cannot be regarded as mere exceptions in otherwise "healthy" experiences of economic development. These practices were an integral part of the pattern of industrialization followed by these local societies during the economic "miracle." In general, illegal activities were part of the informal economy. For local actors, including the relatively more powerful ones, it was difficult to separate out the advantages of informality from its neg-

[57] Archivio Camera di Commercio di Vicenza, 1968–XXVI, Albi e ruoli commerciali, Ditte cessate, folder Sezione orafi, Corrispondenza varia.

ative consequences. For example, since the gold processed in Vicenza was almost entirely smuggled into the country and bought by the leading firms, they found it hard to report unscrupulous entrepreneurs. The leading firms profited more than anybody else from the general atmosphere of silence and complicity. Moreover, as the following example shows, both the public authorities and the leading entrepreneurs already knew who the culprits were. "Squealing on" your neighbor was simply useless and costly.

At the end of the 1960s, when the international price of gold (both official and smuggled) started to go up, a group of German traders based in Pforzheim contacted Vicenza's leading firms. Vicenza's jewelry was very competitive, and Germany was one of its prime markets. The rising price of gold prompted the German traders to propose a formal agreement to the Italian producers. The Germans would keep providing Vicenza's manufacturers with raw materials and orders, but the latter had to enact some forms of self-discipline so as to shelter the German traders from possible frauds. This was a unique opportunity to impose a degree of order on the local economy and crack down on gray-market activities. Some local actors thought that Vicenza's industrial elite could shift the local sector to a new equilibrium in which illegal practices were definitively discouraged.

Between 1969 and 1970, a select group of jewelry producers from the whole province met to discuss the creation of a consortium, called Unionorafi, devoted to monitoring and promoting local production and trade.[58] This group included all the leading industrialists (except one) and several renowned artisans who had built their fortunes on exports. The intention was to set up a committee whose main task was to single out Vicenza's law-abiding producers, who would then be invited to join the consortium. As one of the members of the newly founded committee argued, "It is necessary that all the founding partners be beyond reproach and criticism, and therefore that they enjoy complete mutual trust in each other."[59] In a way, the consortium was supposed to formalize the informal ties that linked the members of the local industrial elite to each other and to the plethora of small firms that the economic boom had brought about.

---

[58] Archivio Camera di Commercio di Vicenza, Sezione Archivio del Centro Produttività Veneto, folder Unionorafi.

[59] Ibid., dated 26 May 1969.

The applications for membership were supposed to be scrutinized in collaboration with the public authorities (the assaying lab of the Chamber of Commerce participated in the initiative). Successful applicants were then invited to sign a solemnly phrased pledge in which they committed themselves to following the consortium's rules. The alternative solution, which called for the selection of the "obviously honorable" few, was discarded after some discussion. By April 1970, the initiative seemed to be gaining momentum. Almost one hundred firms with approximately 1,500 employees (a third of the entire industry) applied for membership. The leading firms in the founding committee had apparently called their subcontracting partners in. In May, however, one of the artisans in the founding committee argued that "it would be better to wait for the situation to change. Many wholesalers have broken the agreement and still buy fraudulent jewelry."[60] Indeed, the wholesalers' behavior triggered a chain reaction that led to generalized defection. In August, the same artisan advised against the official inauguration of the consortium on the grounds that not only the wholesalers, but also some larger companies cheated on gold fineness. He reckoned that only ten to fifteen companies could still be counted in, not nearly enough for the consortium to work. He also noticed that even the jewelry workers' union, concerned with the prospect of a general firm selection, opposed the creation of the consortium. Unsurprisingly, the initiative was first postponed and then quietly called off.

The significance of this episode, which was only one of the attempts at curbing gray-market activities in Vicenza, is threefold. First, the failure of the consortium shows that, at least in some industrial districts, internationalization alone is not sufficient to promote a higher degree of formalization of socioeconomic relations. In Valenza Po, the export boom led to the partial restructuring of economic relations when the independent artisans mobilized to exploit the opportunities offered by the contact with international markets. These artisans challenged the role of the local entrepreneurial elites in the broad area where the formal and informal sectors met. In Vicenza, such a political challenge did not arise, at least not in the postwar decades. The Venetian city did not promote institutions such as Valenza Po's permanent exhibition or Export-Orafi. Once a local equilibrium, based on a specific pattern of relations between the formal and informal economies, develops, it tends to get locked in by creating interest groups and political alli-

---

[60] Ibid., dated 22 May 1970.

ances. Second, the comparison with Valenza Po suggests that formalization within rule-bound institutions is more likely to emerge where commercial activities are firmly embedded in local society. Where local wholesalers and traders dominate the market, as in Valenza Po, "unfair" competition and general defection are less likely to develop. In Vicenza, extralocal traders had an interest in playing one manufacturer off against another and supporting the local informal economy. Third, this episode shows that seemingly suboptimal equilibriums can be quite successful even over a long period. Vicenza's jewelry industry grew enormously and expanded abroad during the postwar decades, despite the instances of cutthroat competition and defection that marred its development. There is little doubt that Vicenza's agents turned informality into a competitive advantage.

In Vicenza, informal (and even illegal) activities and the threats of cutthroat competition did not lead to a vicious circle that precipitated the collapse of the local system. Illegal practices such as cheating on gold fineness were generally tolerated because they provided means of survival for the weaker agents in times of crisis. Overall, these practices increased the flexibility built into the system and preserved a high degree of cohesion in the entrepreneurial "class." Most important, the leading firms had a tight grip on some of the key activities that regulated local economic change. It was widely acknowledged, for example, that access to credit was "often maneuvered politically, even on the local level." These maneuvers reinforced the "chain of patronage-based politics."[61] The cohesion between local entrepreneurs was enhanced and reproduced by their political affiliation. An uninterrupted chain of political connections linked the ministerial bureaucracies to the local constituencies. On the national level, public aid flowed through the channels controlled by the Christian Democratic Party.[62] Archival sources suggest that in the years of the economic boom many jewelry firms in the Vicenza area, regardless of their size and stage of development, profited from this flow of public money,

---

[61] Amministrazione Provinciale di Vicenza, *Problemi dello Sviluppo Economico e Sociale del Vicentino* (Vicenza, 1965), 109–10.

[62] About this aspect of the region's industrialization, see Giovanni Luigi Fontana and Giorgio Roverato, "Processi di settorializzazione e di distrettualizzazione nei sistemi economici locali: Il caso Veneto," in Franco Amatori and Andrea Colli, eds., *Comunità di Imprese: Sistemi Locali in Italia tra Ottocento e Novecento* (Bologna, 2001), 553–57. The authors, however, deny that state intervention was among the main causes of the region's development, which were primarily endogenous to local society.

borrowed at very convenient rates.[63] At the local level, banks such as Banca Popolare del Veneto and Banca Cattolica del Veneto had a long-standing tradition of patronage-oriented intervention in Vicenza's economic life.[64] It was also through these institutions, in addition to face-to-face relations, that Vicenza's entrepreneurial elite preserved its control over the local economy, thereby preventing informality from becoming disruptive.

The development of Vicenza's jewelry industry in the twentieth century confirms the thesis that small-scale industrialization is a path-dependent process that is highly sensitive to specific local conditions. Of the three Italian gold-jewelry districts, Vicenza would appear to have been the best candidate for a long-term specialization in artisanal jewelry. After all, the Venetian city had a century-long tradition in this field. Vicenza's trajectory along this path, however, was deflected in the first two decades of the century, when the city specialized in highly mechanized production. Social conflict was the main force that led to this outcome. The new trajectory towards the selection of a few large firms was interrupted after World War II, when the local industrial elite started to promote start-ups in order to keep up with increasing demand. This outcome had an obviously political dimension, too. The defeat of the labor movement earlier in the century left the leading firms' strategies unchallenged. It is interesting to compare Vicenza's developmental pattern to that of Valenza Po. In Vicenza, the local economic structure changed in sync with demand. The shrinking demand of the 1930s led to the survival of fewer and larger firms. The demand expansion of the postwar era was met by a proliferation of small firms, but also by the increasing weight of larger companies in the local economy. This pattern was the outcome of a long-term strategy through which Vicenza's leading firms tried to combine flexibility and control. In Valenza Po, by contrast, increasing demand did not correlate at all with changes in economic structure. There, the distribution of firms by size remained remarkably stable. No single strategy was allowed to prevail in Valenza Po, where the existence of competing factions (notably the left-wing artisans and the Catholic traders after World War II)

[63] Archivio Camera di Commercio di Vicenza, Archivio Storico, Anno 1956, Faldone 882, Finanziamenti Piccole e Medie Imprese. In one month alone, December 1956, ten jewelry firms received loans for almost fifty million lire. The interest rate was 6.5 percent.

[64] See, for example, Emilio Franzina, *Grandi Artigiani e Piccole Imprese* (Vicenza, 1995), 97–98.

led to ongoing compromises. The stability of the local economic structure was the material embodiment of these compromises.

Another fruitful comparison between Vicenza and Valenza Po concerns the character of the relations between local economic and social actors in the two contexts. Whereas the export boom in Valenza Po led to an increasing formalization of relations within rule-bound institutions, economic globalization in Vicenza tended to reproduce personal and patronage-based practices. In the case of Vicenza, the sources do not show a decisive shift in the continuum between formal and informal relations. This difference is consistent with the notion that rule-bound practices are the outcome and the sign of conflicting strategies. Rule-bound institutions are more likely to develop, and impersonal trust is more likely to replace face-to-face negotiations, where conflict is potentially more disruptive. Given the lack of organized challenges to the elite's power in Vicenza, it is not surprising to see personal relations and patronage reproduce themselves undisturbed.

A Pyramid of Trust: The Development
of Arezzo's Jewelry Industry

IN her transcribed oral autobiography, Nara, one of the founders of Prato's feminist movement, recalls the story of how her father, a sharecropper, got to leave his family's farm and settle on a farm of his own:

> [My dad] was pruning the olive trees one day, when a lawyer who lived near the farm happened to pass by. . . . My dad was in the tree. He said hello to him and struck up a conversation with him till [the lawyer] left. When [my dad] climbed down the tree, he saw a bag on the side of the street. He opened it and found a lot of money and documents. He read them and discovered that they belonged to the lawyer. He decided to go to the villa and return the bag. The *signore* was most impressed and told my dad, "For what you have done, whatever you need, you ask me, and I'll do my best to help you out." One day, after a fight with his brothers, my dad felt really down. He ran into the lawyer, who asked him, "What's wrong?" and he said, "We quarrel a lot at home. If I could find a little farm for myself, I would jump right on it." The lawyer replied, "Go look for one." So my dad said, "What about the farm of Marquis Nicolini?" "There are seventy applications for that farm [the lawyer said], but I'll go talk to the marquis." And sure enough, when the marquis heard about my dad's act of honesty, he signed a sharecropping contract with him. This was 1922, a special year. Dad was a socialist. They called him Filippo because he always defended Turati.[1]

With its fable-like narrative, this story captures something very real about the social world of the Tuscan sharecroppers (mezzadri) in the early twentieth century. It was a world made up of personal relations, hierarchical power structures, and constant family and class conflict. It was also a world in which informal arrangements made all the differ-

---

[1] Maricla Boggio, *La Nara: Una Donna Dentro la Storia* (Vibo Valentia, 1991), 11–12.

ence between fortune and misery, in which loyalty was one of the highest values, and yet mistrust permeated the relations between *contadino* and *padrone*. Patronage, as the story nicely shows, was key to social advancement. Yet, as we will see, the sharecroppers' struggles were directed above all at gaining a degree of formalization and, therefore, protection from the abuse of the landowners. What, if anything, has survived of that world so as to affect the economic and political development of the Tuscan industrial districts of small specialized firms?

In this chapter I will address this question by looking at the development of the jewelry industry of Arezzo, a Tuscan city halfway between Florence and Perugia. Obviously the impact of rural relations on small-scale industrialization was significant in Valenza Po and (to a lesser extent) Vicenza as well. But I focus this broad discussion on Arezzo for two main reasons, the first empirical and the second historiographical. In this Tuscan city, small-scale industrialization emerged quite rapidly in the 1960s and 1970s from the ruins of the two pillars that had sustained the local economy for decades, that is, sharecropping in the countryside and a few metalworking companies in the city itself. In 1951, even within the boundaries of the city area, 48 percent of the gainfully employed population worked primarily in agriculture. More than three-fourths of these agricultural workers were sharecroppers. Twenty years later, only 9 percent of the population of Arezzo was employed in agriculture, and sharecropping contracts had all but disappeared.[2]

The rapidity and extent of this transformation make the analysis of Arezzo's transition to industrial society particularly interesting. This does not make Arezzo typical of all of northern and central Italy. Scholarship on this topic over decades has collected many examples of change, whose peculiarities increase with the level of attention to detail paid by historians in each case. Anna Bull and Paul Corner have distinguished two broad models of transition from rural society in northern and central Italy: many areas of northeastern Italy, including the section of northern Lombardy they studied in detail, experienced a gradual and relatively peaceful trajectory in which agricultural and industrial work coexisted at the family level for decades or even centuries;

---

[2] After many years of negotiations, the stipulation of new sharecropping contracts was banned in 1964 (Law 756 approved on 15 September 1964). Existing contracts were grandfathered under radically novel conditions, far more favorable to the peasants than traditional mezzadria allowed for.

in other areas, such as the Marche region on the Adriatic coast, rural society changed much more rapidly, amidst much conflict, and after massive relocation of families and individuals from the country to the cities.[3] Arezzo exemplifies this latter model in a particularly stark and poignant way.

Nevertheless, and this brings me to the second reason for focusing on Arezzo, the literature on industrial districts and the Third Italy has downplayed conflict and enshrined harmony, trust, and cooperation as fundamental traits of both Italian rural society and small-scale industrialization, and this without a great deal of attention to local variations. This tendency has been especially evident in dealing with areas traditionally dominated by sharecropping (*mezzadria*), such as Arezzo. There is a glaring and puzzling gap between the literature on small-scale industrialization and that on the crisis of sharecropping in the central decades of the twentieth century.[4] The literature on small-scale industrialization emphasizes collaboration between members of the sharecropping family, as well as between genders and classes. Most studies of the end of sharecropping, by contrast, emphasize class conflict and tensions between genders and generations. The former sees continuity and gradualness in the process of industrialization; the second sees abrupt change and dislocation. It is almost as if the two literatures were describing two distinct social spaces and historical periods.

This problem is compounded by the fact that mezzadria produced its own ideology of trust and social cohesion. The Fascist regime, building on a centuries-old discourse, attempted to propagandize the social order of mezzadria as a model of harmony. The hierarchical relations within the patriarchal peasant family, headed by the paterfamilias (called *capoccia* in Tuscany) were portrayed as a microcosm of society at large, itself headed by *il Duce*. The customary and personal relations between pater familias and landowner were in turn presented as the epitome of trust-informed class collaboration. For many social theorists and policymakers, mezzadria was the social coronation of the Fas-

---

[3] Anna Cento-Bull and Paul Corner, *From Peasants and Entrepreneurs: The Survival of the Family Economy in Italy* (Providence, 1993).

[4] The literature on the collapse of mezzadria in north-central Italy is almost as extensive as that on the Third Italy. See, for example, L. Radi, *I Mezzadri: Le Lotte Contadine nell'Italia Centrale* (Rome, 1962); Arrigo Serpieri, *Scritti Giornalistici 1947–1958* (Rome, 1971); F. Bogliari, "Il movimento per la trasformazione della mezzadria," in *Stato e Agricoltura in Italia 1945–1970* (Rome, 1980, 161–204; Elisa Bianchi, *Il Tramonto della Mezzadria e i Suoi Riflessi Geografici* (Milan, 1983).

cist political revolution. The modern scholars who stress the smoothness and nonconflictual transition to industrial society in the Third Italy tend to argue for strong continuities with the rural past, thereby validating—at least implicitly—this long-standing interpretative tradition. After all, they argue, the survival of the family as a production unit and cooperation between firms and other institutions seem to suggest that the social order of mezzadria lives on in the world of modern artisans and small-scale manufacturers.

It is the contention of this chapter that the continuities between mezzadria and small-scale industrialization do not lie in presumed cooperative relations between family members and social classes or in ill-defined notions of entrepreneurship. Two aspects of mezzadria, both strongly emphasized in the literature on the history of sharecropping and ignored in the literature on the Third Italy, have survived its demise in the1960s. The first continuity lies in the coexistence of the vertical ties of patronage and the horizontal ties of class organization. This multiplicity and flexibility of social roles was typical of the sharecroppers' world and informed the negotiations that took place during the economic miracle. But equally important—and this is the second continuity—was the legacy of the mezzadri's struggles in the pre-Fascist and immediate postwar years. The struggle against the discretionary power of the landowners during the 1940s and 1950s led to the establishment of organizations and institutions capable of promoting formal relations and class-based agendas. The importance of the struggles between peasants and landlords in postwar central Italy cannot be easily dismissed; such conflicts were crucial to the shift from a rural to an industrial society. In other words, to make sense of this transition, one must place conflict, rather than harmony, at center stage, and this is as valid for Arezzo as for many other Italian areas. In this limited sense, Arezzo was indeed representative of a much larger process.

Arezzo's industrialization also demonstrates the contingent and discontinuous nature of social and economic change in many portions of the Third Italy, as well as the importance of gender as an analytical category. A vast hierarchical network of small and medium-size businesses emerged in Arezzo after World War II out of the mutual reinforcement of two distinct strategies. On the one hand, a pioneer jewelry company, destined to become the world's largest firm in the trade, began to promote subcontracting relations in order to reap the benefits of the informal economy (gold smuggling, tax evasion, highly flexible labor practices, etc.). On the other hand, the local unions and public authorities supported and validated this process of decentralization as the only viable alternative to the threats of deindustrialization and feminization of the workforce. Both jewelry and clothing, the two new industries in town, tended to employ a disproportionate number of women, whereas recently urbanized men found it hard to gain access to stable manufacturing jobs. The promotion of small-scale entrepreneurship put an end to this "unhealthy" economic trend and turned Arezzo into an industrial district employing an army of male "artisans." Of course what constituted healthy and spontaneous development remained controversial for many years. Family businesses had to be reinvented almost from scratch in Arezzo. For example, in the late 1940s and early 1950s hardly any local actor predicted the growth of the jewelry industry. Former mezzadri were then looking for stable jobs as factory workers in the few and dwindling local engineering companies, rather than as partly independent entrepreneurs. When these companies went under and the prospect of proprietorship emerged as an alternative, the large jewelry company, organized labor, and local authorities came to an agreement. The result was small-scale industrialization: a political solution to the class, generational, and gender tensions that had beset Arezzo's social life in the postwar years.

The Rural Roots of Small-Scale Industrialization in Arezzo

The continuity between sharecropping (mezzadria) and small-scale industrialization is one of the main historical arguments overtly espoused by the literature on the Italian industrial districts. According to many scholars, sharecropping prepared the ground for the post–World War II entrepreneurial boom by creating a class of dispossessed and combative former peasants with a degree of managerial skills, acquired through the supervision of their numerous family members.[5] The interaction between these untapped entrepreneurial abilities and the town-based crafts triggered a proliferation of small businesses and enabled Italian light industry to profit immensely from the market expansion of the 1950s and 1960s. For example, Arnaldo Bagnasco, the

---

[5] See Fuà and Zacchia, *Industrializzazione Senza Fratture*; and Paci, *Famiglia e Mercato del Lavoro*. Putnam builds on this tradition in *Making Democracy Work*.

sociologist who coined the term *Third Italy,* calculated the correlation coefficients between self-employment (or partially autonomous employment, including mezzadria) in the countryside at the beginning of the century and dispersed entrepreneurship in the decades after World War II. The high values for the northeastern and central provinces of the country led him to argue that "the development of small-scale industrialization is likely to find its particular conditions in terms of labor market and artisanal entrepreneurship in specific social formations in the countryside."[6]

Although Bagnasco is right in linking the history of rural society to the development of networks of firms after the war, these kinds of measurements tend to obscure the painful and conflict-ridden demise of sharecropping by conceptualizing it as a coherent and self-preserving social system. In fact, mezzadria varied widely from region to region and changed in significant ways after its establishment in the wake of the Black Death in the fourteenth and fifteenth centuries. This transformation accelerated in the late nineteenth century both for structural reasons (such as the increasing demographic pressure on the land and changes in technology) and for political ones (the spread of socialism and social Catholicism in the countryside). Fascism became a mass movement precisely in the sharecropping areas of northern and central Italy, as a reaction to the mezzadri's struggles in the aftermath of World War I, which had led to a radical redistribution of power in the countryside.[7] The Fascist restoration was followed by another wave of struggles in the late 1940s and early 1950s, which paved the way for the demise of sharecropping in the 1960s. In sum, mezzadria should be examined as an extremely contested and dynamic set of social relations, rather than as a system or a self-contained social formation. In the following pages I will discuss three much-debated historical questions concerning modern mezzadria by drawing on examples taken from the countryside surrounding Arezzo: the degree to which sharecroppers could be regarded as entrepreneurs; the character of the relationships between the landowners and the mezzadri; and the extent to which mezzadria fostered cooperation within peasant families. The

---

[6] Arnaldo Bagnasco, *La Costruzione Sociale del Mercato* (Bologna, 1987), 94.

[7] The classic study in the English language on the rise of Fascism in the countryside of northern and central Italy is Adrian Lyttelton, *The Seizure of Power: Fascism in Italy, 1919–1929* (Princeton, 1987).

discussion of these questions leads to a reappraisal of the historical links between sharecropping and small-scale industrialization in the Third Italy.

The issue concerning the sharecroppers' entrepreneurial skills is particularly difficult to address, since the notion of entrepreneurship is so ill defined. The classic form of mezzadria was based on four "principles," of which the farms of Arezzo's *contado* offered typical examples: the distinction between land and capital, owned by the landlord, and the labor force, provided by the peasant family as a whole, which often comprised three generations; the equal division of the cultivation expenses between the owner and the peasant family; the equal division of the revenue between the same parties; and finally the landlord's right to organize cultivation at his or her discretion.[8] Despite these general similarities, mezzadria varied widely according to local conditions. As far as the sharecroppers' entrepreneurial role is concerned, one of the most important differences concerned the ownership of the livestock. Whereas in Tuscany the landlord provided all the livestock necessary to the management of the farm, in Emilia and in the Marche the sharecropping family was supposed to join the contract with half of the animals. Since livestock was the most expensive part of the farm's current assets, this was a remarkable difference. It was a common exercise in the economic literature to compare the two systems, either to praise the Emilian model for its incentives,[9] or to condemn it for its unfair partition of the risks between such unequal "partners."[10] The current literature on industrial districts simply ignores these differences, since they hardly affected later developments. It would be very hard to argue, for example, that the sharecroppers of the Marche, by virtue of their being endowed with more capital, promoted small-scale industry more swiftly and effectively than their Tuscan counterparts.[11] The lack of correlation between mezzadria and small-scale industrialization on a more analytical level is suggestive of the difficulties faced by the scholars who claim strong continuities.

[8] Pier Francesco Serragli, "Le agitazioni dei contadini e l'avvenire della mezzadria," in *La Mezzadria negli Scritti dei Georgofili* (Florence, 1935), 178. The article was originally published in 1920.

[9] Zeno Vignati, *Andamento dei Redditi in Aziende Mezzadrili Aretine e Maceratesi: Ottennio 1925–1932* (Arezzo, 1938).

[10] Sidney Sonnino, "La mezzadria in Toscana," in *La Mezzadria negli Scritti dei Georgofili*, 69. The article was originally published in 1875.

[11] If anything, the opposite seems to be true. See Blim, *Made in Italy*.

More generally, it is hard to understand what is meant by entrepreneurship at such a highly abstract level. To view the mezzadri as risk takers, for instance, is fundamentally correct, but it ignores decades of conflict over the fairness and desirability of this arrangement, summarized in the formula "risk without control." The imbalance between risk sharing and control over the production process was one of the main contradictions that plagued the peasants' lives. One of the most common criticisms moved against mezzadria was that this contract promoted risk sharing between the owner and the peasant family, represented by the pater familias, but it simultaneously restricted management decisions to the landlord and his administrative agent, the *fattore*.[12] Even in areas like Tuscany, where the sharecropping family owned very little capital (and therefore shouldered a smaller share of the risks), peasants had to put down steep sums of money every season to buy half of the agricultural supplies, which led them to run debts in favor of their landlord. If anything went wrong, risks were indeed shared, but from the peasant's point of view this was more of a form of exploitation than an entrepreneurial privilege. In the Tuscan case, the peasants' position worsened in 1938, when the Fascist authorities decided to generalize the Emilian model of shared livestock to all sharecropping areas.[13]

There is no doubt that the sharecroppers had a direct stake in the productivity of the farms on which they lived, but this did not translate into extensive managerial functions, from which they were often coercively excluded. In the Fascist era, for example, some observers saw the general state of indebtedness that plagued the mezzadri as a powerful disincentive to innovation and "diligent" work: "It is sufficient [for the mezzadri] to produce something, barely enough not to be evicted from the farm. Why should they work more to repay a debt that the creditor can hardly exact anyway?"[14] The supporters of mezzadria as a social and economic order, by contrast, insisted on its collaborative dimension, and went as far as to see Tuscan sharecropping as a rural version of the human-relations experiments that were being carried out in some American factories.[15] A revealing historical exam-

[12] Danilo Agostini, *Osservazioni sull'Evoluzione in Atto nelle Mezzadrie di Alcune Provincie* (Padova, 1967), chap. 1.

[13] Tito Trombetta, "La mezzadria nell'industria," *Rivista di Politica Economica* 30 (1940): 15.

[14] Augusto Traxler, *Corporativismo e Mezzadria* (Pisa, 1934), 12.

[15] Albano Milani, *La Riforma Agraria: La Mezzadria* (Florence, 1946).

ple of the economic contradictions and political tensions that belied the mezzadri's alleged entrepreneurial role is provided by the estate of Maria Budini-Gattai, located approximately thirty miles north of Arezzo. In 1944, the landlady published a collection of imaginary letters to "her" sharecroppers, in which she extolled mezzadria as a divinely ordained system. Her idea of the sharecroppers' entrepreneurial abilities was typical of her social class: "To calculate the compensation for your [the mezzadri's] work is your specialty: I have seen you exceed the proficiency of an accountant, and not by using paper and pencil but just your mental abilities."[16] Documents in Arezzo's Archivio di Stato, however, clearly show that the landlady could make crucial managerial decisions, which affected her mezzadri's lives, in total disregard of their "mental abilities." In the summer of 1938, Budini-Gattai tried to restructure her estate, which employed sixty families and more than three hundred people, by shifting from vine growing to the production of tobacco. The project entailed the eviction of twenty-six families. The mezzadri turned to the Fascist authorities for help, and only the intervention of the prefect and his promises of subsidies to the landlady prevented the tensions from escalating into an open confrontation.[17]

If viewing the sharecroppers as entrepreneurs mystifies the features of the relationship between the landlord and the head of the peasant family, which was the backbone of the mezzadria system, what were the actual features of this relationship? The mix of coercion and collaboration, and of dependence and autonomy, typical of mezzadria makes it difficult to characterize the class nexus at the heart of sharecropping in general terms. Supporters of the contract argued that "the fundamental characteristic of mezzadria is the trust-informed nature of the relationship [between landlord and peasant]. Its success, therefore, depends essentially on trust and collaboration."[18] It was widely acknowledged, however, that there were clear limits to the landlord's ability to monitor the sharecropper's activities. The possibility of cheating made some observers argue that "the relationships between landlords, agents, and sharecroppers are often marred by a sense of mistrust that

---

[16] Maria Budini-Gattai, *La Vita nei Campi: Lettere ai Miei Coloni* (Florence, 1944), 45.

[17] Archivio di Stato di Arezzo, Prefettura, Gabinetto, vol. 98, folder Vertenze sindacali.

[18] Vincenzo Visocchi and Mario Periccioli, *La Mezzadria e il Suo Avvenire* (Florence, 1952), 4.

damages the functioning of the farms."[19] Indeed, the mezzadri were routinely accused of "cheating" their landlords by hiding part of the products, a practice that compensated the peasants for the high volatility of the crops' yields. Turning one of the mezzadri's slogans (*La terra è di chi la lavora*, or "The land belongs to those who work it") on its head, Arezzo's embittered small landowners dismissed the sharecroppers' demand for ownership by noting in 1947 that "a good does not belong to its owner, but to those who enjoy it,"[20] meaning the guileful peasants who routinely grabbed far more than their rightful share.

This diversity of assessments stemmed from a fundamental ambiguity at the core of the mezzadria contract. The double status of the head of the sharecropping family as an employee and an "entrepreneur" made the regulation and enforcement of the contract very difficult. It was impossible to stipulate contracts capable of anticipating every circumstance. Indeed, the strength and the weakness of mezzadria lay precisely in its ability to adapt to ever-changing conditions though informal negotiations. This was recognized at the time: "The subordination of the sharecropper . . . and his having an interest in the farm revenue . . . create a particular kind of relationship that cannot be regulated by [contractual] norms. [The contract] must work on the basis of mutual esteem and trust."[21] Indeed, both the supporters and the critics of mezzadria agreed on the personal and informal nature of the contract. The landlord was supposed to be much more than the farm owner: "The landlord was . . . at the same time the boss and the protector and trustee of the peasants. He was their political representative and the ultimate judge of their conduct, thus capable of rewarding them with remarkable favors or removing them from the contract with a nod of his head."[22] As a Tuscan aristocratic landlady argued, "The landlord is not only the person with whom [the peasant] establishes a relationship of subordination. He is also something of a father or older brother for the mezzadri. He witnesses the births of their children and takes them to the baptismal font [as their godfather]. He follows them in their studies."[23] The supporters of mezzadria maintained that these kinds of

---

[19] Mario Tofani, *La Mezzadria dall'Assemblea Costituente alle Leggi Agrarie* (Bologna, 1964), 122.

[20] Archivio di Stato di Arezzo, Prefettura, Gabinetto, vol. 145, folder Patti di mezzadria.

[21] Luigi Bottini, *La Mezzeria nello Stato Corporativo* (Florence, 1932), 49.

[22] Ernesto Brunori, *Mezzadria in Crisi* (Padua, 1961), 22.

[23] Ibid., 139.

patronage ties fostered trust and collaboration between social classes. The critics emphasized the semifeudal and anachronistic nature of the personal ties between landlord and sharecropper. Precisely because of the pervasiveness of these informal arrangements, which increased the landlords' discretionary power, the sharecroppers organized and struggled for decades to put as many matters as possible on paper. From the beginning of the century onwards, customary and personal norms, which involved a specific farm, the peasant family, and the landlord, coexisted uneasily with impersonal collective contracts stipulated by the representatives of the sharecroppers and the landowners, viewed as social classes with conflicting interests.

Sydel Silverman addressed the coexistence of patronage and class mobilization by arguing that the social distance between peasants and landlords was paradoxically coupled with an ethos of "community" to form the distinctive anthropological traits of mezzadria in central Italy.[24] Unlike the southern peasants, who worked for a wage as laborers and lived in towns under the direct control of the local urban elites, the sharecroppers of central Italy lived on the farms and had a more cooperative relationship with the propertied classes. At the same time, the lack of direct control by the landlords and the possibility of developing a distinct rural identity allowed the sharecroppers to conceive of themselves as a social class and promote elaborate forms of collective action both before and after the Fascist era. From this perspective, patronage ties are compatible with other forms of social organization. This approach resonates with more recent reinterpretations of the social and political origins of the Italian industrial districts. After defining patronage as "a distinctive form of power deriving from control over valuable information,"[25] David Moss noticed that the world of mezzadria, with its relatively long tenancies and extensive contacts between landowners and sharecroppers, was permeated with networks of communication in which individual reputations both for loyalty in patronage relations and for trustworthiness in horizontal alliances among sharecroppers could be established and monitored. He also notes that in the industrial districts of small firms, "the horizontal and

---

[24] Sydel Silverman, "Agricultural Organization, Social Structure, and Values in Italy," *American Anthropologist* 70 (1968): 1–20.

[25] David Moss, "Patronage Revisited: The Dynamics of Information and Reputation," *Journal of Modern Italian Studies* 1 (1995): 67.

vertical flows of valuable information reproduce the circuits of the sharecropping period."[26]

This complex coexistence of vertical and horizontal ties, and of contractual and informal relations, was highly unstable and subject to ongoing redefinition. In the course of the twentieth century, Tuscan sharecroppers struggled to challenge the arbitrariness of patronage ties and establish more formalized relations with the landowners. The spread of literacy, the experience of the Great War, and the success of socialist and Catholic propaganda drastically reduced the appeal of "tradition." In the pre-Fascist years of violent confrontation in the countryside, the mezzadri and their "subversive" organizers found a common platform that partially overcame the bewildering diversity of local conditions. In 1919 and 1920, the sharecroppers' most common requests were the replacement of customary norms with written pacts and the abolition of all the norms that called for acts of submission and deference to the landlords.[27] The acceptance of these requests was the most important accomplishment of the struggles after World War I. Even Fascism did not succeed in promoting the return to customary norms. Instead, the Fascist authorities tried to crystallize the system with the 1928 *Carta della* Mezzadria, a set of guidelines that—for all their biases in favor of the landlords—set relatively clear standards for the stipulation of sharecropping contracts.

The drive towards more formalized relations and collective action continued after World War II. The largest sharecroppers' union, Federmezzadri, won several crucial strikes in the late 1940s and early 1950s. Two of the sharecroppers' main gains included the increase of the peasants' share of the products, which in some areas rose to 60 percent, and the suspension of evictions, which became practically impossible. At the same time, most political forces, notably the socialist and Communist parties as well as the Christian Democrats, called for the gradual but radical transformation of mezzadria. Whereas the Catholics favored solutions leading to the spread of small-scale ownership, the left-wing parties leaned towards the creation of cooperatives. In both cases, the postwar return to democratic rule was viewed as fundamentally incompatible with the preservation of mezzadria. Revealingly, during the post–World War II phase of social unrest in the country-

---

[26] Ibid., 74.

[27] Giuseppe Tassinari, "Le recenti agitazioni nell'Italia centrale e le condizioni economiche dei mezzadri," in *La Mezzadria negli Scritti dei Georgofili*, 193–214.

side, the language of tradition was spoken only by the landlords, especially the small-scale ones. Typically, the sharecroppers and their representatives demanded the strict enforcement of the newly stipulated collective agreements.[28] This ongoing drive towards collective bargaining and more formalized relations gradually led to the demise of sharecropping. A series of legislative measures facilitated the peasants' access to landownership and made the stipulation of sharecropping contracts extremely cumbersome for landlords. By the mid-1960s, the long history of mezzadria had reached the end of the line.

So far I have viewed the mezzadri as a unified class whose spokesmen were the heads of the households. This is how the Fascist authorities and the landlords conceived of the peasants, and how some modern scholars continue to approach the issue of the historical continuities between sharecropping and small-scale entrepreneurship. There is no doubt that the power of the *capoccia* (as the pater familias was called in Tuscany) was great. He might have played a subordinate role vis-à-vis the landlord and his agents, but at least on paper he was the undisputed master in his own house. Indeed, to coordinate the work of a dozen family members belonging to three generations was certainly a daunting task—a "managerial" skill that could be transferred to other activities. An exclusive focus on the prerogatives of the patriarch, however, glosses over the conflicts among genders and generations that beset the sharecroppers' households. To understand the historical links between mezzadria and small-scale industrialization, it is necessary to open the black box of the household and refrain from taking collaboration and coordination for granted.

The myth of mezzadria as an endangered social formation based on harmony and cooperation between classes and family members peaked during the Fascist era. The relationship between class harmony in the countryside and obedience within the peasant families was an integral part of the Fascist conception of mezzadria. This contract promoted "a form of economic collaboration between capitalists and workers, and as such it foster[ed] cooperation and solidarity between the productive forces." Harmony between classes found its pillar in the solidarity within the peasant family: "The working unit is not the

---

[28] See Archivio di Stato di Arezzo, Prefettura, Gabinetto, vols. 145 and 186. In this phase, the partition of most products, as well as other issues, often triggered violent confrontations. The landlords' appeal to traditional practices usually fell flat, though the attitude of many civil courts favored the owners.

individual but the family, which leads to the formation and reproduction of families which are large, well disciplined, and under the authority of their leader."[29] These ideological pronouncements flew in the face of the fact that Fascism achieved power in the wake of first wave of organized conflict in the countryside of northern and central Italy. This conflict had important generational and gender dimensions that belied the Fascists' language of obedience and family harmony.

One of the most interesting aspects of the conflicts of the late 1910s and early 1920s was that open (and often violent) confrontation coincided with a period of relative prosperity for the sharecroppers. Postwar inflation benefited the mezzadri by devaluing their debts and allowing some of them to buy portions of their farms. The coexistence of violent conflict and relative economic prosperity was a puzzling phenomenon for contemporary observers.[30] While the experience of World War I and the political competition between the socialist and the Popular (Catholic) parties cannot be dismissed as causal factors, one of the most interesting explanations of this coexistence was that higher monetary incomes increased the tensions within the sharecropping families. Since most resources were managed by the *capoccia*, younger members of the family grew particularly impatient of the elders' authority in periods of rising income. In periods of prosperity family "solidarity" became particularly strained. Economic tensions combined with latent social conflicts. For example, the preservation of a well-defined ratio between labor and land was key to the success of mezzadria. One person per hectare was the usual rule. As mortality declined, demographic pressure on the land increased. This made the *capoccia*'s (and the landlord's) control over family members ever more crucial to economic profitability.[31] Such control affected all kinds of decisions, including if and when to get married and the possibility of migration—options that became more available in periods of prosperity. In such periods, tensions within the family often tended to be redirected against the landlords. It was less disruptive to openly question class solidarity than jeopardize family cohesion.

Fascism managed to hold these tensions in check for two decades by repressing class mobilization in the countryside. But after World

---

[29] "La mezzadria nello stato fascista cooperativo," in *La Mezzadria negli Scritti dei Georgofili*, 247.

[30] Serragli, "Le agitazioni dei contadini," 170.

[31] Cristina Papa, *Dove Sono Molte Braccia E' Molto Pane* (Perugia, 1985), 60–70.

War II conflicts exploded with unprecedented violence throughout central Italy. Once again, it was not poverty but relative prosperity that ignited the wave of unrest. The mezzadri had fared better than most other social classes during the war, and they saw the collapse of Fascism as a long-awaited opportunity to challenge the mezzadria system. There is plenty of evidence showing the generational dimension of this conflict. Younger peasants were at the forefront of the struggle, carried out at once against the landlords and the patriarchal order.[32] It was no coincidence that the main goal of the protesters in the late 1940s and early 1950s was to break the estates into smaller units that "natural" nuclear families could cultivate and eventually buy. In February 1949, one of Arezzo's associations of landlords (Assoagricoltori) noted with dismay that many sharecroppers were in fact buying portions of their estates. In March 1948, a landowner from Terontola, south of Arezzo, denounced that "The peasants' illusion . . . not just of pursuing better economic conditions, which is natural, but of being entitled to rob the owners of their property makes the younger generations—especially the younger generations—restless and unreasonable."[33] Just how unreasonably younger mezzadri could behave is shown by the increasing number of litigation cases involving owners and peasants. In March 1948, for example, a young sharecropper from Bucine, west of Arezzo, had just succeeded his father to the position of *capoccia*. His first act as head of the family was to refuse to move to a less productive farm, as the informal agreement between his father and the landlady mandated. The contentious young peasant brought the landlady to court and won the case, maybe also because she was the widow of Bucine's former Fascist mayor.[34] As this example nicely shows, class "harmony" and patriarchal authority collapsed at the same time. Moreover, the conflicts of the late 1940s show that the crisis of mezzadria as a social and political order preceded the flight of the mezzadri from the countryside to the factories. The crisis of mezzadria after World War II exposed the coercive, rather than cooperative, nature of the relations within the sharecropping families.

While generational conflicts were at the core of mezzadria's final crisis in the decades after World War II, gender tensions cannot be dis-

---

[32] Tofani, *La Mezzadria*, 47–50.

[33] Archivio di Stato di Arezzo, Prefettura, Gabinetto, vol. 186, Agricoltura 1948, folder Patti di mezzadria.

[34] Ibid.

counted either. The role of women in sharecropping families was based on a rather well defined sphere of activities. The female head of the household, usually the *capoccia*'s wife, was in charge of feeding the family's chickens, rabbits, and pigs, of cultivating the garden, of gathering mushrooms and chestnuts, and of carrying out nonagricultural activities such as weaving. Of course, women were also supposed to work in the fields whenever the need arose. These distinctively female activities did not belong to a "private" sphere any more than those carried out exclusively by men, such as the slaughtering of pigs or the production of wine. Some of the distinctively "feminine" tasks actually linked the family directly to the local market. The sale of eggs, small animals, and manufactured goods provided the family with cash, whereas men's work was paid with half of the produce (wine, pork meat, and so on), which was usually stored and consumed within the family itself. According to Cristina Papa, women concentrated their efforts on the assets that were either owned by the family (e.g., small animals) or that enabled the family to bypass the landlord and promote a direct link with the market (e.g., textile work). In both cases, women's activities developed outside of the class nexus between the landowner and the *capoccia*, which was the backbone of the mezzadria system.[35]

The "privileged" relationship between the male head of the household and the landlord also prevented male family members from engaging in nonagricultural activities, which explains why the figure of the peasant–factory worker was traditionally rare in sharecropping areas before the 1950s. Conversely, the distinction between family- and class-oriented activities informed the nonagricultural work carried out by young peasant women. The daughters' wages, just like the revenue of the poultry pen, were supposed to contribute to the family survival. Although job opportunities for young women were scanty in much of Arezzo's *contado* before the 1950s, this approach to women's activities affected the behavior of urbanized workers, who interpreted female work as a subordinate contribution to the family economy. When industrial jobs became available for women (especially young and unmarried ones) and good jobs for men began to dwindle, this put a severe strain on what was largely perceived as the natural order among genders, classes, and generations. Small-scale entrepreneurship emerged as an appealing (albeit problematic) solution to the threat of social decay.

[35] Papa, *Dove Sono Molte Braccia*, 124–27.

Over a period of less than two decades, the crisis of mezzadria in Arezzo and the rest of Tuscany led to "a countryside without agriculture and an agriculture without young people."[36] Anthropologists and other social scientists have explored the consequences of the collapse of this centuries-old social order, which had been instrumental in shaping the renowned *bel paesaggio* of Tuscany, and they have investigated the "collective amnesia" of the younger generations.[37] The museums of peasant culture that dot the Tuscan countryside preserve traces of a world that is lost to all but the local elders. Perhaps the long duration of the crisis, protracted by the authoritarian measures of the Fascist regime, partly explains the suddenness of the final transformation. Indeed, the new social order, based on small-scale industry and dispersed entrepreneurship, did not develop smoothly from the legacy of the rural past. As will become clear in the rest of this chapter, the path to small-scale industrialization was tortuous and dotted with the unexpected consequences of conflicts and compromises. There was little in traditional mezzadria that anticipated later developments. The resurgence of family artisanal work under the supervision of the pater familias, for example, emerged in a different form after bitter conflicts and the collapse of alternative social arrangements. The main continuity between mezzadria and dispersed entrepreneurship was the problematic coexistence of patronage relations and class mobilization, which shaped a social order where multiple roles and fuzzy social identities were the rule rather than the exception. In sum, a social order that had survived in its fundamental traits for more than six centuries did not die without leaving traces. Historical analysis, however, must resist the temptation to take homologies for continuities.

No Work for Father: Arezzo's Industrial Transformation after World War II

The rather sudden collapse of mezzadria in the 1950s and early 1960s led to the rapid depopulation of Arezzo's countryside. The sharecroppers' migration occurred in two distinct flows: one from the valleys of

---

[36] Ivo Biagianti, *Lavoro, Industria e Cultura: Storia delle Trasformazioni sel territorio Aretino* (Arezzo, 1990), 99.

[37] See, for example, Pietro Clemente, *Cultura e Mezzadria Toscana tra Ottocento e Novecento* (Terranuova Bracciolini, 1985).

the province to other parts of Tuscany and to northern Italy, and one from the valleys to the town of Arezzo and a few other industrializing centers in the province, such as Sansepolcro (home to the food-processing firm Buitoni) and the upper valley of the Arno River. The overall balance of these two flows was negative. The province as a whole lost more than 24,000 inhabitants from 1951 to 1971, when population stabilized at a little over 300,000. Indeed, depopulation was particularly severe in the marginal areas of the province. Casentino, the uppermost stretch of the Arno valley, lost almost 25 percent of its population between 1951 and 1971, with emigration peaking in the late 1950s.[38] A large portion of these former peasants moved to Arezzo. The population of the provincial capital increased from 67,000 in 1951 to 87,000 twenty years later. If we consider only the urbanized portion of the rather extensive city area, the population rose from 39,000 to 71,000 over the same period. A survey carried out by the municipal authorities in 1967 reported that 55 percent of the families who had migrated to Arezzo in the previous five years came from the province. The average size of these families was 2.5 individuals, significantly smaller than the provincial average—which was 3.8 individuals in 1961.[39] This suggests that most of the immigrants lived in nuclear families that had split from the multigenerational households typical of mezzadria. The shrinking size of sharecropping families in the 1950s and 1960s confirms this hypothesis. The size of the average family of mezzadri in the province of Arezzo decreased from 5.8 individuals in 1952 to 4.9 in 1961 to 3.3 in 1969.[40]

For all the entrepreneurial skills ascribed to the mezzadri by modern scholars, the competencies of these immigrants were a source of concern for the public authorities and the local industrialists. As the manufacturers' association noted in 1955, "The flight from agricultural to industrial work is a phenomenon of massive proportions, which in the province of Arezzo involves thousands of workers who crowd the labor market every year. The opportunities of employment are scanty, since most of this workforce is made up of completely unskilled

---

[38] Data from R. Leoni, T. Bensi, and B. Boschetto, *Guida Statistica alla Realtà Socioeconomica Aretina* (Milan, 1976).

[39] "Un aspetto dell'immigrazione nel comune di Arezzo," *Notiziario del Comune di Arezzo*, April 1967.

[40] Alfio Savini, Guido Occhini, and Carlo Salvicchi, *Ricordi, Immagini, Documenti: Pezzi di Storia Sindacale dell'Aretino 1944–1989* (Cortona, 1989), 36–37.

labor."[41] In fact, many of the immigrants ended up joining the swelling ranks of the unemployed and underemployed. The unemployment rate reached two-digit figures in the early 1950s and forced public authorities to intervene with a series of public work projects.[42] Dialma Bastanzetti, the owner of a metalworking firm in Arezzo that employed between thirty-five and forty workers, received forty job applications in 1953. Many of the applicants were ex-peasants who had left the farm with little more than a letter of recommendation from the local priest, though a few had managed to tap the bishop or even the mayor of Florence.[43]

Many male ex-sharecroppers aspired to land a secure job in one of Arezzo's engineering companies. Their timing could not have been worse. Soon after the end of the war, Sacfem, the largest company in town, specializing in the construction and repair of railroad cars, entered into a period of crisis that lasted more than forty years. Sacfem, known to the people of Arezzo simply as the *fabbricone* (big factory), had been founded in 1907 by a group of Florentine capitalists who chose Arezzo rather than Pistoia as the site of the plant after a consortium of local associations (the city government, the Chamber of Commerce, two banks, and the workers' Friendly Society) allocated 134,000 lire for building expenses.[44] This was the first of a series of public "gifts" that Arezzo's authorities bestowed on Sacfem, viewed as the essential basis for the city's industrial development. Nevertheless, the *fabbricone* remained one of the weakest links in a chain of financial ties that bound several large-scale steelmaking and engineering concerns to the state-owned railway company. Employment soared temporarily during World War I, when the company had more than a thousand male workers, but the postwar crisis brought a first wave of layoffs. From the beginning, Sacfem's workers acted as the political vanguard of Arezzo's small working class, and a strong tie developed between the town and the factory. The workers' occupation of the plant in September 1920, for example, seemed to place Arezzo on the map of the

[41] Associazione Industriali della Provincia di Arezzo, Verbali Riunioni, meeting held on 17 December 1955, 215.

[42] Archivio di Stato di Arezzo, Prefettura, Gabinetto, vol. 234, folder Lavoro e Previdenza Sociale 1950–51.

[43] Archivio di Stato di Arezzo, Archivio di Dialma Bastanzetti, vol. 4.

[44] "Sacfem: Una storia di ricatti sulla pelle della città," *Arezzo Comune*, August 1974. See also "Dal Fabbricone alla Gepi," in Savini, Occhini, and Salvicchi, *Ricordi, Immagini, Documenti*, 60–84.

nationwide labor unrest known as *biennio rosso*. Struck by the Great Depression and on the verge of filing bankruptcy, in 1933 Sacfem was taken over by Bastogi, a large Rome-based concern specialized in railway materials. World War II brought with it another generous batch of state orders but also the devastating bombings of 1943.

The reconstruction years were particularly difficult for Sacfem and consequently for Arezzo's working class. Labor unrest was endemic to the engineering factory. Tensions peaked in the summer of 1948, when in the aftermath of a strike, the carabinieri searched the plant and the workers for hidden weapons.[45] Although no arms were found, it became clear that Sacfem's destiny was much more than an economic issue. Arezzo's mayors and prefects routinely pleaded with the Ministry of Transportation for orders. Throughout the 1950s, only the repeated interventions of the local public authorities convinced the company to spare the plant. For example, in 1954 the commune gave Sacfem 2.5 million lire to help the company relocate to a large area south of the town center.[46] Despite this citywide mobilization, employment at Sacfem fluctuated wildly, following the erratic course of state orders. This instability was somewhat ironic, since the town's attitude towards Sacfem was founded on the supposed contrast between the reliability of heavy industry and the volatility of consumers' goods markets. Another contrast was even more important to shaping the local political culture: Sacfem was the symbol of male industrial employment, viewed as vital to the future of the city, whereas the newer local booming industries (that is, the gold jewelry and clothing trades), were dominated by female work and were therefore regarded as peripheral to the city's long-term development.

The attitude of the local political culture towards male work explains the growing involvement of Arezzo's working class and public authorities with Sacfem's destiny in the 1960s. Such involvement was disproportionate to the actual importance of the factory to the local economy. Although Sacfem and the engineering industry as a whole had failed to absorb the onslaught of the rural immigration during the economic boom, the entire city mobilized repeatedly during the 1960s to defend "Arezzo's only heavy industry." The tension peaked again in May

---

[45] Archivio di Stato di Arezzo, Prefettura, Gabinetto, vol. 221, folder Sacfem 1948–1950.

[46] "Una serrata requisitoria contro la Sacfem nella seduta notturna del consiglio comunale," *La Nazione*, Cronaca di Arezzo, 30 May 1967.

1967, when the company, which had diversified into the production of construction materials and agricultural and textile machinery, proposed to the city government another relocation of the plant to the outskirts of town and the transformation of the old site into a residential area. Moreover, ridden with debts, the company proceeded to fire more than one hundred workers. The reaction of the unions and public authorities was immediate. Sacfem's workers struck for two weeks, and then occupied the plant.[47] On June 17 a general strike paralyzed the city. Even the retail stores closed for an hour as thousands of people "of all social conditions" marched in the town center.[48] The jewelry and clothing workers launched a public subscription in support of the seven hundred strikers. Despite Sacfem's openly speculative strategy, the city government gave in once again, the only concession to the public interest being the transformation of part of the factory area into a park. Unsurprisingly, the construction of the new plant was slow and costly, and employment at Sacfem never picked up again.

Conflicts and suspicions of bad faith did not subside in the following years. Despite the sale of the old area at a nice price, the company's debts reached 20 billion lire in the early 1970s, when the director of Bastogi privately complained, "We should have closed in 1967. Our mistake has been to be sensitive to Arezzo's social problems."[49] The strained relationship between the city and the company dragged on for years, until the company closed down definitively in 1988. The most interesting aspect of this relationship lies in its ability to forge a united front of many of Arezzo's political actors under the banner of a "healthy" industrial development. As the Communist mayor of Arezzo declared in 1967, at the height of social tension, "We are convinced that the future of Arezzo . . . is an industrial future and that consequently a heavy industry must be preserved at any cost."[50] This future was based on large-scale industry, male employment, and a combative and unionized working class. Sacfem represented for the mayor, as well as for many of Arezzo's citizens, an ideal path that the local economy sought to travel. For them small-scale businesses and dispersed entrepreneurship were anything but a natural and consensual outgrowth of the area's rural past.

[47] *La Nazione*, Cronaca di Arezzo, 13 June 1967.

[48] *La Nazione*, Cronaca di Arezzo, 18 June 1967.

[49] Archivio di Stato di Arezzo, Archivio Sacfem, Corrispondenza 1969–73, letter dated 1 March 1972.

[50] *La Nazione*, Cronaca di Arezzo, 28 June 1967.

The history of Sacfem and its relationships with Arezzo's social forces can be viewed as an example of politically informed economic change. Much of Arezzo's population reacted to the company's ongoing threats of defection by forging a close-knit network of social ties that included the high-level negotiations between the local authorities and the Ministry of Transportation and the collective action promoted by the male-dominated unions, not to mention public opinion at large. As is often the case, however, this process of "community" creation set the boundaries between the initiatives that had to be defended "at any cost" and the social changes that remained outside of the sphere of community intervention. The foremost goal of the city's mobilization in support of Sacfem's workers was to stop the relentless process of feminization of local industry, although this rationale was seldom articulated as such. As table 5 shows, the male workforce employed in the manufacturing industry declined sharply in relative terms, decreasing from 77 percent in 1951 to 58 percent in 1971. At the same time, agricultural work became almost exclusively masculine, rising from 63 percent in 1951 to a stunning 87 percent a decade later. If anything, these data underestimate the actual number of women employed in the manufacturing industries since, as we will see, undocumented homework became widespread in the clothing and jewelry industries during the 1950s and 1960s. Clearly, getting an industrial job in Arezzo was much easier for women than for men. Coupled with lingering unemployment, this situation heavily affected the power relations within immigrant families. Many unskilled male workers alternated between agricultural and industrial work, especially in the volatile construction sector. The gap between the new economic uncertainties and the mythical patriarchal order of mezzadria could not have been wider.

Meanwhile, throughout the 1950s and 1960s, female workers saw unprecedented employment opportunities, above all in the clothing industry. Like Sacfem, this activity owed its origins to circumstances external to local society, and it relied heavily on state support. The relationships between the clothing industry and local society, however, developed along quite different tracks. Lebole, the largest clothing company in Arezzo specialized in menswear, was founded in 1951 by a family of Venetian entrepreneurs drawn to the area by the opportunity to tap the fast-growing supply of cheap female labor. Lebole grew rather slowly in the 1950s, when it was customary for the company

TABLE 5
Sex Structure of Arezzo's Economy

	Agriculture		Manufacturing Industry		Total	
	Male	*Female*	*Male*	*Female*	*Male*	*Female*
1951	9,208	5,360	3,595	1,053	21,277	9,060
	(63.2)	(36.8)	(77.3)	(22.7)	(70.1)	(29.9)
1961	5,865	842	5,422	3,183	22,372	7,452
	(87.4)	(12.6)	(62.9)	(37.1)	(75.0)	(25.0)
1971	2,554	662	7,483	5,379	22,828	10,876
	(79.4)	(21.6)	(58.2)	(41.8)	(67.7)	(32.3)

Source: Elaboration from R. Leoni, T. Bensi, and B. Boschetto, eds., *Guida Statistica alla Realtà Socioeconomica Aretina*, (Milan, 1976), 133–47. Manufacturing industry does not include the building sector, dominated by male employment.

Note: Percentages are given in parentheses.

to rely heavily on homework and subcontracting.[51] The turning point occurred in 1962, when the Lebole family sold half of the company's stock to state-owned Lanerossi. With the decisive contribution of public money, the new company, called Lebole Euroconf, relocated to a large plant in the outskirts of town. Employment at Lebole soared, increasing from a few hundred workers in the late 1950s to 2,700 in 1962, 4,100 in 1967, and more than 5,000 in 1971.[52] Almost 90 percent of these workers were women. The Lebole brothers used their political connections to open up another company, Giole, at Castiglion Fibocchi, ten miles west of Arezzo. This soon became the second largest plant in the area, with more than 1,000 workers in the late 1960s. Although homework remained common,[53] the clothing industry as a whole grew more and more concentrated, as mass production and standardization became the hallmarks of the garments "made in Arezzo." The average firm size increased from 2.6 employees in 1951 to 25.9 twenty years

[51] Archivio di Stato di Arezzo, Prefettura, Gabinetto, vol. 196, folder Disoccupoazione Operaia Pratiche Generali.

[52] Provincia di Arezzo, "Quattordici Tesi per un Dibattito sui Problemi e sulle Prospettive dell'Industria delle Confezioni in Serie," August 1976, typewritten memo preserved at Arezzo's Public Library.

[53] See Provincia di Arezzo, *Il Lavoro a Domicilio* (Arezzo, 1976).

later. Moreover, by the early 1970s approximately half of the clothing employees in the province worked in the two large plants founded by the Lebole brothers.

Work conditions in these factories were quite difficult. A worker at Lebole recalls, "Orders and reproaches were imposed on us by shouting, insulting, and even throwing objects at us. The management adopted mechanisms for the control of production. A panel made of lightbulbs was introduced, each bulb corresponding to a worker. When one of us did not follow the work schedule, a red light went off."[54] Although unionization drives improved conditions from the late 1960s on, the pace and nature of work remained taxing. Local society came to terms with the character of industrial female work in the area in the fall of 1965, when a worker committed suicide during her lunch break by throwing herself under a passing train. The local press immediately attributed the incident to the consequences of the newly adopted "American" system of productivity incentives.[55]

In the 1960s, concern for the plight of the female factory workers gained center stage. Revealingly, however, this concern was expressed above all in the language of psychiatry. In 1962–63, the director of Arezzo's psychiatric hospital collaborated with other doctors toward a wide-ranging study of female factory workers in the area.[56] He handed out thousands of questionnaires to the women who worked at Lebole and at Gori & Zucchi, the largest jewelry company in town. He then proceeded to conduct hundreds of interviews with the subjects that had exhibited "neurotic" or even "psychotic" tendencies. Although only 4 percent of the workers showed flagrant symptoms of mental illness, the study revealed that 29 percent of the workers suffered from "neurotic dispositions" (*disposizioni nevrosiche*). The doctors' conclusions did not condemn female factory work outright, but they warned that "work acts as a neurotizing factor for women more often than for men."[57] This pathologizing attitude was not restricted to the medical profession. The unions carried out several surveys on the mental health of the workers, and the results were startling: One-third

---

[54] Savini, Occhini, and Salvicchi, *Ricordi, Immagini, Documenti*, 124–25.

[55] "Arezzo: Nevrosi a catena con il ritmo americano," *L'Unità*, 18 November 1965.

[56] Alfonso Granati, Marino Benvenuti, Franco Angeleri, and Renato Lenzi, "Aspetti biologici e psicologici della donna al lavoro," in Istituto Italiano di Medicina Sociale, *Atti del Convegno Nazionale di Studio su "Il Lavoro della Donna" Salerno 22–23–24 novembre 1963*, vol. 1 (Rome, 1965), 116–77.

[57] Ibid., 173.

of the workers reported suffering from "neuroses" and "nervous breakdowns," and one-fourth of them had sought professional help.[58] In the wake of these reports, the municipal authorities organized a conference on women's industrial work. The themes discussed included "internal migration; biological disadvantages; unfavorable social and cultural factors; and production systems and psychiatry."[59]

Although the unions and the local authorities were not willing to go so far as to wage war on women's factory work as such, the clothing industry provided the "social disease" with which "healthy" economic development, embodied by Sacfem, was contrasted. Revealingly, the sources are almost silent about the fate of the thousands of women, approximately half of the clothing workers in the late 1960s, who worked in small factories or at home. Even the local unions saw homework and the informal economy that supported it as a lesser evil, a minor consequence of the general problem affecting Arezzo's economy, that is, the "monopolistic" exploitation of female labor by powerful "alien" concerns.[60]

GORI & ZUCCHI AND THE ORIGINS OF AREZZO'S JEWELRY INDUSTRY

The astounding and sudden success of the jewelry industry in Arezzo should be set in the context of a rapidly changing social and economic structure at odds with the aspirations of many local actors. At first sight, Arezzo's jewelry industry in the late 1950s and early 1960s did not differ significantly from the clothing sector. Dominated by one powerful firm, Gori & Zucchi, which employed increasing numbers of unskilled women, the jewelry trade did not seem a promising candidate for the resolution of local tensions. As late as 1950, a detailed survey on Arezzo's artisanal economy carried out by the Chamber of

[58] ACLI, "Inchiesta sulla 'Condizione Operaia" (Arezzo, 1967), typewritten memo preserved at Arezzo's Public Library.

[59] "La Donna nel Lavoro Industriale," *Notiziario del Comune di Arezzo*, April 1967.

[60] The distortion of Arezzo's industrial development was confirmed by its rapidity and lack of continuity with agriculture: Industrialization has developed "with no ties whatsoever with the rural problems. It has damaged the countryside by prompting the unchecked flight of young workers and the virtual neglect of agriculture," in Provincia di Arezzo, *Primo Convegno sulla Situazione Economica della Provincia di Arezzo* (Arezzo, 1966), 42.

Commerce did not even mention gold jewelry as a local specialty. Moreover, the report noted that the increasing concentration of production and the crisis of traditional craftsmanship cast a gloomy shadow on the prospects for artisanal initiatives in the area.[61] The situation changed radically in the 1960s, when the combined strategies of Gori & Zucchi, the unions, and the public authorities led to the proliferation of male small-scale entrepreneurship and to the redefinition of Arezzo's social and economic identity.

Gori & Zucchi was founded in 1926 by Leopoldo Gori, a former socialist-turned-Catholic gold recycler from Siena, and Vittorio Zucchi, a goldsmith from Arezzo. Gori's commercially minded management was key to the company's success.[62] The bases for the postwar expansion were laid in the 1930s, when the company's employees increased from less than twenty to almost two hundred. This early growth was based on the mechanization of several production phases, such as metal casting and chain manufacturing. By the mid-1930s the company was already well connected to the highest spheres of Roman politics. When Mussolini launched the "gold to the Fatherland" campaign in December 1935, after the invasion of Ethiopia and the international sanctions against Italy, Gori & Zucchi became the largest producer of the faux-gold wedding rings, which party officials gave Italian wives in return for their authentic bands and patriotic fervor. Chain making was the other major specialty.[63] The first machines for chain production were imported from Germany, especially from Pforzheim, which was at the time Europe's main manufacturing center in the field. These machines were significantly improved by a group of technicians at Gori & Zucchi in order to produce more sophisticated items. From the first experiments of this period to the introduction of numerical control in the mid-1980s, these machines allowed the ongoing creation of marginally different chains. In this sense, they represented a monument to flexible specialization.

However, the main innovations did not concern mechanization but the products themselves and the manner of their commercialization. In the mid-1930s, Gori & Zucchi patented a new plating process that

---

[61] Archivio di Stato di Arezzo, Prefettura, Gabinetto, vol. 219, folder Camera di Commercio.

[62] For a short but less than impartial history sponsored by the company itself, see Mario Guidotti, *Viaggio nel Pianeta dell'Arte Orafa* (Milan, 1966).

[63] Lucio Fabbriciani, *Partecipazione Umana e Competitività Aziendale* (Milan, 1995), 45–46. This is the company-endorsed history of Gori & Zucchi, largely based on a series of

made gold jewelry available to the larger public. The company succeeded in shifting the attention of part of the public from the weight of the artifact to the "quality" of the gold used. In order to achieve these goals, the symbolic value of gold had to be fully exploited by using high-fineness metal in small quantities. At the same time, the demand for this sort of "purity" had to be created by insisting on its importance. This persuasion effort became evident after the war. In 1957, the company started to sell its products with a "certificate of guarantee" that stated that the company's jewelry, bearing the mark Uno-A-Erre, constituted "superior-quality gold works of controlled fineness." A few years later, Gori & Zucchi launched a series of products that tended to reinforce (or even invent) mass rituals involving the exchange of gold. The "love medal" to be given as an engagement gift (1961) and the "mom's medal" for the celebration of Mother's Day (1964) were the most popular examples.[64] The purity and reliability of the material—always 18-carat gold—were effectively presented as symbols of other less tangible forms of virtue.

On the basis of this commercial and industrial strategy, Gori & Zucchi experienced a phase of tumultuous expansion in the 1950s. The number of employees rose from 161 in 1951 to almost 700 in 1956 and more than 1,000 in 1960. In that year, the company became the largest jewelry exporter in Europe, and two years later, with more than 1,200 employees, it already qualified as the largest gold jewelry producer in the world. Between 60 and 65 percent of these workers were women. In the late 1950s, almost 60 percent of Arezzo's 1,900 gold-manufacturing workers were directly employed by Gori & Zucchi and another medium-size company, Patrassi & Domini, which employed approximately 170 workers. The latter firm, founded in 1945 by former workers at Gori & Zucchi, was one of the earliest offshoots of Arezzo's leading firm. Its commercial strategies bore the unmistakable imprint of its more powerful competitor. In 1966, for example, Patrassi & Domini launched the "Highway Medal, the only one officially blessed by the Franciscan Fathers."[65]

---

interviews with Leopoldo Gori. Although shamelessly celebratory, the book provides a wealth of information on the company's strategies and on its leader's perspectives.

[64] On Gori & Zucchi's promotional campaigns see Giacomo di Iasio, "La Gori & Zucchi e la pubblicità," in Gori & Zucchi, *Sessanta Anni di Arte Orafa* (Montepulciano, 1986), 179–85.

[65] Advertisement in *L'Orafo Italiano*, October 1966.

The other side of the coin of Gori & Zucchi's widely advertised accuracy and reliability consisted of quite unscrupulous labor practices. Of course these practices made Arezzo's jewelry very cost competitive, first in the domestic market, and from the late 1950s on, worldwide. The company tapped the increasing reservoir of rural immigrants in two radically different way. First, it promoted an internal labor market for a select group of male workers who in later years would initiate the first entrepreneurial boom. Second, the company employed a large number of unskilled women who could be officially hired, informally employed as home workers, or both. The two strategies were adopted at the same time soon after the end of the war. In the early 1950s Gori & Zucchi established a training department in which select workers were taught not only technical drawing and the rudiments of mechanical engineering but also math and "general culture." Even more important, in 1948 Gori & Zucchi set up an elaborate system of productivity bonuses for its male workers. As one of the company's engineers recalled, these select workers were given a stake in the company's profits:

> A remarkable portion of the profits, half of them, was distributed to the employees. But not haphazardly. . . . Instead, the program worked on the basis of an evaluation system that the unions would now call outrageous. Every three or four months, each foreman made an evaluation of the workers in his department on the basis of a scale of values that was in turn used to calculate the amounts to be given to each worker as a productivity bonus. . . . Everybody made himself busy. The slackers and the grumblers were rare. The incentive was strong and it raised a lot of enthusiasm.[66]

Women's work conditions were quite different. Although Gori & Zucchi has always denied that it made use of homework, this practice was already widespread in the late 1940s, at the height of demand for gold jewelry in the domestic market. The engineer's words can be contrasted with one of the rare examples of open protest against jewelry homework in Arezzo. In 1949, the women's section of the Confederazione Generale Italiana del Lavoro (CGIL), the Communist-led union, sent an exposé to the provincial Department of Labor claiming that

[66] Quoted in Fabbriciani, *Partecipazione Umana*, 51.

Gori & Zucchi often distributes homework to its own female employees, thereby avoiding the regular employment of new workers. . . . The same company hands out homework to women whose daily wages range from 100 lire to a maximum of 300 lire and who are forced to work for ten or twelve hours a day to make that much. These are workers who are reported neither to the health insurance administration nor to the social security office.[67]

Public authorities knew perfectly well that illegal homework was becoming very common in both the clothing and the jewelry industries, but they tolerated it as a way of reducing the lingering unemployment and naturalized it as an expected part of the generally "unhealthy" economic development of the province. In his official monthly report on the economic conditions of the province, Arezzo's prefect noted as early as June 1946, "There are hundreds of home workers [in Arezzo], most of whom are women. The rural vocation of the area would recommend the development of agriculture-related industries, but that type of initiatives has always been rare. Whereas unemployment decreases in the rural areas, it goes up in the capital."[68] With the initial endorsement of the public authorities, homework grew into a generally accepted practice, especially in the jewelry sector.

Despite their obvious differences, Gori & Zucchi's highly gendered labor practices had one common element, that is, their personal and discretionary nature. Until the early 1960s, a priest's letter of recommendation was necessary to be hired. Since small thefts of precious metal were a constant temptation for the workers, the company's management required some guarantee of honesty and trustworthiness. In fact, minor cases of embezzlement were very common,[69] and the workers were searched every day on the basis of a lottery mechanism. Whereas in the case of the male workers discretionary practices were mitigated by the seemingly objective "scale of values" through which the management calculated productivity bonuses, the female employees' compensation was based on a straightforward system of piece-

---

[67] Archivio di Stato di Arezzo, Prefettura, Gabinetto, vol. 196, folder Disoccupazione Operaia—Pratiche Generali, letter dated 11 January 1949.

[68] Archivio di Stato di Arezzo, Prefettura, Gabinetto, vol. 130, folder Relazione Economica Giugno 1946.

[69] "The workers who came straight from the farms had the flaw of petty thefts. If you gave them a kilogram of paint and half that much was enough for the job, they took home the rest." Fabbriciani, *Partecipazione Umana*, 23.

work. During the peak season, they were often asked to take some work home without overtime pay. Paternalistic practices were reinforced by the periodic awarding of "loyalty" prizes for longtime employees and by other company rituals.[70] More generally, it was insistently suggested that a job at Gori & Zucchi was for life.

The "traditional" nature of these practices should be underlined: Gori & Zucchi's proprietors tried to build on the tradition of patronage-based relations typical of mezzadria. However, paternalism was only one side of modern mezzadria, the other being class mobilization. The company's young workers were relatively quick to resort to collective action when the opportunity arose in the early 1960s. A wave of strikes stirred the area in February 1962.[71] Part of a general campaign organized by the Communist-led union (CGIL), these strikes involved both Gori & Zucchi and Lebole, the twin symbols of Arezzo's recent industrialization. Revealingly, the main slogan of the mobilization drive was gender equality. In the case of Gori & Zucchi, the two bones of contention were the discriminatory and discretionary system of productivity bonuses and workers' classification. The employees were divided into eight categories according to their qualification and gender. In addition to being excluded from the distribution of bonuses, no woman could be paid more than any man, regardless of category: that is, the best-paid women earned only as much as the lowest category of men. The union's platform called for the establishment of only two categories, independent of gender, and for the equal distribution of the workers' share of the profits.[72] In addition to these economic complaints, the union questioned safety standards and the pace of work, generally regarded as repetitive and grueling.

After two weeks of strikes and negotiations, the union obtained a partial victory. The bonus system was dismantled, but workers were

---

[70] Archivio della Camera di Commercio di Arezzo, vol. XIII-8-2, Premio Gori e Zucchi, folder Secondo Convegno Orafi Dettaglianti, pamphlet entitled "Costituzione Gruppo Lavoratori Anziani Gori e Zucchi" dated 10 October 1962.

[71] "Si accende la lotta nella grande azienda aretina," *L'Unità*, 11 February 1962. For a short reconstruction of the events from the union's perspective, see Savini, Occhini, and Salvicchi, *Ricordi, Immagini, Documenti*, 178–92. The industrialists' association was caught by surprise at the suddenness of the strikes: "The movement has occurred in quite a peculiar way. The employees have stopped working before putting forward a specific platform and without any warning." Archivio di Stato di Arezzo, Fondo Bastanzetti, vol. 4, letter dated 20 February 1962.

[72] Fabbriciani, *Partecipazione Umana*, 74–75.

divided into six categories based on skill. Given the highly gendered patterns of skill formation at Gori & Zucchi, this meant that gender inequality lived on in practice. Nevertheless, the company had to come to terms with organized class confrontation. Much to the proprietors' surprise, the elections for the workers' representatives called in the wake of the strike gave the Communist-led union the majority of the votes.[73] This "tragic turn," as Gori called it,[74] put an end to paternalistic practices and turned the company into a hotbed of labor conflict for the next thirty years. Although Gori took this transformation as a personal defeat inflicted upon what he himself called "enlightened despotism,"[75] the events at Gori & Zucchi should be set in the larger context of Arezzo's social and political tensions. The union's campaign for gender equality was a direct response to the increasing feminization of the industrial workforce, and it affected all the other large companies in the area.

What did the union mean by gender equality? It would be naive to take the union's motivations at face value. Despite its calls for equality within the factories, the union never addressed the issues of homework and of the burgeoning development of family businesses, institutions that were plagued by even more blatant gender inequalities. As we will see in the next paragraphs, the left-wing unions advocated the promotion of small-scale entrepreneurship and simply ignored the problem of undocumented female labor. Gender equality within the factories was above all the ploy through which the unions set out to redefine the rules of the game. After the strike, Gori & Zucchi's expansion came to a close, and a vast network of subcontracting relations between the company and small-scale firms emerged, inaugurating a new phase of Arezzo's social and economic life. This phase saw male skilled workers as protagonists, Gori & Zucchi as a somewhat reluctant sponsor, and the unions and public authorities as arbiters. The female factory and home workers remained outside this newly stipulated social contract. They were either the all-too-visible sign of social decay, as was the case with the overworked and exploited women in the factories, or the invisible symbol of the informal economy, as was the case with home workers. In both cases, female industrial employment was a disease to be cured. The cure for Arezzo's "unhealthy" development

---

[73] "Il significato del voto alla 'fabbrica dell'oro,' " *L'Unità*, 24 March 1962.

[74] Fabbriciani, *Partecipazione Umana*, 68.

[75] Gori's own words. Ibid., 72.

turned out to be neither agriculture-related industrialization nor the promotion of state-sponsored heavy industry, as the public authorities had anticipated. Small-scale businesses became the "therapy" that a variety of local actors had been looking for.

A City of Entrepreneurs: The Rise of Small-Scale Businesses in Arezzo

In the wake of the 1962 strike, Arezzo's jewelry industry developed into a hierarchical structure of subcontracting relations. This "pyramid," as it has been defined by local observers,[76] retained Gori & Zucchi at its apex; a gradually growing number of medium-size firms that combined subcontracted and independent work at the lower level; a much larger number of officially registered small businesses with no direct contact with the market farther down in the hierarchy; and finally, at the bottom, an even larger group of undocumented home workers active in the peak seasons. Until the early 1960s, Gori & Zucchi had exerted a remarkable degree of control over this process of firm proliferation. Despite its fast growth, the large company had not been able to meet the booming demand for cheap gold jewelry in the domestic and—from the late 1950s on—international markets. Consequently, Gori & Zucchi had started to farm out an increasing portion of its production. Moreover, as we will see in more detail later, the company used subcontractors as part of a comprehensive strategy to minimize tax expenses and legal risks. As table 6 suggests, however, the vast majority of the jewelry made in Arezzo was still sold with Gori & Zucchi's hallmark and brand name, Uno-A-Erre. As late as 1961, only eight firms had an official hallmark for gold jewelry production, even though the industrial census of that year reported more than a hundred jewelry firms in the Arezzo area (see table 6). Most of these businesses only worked as subcontractors, and thus did not need to apply for a hallmark.

[76] See, for example, Paolo Peruzzi, "Organizzazione e Gestione delle Imprese Orafe Aretine," laurea thesis, University of Siena, 1980–81, 19–22. Even Gori & Zucchi's "endorsed" company history accepts this metaphor: See Fabbriciani, *Partecipazione Umana*, 432–34.

TABLE 6
Gold Jewelry Hallmarks in the Province of Arezzo

Year	Hallmarks	Year	Hallmarks
1951	3	1971	48
1952	4	1972	59
1953	5	1973	79
1954	5	1974	95
1955	6	1975	112
1956	6	1976	132
1957	6	1977	146
1958	7	1978	165
1959	8	1979	186
1960	8	1980	200
1961	8	1981	227
1962	12	1982	271
1963	14	1983	310
1964	17	1984	354
1965	18	1985	413
1966	21	1986	450
1967	24	1987	540
1968	33	1988	623
1969	37	1989	711
1970	40	1990	810

Source: Data provided by the Chamber of Commerce of Arezzo.

This situation started to change after the outbreak of class confrontation within Gori & Zucchi in 1962. The further growth of the company, still regarded as a possibility before the strike, was no longer a viable strategy. At the same time, a new generation of skilled workers "came of age" at Gori & Zucchi and started to open up their own businesses, also as a reaction to the end of the "generous" mechanism of productivity bonuses brought about by the strike. Although the ties

TABLE 7

Arezzo's Gold Jewelry Firms and Gori & Zucchi/Uno-A-Erre's Employees

Year	Firms	Employees	Employees per firm	Gori & Zucchi's Employees (%)
1951	4	215	53.7	74.9
1961	106	1909	18.0	57.6
1971	141	3129	22.2	44.7
1981	555	5028	9.1	25.8
1991	1208	9283	7.7	9.1

Sources: For 1951, Archivio della Camera di Commercio di Arezzo, Folder B 13–8–1/2 Industria Meccanica Orafa, document titled "Problemi dell'industria orafa," Report of the Chamber of Commerce of Arezzo, 6 May 1958. For 1961, 1971, and 1981 elaboration from Carla Cattaneo, Edoardo Sabbadin, and Roberta Virtuani, *Il Settore Orafo: Strategie di Prodotto, di Marketing e di Area* (Milan, 1993), 106. For 1991, personal communication to the author by the Chamber of Commerce of Arezzo. All these data were originally collected for the industrial censuses carried out by the Italian Bureau of Statistics (ISTAT).

between this new batch of entrepreneurs and their powerful ex-employer remained close, these firms enjoyed increasing opportunities for independent action, as wholesalers from Florence, Milan, and elsewhere started to flock to Arezzo. As a consequence, the number of hallmarks (and of Gori & Zucchi's potential competitors) increased relentlessly throughout the period, signaling the growing independence of the small-scale entrepreneurs. The importance of Gori & Zucchi in the local economy remained remarkable, but it decreased in relative terms after the mid-1960s. As late as 1971, more than 40 percent of Arezzo's official jewelry workers were directly employed by the company, but twenty years before, Gori & Zucchi's share had been almost twice as large.

Before examining Gori & Zucchi's strategy vis-à-vis the small-scale jewelry businesses, it is worth noting that Arezzo's entrepreneurial boom did not develop as a reaction against the workers' increasing unionization. The left-wing unions and political parties played an active role in fostering and shaping the proliferation of "artisanal" firms. On the national level, this strategy was consistent with the Left's attempts to promote the alliance between the working class and the "industrious middle strata" (*ceti medi produttivi*), an alliance that was to pave the Italian way to socialism.[77] The Communist Party (the most powerful political force in Arezzo) articulated its attitude towards small-scale capitalism at its Eighth Congress in 1956. The enemy of socialism was monopoly capital. Artisans and small bosses needed to be protected and supported so as to create the conditions of prosperity and political consensus that would pave the way for a gradual transition to a socialist economy. This political and ideological attitude was extremely resilient. Even after the economic boom, when the number of "artisanal" firms grew exponentially, reaching 2.6 million in 1968, the Communists kept viewing petty capitalism as the healthy core of the Italian economy. The tenth thesis voted by the party's Fifteenth Congress in 1979 still argued that "we must fight monopolistic positions and support those public, private, and cooperative initiatives that realize the goals of planning (*programmazione*). A special function will be carried out by the free associations of landowning farmers; artisans; small and medium industry; and the private activities in the service sector."[78] This long-term positive assessment partially blinded the party's leadership to the contradictions inherent in the country's small-scale industrialization, such as high levels of exploitation, the disregard of labor standards, widespread tax evasion, and generally the development of a thriving informal economy. Whereas these problems were very present to the grassroots militants of the party, the leadership kept putting the construction of political consensus before the protection of workers, the promotion of social justice, and the fight for the respect of legal norms.

Arezzo provides a particularly revealing example of the ways in which these national guidelines were received at the local level. Even before the strike of 1962, the local Communist Party launched a campaign against "industrial monopolies" that was meant to provide the burgeoning small-scale entrepreneurs with the aggressive political representation of their interests. Typical in this regard was the Communists' accusation of unfair and collusive practices involving the local electric monopoly (Stelt-Valdarno) and Gori & Zucchi, charged with enjoying much lower rates than smaller companies.[79] By the same

[77] See, for example, the Acts of the Eighth Congress of the Italian Communist Party as reported by Paolo Cantelli, *L'Economia Sommersa* (Rome, 1980), 59.

[78] Partito Comunista Italiano, *XV Congresso del Partito Comunista Italiano: Atti e Risoluzioni* (Rome, 1979), 636.

[79] "Il monopolio elettrico mette in crisi le piccole industrie orafe di Arezzo," *L'Unità*, 20 April 1960. This accusation was part of a more general campaign in support of the

token, the local Communists accused the large company of enjoying privileged credit relationships with the local banks and of monopolizing the supply of raw gold in the area.[80] Given these constraints, small-scale businesses were forced to compete among each other, thereby benefiting their powerful subcontractor. In this context, "true" competition was thwarted, and small firms were little more than "safety valves" for the large concern. Therefore, the Communists' paramount task was

> To unmask before public opinion the predatory nature of the large jewelry concern's behavior vis-à-vis its workers as well as the small and medium-scale jewelry firms. . . . This task must promote a general struggle that will end exploitation and discrimination by fostering solidarity between all the industrious classes of our city for the healthy and harmonious development of our economy."[81]

The campaign against Gori & Zucchi laid the foundations for a broad consensus in support of small-scale industrialization. The "health and harmony" of the local economy was predicated on the development of small businesses.

In retrospect, the political strategy of the local Communists appears woefully overdetermined. Far from being an endangered social class, small-scale entrepreneurs were rapidly becoming the most dynamic section of the city's economy. Moreover, the proliferation of small firms constituted more of an opportunity than a threat for Gori & Zucchi, despite the risk of unwelcome competition. The relationships between the large company and the growing army of small-time bosses were highly informal. The supply of gold and other raw materials, the manufacturing process, and the commercialization of jewelry all took place across the boundaries of the large firm. Gold smuggling, the bending of labor regulations, and pervasive tax dodging wove ties of trust and loyalty between the large company and its subcontractors. By informal means Gori & Zucchi gave smaller firms a stake in the company's profits, but it also bound them to a code of secrecy and complicity. In

---

nationalization of the electric industry, which was carried out in 1962 with the establishment of ENEL.

[80] "L'intera economia aretina fa le spese della prosperità della Gori & Zucchi," *L'Unità*, 23 August 1960.

[81] Archivio della Camera di Commercio di Arezzo, vol. 13, Oreficeria IGE 1960–66, folder 14, Partito Comunista Italiano—Comitato Comunale Arezzo, "Per l'Organico Sviluppo dell'Industria Orafa nella Città di Arezzo," typed pamphlet dated 22 June 1960.

the 1960s and 1970s Arezzo boomed into a thriving informal economy, whose construction involved many of the city's social classes and political institutions. The Left chose to condone the development of informal relations, in a sense betraying what had been the main goal of decades of struggles in the countryside.

One venue in which informal—even illegal—relations thrived was the market for raw gold. Gori & Zucchi could count on three main sources of gold supply, two of which were legally compatible with the state monopoly on gold trade. The official channel linked the government's Office of Foreign Commerce (Ufficio del Commercio Estero) to the authorized dealers (regular banks and specialized gold banks) and, occasionally, to the national goldsmiths' association (see chapter 6). A remarkable amount of official gold was temporarily imported—mostly from Switzerland—in order to be transformed into jewelry. The Swiss agents, usually banks acting on behalf of European and American traders, remained the legal owners of the metal throughout the chain of transactions. Finally, gold was smuggled into the country by an array of more or less "shady" agents who could sell the metal at highly competitive prices or retain its ownership. As we will see in chapter 6, the role of the Swiss banks was crucial at this stage as well.

Although it is impossible to assess the relative importance of these supply channels with any accuracy, legal sources made up a very small percentage of the total supply of gold. In 1969, for example, Gori & Zucchi purchased 7,856 kilograms of pure gold but processed 17,762 kilograms.[82] More than half of the metal, therefore, was processed on behalf of the customer. "Illegal" gold, then, represented the larger share of the total supply. Gori himself assessed the share of legal trade nationally at extremely low levels: "2 percent for precious stones, 4–5 percent for gold jewelry, and 40–45 percent for sterling silver production."[83] It was far from easy to hide tons of pure gold, and the risks of being caught were high. The adoption of subcontracting practices provided the main strategy adopted by Gori & Zucchi to reduce and spread such risks. Part of the gold was processed and transformed into by-products, for example chains or findings (jewelry parts), and then turned over to smaller companies for the finishing processes. Once the

[82] Archivio della Camera di Commercio di Arezzo, vol. 13, Oreficeria Varie IGE, typewritten sheet not included in a folder.

[83] Archivio della Camera di Commercio di Arezzo, vol. 13, Oreficeria Varie IGE, folder IGE Atti più importanti, sottofascicolo Appello della Gori & Zucchi (aprile 1969), 11.

jewelry was ready to be sold to the customer, it could be invoiced for part of its value or not invoiced at all. By subcontracting part of its production, Gori & Zucchi increased the turnover of a raw material that the company possessed illegally. Moreover, if the tax police paid the subcontractor an unwelcome visit, Gori & Zucchi could pretend not to know anything about the metal. Finally, the use of homework and undocumented labor could be turned over to the subcontractors as well, thereby reducing the risks of fines by the labor department.

Exports were carried out by equally informal means. As was the case in Vicenza and—to a lesser extent—Valenza Po, highly informal relations with foreign agents were the key to the international success of Arezzo's jewelry. In an interesting document found in the archive of Arezzo's Chamber of Commerce, Gori outlined a dispassionate analysis of the Italian jewelry industry's astounding international success. The note, probably penned in 1971, was meant to inform the president of the chamber about the consequences of an impending tax reform, which would have led to the adoption of a tax on value added (the Imposta sul Valore Aggiunto, or IVA) rather than on transactions (the Imposta Generale sulle Entrate, or IGE). Adopting a tone at odds with his usual rhetoric, Gori placed tax dodging and gold smuggling at the basis of Italy's competitiveness in the international markets: "There is no doubt that without this risky and abnormal competitiveness, Italy's success in the gold jewelry trade would never have taken place."[84] Gori went into some detail explaining how the meager margins of jewelry producers would be completely eroded if they had respected the tax code. The president of the chamber dotted the memo with question marks, probably more surprised by the document's straightforward style than by its content. To get his point across even more clearly, Gori attached a handwritten note by Gori & Zucchi's chief accountant, sketching the relationships between Arezzo's company and some of its foreign customers:

> I told [the Belgians] that starting from the first of January [1972] we will not be able to operate as we did in the past and that we will have to send everything by Sabena . . . with regular invoices. They told me that it would be the end of their relationship with Gori & Zucchi and that they would certainly find someone who

[84] Archivio della Camera di Commercio di Arezzo, vol. 13, Oreficeria Varie 2, document not included in any folder, bearing the title "Oreficerie e gioielli italiani nei mercati esteri e nelle zone franche. Rapida indagine."

could replace us. Even the Germans, despite the steep fines and forced labor they inflict on tax dodgers, keep importing undocumented merchandise, which many wholesalers . . . are glad to buy and which they resell just as illegally. They easily find customers willing to shoulder the risks. For the stones . . . it is almost all illegal work as well.[85]

The main intent of the document was to remind the state officials that Gori & Zucchi, despite its size and power, was just a link in a chain of informal relations that offered as many opportunities as constraints. The roots of these illegal practices lay well beyond the company's control: These practices informed a complex game in which Gori & Zucchi was but one player.

These highly informal strategies were quite successful in transforming Arezzo into a city of entrepreneurs who were, not unlike the old mezzadri, simultaneously their own bosses and the humble clients of a powerful patron. The success of these practices triggered the exponential proliferation of jewelry firms. According to a union leader, however, as late as 1997 many of the 1,200 firms that crowd Arezzo's jewelry industry today still obtained the vast majority of their gold ("99 percent," in his own words) from Gori & Zucchi, now officially called Uno-A-Erre.[86] Having a stake in their own businesses, subcontracting entrepreneurs did not have powerful incentives to betray their "patron." Instead, they needed the company's protection and political clout to weather difficult times and dodge the potentially thwarting controls of the public authorities. Paradoxically, Gori & Zucchi's own employees were more of a threat to the company. They had inside knowledge of its practices and could even collect evidence of illegal transactions, evidence that could be used directly against their employer. In Gori's words, "The impossibility of respecting formalities has allowed blackmailers and envious competitors to smear the [company's] name with slanderous accusations."[87]

This is precisely what happened in the mid-1960s, when Pierluigi Todisco, a commercial agent regularly hired by Gori & Zucchi to manage sales in the company's Rome office, started to collect information about gold smuggling and tax dodging in a "big book that he was

[85] Ibid.

[86] Oscar Ceccherini, interview by author, January 1997.

[87] Archivio della Camera di Commercio di Arezzo, vol. 13, Oreficeria Varie 2, folder 1-tris, undated typewritten document (probably last months of 1970).

wont to show as a warning."[88] Overt blackmailing followed the warnings. Despite the company's attempts to discharge the troublemaker, Todisco proved relentless in using his information to silence his employer, all the while taking advantage of his position by embezzling increasing sums of money. Through means that remain mysterious, however, Gori succeeded in having Todisco charged with embezzlement. In 1967 the Tribunal of Rome sentenced him to almost three years in jail. As soon as Todisco got out of jail, he enacted his vendetta. In late 1970 he turned his famous book over to the tax police and collaborated actively with the investigators. Gori himself and three other "loyal" white-collar employees were charged with tax evasion and falsification of accounts for 16 billion lire over a period of three months in 1964.[89]

For those who followed the trial, the emperor had no clothes.[90] Unsurprisingly, however, the consequences of Todisco's revenge were far from disastrous for Gori & Zucchi. The company had to pay a fine, but it carried on its business as usual. Well connected to the highest-ranking Christian Democrats in the national government, the company had already obtained a series of fiscal amnesties in 1958, 1963, and 1968. What Todisco had overlooked in his painstaking scheme was that there was relatively little to expose. Public authorities were aware and understanding of Gori & Zucchi's illegal activities. More disconcerting— but explainable in the light of this chapter's analysis—was the almost complete silence of Arezzo's left-wing parties and labor movement. The same actors who had launched a campaign to expose Gori & Zucchi's illegally low electric bills ten years before, stood by almost silently throughout this potentially explosive scandal. The local conservative newspaper could argue, without any danger of being contradicted, that "the majority of the public opinion has sided instinctively with the industrialist."[91] The unions knew very well that the company was no longer unique in its less-than-pristine practices. The most promising and vital part of Arezzo's economy was predicated on an ever-growing network of trust and complicity.

---

[88] Archivio della Camera di Commercio di Arezzo, vol. 13, Oreficeria Varie 2, document not included in any folder and bearing the title "Ex-fallito nel 1955."

[89] "Frodato il fisco per 16 miliardi," *L'Unità*, 20 January 1971.

[90] The Italian archival laws will make these records available in 2050.

[91] "Sorpresa e disagio in città per la vicenda Gori & Zucchi," *La Nazione*, 21 January 1971.

Whereas Gori & Zucchi could use its political power and its strategies of decentralization to keep public authorities at bay, other local firms were not as successful. Revealingly, the two main victims of police controls in the 1960s were medium-size companies, precisely those that enjoyed neither Gori & Zucchi's clout nor the small businesses' invisibility. In both cases, however, the network of political ties that linked local and national actors was instrumental in minimizing the damages. The first case occurred in 1965 and concerned Piombanti & Borgogni, a firm that employed approximately fifty workers on the outskirts of town. The tax police paid the firm a visit in April and asked for invoices documenting the purchase of the gold in stock. The proprietors could only reply that the whole industry manufactured "illegal" gold. The officers were unimpressed, and the firm had to appeal to the provincial tax office (Intendenza di Finanza) arguing that "gold jewelry firms, especially the smaller ones like ours, survive by manufacturing the metal on behalf of the customer, even though there can be undeniable difficulties in the formal regulation of these economic relationships."[92] The appeal was rejected on account of the remarkable amount of gold (and profits) involved: Over a year and a half the firm had received more than 100 kilograms of pure gold and produced 137 kilograms of jewelry. The firm was sentenced to pay a seven-million lire fine and a three-million refund.

The second case occurred in 1967 and concerned Patrassi & Domini, the second largest jewelry firm in town. The pattern was the same, and the fine commensurate to the importance of the firm: a million and a half lire for tax evasion. The consequences of these incidents were dire for their "victims." Patrassi & Domini reduced its employment from 180 workers to 70. Many of the dismissed workers proceeded to open up their own businesses with the support of their former employer. Moreover, the fiscal controls killed one of the few instances of formal partnership between Arezzo's jewelry firms, that is, the consortium that Patrassi & Domini and Piombanti & Borgogni had formed in the late 1950s to deal with Milan-based wholesalers.[93]

The reaction to such a serious attack on the informal economy was immediate and comprehensive. In September 1967 the president of the

[92] Archivio della Camera di Commercio di Arezzo, vol. 13–8–1/2, Industria Meccanica Orafa, folder Creazione di un Laboratorio di Analisi Metalli Preziosi.

[93] Of course it was no coincidence that the victims of police controls were the two most visible firms in the area after Gori & Zucchi. The name of the consortium was RIOA-Rappresentanze Commerciali Orafe Aretine. See Archivio della Camera di Commercio di Arezzo, vol. 13, Oreficeria IGE Anni 1960–66, folder 14, Arte Orafa.

Chamber of Commerce wrote to the prefect of Arezzo asking him to plead with Patrassi & Domini's banks for credit extensions.[94] Gori himself stepped in and wrote to Arezzo's Christian Democratic patron and powerful member of the Senate, Amintore Fanfani, lamenting the consequences of this "unfortunate fiscal incident."[95] Gori also wrote to his longtime friend Giulio Andreotti, then minister of industry and pillar of the Christian Democratic regime, arguing that Patrassi "needed to be defended as far as the invoices were concerned."[96] This connection proved to be extremely productive. Andreotti wrote back in December 1968 assuring Gori that an amnesty for tax dodging would soon condone 70 percent of the evaded revenue.[97] Informed of these positive developments, the president of the national goldsmiths' association gratefully wrote to Andreotti: "I want to thank [you] wholeheartedly for your precious protection in our favor."[98]

As these incidents clearly show, small-scale industrialization in Arezzo was predicated on the creation of a network of social and political relations that grew in both scope and flexibility as the economic boom developed. The erratic character of state control reinforced the ties of complicity that linked the large company to the rest of the city. It became apparent that, while organized labor had stemmed the growth of Gori & Zucchi itself, the public authorities would not allow Arezzo's medium-size firms to achieve Gori & Zucchi's scale and power unless they reformed their ways, which they could not do. The formation of family businesses and small firms became not only a sign of social achievement but also one of the few economic strategies open to the city's economic elite, who started to promote their development. Far from being the natural outcome of rural traditions, these relations were forged in conflict and emerged out of political alliances. The relative passivity of the state authorities, for example, was also a consequence of the consensus that developed around the virtues of small-

[94] Archivio della Camera di Commercio di Arezzo, vol. 13, Oreficeria Varie IGE, untitled folder, letter dated 26 September 1967.

[95] Archivio della Camera di Commercio di Arezzo, vol. 13, Oreficeria Varie IGE, folder IGE Atti più importanti, sottofascicolo Appello della Gori & Zucchi (aprile 1969), 13.

[96] Archivio della Camera di Commercio di Arezzo, vol. 13, Oreficeria Varie IGE, untitled folder, letter dated 4 February 1968. The alliance between Gori and Andreotti had been forged in November 1966, when Andreotti, then head of the Ministry of Industry, paid an official visit to Gori & Zucchi's new plant.

[97] Archivio della Camera di Commercio di Arezzo, vol. 13, Oreficeria Varie IGE, not included in a folder, letter dated 9 December 1968.

[98] Archivio della Camera di Commercio di Arezzo, vol. 13, Oreficeria Varie 2, folder 1, letter dated 8 November 1968.

scale industrialization and the informal economy, consensus that extended to large sections of organized labor. It was through these kinds of political negotiations that Arezzo acquired its new identity of "city of gold," developing into one of the richest towns in Italy. Between 1951 and 1971, per capita income increased sixfold, the fourth largest jump in Italy and the largest in Tuscany.

A variety of processes triggered the proliferation of small businesses in Arezzo: the large firm's deliberate strategies; the tax authorities' controls over medium-size firms; the unions' militant activities and their resistance to the feminization of industrial labor; and the open support of the local (and national) Left. These processes also affected the practices of the new entrepreneurs. The flexibility of the social context in which they operated enabled the small-scale entrepreneurs to play multiple and overlapping social roles. Although their need for protection, credit, and reliable market connections tied them to their more powerful patrons, small-scale entrepreneurs learned very soon how to take advantage of the opportunities offered by an increasingly open economy. The social origins of the jewelry small-scale entrepreneurs were rather diverse. Some of them were sons of sharecroppers who, after a few years as factory workers, mobilized their family resources to open up their shops. A couple of brother-entrepreneurs recalled, "We started off by asking our parents [to make] a sacrifice: They sold the cows, the chickens, and an oven. We built our machines in the cellar and began working night and day."[99] Others came from families who had urbanized one generation before. Most of them had already had some experience in the gold jewelry trade. One study, based on a small sample of fifty small-scale industrialists (rather than "artisans"), reported that 62 percent of them were blue- or white-collar workers prior to the establishment of their firms.[100]

The negotiation of multiple roles by would-be entrepreneurs began even before the establishment of "independent" businesses. In a letter to another of his Christian Democratic friends, Minister of Finance Antonio Gava, Gori noted with a combination of dismay and amusement that "a multitude of gold jewelry workers keep working at home after the end of their shifts in the factory, and they sell their merchandise

[99] Quoted in Fabio Rossi, "Profilo Sociologico dell'Imprenditore nell'Area Intercomunale Aretina: Un'Indagine Esplorativa a Livello di Piccola e Media Industria" laurea thesis, University of Florence, 1983–84, 119.
[100] Ibid., table 23.

either to another firm or to small wholesalers who supply them with gold. Many of these shops are completely clandestine."[101] Of course, many of these workers and entrepreneurs *in pectore* could rely on the work of their family members. After all, their wives had already acquired some experience by working for the industrialist. It was now time for them to work for their husbands and families. According to the local lore, some of the workers most successful at this strategy were also union leaders, who took advantage of their social and political connections to attain proprietorship.[102]

The reinvention of the family as a production unit gave the pater familias the opportunity to take full advantage of informal relations and shifting social roles. The multiplicity of the workers-entrepreneurs-paterfamilias–union activists' social life did not decline once they opened up their shops. As in Prato and many other Italian centers of small-scale industrialization, business opportunities often arose from the availability of dismissed machinery in the local market.[103] Gori himself is reported to have sold some of his old chain-making machines to his former employees, before establishing MGZ (Macchine Gori & Zucchi), a company specialized in the production of machinery for the production of gold jewelry. After years of experience in the factory, these workers could purchase the machines and start their production, sometimes in the basement of their homes.[104] As already mentioned, these shops were simultaneously a resource and a threat for Gori & Zucchi and the few other medium-size companies in the area. But for the small entrepreneurs, this ambiguity was rife with opportunities for social advancement and economic success. They combined subcontracting with more independent work and enjoyed the competitive advantages offered by the informal economy by playing off one "patron" against another. The downside of this wealth of opportunities was lack of stability and the need to rely on personal ties.

Here is an example of the way such instability created opportunities for social mobility. Livio C., after laboring for a few years as a factory worker, opened a shop with his wife Rita B. and a few machines for

---

[101] Archivio della Camera di Commercio di Arezzo, vol. 13, Oreficeria Varie 4, folder IGE sui Prodotti Orafi—Lettera al Ministro Gava, dated November 1970.

[102] Oscar Ceccherini, interview by author, January 1997.

[103] For Prato, see, for example, Gabi Dei Ottati, *Tra Mercato e Comunità* (Milan, 1995), chaps. 4–6.

[104] Fabbriciani, *Partecipazione Umana*, 435–36.

the microfusion of gold jewelry.[105] After being in business for a few months, in 1969 Livio had to close shop and sell the machinery to a more successful small firm, FOA, which hired the couple, too. Livio was appointed foreman of the small microfusion department. But at thirty-five, he was eager to regain his independence. To this purpose, he started to embezzle gold from his new boss with the cooperation of his wife. The metal was sold to another of FOA's employees, who in turn placed it in the local market. Once caught and arrested in September 1971, Livio confessed to having stolen seven kilograms of gold in less than a year and was sentenced to eight months in prison. Though far from typical, Livio's career nicely captures the opportunities as well as the dangers of the social world of Arezzo's small entrepreneurs. By the early 1970s, small entrepreneurship had developed into a positively sanctioned social norm, a goal to which many male jewelry workers aspired. "Independence" was almost a synonym of masculinity. (The Italian expression for wage or salaried labor is *lavoro dipendente*). However, it was common to slide from the position of small-scale boss back to that of worker, and the social pressures to climb the social ladder again led some to take advantage of the network of personal relations that constituted the local economic life.

Since the late 1970s, Arezzo's jewelry industry has been approaching Becattini's model of an industrial district, without, however, erasing its peculiarities.[106] Gori & Zucchi's leadership has remained crucial, but the company has also unwillingly nurtured competing networks of firms, which no longer depend on it for the supply of raw materials and the marketing of their production. According to one of my interview partners, a prominent union leader, a tacit norm developed according to which entrepreneurs had to choose between cooperating with the large company, thereby relinquishing some autonomy in exchange for protection and security, and joining the growing number of its competitors, themselves organized in networks of subcontracting relations.[107] Illegal homework, still dominated by female labor, has remained something of an open secret, tolerated today much as it was a generation ago. In other words, the kind of pyramid structure that I have described in Valenza Po's case has also developed in Arezzo, ex-

<hr/>

[105] "Condannati marito e moglie per furto d'oro in fabbrica," *La Nazione*, Cronaca di Arezzo, 6 February 1972.

[106] For an overview of Arezzo's jewelry industry in the 1980s and early 1990s, see CENSIS, *L'Economia Aretina Oltre il Riaggiustamento* (Milan, 1986).

[107] Oscar Ceccherini, interview by author, 17 January 1997.

cept that a single company—rather than a plurality of firms—is placed at the top.

Despite its persisting influence, however, the relationships between Arezzo's society and Gori & Zucchi/Uno-A-Erre have changed considerably in the course of the last two decades. In 1980 the company restructured by forging an alliance with Centaur International, an affiliate of Elie de Rothschild's group and a leading gold-mining and trading company. Centaur acquired 49 percent of the company's stock, while the Gori and Zucchi families retained 30 and 21 percent respectively. This was only the first of a series of financial transactions between the company and prominent international actors. In 1999, a major overhaul of the company's assets by Deutsche Morgan Grenfell (a global investment back affiliated with Deutsche Bank) led to the temporary withdrawal of the founders' families, who, however, were forced to reacquire the stock three years later. This process of internationalization has also affected production. In the face of declining demand for its products, the company decided to relocate a considerable portion of its manufacturing activities to Jordan, where a major plant began operations in 2002. This decision has not only drastically reduced the company's labor costs but also allowed it to bypass the steep protective barrier raised by the United States against European jewelry. In the meantime, the workforce at the Arezzo plant declined from more than 800 in the early 1990s to 440 a decade later.[108] The company is currently making plans for further job cuts in the face of mounting labor unrest. Unsurprisingly, as Gori & Zucchi underwent this process of internationalization and the horizon of its operations expanded, its embeddedness in Arezzo's society, measured, for example, by the number of its local subcontractors, decreased significantly.[109] But several medium-size firms, some of them founded by Gori & Zucchi's former employees in the 1960s and 1970s, have stepped up to replace the large company's original role as supplier of materials and information to an army of small-time bosses whose numbers have only recently begun to decline.

It was primarily to monitor and regulate the tumultuous growth of the district from the late 1970s to the early 1990s that Arezzo's public authorities and leading companies established a series of institutions

---

[108] Andrea Milluzzi, "Arezzo, Uno A Erre licenzia, si aggrava la crisi dell'oro," http://www.liberazione.it/giornale/050527/LB12D69A.asp, accessed on 29 January 2006.
[109] Falzoni, "Il Distretto Orafo."

meant to promote trust and cooperation among local agents. Some of these institutions were similar to the initiatives undertaken in Valenza Po. For example, in 1980 the industrialists' association and the Chamber of Commerce established an international fair (Mostra Internazionale dell'Oreficeria e dell'Argenteria Aretina) to be held once a year to promote Arezzo's production and expand the small artisanal firms' opportunities to export their production without having to rely on intermediaries. The city government provided the financial and organizational resources to build a state-of-the-art conference center at the edge of town, where the fair and other promotional initiatives could take place. At the same time, the industrialists' association also founded several consortiums among firms with the goal of institutionalizing and monitoring some of the informal relationships that had developed between larger and smaller companies. The reception of these initiatives, however, was lukewarm at best. According to a survey carried out in 1989, only 5 percent of Arezzo's companies entertained regular contacts with a consortium.[110] As in Valenza Po, consortiums (and by extension other institutions) only worked when embedded in multiple networks of relations. It was not enough for a local organization to conjure up a plausible institutional solution to a widely perceived problem for that solution to work.

As in Valenza Po, in Arezzo the promotion of trust was a highly contentious and even contradictory process. Trust was both cemented by ties of complicity within a growing informal sector and promoted by the creation of specific institutions meant to curtail and monitor informal relations. The foremost example of this tension was SAGOR (Servizio di Analisi e Garanzia dell'Oreficeria), a company for the assaying of precious metals and jewelry founded in 1990 by the local Chamber of Commerce with the support of Uno-A-Erre and other leading jewelry companies. The main service offered by SAGOR is the voluntary certification of local jewelry through the granting of a hallmark depicting Arezzo's Chimera, the famous Etruscan bronze sculpture. In the promoters' words, the company "offers through its services the possibility to enhance [trust] among producers, intermedia[rie]s, and retailers."[111] Even though the Italian state had already established and

---

[110] Carla Cattaneo, Edoardo Sabbadin, and Roberta Virtuani, *Il Settore Orafo: Strategie di Prodotto, di Marketing e di Area* (Milan, 1993).

[111] See the company's web site at http://www.sagoritalia.it/Eng/chisiamo_eng.htm, accessed on 29 January 2006. The web site erroneously translates the Italian *fiducia* with

perfected a complex system of controls and sanctions to punish frauds,[112] cheating on gold fineness was widely regarded as one of the main ways in which improvised artisans undermined the national and international reputation of Arezzo's jewelry. Leopoldo Gori of Gori & Zucchi and Uno-A-Erre had campaigned relentlessly to reform the national law on gold fineness standards, partially succeeding at the end of the 1960s. Even though his company had greatly benefited from the development of Arezzo's informal economy, Gori saw local artisans as a potential threat and a source of unfair competition. The wild proliferation of small-scale firms through the 1970s and 1980s convinced the town's industrial elite that national sanctions were not enough to "moralize" the industry and that locally based measures were called for. Therefore, the foundation of SAGOR should be set in this historical context of tensions between the world's largest gold jewelry producer and its often unruly offshoots. In this case as well, a trust-promoting institution was embedded in contentious political negotiations that only historical analysis can reveal. Although SAGOR is portrayed by its promoters as a success, only a fraction of Arezzo's firms avail themselves of its services. More important is the institution's rhetorical and symbolic power in the international arena, where its existence is heralded as a major strength of Arezzo's district in the mounting competition with the supposedly less trustworthy jewelry producers based in southern and eastern Asia.

Arezzo's recent history demonstrates in a particularly clear way the constructed nature of economic relations in much of the Third Italy. Here notions of community had to be invented from scratch, and it was only after the development of extensive networks of political relations that small-scale industrialization took off, corroborating Granovetter's argument that there is a link between embeddedness and vertical disintegration. But economic action was not embedded in rigid structures of relations and meanings. Rather, multiplicity of roles and networks, consistently with my definition of social capital, was a dis-

---

"confidentiality level," rather than "trust" or "confidence." Almost as a slip of the tongue, the erroneous translation aptly connects trust and secrecy, nicely fitting with my analysis.

[112] I examine these negotiations over gold fineness and their relationships with trust and economic structure in chapter 7 of this book and in "Negotiating the Gold Standard: The Geographical and Political Construction of Gold Fineness in Twentieth-Century Italy," *Technology and Culture* 43 (April 2002): 291–314.

tinctive trait of small-scale industrialization in Arezzo. The close relationship between proprietorship and socialist politics in early-twenti-
eth-century Valenza Po (chapter 1), the interplay between public
appointments and economic patronage in post–World War II Valenza
Po (chapter 2), and the conflictual relation between cooperative action
and proprietorship in Vicenza (chapter 3) are other examples of this
richness and diversity of social and political ties, which enhanced the
flexibility of the economic system and spread the risks and the opportunities of economic competition. But a functionalist explanation of
this pattern would miss the conflictual and contingent nature of its development. The multiplicity and flexibility of roles in the three Italian
jewelry districts were the products of particular conflicts and compromises. Class struggle and the reinterpretation of patronage relations
are necessary ingredients of any historical explanation of these experiences. Moreover, multiplicity of roles was tightly linked to the distinctive interplay between the local formal and informal economies in the
three towns. Most actors negotiated their lives at the border between
formal and informal relations, trying to enhance their opportunities of
success or limit the damages of failure.

As we have seen at the beginning of this chapter, the presence of
multiple social roles was one of the hallmarks of modern mezzadria.
The *capoccia* (the male head of the household), for example, was simultaneously employee and entrepreneur, client and pater familias, head
of a unit competing in the market and member of an increasingly organized social class. This multiplicity of roles was simultaneously one of
the main strengths of mezzadria and one of the principal causes of its
collapse. The similarities with the condition of the small entrepreneurs
after World War II are striking and far from coincidental. Small-scale
proprietors also were simultaneously their own bosses and the clients
of more powerful patrons, always in need of protection and always
ready to take advantage of opportunities to increase their autonomy.
Arezzo's history, however, shows that these similarities were not the
product of a smooth evolutionary process. Mezzadria did not gradually and painlessly evolve into small-scale industrialization. The homologies between the two systems were the outcome of political conflicts and compromises; they were the product of the political
construction of the local economy.

If trust and collaboration should not be taken for granted in the context of mezzadria, this is even more true for small-scale industrialization. In Arezzo, trust was above all the flip side of complicity; confi-

dence was inextricably linked to confidentiality. Gori & Zucchi and the city's other leaders gave many of the town's residents a stake in the construction and reproduction of a growing informal economy, protected by extensive connections with state officials and powerful global players (the Swiss banks among others). In this case, it was the construction of an informal economy that produced the ties of community, rather than vice versa. These kinds of negotiations have made Arezzo very prosperous, but they also have created a society at odds with its own history and with the hopes of its weakest members. The mezzadri's aspirations for social justice and legal fairness have largely gone unfulfilled. After half a century of leftist governments, in 1999 Arezzo's citizens elected a mayor belonging to Berlusconi's party. As in many other Italian cities, the twenty-first century began with the unholy marriage of civil and political societies, finally reconciled in the celebration of the entrepreneurial spirit.

The Epistemology of Craftsmanship:
Patterns of Style and Skill Formation

SINCE the economic "miracle" of the 1950s and 1960s, Italy has carved out a distinctive niche in the international division of labor. "Made in Italy" has become a synonym of style and fashion, and Italian firms have gained an unparalleled reputation for artisanal beauty in a variety of industries, ranging from furniture to clothing. Much of this production is carried out in places similar to the jewelry towns examined in this book, where thousands of small and medium-size firms cooperate and compete by specializing in different stages of the manufacturing and marketing processes of specific goods. What does it mean for specific places to be the sites of unique craft skills? How are these collective competencies produced, reproduced, and negotiated in the face of local and extralocal challenges? This chapter aims at providing a historical answer to these questions by examining the ways in which knowledge was produced and transmitted in Valenza Po and Arezzo.

The notion that knowledge plays an important role in shaping the organization of social and economic activities has drawn much attention in recent years. In particular, a sizable literature relates the spatial agglomeration of firms to the importance of knowledge flows for the gaining of competitive advantages by specific areas and companies.[1] A common claim in this literature argues that spatial and social proximity among firms allows the development of trust-informed relationships, which in turn make communication of new information and learning of new skills effective through processes of emulation and (at least provisional) cooperation.[2] The literature on the Italian industrial

---

[1] See, for example, Peter Maskell and Andres Malmberg, "Localized Learning and Industrial Competitiveness," *Cambridge Journal of Economics* 23 (1999): 167–85. Many recent studies owe their conceptual framework to the pathbreaking study by Michael Porter, *The Competitive Advantage of Nations* (New York, 1990).

[2] See, for example, Ian R. Gordon and Philip McCann, "Industrial Clusters: Complexes, Agglomeration and/or Social Networks?" *Urban Studies* 37 (2000): 513–32. For a critique of this argument from a geographical perspective, see Ash Amin and Nigel

districts has greatly informed (and contributed to) this debate in at least two main ways. First, this literature has emphasized the importance of informal relations and venues by building on Alfred Marshall's notion of the "industrial atmosphere," a primarily cognitive concept that he developed by examining several clustered industries in Britain at the end of the nineteenth century.[3] Second, the literature on the Italian industrial districts has discussed in great detail the role played by formal institutions, such as company-based training programs and technical schools, in the production and diffusion of knowledge.[4] In this case as well, however, much of this literature tends to take cooperation, trust, and social consensus for granted. And yet, this chapter will show that access to knowledge and its meanings raised a number of extremely contentious issues in the jewelry towns, and that much of this conflict stemmed from the coexistence of formal and informal relations. Therefore, in this chapter I will focus on the politics of knowledge, that is, the struggles over knowledge and its relationships with power.[5]

The main thrust of this chapter is to show how cognitive and social relations are mutually constitutive and how political negotiations embed knowledge in specific networks of personal and institutional relations. The realization that knowledge and economic action are both embedded in changing networks of social relations provides a powerful antidote to viewing the "market" and "cognitive patterns" as disembodied forces endowed with their internal logic of development.

Thrift, *Cities: Reimagining the Urban* (Cambridge, 2002), especially chapter 3. For a valuable—albeit problematic—evolutionary perspective and for a useful review of the literature, see Bart Nooteboom, "Innovation, Learning and Industrial Organisation," *Cambridge Journal of Economics* 23 (1999): 127–50.

[3] Giacomo Becattini has been particularly involved in the development of the Marshallian notion of industrial atmosphere. In English, see especially Giacomo Becattini, "The Marshallian Industrial District as a Socio-Economic Notion," in Pyke, Becattini, and Segenberger, *Industrial Districts*, 37–51.

[4] See, for example, Sebastiano Brusco and Ezio Righi, "Enti locali, politica per l'industria e consenso sociale: L'esperienza di Modena," in Sebastiano Brusco, *Piccole Imprese e Distretti Industriali* (Turin, 1989), 435–60. For a more general discussion on technical education, see Aurelio Alaimo, *Un'Altra Industria? Distretti e Sistemi Locali nell'Italia Contemporanea* (Milan, 2002), 30–35.

[5] The neglect of issues of power in the literature on knowledge and economic change is somewhat puzzling, given the Foucauldian emphasis on the fungibility of knowledge and power. See, for example, Michel Foucault, *Power/Knowledge: Selected Interviews and Other Writings, 1972–1977* (New York, 1980). Of course a Foucaldian reading of such neglect, however valuable, exceeds the scope of this book.

Conversely, a focus on the production of cognitive patterns avoids the reification of social networks by drawing attention to the conflicts and compromises through which unequal actors produce and give meaning to different kinds of knowledge in order to preserve or challenge the organization of their lives. By struggling over knowledge, actors produce and reshape the networks in which they are embedded.

Crucial to the argument of this chapter is the distinction between tacit and explicit knowledge. Tacit knowledge can be defined as the kinds of skills that are not codified in routines of explicitly stated rules.[6] The manual and mental abilities of the artisan fit this definition. Michael Polanyi, the philosopher and scientist who first explored the relevance of tacit knowledge to a wide variety of social phenomena, took the relationship between master and apprentice as one of its purest illustrations.[7] Polanyi believed tacit knowledge to be embedded in communities of practice, and in this sense the concept accounts for at least part of what Marshall meant by industrial atmosphere. Polanyi believed that tacit knowing cannot be reduced to its components, in the sense that it tends to link up with other complementary skills and forms of knowledge in an open and ever-provisional process.[8] One of the implications of this conception is that tacit knowledge weaves social ties that are unstable and dynamic, in perennial tension between an exclusionary ethos defined by personal relations on the one hand and the need to tap collective resources of cognitive and organizational skills on the other.[9] This tension makes sense of the often uneasy coexistence of competition and cooperation in social contexts, such as the Italian industrial districts, where the importance of tacit knowledge is paramount.

[6] For a taxonomy of different forms of tacit knowledge and for an attempt at systematizing the literature on tacit knowledge as it relates to management studies, see José Castillo, "A Note on the Concept of Tacit Knowledge," *Journal of Management Inquiry* 11 (2002): 46–57.

[7] Michael Polanyi, *The Tacit Dimension* (Garden City, N.Y., 1966), 30.

[8] It was by virtue of this openness and provisional character that Polanyi believed science to be shot through with tacit knowledge. For a philosophical critique of Polanyi's insights and a more general attack on the notions of tacit knowledge and practice, see Stephen Turner, *The Social Theory of Practices: Tradition, Tacit Knowledge, and Presuppositions* (Chicago, 1994).

[9] I purposely use the terms *collective* and *communal*, rather than *public*, to emphasize the fact that access to knowledge in industrial districts is not necessarily a publicly sanctioned right subject to inclusive rules of membership. My terminology is consistent with

Even though the distinction between explicit and tacit knowledge is of great heuristic and epistemological value we should avoid its reification at the ontological level.[10] Polanyi himself was careful to view the two kinds of knowledge as poles in a dynamic continuum, rather than mutually exclusive entities. The boundaries between different kinds of knowledge are contingent on specific patterns of action, rather than set once and for all. Certain kinds of tacit knowledge can be made explicit and vice versa, and very few social interactions rely on only one kind of knowledge.[11] Many struggles in the jewelry towns developed over attempts to move the boundary between explicit and tacit knowledge in a specific direction.

In the jewelry towns, knowledge was political "all the way down," not only in its relations with the state and extralocal market agents but also in its local and collective dimension. Information about styles and market opportunities spread within communities that attempted (mostly in vain) to police their boundaries and protect themselves from outsiders—tax officers as well as recent immigrants. By the same token, the transmission of knowledge had to tread a fine line between the exclusionary and personal relations of apprenticeship and family ties on the one hand and the democratic ethos of public education on the other. The power of social interaction was nowhere as evident as in the construction of local knowledge. This kind of knowledge needed to be simultaneously protected from the instrumentality of the market, lest it lose its collective dimension, and sold to the highest bidder in a highly competitive context. "Made in Valenza" (or Vicenza, or Arezzo) was at the same time a marketing label and a moral statement. These towns owed their very livelihood to the nurturing of unique forms of knowledge, but their uniqueness was made vulnerable every time it was put to value or exploited. Of course the solution to this tension could only be provisional and as politically charged as its origins.

---

the argument in Cristiano Antonelli, "Collective Knowledge, Communication and Innovation: The Evidence of Technological Districts," *Regional Studies* 34 (2000): 535–47.

[10] This is a point made, for example, by Jeremy Howells, "Tacit Knowledge, Innovation and Economic Geography," *Urban Studies* 39 (2002): 871–84.

[11] For a recent discussion on the politics of tacit knowledge and its different incarnations by a pioneering scholar in the field, see Harry Collins, "Tacit Knowledge, Trust and the Q of Sapphire," *Social Studies of Science* 31 (2001): 71–85. Collins was instrumental in bringing the notion of tacit knowledge back onto the agendas of historians and sociologists of science. See his "The TEA Set: Tacit Knowledge and Scientific Networks," *Science Studies* 4 (1974): 165–86.

THE REINVENTION OF CRAFTSMANSHIP

Despite countless later claims to the contrary, Italy in the early twentieth century was hardly a promising candidate for world leadership in the production of gold jewelry. Cellini's days were long gone, and most observers' general impression of Italy's jewelry production was one of decline and parochialism. Art nouveau, the style that had renovated French jewelry at the end of the nineteenth century, came to Italy only after 1906, when an international show in Milan exposed the boorishness of most Italian designers. In the meantime, however, Cartier was already revolutionizing the Parisian scene by setting precious stones, the symbols of eternal worth, on supports as ephemeral as silk ribbons. Of course this display of extravagance was above all a reaction to the popularization of taste and the increasing mechanization and standardization of production, those archenemies of the luxury trades. But even in the field of "popular" gold jewelry, Italian production did not fare too well. The first waves of mass tourism did go some way toward resurrecting of the quaint "Renaissance" styles so familiar to the northern European middle classes venturing into the streets of Florence and Venice on their toned-down versions of the aristocratic Grand Tour, but most Italian stores were flooded with relatively cheap German jewelry.

Despite Italy's glorious tradition, official exports of gold jewelry were close to nil until the mid-1950s. The most common explanation of this decline was the lack of interaction between the worlds of art and industry in the Italian jewelry shops. According to Carlo Felice, a prominent jewelry expert of the 1920s, potential style innovators retreated to the sterile abstraction of the art schools, while the craftsmen "worked by hand with an idle mind, and with the same apathy and the same lack of sensibility as machines."[12] Felice went as far as to say that "at present—this is self-evident—there is no Italian jewelry-making to speak of." All that Italy could boast was at best a few good jewelry makers.[13]

Exaggerations about Italian gold jewelry became commonplace again after the export boom of the 1950s and 1960s, but of course the exaggeration bore the opposite sign. Now observers marveled at the astounding and sudden international success of Italian jewelry. The de-

[12] Carlo Felice, L'Oreficeria (Milan, 1927), 104.
[13] Ibid., 110.

signer and critic Guido Gregorietti reported with pride that in 1970 almost 85 percent of the gold jewelry imported by West Germany and half of that imported by France came from Italy. The reason for this success? "Thirty centuries of history have refined the sensitivity of Italian goldsmiths to every cultural renewal. They accept these [renewals] with the full awareness of their own experience, the refinement of their artistic taste, and their inborn creative genius."[14] Even serious semiacademic publications used this kind of rhetoric. After reporting that in 1978 Italy processed more gold than the combined total of all the other European countries, Luigi Stella and Fabio Torsoli, two leaders of the Italian gold jewelers' association, gave four reasons for this success. Reason number one was tradition, followed by advanced technology, the "well-known good taste of Italian producers," and finally the extension of the domestic market.[15]

The invention of this myth that twentieth-century Italy's gold jewelry trade owed its success to a long-standing tradition of craftsmanship took place in different ways in the three "gold towns," and it often involved heated debates. In the spring of 1957, when the Italian producers were experiencing their first international successes, Guido Invernizzi, the president of the gold jewelry manufacturers' association and Milanese craftsman, sent a harshly critical letter to Gori, accusing his business practices of being the fundamental cause of the trade's problems. The main target of Invernizzi's accusations was the intense mechanization at Arezzo's Gori & Zucchi, soon to become the largest gold jewelry company in the world. His argument was well structured. First of all, gold jewelry, the luxury good par excellence, should not be manufactured by the cost- and price-reducing technologies adopted by other metalworking industries. The quest for economies of scale betrayed the spirit of goldsmithing. Gori's practices "attempt to sacrifice the traditional entrepreneurship, the ingenuity, and the very preciousness of artisanal goods in the name of mass production, which is mechanized and thus debased by considerations of quantity and price." Second, the application of the principles of mass production to the jewelry industry had a damaging economic consequence since they led to the constant saturation of the market and to recurrent crises of

---

[14] Guido Gregorietti, *Italian Gold, Silver, and Jewelry: Their History and Centres* (Milan, 1971), 21.

[15] L. Stella and F. Torsoli, "Aspects of the Industrial Demand as to Jewellery: Case Study of a Typical Country," in Quadri-Curzio, ed., *The Gold Problem*, 140.

overproduction. Finally, the necessity of reducing prices caused the deterioration of quality and, most important, encouraged the pursuit of illegal behaviors such as the violation of labor and fiscal standards to the point of "canceling the boundaries between legality and illegality." For these reasons, Invernizzi concluded, Gori's practices were "at this moment one of the greatest dangers for all jewelry traders, and not only for the Italian ones."[16]

Gori resented these accusations and pointed out that the concept of luxury was historically relative. Like TV sets and automobiles, gold jewelry was becoming an integral part of modern life. Therefore, reducing the cost and price of jewelry could extend its market as had been the case with other industrial goods. Moreover, opposition to this trend towards the democratization of consumption was tantamount to resurrecting the policies of the Fascist regime: "The nostalgic policy of collective and fixed prices has collapsed with corporatism and the unsound principles of economic autarchy. Fair competition is not only the expression of untamed liberty but also the irresistible dynamic impulse towards perfection." Despite this apology for capitalist modernity, Gori also paid lip service to the nobility of craftsmanship by pointing out that Gori & Zucchi's mechanized processes were not meant to replace the artisans' touch, but to spare the "craftsmen" on the company's payroll many menial tasks and provide them with inexpensive and reliable semifinished products: "No deterioration of quality, but only convenience and swiftness in the supply of materials, from which man—and man only—draws the expression of his creative personality with the signs of his art."[17] Therefore, Gori's production embodied simultaneously the modernity of competition and mass consumption on the one hand and the traditions of creativity and uniqueness on the other. Gori's practices were not unfair, but the same could not be said of many of his competitors, who were always ready to undermine his technical (and moral) superiority by all kinds of treacherous means.

The correspondence between Gori and Invernizzi shows that the debates about craftsmanship tended to assume the connotations of a morality play, in which the impersonal rules of modern competition were contrasted with a mythical world of personal agreements and tacit re-

---

[16] Archivio della Camera di Commercio di Arezzo, vol. 13, Oreficeria Varie, IGE 4, folder IGE Atti più importanti, Invernizzi's letter to Gori, dated 8 May 1957.

[17] Archivio della Camera di Commercio di Arezzo, vol. 13, Oreficeria Varie, IGE 4, folder IGE Atti più importanti, Gori's letter to Invernizzi, dated 4 June 1957.

spect of aesthetic standards. These ideological concerns had a long history in the Italian jewelry towns. Both in pre-Fascist Valenza Po and Vicenza, as we have seen in chapters 1 and 3 respectively, craftsmanship and socialism were closely linked, albeit in partially contradictory ways. Before the war, and especially before the rise of Fascism, the debate about craftsmanship hinged on the tension between individualism and competition on the one hand and the values of equality and cooperation on the other. After the war, the main ideological contradiction was that between the world of production, where artisanal practices tended to be associated with the values of grassroots democracy and the ethos of social equality, and the world of consumption, where the same practices supported the preservation of high-quality standards and elitism. This latent contradiction exploded during the economic "miracle" of the 1950s and 1960s, when the unprecedented expansion of the domestic market was matched by the globalization of Italian jewelry. An observer from Arezzo argued in 1950 that the increasing prosperity and the rise of mass media were promoting the convergence of taste towards a generic "modern style": "The general taste of the artisan's customers has changed in recent years. Even among the rural and working classes we have experienced a remarkable realignment towards the suggestions of current fashion and standardized taste."[18] What then constituted a genuine artisan in the new context of global competition and mass consumption, and what were the political implications of craftsmanship?

Both the Christian Democrats and the Communists supported the spread of locally based artisanal economies, although for different reasons. The Catholics extolled family businesses, as well as the creation of networks of small independent producers, as institutions fully compatible with the social teachings of the church. The Left, by contrast, saw the artisanal economy as an antimonopolist system potentially endowed with collectivist tendencies to be encouraged.[19] In both cases, however, the role and identity of the new artisan in an increasingly globalized economy were ill defined. Although it was apparent that

[18] Archivio di Stato di Arezzo, Prefettura di Arezzo, Gabinetto, vol. 219, Industria e Commercio, folder Camera di Commercio.

[19] For the relationship between Catholicism and small-scale entrepreneurship in postwar Italy, see Arnaldo Bagnasco and Carlo Trigilia, *Società e Politica nelle Aree di Piccola Impresa: Il caso di Bassano* (Venice, 1984); for the Communist case, see see Arnaldo Bagnasco and Carlo Trigilia, *Società e Politica nelle Aree di Piccola Impresa: Il caso della Valdelsa* (Milan, 1985).

the typical artisan who worked in the jewelry districts was quite different from the all-around independent producer of preindustrial societies, a definition of his social and political status was elusive. At stake in this process of definition were not only claims to the values of morality and beauty with which craftsmanship was associated, but also more mundane advantages in terms of fiscal and labor practices, since the legal standards for artisanal firms were much more flexible than for industrial companies. Therefore, whereas the "genuine" artisan remained the ideological model for the industry, the practice of craftsmanship also nourished the worst kind of opportunism. Unscrupulous agents could usurp the title of artisan for their basest interests.

The laws that regulated the artisanal sector and distinguished between artisanal and industrial firms fueled conflicts and ambiguities, rather than dissipate them. During the economic boom, the matter was addressed by two laws issued in 1956.[20] According to these laws, no exam was necessary to be listed as an artisan. The discriminating variables were the quality of the work process, which could not be entirely mechanized, the firm's size, and the legal status of the firm (only companies of people, as opposed to corporations, could be regarded as artisanal). Artisans could not employ more than ten apprentices and ten workers (five and five in the case of partly mechanized production processes). However, the laws had a big loophole. In the case of traditional artistic trades (*mestieri artistici tradizionali*), there was no size constraint. Only the exclusion of incorporated companies remained valid, the rationale being that the bosses of nonincorporated companies usually participated manually in the work process. Gold jewelry production was included in this category at the end of the 1950s. Therefore, in that trade the legal status of a firm said very little about its actual practices. It was not uncommon for a fully mechanized jewelry company with more than fifty workers to be listed as artisanal and thus enjoy preferential treatment by the tax and labor authorities.

These ambiguities showed all their rhetorical and political power in the rivalry between Valenza Po and Arezzo, respectively the most "artisanal" and "industrial" centers in the Italian gold jewelry industry. As we have seen in chapter 2, after World War II, Valenza Po became the site of a militant group of left-wing artisans who shaped the development of the Piedmontese town in the 1950s and 1960s through the establishment of institutions (the collective export company and the

[20] Law no. 860 issued on 25 July 1956, and no. 1533 issued on 29 December 1956.

permanent exhibition) specifically geared to their needs. Valenza Po's small-size producers were perfectly aware of the political nature of these institutional initiatives: "The protection of the artisan in his individuality . . . is recognized by all ideologies as a vital and irreplaceable element. Therefore [such protection] finds its rightful place in the local economic programs. Our conception shows its practical consequences in the social distribution of prosperity, which is very different from that typical of the other Italian centers grown rich by working in our industrial sector."[21] The "typical center" in this quote was obviously Arezzo. Gori & Zucchi, the largest jewelry company in the world, was accused of simultaneously promoting Taylorism in its own plant and inequality in Arezzo's society at large. Valenza Po, by contrast, presented itself as a model for all artisanal centers in Italy. Its astounding international success of the late 1950s and early 1960s, Illario argued in 1966, had relied on artisanal cooperation, epitomized by the permanent show and the collective export company: "It is necessary to be united, to understand that an isolated artisan is doomed. Either the artisan is part of a group or he stands alone helpless."[22] Collective action was what distinguished Valenza Po's artisans from both preindustrial craftsmen and the jewelry manufacturers of other Italian districts. And the ability to cooperate and translate cooperation into competitiveness in the new global market allowed Valenza Po's artisans to avoid aesthetic compromises in the quality of their production.

Gori and other leaders of Arezzo's economy bitterly rejected this self-congratulatory interpretation of Valenza Po's techno-economic and social practices. At stake were problems of tax and labor regulation, as well as issues of image and commercial promotion. Throughout the 1960s, Gori adopted two largely incompatible rhetorical strategies to challenge the identification of Valenza Po with craftsmanship and Arezzo with mass production. First, he argued relentlessly that all jewelry producers manufactured "art objects," which formed "a homogenous and indivisible entity." The special status granted to the "artisans" of Valenza Po, therefore, was misplaced.[23] Arezzo's output was equally artistic. Second, he set out to attack Valenza Po's image as a center for high-end jewelry. When the price of gold started to

---

[21] A. Cavallero, "Un giusto riconoscimento," *L'Orafo Valenzano*, February 1964, 15.

[22] "Le realizzazioni del Centro Orafo Valenzano," *L'Orafo Valenzano* 8 (May 1966), 21.

[23] Archivio della Camera di Commercio di Arezzo, vol. 13, Oreficeria, IGE, Anni 1960–66, folder 8, Riforma del sistema di riscossione, Gori's note dated 12 April 1963.

fluctuate after 1968, both the national television company (Radio Tele-
visione Italiana, or RAI) and Italy's most prestigious newspaper (*Corriere della Sera*) paid considerable attention to the possible consequences of the new economic conditions on Valenza Po's economy,
while they largely ignored Arezzo. Gori's angry response to the media
was that only 10 percent of Valenza Po's firms produced high-quality
artisanal jewelry. "Valenza's thousands of artisans are by and large just
home workers, even though they are not reported as such, and they
perform work that is entirely mechanized."[24] The purpose of this
system, Gori argued disingenuously, was to dodge all fiscal, labor,
and social security standards. Whereas Valenza Po was falsely "aristocratic," Arezzo was genuinely "democratic." The president of
Arezzo's Chamber of Commerce argued that Arezzo's sophisticated
technical practices had made gold jewelry accessible to even the hum-
blest population strata. Arezzo's production, valued at more than 400
billion lire, consisted mostly of "small items of popular use."[25] But by
pointing out simultaneously the homogeneity of the industry and its
fractures (and the "artistic" and "popular" character of Arezzo's production), Gori and his allies proved ill equipped to implement a coherent and politically effective strategy.

These ideological debates stemmed from three related sources of ambiguity. The first source resided in the dual use of gold jewelry as a
consumer good and as part of families' saving and hedging strategies.
Concerns of style and taste were of primary importance for the buyers
who conceived of gold jewelry as a fashion good, whereas the sheer
weight of a piece of gold jewelry and its market price largely determined the decisions of the "hoarders," as they were often referred to in
the trade literature. Arezzo was specialized in the production of simple
rings, chains, and medals, which were the typical goods exchanged
during family rituals (baptism, marriage, communion, etc.) as a form
of inflation-proof savings. By contrast, Valenza Po's typical production
consisted of more elaborate jewelry, which involved the use of precious
and semiprecious stones and was more susceptible to fashion changes.
In this regard, therefore, Gori's claim that jewelry production was a
homogenous activity represented a disingenuous attempt to obtain the
legal and cultural advantages of the "artisan" label.

[24] Archivio della Camera di Commercio di Arezzo, vol. 13, Oreficeria, Varie 2, folder
IVA oreficerie, handwritten note, dated June 1972.
[25] Ibid.

But Gori was quite right in pointing out the mechanized nature of Valenza Po's production processes. This was the second source of ambiguity. Differences in firm size and technological practices correlated rather weakly with differences in the type of jewelry produced. Once again, a gap divided ideology and practice. Valenza Po's self-image was one of technological stability and continuity. After describing in detail a sixteenth-century engraving showing a German goldsmith's shop, local craftsman and historian Franco Cantamessa noticed with pride that "the tradition of our craftsmanship has allowed our tools to remain much the same. . . . We can argue that gold jewelers' craftsmanship has survived unchanged to our time precisely because it is an activity that does not need sophisticated technology."[26] But actual technical practices had changed quite significantly during the economic boom of the 1950s and 1960s. Many articles in the periodical of the local jewelry manufacturers' association, *L'Orafo Valenzano*, testify to the attention paid by Valenza Po's producers to technological innovations. The productivity advantages of sophisticated techniques such as microfusion and ultrasound polishing were widely advertised, and the journal praised Valenza Po's manufacturers for their technological receptivity.[27] The journal's technological discussions were as sophisticated as the machines it advertised. In reply to the letter of two concerned manufacturers about guillocher machines, for example, the journal pointed at technology's inherent flexibility and argued, "What matters in most cases is not the possession and the use of a machine, but the criteria with which one utilizes it and the originality of the results that one manages to obtain." The modern craftsman, the journal argued, was in an ideal position to exploit this flexibility fully: "The goldsmith must take advantage of all technical and scientific resources so as to direct their power towards the goal of [achieving] eclecticism and originality."[28] In fact, the success of Valenza Po's "artisanal" jewelry relied heavily on the mechanization of key production processes, albeit a mechanization over which the artisan exercised considerable control.

Craftsmanship in Valenza Po did not mean lack of mechanization and technological sophistication. By the same token, mechanization in

---

[26] Franco Cantamessa, "Oggi come ieri," *Valensa d'na Vota* 1 (1986): 30.

[27] On microfusion, see *L'Orafo Valenzano* 6 (May and August 1965); on ultrasound polishing, *L'Orafo Valenzano* 6 (October 1965).

[28] "Diamantatrici e macchine a guillocher sono utensili 'a doppio taglio'?" *L'Orafo Valenzano* 6 (November 1965), 26–27.

Arezzo did not necessarily mean large-scale production. Chain-making machines, for example, were a rather sophisticated and highly "divisible" technology, which could be adopted just as efficiently by small as large companies. High expenses for raw materials, rather than the cost of fixed capital, constituted the main barrier to entry into the industry. The main source of economies of scale in mechanized jewelry plants came from the wear-and-tear losses of gold, which were then recuperated and recycled. The firms that processed gold belonging to the customer usually agreed on a percentage of metal loss higher than the actual one, thereby making a tax-free profit. Larger plants enjoyed a disproportionate access to this source of income.[29]

Despite this scale-related advantage, small firms could be highly profitable even in the mechanized segment of the industry. Starting up a new firm became even easier after 1970, when Gori & Zucchi diversified into the production of jewelry machinery by founding a company called MGZ. The skilled workers who tended and repaired chain-making machines (*meccanici catenisti*) were by far the best-paid employees in Arezzo. More than half of their wages consisted of under-the-counter handouts, especially in the small and medium-size firms.[30] This form of payment was above all an incentive to keep key skilled workers from starting up their own firm. Many chose proprietorship none the less, becoming "artisans" in the legal sense of the term. At the end of the 1970s, approximately 550 of the 600 jewelry firms in Arezzo were officially "artisanal," despite their adoption of mechanized processes and the relatively standardized character of their production.

In their negotiations with government officials (and with each other), local actors often employed categories borrowed from the language of state bureaucracy, despite the fact that these categories only partially fit social and economic relations at the local level. The relationships between individual firms on the one hand, and networks of producers, commercial agents, and political actors on the other constituted the third and final source of ambiguity. Both Gori and his rivals took the firm as the main focus of their polemic statements, even though in both Valenza Po and Arezzo jewelry was manufactured and distributed by networks of actors (some of whom did not even constitute a firm in the legal sense) linked by informal subcontracting rela-

[29] Luigi Illario, *Le Imprese Orafe* (Alessandria, 1959), 80–85.
[30] Peruzzi, *Organizzazione e Gestione*, 96–98.

tions. In this context, the firm was little more than an ideological construction used by key local actors in their negotiations with the state. Therefore, the attempts to distinguish between artisanal and industrial companies was doomed to failure. Production practices in Arezzo and Valenza transgressed the boundaries between artisanal and industrial manufacturing. In both towns, most jewelry was produced by combinations of "artisanal" and "industrial" processes. The challenge for traders was to stress the artisanal aspect of their wares for financial as well as promotional reasons. But the coexistence of vastly different practices in the same towns, practices ranging from fully mechanized and technologically advanced processes to seemingly "traditional" handwork, constituted a remarkable competitive advantage. In sum, the modernity of craftsmanship in the jewelry districts did not reside only in its recent invention but also in its practical and ideological flexibility.

HISTORICAL PATTERNS OF STYLE FORMATION

While the notion of craftsmanship assumed a variety of meanings for different actors, the jewelry towns shared some fundamental patterns for the creation and transmission of knowledge about style and fashion changes. In this context, Marshall's notion of the industrial atmosphere is particularly fruitful. I take Marshall to mean that skills, technical information, and other forms of knowledge should be viewed as emergent properties that do not reside in any single node of local networks but develop in a nonlinear fashion from the interactions among a variety of actors.[31] My contention is that in the jewelry towns these patterns emerged historically from the personal and informal relations that constituted the backbone of local social life. Information about styles and fashion, for example, was not routinized within formal institutions; instead, it spread by word of mouth in countless informal occasions. This guaranteed first of all that knowledge could not easily become proprietary. Therefore, no single agent could earn a monopoly rent over it. Second, informal networks guaranteed that local actors could come up

---

[31] The notion of "emergent property" was developed by C. D. Broad in the 1920s. The nonlinearity of these patterns describes their ability to trigger self-reinforcing ("positive feedback") mechanisms. See Brian Arthur, "Positive Feedbacks in the Economy," *Scientific American*, February 1990, 92–99.

with a plethora of variations on any stylistic theme, subject them to the evaluation of the market, assess the market's response, and read-just their practices on the basis of the new information. These feedback mechanisms enhanced the flexibility of the local economies and opened up avenues for the recognition of new "talent," thereby foster-ing political consensus and legitimizing the local social structure.

This understanding of the jewelry towns' epistemic—and aes-thetic—patterns leads to the reappraisal of a central theme in labor his-tory, the supposedly inevitable divorce of notions of beauty and taste from the world of production in the course of industrialization. In the jewelry towns, as in many other Italian artisanal centers, this separa-tion never took place. Even though local producers had to negotiate their positions vis-à-vis the professional trendsetters located in Paris, Milan, or Rome, and despite the fact that specialization and division of labor at the local level made the all-around craftsman of preindus-trial times relatively uncommon, small-scale producers understood taste and beauty as products of their local networks. The beautiful piece of jewelry—be it a refined brooch encrusted with pearls and pre-cious stones or the perfectly manufactured gold chain with an innova-tive pattern—bore the name of one author. But local jewelers were fully aware of the crucial role played by their colleagues and fellow citizens in sharing advice and information, more or less willingly, within infor-mal networks of relations. They understood that, at least in some sense, their jewelry was indeed "made in Valenza Po"—or "made in Arezzo." While the main directives of taste were set elsewhere, Italian artisans preserved a high degree of control over its local—and collec-tive—reinterpretation. Neither the formal rules of organized labor nor the state's preoccupation with educational standards successfully chal-lenged the power of locality to shape distinctive aesthetic cultures.

This link between locality and beauty also had an important gender dimension. Leora Auslander's analysis of the French furniture indus-try shows how preoccupations with taste and beauty were "femi-nized" in the course of the industrialization process by moving from the realm of production to that of consumption. As French artisans lost their independence, they also relinquished their willingness to articu-late aesthetic standards in the public sphere of class organization.[32]

---

[32] See Leora Auslander, "Perceptions of Beauty and the Problem of Consciousness: Parisian Furniture Makers," in Lenard R. Berlanstein, ed., *Rethinking Labor History* (Ur-bana-Champaign, 1993), 149–81.

This is not what happened in the towns of northern and central Italy. Here the preoccupation with beauty and taste has assumed a distinctively masculine character through its link with small-scale entrepreneurship. In Valenza Po, for example, competition among craftsmen over stylistic accuracy and innovation can be witnessed in bars and clubs all over town.

While these were general mechanisms at work in all the jewelry towns, there were significant differences in the ways knowledge about styles was produced and spread at the local level. The case of Valenza Po is particularly interesting because of the central role played by fashion changes in the economy of the Piedmontese town from a relatively early date. Nevertheless, documentary evidence about this important topic is scanty at best. I worked around this evidentiary problem by interviewing a group of jewelry makers or traders in their sixties and seventies who were well connected both politically and economically. These interviews have allowed me to trace the path followed by Valenza Po's jewelers in their stylistic negotiations with the domestic and international markets. The available documentary evidence backs up oral testimonies. But these interviews also offer valuable insights into the ways in which local actors interpret past changes and conceive of their town's future. As is often the case with oral history, these informants proved to be not only useful observers but also subtle ethnographers.[33]

A commercial crisis turned Valenza Po from a minor artisanal center into a powerhouse of stylistic innovation.[34] The World War I–related paralysis of the jewelry trade was followed by a brief but remarkable upsurge of pent-up demand, which spurred the unprecedented proliferation of start-ups (see chapter 1). By the early 1920s, however, the demand boom was over. In order to defend their newly achieved positions in the local economy, dozens of jewelry firms radically changed their commercial practices by hiring a traveling agent or, more often, by turning one of the founding partners into a traveling salesman. It was only natural for these agents to concentrate on the south of Italy, the area of the country where the demand for gold jewelry was rela-

[33] The literature on oral history is vast. See at least Paul Thompson, *The Voice of the Past: Oral Hisrtory,* 3rd ed. (Oxford, 2000); and John Foley, *The Theory of Oral Composition: History and Methodology* (Bloomington, 1988).

[34] By "innovation" I mean the commercial adaptation of radical stylistic changes (which we might call "inventions"). Valenza Po, for reasons that will become clear in the next paragraphs, never had the power and clout to reorient taste autonomously.

tively higher and local supply was lower.[35] Ezio De Ambrogi (b. 1923), the retired heir to one of Valenza Po's most successful commercial offices, recounted his father's memories of these early business trips: "They stayed away three or four months at a time. . . . You can imagine what it meant in 1925 or 1930 to travel to Canicattì or Caltanisetta [Sicilian towns], to Puglia, to the Albanian villages of Puglia and Calabria by all kinds of means of transportation."[36]

From these trips, Valenza Po's salesmen returned with something more valuable than cash and promissory notes. They also began to gauge personally the bewildering diversity of Italy's local tastes. But learning the subtle differences between local jewelry traditions was only the first step of a two-pronged strategy. De Ambrogi's analysis is quite pointed: "Every single area had its very own jewelry with its very own tradition. . . . They all had their goldsmiths who produced according to their particular taste. Valenza's tradesmen disrupted this. They borrowed ideas, but at the same time they created a common Italian taste for jewelry, even though some designs came from Germany, France, and other countries."[37] Starting in the interwar years, Valenza Po's producers and traders invented an "Italian" style by acting as the *trait d'union* between the local markets in the peninsula and the international capitals of jewelry design, above all Paris in France and Pforzheim in Germany.[38] The first informal contacts between Valenza Po and the international designers were established in these years. Ginetto Prandi (b. 1930), once one of the most accomplished craftsmen in town, confirms this reconstruction: "We saw some enormous catalogues of designs. . . . The designers from Paris showed up in town, and everybody in Valenza bought them."[39] Of course these were old designs that were not in vogue in Paris anymore, but the establishment of these networks of personal relations constituted the first step towards the globalization of Valenza Po's jewelry.

One of the main strengths of Valenza Po as a manufacturing center was precisely its liminal position between networks as different as the world of international luxury on the one hand and that of the southern

---

[35] Even today, the southern regions account for almost two-thirds of the gold jewelry purchased in Italy every year.

[36] Interview by author, October 1996.

[37] Ibid.

[38] On Pforzheim's jewelry industry, see Wolfgang Pieper, *Gescichte der Pforzheimer Schmuckindustrie: Ein Beitrag zur Geschichte des Nordschwarzwaldes* (Gernsbach, 1989).

[39] Interview by author, October 1996.

Italian peasant towns on the other. But it would be a mistake to see Valenza Po's role as simply one of popularization. While countless Parisian designs were adapted by the Piedmontese manufacturers to a less privileged public, Valenza Po also developed some examples of artisanal excellence that operated in the opposite direction, transforming relatively "popular" jewelry into exclusive items. The case of the Illario brothers is certainly the most revealing in this regard. We have already met Luigi, the future Christian Democratic patron and political leader. His older brother, Carlo, was the stylistic and technical brain of the family company, founded in 1920 and destined to become the symbol of Valenza Po's high-quality jewelry from the 1920s to the 1970s. Carlo began his career as an agent for several Pforzheim-based companies in the Italian market. In the 1920s, the German center was specialized in gold jewelry richly encrusted with synthetic stones. Carlo began to make copies of this jewelry but replaced synthetic stones with authentic ones. The Illarios thus became the suppliers of the Italian royal family and of several prominent Fascist leaders. The firm's artisanal proficiency soon attracted the attention of several Parisian *maisons*. Illario's trips to Paris, where he is said to have sold his creations to the most prestigious names of *haute joaillerie* directly from his hotel room, have become legendary in Valenza Po.[40]

It would be hard to overestimate the impact of these early contacts between Valenza Po's manufacturers and the domestic and international markets on the economic boom after World War II. The local tradesmen hardly waited for demand to pick up again after the end of the conflict. They immediately set out to reweave the commercial ties severed by the war. The Parisian hotels visited by Carlo Illario were a far cry from the situations encountered by the majority of Valenza Po's salesmen in their trips to the towns of postwar Italy. De Ambrogi's tale of a particularly adventurous business trip to Puglia, undertaken with his father in the late 1940s, brings back to life a world rife with risk and bound by a tacit code of honor:

> My father had always had a clientele in the south. We set out to deal with that old clientele again. . . . We got to Termoli, and [the customers] came to pick us up with their carriage to climb up to Chienti, near Foggia. . . . It was an Albanian village; they spoke Albanian. The store owner was the son of one of my fathers' old

[40] This information was provided by Ezio De Ambrogi in his interview and confirmed by Aldo Annaratone and Ginetto Prandi.

customers. . . . His father had died during the war. So he received us in his austere-looking building. The other dwellings were huts were they slept all together: children, grown-ups, and animals. That was the only building. He sold everything in town. He sold pasta, rice, and he also sold jewelry for the weddings. So there we were. They put us up for three days before a word on the business deal was mentioned. . . . Three days on the balcony talking and discussing nothing in particular, and right before we left, the deal was made.[41]

Throughout the 1950s, Valenza Po's manufacturers and traders took advantage of these diffused contacts to keep a tight hold on taste changes in the domestic market, as they continued their slow but relentless activity of standardization.

In the 1950s, Valenza Po's manufacturers and traders started to reap the benefits of their extensive web of commercial relations. The information flowing from places as diverse as Paris and the Albanian-speaking villages of southern Italy converged in the streets of Valenza Po. The town itself became an open shop in which information circulated almost freely through the daily contacts and conversations typical of a small provincial center. A regained access to uncensored political debate also created a public arena for the exchange of knowledge relevant to the jewelry trade. The interviewees were unanimous in describing the exhilarating atmosphere of those years. Ginetto Prandi gave a vivid portrait of the jewelry makers' social life during the economic boom:

The strength of Valenza was that of having a thousand artisans among whom there were five hundred who copied, and others who just got by. But every day in order to survive . . . you grabbed a pencil, sketched something, took a piece of gold, and played with it. And you got one good idea out of ten you tried. . . . Ideas popped up . . . new ways of setting stones, for example. Who knows how you came up with it. . . . I think that when someone comes up with an idea, he usually tries to keep it for himself. . . . But within a month—not a year, a month—everyone in town knew how to do the same thing. That meant that one shared his innovation with others [just] by minding his own business. And this is possible only where there is the artisan who goes to the bar

---

[41] Interview by author, October 1996.

and almost unwillingly talks to one person, then talks to the other person, and not just about major techniques but also about trifles, such as a gadget to emery a particular piece of jewelry. . . . They came up with new things as they went. Nobody even knew how a certain thing got invented.[42]

Prandi's description is particularly valuable because it highlights how ecological notions, such as emergent property and feedback mechanism, are very much part of local actors' self-representation. The notion of knowledge as an emergent property is a somewhat abstract way of capturing the nonquantifiable increase in productivity and inventiveness that emerged from countless conversations over a bottle of wine, in town meetings, or simply on the streets. By the same token, the notion of positive feedback is a theoretical definition of the virtuous circles triggered by the sharing of information between actors motivated simultaneously by the desire to earn a rent on their technical or stylistic innovation and by the need to tap the flow of public knowledge in order to improve and implement the innovation itself.

This conception of local society as a self-contained and self-regulating system, however, contrasts with other narratives and interpretations that emphasize the connections between the town and the larger world—connections fraught with conflicts and tensions. The years of the economic boom saw the development of more systematic contacts with the French designers of *haute joaillerie*. These contacts transformed Valenza Po's producers into "the Japanese of gold jewelry," as accountant and tax advisor Franco Frascarolo put it.[43] Again, this was not a simple process of imitation. The technical proficiency of the local producers and the relatively low costs of their work drew almost all the leading international gold jewelry companies to Valenza Po. By the early 1960s, the Piedmontese town had become one of the main suppliers of high-quality gold jewelry to Cartier, Boucheron, Van Cleef, and later Tiffany and Bulgari. Although the designs came from Paris, New York, or Rome, Valenza Po's artisans enjoyed some leeway in the translation of the original ideas into technically feasible objects. Nonetheless, the ties between these artisans and the French *maisons* remained a relatively well-kept secret for many years. Aldo Annaratone's assessment of these relations combined pride and resentment:

---

[42] Interview by author, October 1996.
[43] Interview by author, October 1996.

In Valenza people still know how to keep it quiet. This is important. Because if I take you downstairs [to the shop] I can show you the hallmarks of Tiffany, Cartier, Van Cleef, Boucheron. Now I can say it, since it not a secret anymore. . . . We made the objects, stamped them with their hallmarks, and [it was like] they had built them themselves. We still do that. All of Valenza does. . . . They sell their creation, and yet they probably don't even know how to make it.[44]

Valenza Po's manufacturers never managed to have their names displayed in the shop windows of Paris and New York. Their weakness vis-à-vis the renowned brand names of high jewelry certainly played a role in this lack of recognition. The Parisian houses entrusted Valenza Po with more and more "responsibilities" precisely because the local informal economy guaranteed secrecy and lower costs. The same informal mechanisms that produced and spread information so effectively also prevented local firms from "making the leap" towards international notoriety. By the late 1960s, however, the somewhat paradoxical relationship between globalization and informality (in the shape of gold and precious stone smuggling, tax evasion, disrespect of labor standards, etc.) had become apparent, and some media wasted no time in exposing it. Unsurprisingly, given Valenza Po's leftist tradition, a Catholic daily newspaper, *Avvenire*, took the lead. The paper ran a series of articles mocking Valenza Po's social relations as a "world à la James Bond," in which salesmen packed Beretta guns under their blazers and "improvised businessmen deal[t] gold and diamonds as if they were cows and pigs."[45] The daily also did not miss the opportunity to highlight the paradox of a Communist-led town in which labor laws were completely ignored. The journalist contrasted these shady practices with the international glamour of Valenza Po's production:

In Valenza, the labor of a skilled worker can be paid up to eight hundred lire per hour, which would not be a bad pay if four out of eight hundred was not handed out under the counter. This means that paradoxically Cartier's and Tiffany's jewelry is produced by a workforce without qualifications or specialization,

[44] Interview by author, October 1996.
[45] "Corrieri-fachiro portano gioielli alla città dell'oro," *Avvenire*, 20 August 1969.

since four hundred lire is the [official] pay of an unskilled metal worker.[46]

By the late 1960s, the "secret" relations between the Parisian houses and Valenza Po's artisans could be exposed without fear of reprisal also because the Piedmontese producers had openly embraced their role of popularizers of taste for gradually wider audiences. This process of popularization was largely based on the imitation of the designs of high jewelry, which Valenza Po's producers had grown to know so well. As the local suppliers of the international brand names multiplied, so did the firms that toned down the jewelry crafted by their better-connected or more proficient competitors. Sometimes trusted suppliers and imitators coincided. A locally famous story about the opportunities and tensions engendered by this process of imitation has a winking cat head as its main character. Three different people told me versions of this story in their interviews.[47] Although some details are less than precise, starting from the time frame, the significance of the incident lies in its paradigmatic character. The story can almost be read as a parable about power and justice, and that is certainly the way the witnesses experienced and recounted it.

In the mid-1960s, Van Cleef and Arpels, the prestigious Paris-based *maison* of top-quality jewelry, contacted Aldo Annaratone and placed an important order for a series of very expensive pieces of jewelry. Annaratone's firm, PARM, was asked to supply the French house with a number of emerald-encrusted cat heads that winked at the amused buyer (as well as at the envious onlooker). The order was carried out with full satisfaction of the commissioner. But Annaratone was a cat lover too, and he let himself get inspired by his very own pet, "a great opportunist of a tabby-cat," and decided to produce his own golden feline. In order to accommodate the pocketbooks of his less wealthy customers, he had to replace authentic emeralds with synthetic stones, and the size of the brooch was not as impressive as its French cousin. But the design was so appealing that it became one of PARM's favorites for several seasons. Indeed, its success was such that one of its local competitors, GAM, decided to launch its own variation on the same theme. That move apparently crossed the line. Van Cleef sued GAM for plagiarism and dragged its director, Franco Frascarolo, down

[46] "Fa i gioielli per Cartier però non è specializzato," *Avvenire*, 21 August 1969.
[47] Aldo Annaratone, Franco Frascarolo, and—indirectly—Ezio De Ambrogi.

to Marseille to withstand a trial. As expected, Van Cleef won the suit, and GAM was forced to pay a steep fine.

While Frascarolo, the imitator, told me this story to illustrate his argument about the fundamentally derivative character of Valenza Po's jewelry, Annaratone, the "adapter," went on to recount the ironic follow-up of the episode. More than twenty years after the trial, when he had just retired, a wealthy German lady who shared Annaratone's passion for cats happened to see PARM's cat head in a catalogue. She decided that this piece had to be the acquisition of her lifetime. The lady had a collection of small but perfect pearls, "a unique treasure." Her trusted jeweler in Germany put her in touch with Annaratone's firm, and the lady placed an order for a life-size cat head encrusted with her pearls. The dream brooch of the German lady became the coronation of the aging craftsman's career and perhaps also the vindication of his life, spent relinquishing control over "his" creations and attaching his name only to their toned-down versions.

This story also hints at the tacit norms that regulated the relations between the French companies and the Piedmontese artisans. Revealingly, Van Cleef sued the imitator but let the "original" popularizer of its design off the hook. After all, the exclusive winking cat head would not have been realized without Annaratone's craft. His derivative activity could be tolerated. It was the price the Parisians had to pay to preserve their fruitful ties with Valenza Po's artisans. But these informal agreements also had clear-cut boundaries and implications. It is tempting to surmise that it was Annaratone himself who turned to his French commissioner for protection from his unwelcome competitors. Whereas he was helpless vis-à-vis the local imitators, the French designer could resort to formal law and institutions to sanction the breach of its patents. Unequal (and yet successful) business relations often negotiate the fine line between personal agreements and formal contracts.

Valenza Po's "old guard" unanimously places the stylistic golden age of local jewelry in the 1960s and 1970s, when information about taste changes flowed relatively smoothly from Paris to an increasing number of foreign markets, passing through the small shops of the Piedmontese town. In fact, this flow was so effective that by the 1980s Hong Kong and other East Asian centers had done their homework and had become Valenza Po's threatening competitors in the global market. Ginetto Prandi's words convey the anxiety triggered by the new scenario: "The quality of some of the objects made in Hong Kong is comparable to ours, and on top of that, they have much lower costs. But they're still mere imitators. And what's Valenza's strength? . . . Within the time it takes them to imitate a model, we have put out three hundred new ones." Imitation, Prandi's argument suggests, is not a trivial activity. It has to be accurate, dependable, and fast. Valenza Po enjoyed a good geographic location and an ideal socioeconomic structure to play the game successfully.

But above all, my interview partners argued, Valenza Po had the right ethos to operate as the *trait d'union* between the exclusivity of the Parisian *maisons* and the profitability of the world's middle-class markets. Nothing outraged the aging craftsmen more than my indelicate comparisons between their hometown and Arezzo or Vicenza. Luciano Lenti cried passionately: "Should we all go where Arezzo is sending us and do machine work in huge quantity? Is this to be the destiny of Italian gold jewelry?" More quietly, Prandi remarked: "In Valenza I had never heard of anyone working by the gram. That was Vicenza's job. We were paid by the object. This ring costs 1,000, this one 1,300 . . ." The combination of institutional and personal relations that was typical of postwar Valenza Po kept local competition within clear-cut boundaries. These norms also defined a community of producers that distinguished clearly between insiders and outsiders. Opportunities for social mobility and the recognition of talent were plentiful, but only within a rather well-defined community. Prandi's words are once again instructive. After complaining about the degeneration of morals, exemplified by the practice of selling jewelry by the gram, Prandi was quick to identify the culprits:

> In Valenza it's been above all the southern immigrants to do that [selling by the gram]. Why? Because the southerner is clearly different from us. He does not have the kind of culture we had in the past [meaning socialism]. . . . They found themselves being jewelry makers much the way they could have become stone cutters. They are not interested in saying: "I am capable of taking a drawing and making the object." What matters to them is that they got themselves a job, and a profitable one at that. That's it. . . . The less proficient they were, the richer they've become.

Prandi's tirade against the southern immigrants, who had not partaken of Valenza Po's socialist culture, exposes first of all the impact of local norms on stylistic and commercial practices. Jewelry production was also a moral activity in which actors had to resist the tempta-

227

tion to make money for its own sake if they wanted to be fully accepted within the local community. Valenza Po's elite theorized this artisanal ethos explicitly. Aurelio Sorrentino, the dean of the local school for jewelry makers, stated in 1949, "It should not be believed that the venal search for profit has always been the priority of the creators of the masterpieces that crossed oceans and mountains to reach the most sumptuous courts of Europe. The artist's moral satisfaction . . . surpasses the attractiveness of the money that measures the price [of the work of art]."[48] Second, Prandi's attitude also reveals the political limitations of a society grown prosperous largely on the basis of an extensive web of personal and informal relations. On the one hand, these relations relied on exclusionary strategies to remain viable. On the other hand, however, informality was generally ineffective at monitoring and policing the community's boundaries. The decadence of morals, embodied by the deterioration of style patterns, remains a constant and yet elusive threat.

The contradictions of informality were even more strident in Arezzo, a town whose economy was dominated by one powerful actor, Gori & Zucchi. Many of Valenza Po's jewelry traders portrayed their rival towns, and especially Arezzo, as lacking the ethos of craftsmanship and therefore as deprived of any real sense of morality. "Arezzo's companies are not goldsmiths, they are metalworking factories (*metalmeccanici*)," Luciano Lenti remarked with disdain. And whereas Valenza Po had agreed upon strict norms of behavior over its relatively long history as an artisanal and socialist center, Arezzo had no past. What represented a threatening exception in Valenza Po (the unscrupulous "southerner" imbued with a purely instrumental rationality) was the norm in Arezzo, a city populated by recently urbanized sharecroppers with very little artisanal and industrial tradition.

Gori and his collaborators in Arezzo tried hard to overcome this perceived handicap in a variety of partly contradictory ways. From the 1960s on, for example, Gori & Zucchi set out to invent a stylistic tradition that was supposedly rooted in the city's long history. This strategy assumed almost pathetic overtones when the company announced with pride that it had succeeded at replicating a particularly difficult Etruscan technique called granulation and consisting of the soldering

---

[48] Archivio Corrente del Comune di Valenza, IX-5/6, Scuola Serale di Disegno "Benvenuto Cellini" 1925–68, Relazione sull'istituzione Scuola Tecnica d'Oreficeria in Valenza.

of minute gold granules on a support. In the same period, the company launched a line of rings directly inspired by the jewelry that Arezzo's peasants wore in the nineteenth and early twentieth centuries.[49] But Gori & Zucchi also tried to combine local and global taste by hiring internationally famous artists such as Salvador Dalí and Giacomo Manzù for the creation of high-profile lines of jewelry. These promotional strategies betrayed the uneasiness of the company's management vis-à-vis Gori & Zucchi's reputation as a profit-seeking standardizer of taste.

In fact, the bulk of the jewelry that Arezzo's producers sold in the domestic and international markets (a quarter of the jewelry exported from Italy in the late 1970s, for example, came from the Tuscan town) consisted of variations on limited typologies of styles. Gori & Zucchi's catalogues displayed a bewildering variety of chains, necklaces, bracelets, rings, medals, and so forth, organized first by stylistic type and second by size, color, and price. Of course fashion changes affected the customers' orders to some degree, but Gori & Zucchi's vast repertoire of relatively simple jewelry was meant to exhaust most possibilities. Whereas Valenza Po's manufacturers and traders had to respond promptly to the exogenous changes of taste imposed by the Parisian *maisons*, Arezzo's company could plan ahead and transform the vagaries of fashion into a predictable routine. Gori & Zucchi had a whole team of designers on its payroll, each of whom was specialized in a line of products. The main task of these designers was to anticipate the marginal changes in customers' taste, but the buyers of Gori & Zucchi's jewelry were mostly concerned with its weight and price, rather than its stylistic features. Marketing strategies, such as the promotion of the mass rituals that involved the exchange of gold, were more important to Gori & Zucchi than the specific design of its production. Hence the mass-production of medals celebrating Mother's Day or Valentine's Day, which became some of the symbols of Gori & Zucchi's production worldwide (see chapter 4).

Institutionalized within formal routines, Gori & Zucchi's knowledge about styles and techniques was also meant to be proprietary. Whereas in Valenza Po information about stylistic and technical innovations enjoyed the multiplying effects of the "invisible hand" of social exchange, Arezzo's leading company was supposed to remain in control of the flow of knowledge as it trickled down the social and economic ladder

---

[49] Ivan Bruschi, "Alle radici dell'arte orafa," in Gori & Zucchi, *Sessanta Anni*, 29–31.

of its subcontractors. Unlike Valenza Po, Arezzo's social landscape was *tabula rasa* before the establishment and development of Gori & Zucchi. In the years of the economic miracle, the town was populated by recent immigrants from the countryside, peasants and sons of peasants who seemed to have no other option than to adapt to the policies enacted by the large company. In a sense, Gori & Zucchi's mechanized technology and Arezzo's recently urbanized workforce complemented each other. Compared with Valenza Po, they both had no past.

But the proprietary strategy of the world's largest jewelry company was the victim of a subtle irony. Gori & Zucchi's knowledge was not only formalized within specific routines, it was also incorporated into the company's machinery. Different chain patterns, for example, required minor variations in the settings of the chain-making machines. A small manufacturer described this pattern of marginal innovations with pride: "When the customer places an order for a particular model, we go down to our engineering department and create the technology or, whenever possible, we modify a machine already in use."[50] Unlike Valenza Po's jewelry, the style of Arezzo's production was a function of machinery, and the knowledge embodied by these machines was readily reproducible precisely because of its formalization.[51] When actors in the informal economy, which had been partly fostered by Gori & Zucchi itself for financial reasons, found access to the company's routinized knowledge, the outcome was explosive. The encounter between the two worlds took place on the factory's shop floor, but its effects radiated throughout Arezzo's society. Even before jewelry-making machines were made available in the local market by Gori & Zucchi itself and other firms, some of the company's workers painstakingly copied the machinery they tended. Then they turned to their family and neighborhood networks to reproduce the machines in their homes' basements:

> During their breaks, these enterprising workers secretly copied on pieces of paper the various components of the machines, measuring their shape with great care. Then at night they drew the machines more accurately, and on holidays they built and assembled

[50] Quoted in Rossi, *Profilo Sociologico*, 109.

[51] Despite the vain rhetoric of the publications sponsored by Gori & Zucchi, my analysis is compatible with that of an art critic hired by the company for its celebration. See Enrico Crispolti, "Arte e produzione possibilità di un'armonia," in Gori & Zucchi, *Sessanta Anni*, 19–26.

them with the help of their ironsmith friend or mechanic relative. These unsophisticated and yet efficient machines, placed in garrets and basements, began to work. This was the origin of almost all the jewelry firms of that period [the 1950s].[52]

In a sense, Arezzo's workers transformed codified information into tacit knowledge by expropriating the former from the large company and sharing (and enhancing) their new skills with their friends and neighbors. Gori & Zucchi' s knowledge was socialized in the informal arenas of family and neighborhood ties. The boundaries of the large company were very porous, and information also leaked through the relationships established among former colleagues. A small-scale entrepreneur spoke fondly of his informal ties with Gori & Zucchi:

Every day I discover that there are things I do not know or do not know how to accomplish! So, many times I find myself in the position of having to get in touch with my former friends and colleagues at Gori & Zucchi who still work there to solve technical problems that in a company like that can be fixed even by the least accomplished line worker.[53]

Through these kinds of contacts, the company acted as a de facto master to dozens, and later hundreds, of "apprentices" who often proceeded to establish their own firms. But unlike Valenza Po, Arezzo's informality bore the sign of the larger company's domination. The strategic decisions affecting local economic life, including what kind of knowledge was spread, were taken by one hegemonic actor.

Despite their very different economic structure, thus, Arezzo and Valenza Po converged towards similar information-sharing patterns. In Valenza Po, the absence of a clearly hegemonic actor and an extremely dispersed economic structure prevented knowledge about styles and tastes from becoming proprietary. At the same time, the informal networks in which such knowledge was generated and spread perpetuated the dispersion of the economic structure. Epistemic networks and production networks reinforced each other from the beginning. In Arezzo, by contrast, local conflict led to the informalization of knowledge transmission, previously routinized and made proprietary within Gori & Zucchi. Arezzo's simpler and more routinized knowledge compensated for the lack of a long-standing artisanal and commercial tra-

---

[52] Fabbriciani, *Partecipazione Umana*, 435–36.
[53] Quoted in Rossi, *Profilo Sociologico*, 91–92.

dition. Even in Arezzo informalization and economic dispersion went hand in hand. This process of convergence between the two towns, however, did not affect the *kind* of knowledge generated. The main source of innovation in Arezzo remained Gori & Zucchi. The emerging social networks challenged the company's hegemony, but they remained dependent on the innovative capabilities of Gori & Zucchi's formal structure and on its extensive ties to the market. In this sense, then, formality and informality were even more inextricably linked in Arezzo than in Valenza Po.

Patterns of Skill Formation

In the jewelry towns, production and transmission of knowledge relied on specific patterns of skill formation. Every new generation needed to be introduced to the technical foundations of the trade. And because of the interweaving of economic and sociopolitical ties, skill formation assumed the traits of a full-blown socialization process in which the new generations learned the explicit and implicit norms of their community. Intergenerational transmission of knowledge took place in two coexisting and yet potentially conflicting arenas: the personal and informal relationship between "master" and "apprentice," and the institutional curricula of the local technical schools. Apprenticeship, with its attention to the practical details of the trade, and formal schooling, with its emphasis on more theoretical skills, were meant to complement each other. But these two patterns of skill formation could also work at cross-purposes. The procedures for the admission to the two institutions were quite different. Formal schooling relied on an ethos of openness and impartiality that was potentially at odds with the personal and discretionary practices of apprenticeship. The two institutions also operated on the basis of different notions of merit, which in turn tended to upset the balance between personal ambitions and social expectations. Nobody was more threatening to the stability of the jewelry towns than an overeducated worker determined to question the foundations of the local social order. Skill formation also constituted a terrain of confrontation between local societies and the state, since education—at least in Italy—is one of the main concerns of public authorities. From a local perspective, one of the main goals of skill formation was the policing of the community's boundaries, but this exclusionary agenda clashed both with the culture of state bureaucrats and with the aspirations of the sections of local society that felt deprived of opportunities for social mobility.

The contradictions between apprenticeship and formal schooling were most evident in Valenza Po. The first school of design of the Piedmontese town was founded in 1852, almost at the same time as the establishment of the first jewelry firms. Revealingly, the school founders were members of the local Friendly Society (Società Operai e Artisti), who admitted to their classes boys older than eight and taught them the rudiments of linear drawing and decoration for four months a year. This was a three-year course that did not require any prerequisites beyond basic literacy. With the introduction of mandatory elementary education in 1859, the official age for admission was raised to eleven. In order to make the curriculum even more compatible with the needs of the local shops, in 1872 the commune transformed the institution into a night school.[54] Although enrollment data for these early decades are not available, the school remained for a long time a marginal institution in Valenza Po's social life. Formal education was little more than an integration of apprenticeship that involved small groups of kids in the idle spring months.

In the early twentieth century, the night school began to be regarded by sections of the growing working class as a venue for social promotion, and therefore it was embraced and supported by the local socialists. This process culminated in 1920–21, when the socialist-led city government took over the school management. The school goals grew more ambitious, aiming at training students "to read and comprehend the drawings of common and industrial objects with confidence and acquire the skills necessary to be creative according to the standards of their trade."[55] Consistently with this program, the school began to offer classes in both jewelry and shoe making, thereby catering to the needs of the two leading local industries. Enrollment increased accordingly, reaching sixty students in 1921.[56] The direct intervention of the local public authorities also changed the purpose of technical and artistic training vis-à-vis apprenticeship. School attendance became gradually more of a preparation course for future skilled workers and less of a mere integration to apprenticeship practices. For example, before

[54] Ratti, "Origini e evoluzione storica," 20.

[55] Archivio Storico del Comune di Valenza, vol. 1094, Scuola Tecnica di Valenza, folder Scuola Serale di Disegno.

[56] Jewelry making remained by far the most popular course, with forty-four students out of sixty.

the commune's takeover, students needed the signature of either their parents or their boss on their absence notes. The new regulations made the parents' signature the only option.

These changes should be set in the context of Valenza Po's class relations and of the state's growing intervention in shaping the purpose and characters of local schools. Despite the socialists' concerns, education remained strictly segregated by class. When the Fascist government set out to reform the national school system in 1923, Valenza Po's elite campaigned to retain a locally based education track at the junior-high level that enabled their children to continue their studies. The city council pleaded with the Ministry of Education by explicitly using the language of class distinction:

> Here [in Valenza Po] industry is very well developed. Therefore, the population is divided into two classes: the workers, who get their children a job in the factories after the sixth grade and have the opportunity to improve their kids' technical education at a thriving night school managed by the commune. . . ; and the class of the owners and manufacturers, who intend to provide their children with higher education and thus wish to have access to courses that allow the continuation of their studies so as not to be forced to send such young kids far away from their families.[57]

A compromise was finally reached by establishing a state technical school (Scuola Complementare Tecnica) for the children of Valenza Po's elite, who upon completion of the three-year course could take an examination and continue their studies at the high-school level.

Although the night school of design remained under the control of the city and kept awarding a terminal degree, the 1923 reform changed its education programs by introducing more academic disciplines such as general culture and geometry, a first step towards the transformation of the school into a complete course of post-elementary studies and its incorporation into the state education system. Moreover, the school management decided to add a fourth and a fifth optional class devoted to the teaching of clay and wax molding. As the teaching became more formalized and abstract, and the ambitions of the teachers and managers grew higher, the attitude of the local population to-

---

[57] Archivio Storico del Comune di Valenza, vol. 1094, Scuola Tecnica di Valenza, folder Scuola Complementare Tecnica, letter of the City Council to the Ministry of Education, dated 25 July 1923.

wards the school of design cooled down considerably. Although enrollment levels averaged approximately one hundred students in the 1920s, more than a third of these students dropped out of the program or simply did not show up for class. In 1929 the director accused the local manufacturers of boycotting the school: "[The industrialists], instead of encouraging the youngsters who are learning the trade in their shops, tell them that drawing is irrelevant, and that the discipline of modeling is absolutely useless."[58] Formal schooling was increasingly regarded as a dubious alternative to apprenticeship rather than a complement to it.

These kinds of complaints continued throughout the 1930s. In 1936, membership in one of the party's youth organizations was made compulsory for all students, which exacerbated the skepticism of large sections of Valenza Po's society towards the Fascist authorities. As a result, enrollment dropped from 102 in 1934–35 to 61 in 1937–38.[59] The authorities' only reaction to this drop in enrollment was to extend the scope of the school courses even further. For the first time, in 1938 girls were admitted to a one-year course for the training of shoe hemmers. Even so, only ten boys and girls registered for the first year of classes in 1940, as the breakout of the war brought teaching to a virtual halt.

The trend towards the formalization of education that had begun during the Fascist era continued in the postwar years. In the late 1940s, the local public authorities, the goldsmiths' association (AOV), and some of the leading companies, including the Illarios, resurrected a reform proposal dating back to 1941 and set out to transform the local night school of design into a day school completely integrated in the state education system. The main innovations included the opportunity for women to enroll in all the classes offered in jewelry making, the introduction of art history and "artistic culture" in the curriculum, and the increase of the minimum age for registration to fourteen. The new school kept students in class for six hours a day and nine months a year. Therefore, the students were encouraged to prioritize formal education and postpone their enrollment in an apprenticeship pro-

[58] Archivio Corrente del Comune di Valenza, IX-5/6 Scuola Serale di Disegno "Benvenuto Cellini" 1925–68, Luigi Ratti's letter to Valenza Po's Podestà dated 19 February 1929.

[59] Archivio Corrente del Comune di Valenza, IX-5/6 Scuola Serale di Disegno "Benvenuto Cellini" 1925–68, Luigi Vaccari's report dated 19 October 1939. Even the school's most prestigious teacher, Luigi Stanchi, was asked repeatedly to become a party member, which he managed to avoid through the end of the war.

gram. The goals of the school grew even more ambitious than in the prewar decades so as to include the training of artisans endowed with that "artistic sensibility" which only the close relationship between master and apprentice could traditionally provide.[60]

In 1951, the relentless campaigning of Valenza Po's politically engaged jewelers of both Catholic and leftist persuasion led to the establishment of the Istituto Professionale per l'Oreficeria (IPO), which in 1955 was appropriately named after Benvenuto Cellini. Relatively generous state funds, integrated by private contributions from the school founders and supporters, allowed the hiring of a first-rate faculty. In 1956, for example, the school opened the first public laboratory in the country specialized in gemmology and appointed Speranza Cavegnago, a self-taught Milanese woman who was the leading Italian expert in the field, as its director. For the next fifteen years the lab appraised precious stones for the local jewelry makers and trained dozens of gemmologists, before closing under the pressure of increasing insurance costs. Drawn to the school by the fame of its teachers and supported by special fellowships, students from all over Italy began to register for the IPO's classes. Enrollment increased from 27 students in 1951 (including the night course) to 190 in 1955.[61] In the late 1950s the commune built a dormitory for out-of-town students, as the school began to attract students from Canada, West Africa, and the Middle East.

This national and international success, however, failed to resonate with Valenza Po's local population. Many local manufacturers regarded the school curriculum as too abstract and as conducive to a sort of cultural arrogance that they found unsuitable to their needs. The local kids who intended to pursue a career as jewelry makers preferred to enroll in an apprenticeship program very early on, sometimes even before reaching the legal working age (fourteen). The families of the local elite, on the other hand, shunned the IPO as too technical and sent their children to Valenza Po's state accounting school or to a *liceo* in Alessandria. By the 1960s, the IPO's ethos, based on openness and impartiality, was very distant from the local firms' culture and prac-

[60] Archivio Corrente del Comune di Valenza, IX–5/6 Scuola Serale di Disegno "Benvenuto Cellini" 1925–68, Relazione sull'istituzione Scuola Tecnica d'Oreficeria in Valenza, 2–3.

[61] "L'Istituto Professionale di Oreficeria 'Benvenuto Cellini' di Valenza," *Rassegna Economica della Provincia di Alessandria* 8 (December 1955): 8.

tices. One of the small scandals engendered by this tension is particularly revealing. In 1965, the school admitted a group of students on a special fellowship granted by the National Board for the Assistance of Workers' Orphans (ENAOLI), who resided in the local dorm for three years. In 1970, however, few of the graduates found a job with Valenza Po's jewelry firms, and those few complained to the mayor about their pay and labor conditions. Embarrassed for the orphans' treatment, the mayor had to admit that he "had been aware for a long time of the fact that some of Valenza Po's jewelry firms have little respect for IPO's graduates and give them inadequate wages."[62]

The school managers themselves had to face the striking contrast between the international success of their classes and their failure to attract local students: "Many students go back to their countries, such as Guinea, Senegal, and Canada, to teach. The Italian students come from all over the country. Only the number of Valenza Po's students decreases every year. This year [1970] only one of the 210 graduates of the local junior high school has registered for our classes."[63] The solution to this lack of local enthusiasm, the managers argued, was the transformation of the IPO into a state art school (Istituto d'Arte), which had a four-year curriculum and awarded a degree valid for the admission to some university-level courses. The reform was implemented in 1970, but it did not change the attitude of Valenza Po's population, who remained skeptical of the school's educational goals and inclusive ethos.

At least until the end of the economic boom of the 1950s and 1960s, formal schooling was not necessary to pursue a career as jewelry maker at any level. Training started very early on, at age ten or eleven, when Valenza Po's kids were informally admitted to the factory premises as shopboys (*garzoncino* or, in the local dialect, *garsunné*). Family and neighborhood connections were key to securing a position for one's children, especially in the best-known shops, and the boy's tasks were ill-defined at best. Ginetto Prandi's experience was the norm: "At that time a father . . . would ask his friend to take his son to work, and [the boy] had to do a little bit of everything. . . . He would go buy some

---

[62] Archivio Corrente del Comune di Valenza, XI–2–2D Associazione Orafa Valenzana, Virgilio Piacentini's letter dated 29 November 1970.

[63] Minutes of the school's board of directors, quoted in Franco Cantamessa, "L'Istituto Professionale d'Oreficeria 'Benvenuto Cellini': Nascita e sviluppo di una scuola a misura di una città di orafi 1950–1970," *Valensa d'na Vota* 5 (1990): 105.

salt for the boss's wife, for example. This would be unthinkable today. But at the same time [the boss] taught him the trade."[64]

Only after a few years, at age sixteen to eighteen, was the boy formally hired as an apprentice. But more years would go by before the apprentice became a productive company member. This was a long and costly process that entailed a series of mutual obligations: "Shopboys remain such de facto, if not by pay, for several years. It is a burden you have to carry with you . . . for years."[65] On the other hand, apprentices, and especially the most promising ones, had to endure years of despotic paternalism from their "masters." Shop labor was organized along the principles of an informal and subtle hierarchy whose most evident sign of distinction was the distance of the worker's bench from the window. (The master sat right by the window, where natural light was best.) The strictness of some masters has marked Valenza Po's collective memory indelibly. Ido Bencini, one of the most proficient postwar modelists, betrayed a combination of respect and awe in his recollection of his master, G. Ponzone:

> Signor Ponzone directed and controlled everything in the factory. He was god almighty. He supervised every saw movement, every passage of sand paper, every soldering, and he always had some advice or reproach. Only after keeping an eye on you for several years, on how you handled the tools or the piece of jewelry you were working on, and on how you handed it over to the stone setter, did his lips finally utter the verdict: "This ring is perfect even without stones." This was a privilege that very few enjoyed, and it was tantamount to a university degree in jewelry making.[66]

Of course enduring the whims of a well-respected master was a privilege in itself, a rite of passage in Valenza Po's social hierarchy that no formal school course could replace.

This pattern of skill formation, which stressed the transmission of tacit knowledge through the personal relationship between master and apprentice, dated back to the establishment of the first jewelry firms in the late nineteenth century. Long-standing companies such as Melchiorre and Illario had trained hundreds of jewelry makers during their history. In these shops promotion was based on the master's rec-

---

[64] Interview by author, October 1996.
[65] Luciano Lenti, interview by author, October 1996.
[66] Quoted in Lenti, *Gioielli e Gioiellieri*, 429.

ognition of the apprentice's talent, and few values were more widely shared in Valenza Po than the necessity to reward artisanal proficiency. But talent is by definition an elusive trait whose recognition, at least in Valenza Po, relied on subjective methods of evaluation. The economic boom of the 1950s and 1960s led to the explosion of the tensions that lay latent in this artisanal ethos. First of all, the introduction of mechanized processes increased the demand for semiskilled workers who would never become proficient "masters." Moreover, labor regulation did not allow for the distinction between "talented" and "untalented" apprentices, and the generation that came of age in the 1960s turned to these formal rules to question the potentially discriminatory practices of the artisanal economy.

The graduates of the local technical schools were particularly likely to resent the personal nature of the master-apprentice relationship, from which they were often excluded. In 1969, for example, a "collective of students and workers" sent a letter to the mayor arguing that "employers in Valenza speculate on their apprentices. They hire them not to teach them a trade but to take advantage of cheap labor." These "apprentices" worked up to fifty-four hours a week, much longer than the legal limit, and they often did piecework, which the law ruled out explicitly for their category.[67] The collective also sent a petition to the Labor Department in Alessandria, signed by several organizations including the local branch of the Communist Party and the Chamber of Labor. In the wake of this kind of incident, the public authorities decided to crack down on apprenticeship, which became more regulated and costly for Valenza Po's firms. Combined with the new generations' more skeptical attitude towards the appeal of jewelry work, this regulation drive led to a veritable crisis of apprenticeship. The number of officially hired apprentices dropped from 1,704 in January 1968 to less than 500 in January 1975.[68] Following the general pattern of the local economy in these years (see chapter 2), the new regulatory zeal swelled the number of the workers engaged in the informal economy, rather than reducing it. Many young workers simply waited even longer to have their position regularized and skipped an official apprenticeship period altogether.

[67] Archivio Corrente del Comune di Valenza, XI–6–6 Legislazione sociale e sicurezza del lavoro 1925–69.

[68] Cantamessa, *AOV,* 139.

Valenza Po's patterns of skill formation were consistent with the town's informal mechanisms of knowledge generation and transmission. The personal and informal relations of apprenticeship were widespread and resilient, and they simultaneously constituted a framework for skill formation, a venue for social promotion, and an arena for the transmission and enforcement of the norms of craftsmanship. But this pattern of informality coexisted uneasily with the drive towards more open and inclusive institutions. The town's public authorities were particularly preoccupied with promoting formal education as part of a strategy to integrate local social life into state institutions. But their strategy clashed with the attitudes and behaviors of local actors, and therefore it was ultimately unsuccessful. The tension between the personal character of apprenticeship, fully consistent with the town's production and epistemic practices, and the open ethos of formal schooling was never resolved, but rather became a long-standing trait of Valenza Po's society.

The tension between apprenticeship and formal schooling informed skill formation in Arezzo as well, but in different ways. During its tumultuous growth of the 1950s, Gori & Zucchi's development was marred by the scarcity of skilled labor in the area. Although many of the company's production processes, such as linking, polishing, packaging, and so on, could be carried out by semiskilled and unskilled labor, the increasing adoption of sophisticated machines for casting and chain-making called for growing numbers of (male) workers with some expertise in metallurgy and mechanical engineering. In this period, the company implemented two parallel strategies. On the one hand, in 1954 Gori & Zucchi established a factory training program devoted to the teaching of technical drawing, mechanical engineering, and metallurgy, as well as general culture and math. On the other hand, the company externalized the training costs by promoting the creation of a public three-year course at the high-school level for the formation of skilled jewelry workers. Starting in 1954, the course was offered by the local technical school (Istituto Professionale), named after Margheritone, a medieval sculptor and architect from Arezzo. The ties between the two institutions were tight: G. Mazzini, the engineer who organized the company's training program, was a teacher at the "Margheritone." He then proceeded to become one of the two chief foremen at Gori & Zucchi.[69]

_____

[69] Fabbriciani, *Partecipazione Umana*, 55.

At least in their initial stages, factory apprenticeship and public education served complementary functions for Gori & Zucchi. The public school trained a pool of prospective skilled workers who were then screened within the company's internal labor market. Throughout the 1950s, an elaborate system of factory committees, which included both workers and managers, was in charge of making proposals for the promotion of individual workers. The "committee of the skilled workers" (Commissione degli operai specializzati), for example, evaluated the proficiency attained by individual apprentices. Another committee, which included only the foremen, distributed the productivity bonuses on an individual and discretionary basis (see chapter 4). Finally, a "committee of the elders" (Commissione degli Anziani), whose membership was limited to the most loyal employees, had a say in general management strategies.[70] Ideally, a large selection of the kids who graduated from the public school were hired by Gori & Zucchi as apprentices and put in the appropriate track according to their loyalty and ability. Thus public education was a way for Gori & Zucchi to socialize the costs and risks of the early stages of skill formation.

In the 1950s, therefore, Gori & Zucchi managed to establish a pattern of skill formation that offered the company the best of both worlds: the open and democratic ethos of public education on the one hand, and the personal and discretionary practices of "artisanal" apprenticeship on the other. But the discretionary power of the large company collapsed in later years under the double attack of unionized labor and state regulation. The cross-class factory committees were dismantled in the aftermath of a major strike in 1962 and replaced by union representatives with a radically egalitarian ethos. Moreover, a 1955 regulation prevented industrial (as opposed to artisanal) firms from choosing all but a small percentage of their apprentices. Instead, Gori & Zucchi had to draw from the lists of the public employment office (Ufficio di Collocamento). In 1968 another law forbade employers from assigning apprentices to assembly-line work.

These events brought Gori & Zucchi's strategy to an end. Skill formation became for the company an increasingly rigid and routinized process that the management was forced to negotiate with potentially hostile actors. But as the company's discretionary and paternalistic practices collapsed, public technical education took off. The students enrolled in the local technical schools that offered courses in jewelry

[70] Ibid., 63–64.

making (the "Margheritone," the technical institute that offered a five-year curriculum, and the art school) increased from 352 in 1961 to more than 1,300 in 1969. Unlike Valenza Po, public vocational education in Arezzo was a success. Informal training was not absent in Arezzo: It was (and is) customary for kids to do some homework in the summer months. This illegal work constituted "one of the earliest contacts, also in a material sense, with gold and silver, and therefore with the city's economic life."[71] But the figure of the shopboy, so common in Valenza Po, was unknown in Arezzo. Vocational education at a public school compensated for this lack of informal factory experience.

Despite these differences, however, public schooling did not disrupt Arezzo's informal economies. The constraints imposed on Gori & Zucchi by state regulation and organized labor made Arezzo's informal networks of small "artisanal" firms even more competitive. Apprenticeship in these smaller firms evolved into an extremely diverse and often exploitative set of practices. The left-wing administrators of the province noticed in the mid-1960s that Arezzo's ratio of apprentices over the total number of workers was twice as high as the national average. These apprentices' wages were 25 to 50 percent lower than workers' wages, and this differential was made even larger by the gap between the wages paid by the large companies such as Gori & Zucchi and those paid by the booming artisanal firms. These data led the administrators to define the indiscriminate use of apprenticeship as a "social evil."[72] There is little doubt that enrollment in a public technical schools became for many of Arezzo's families a defense strategy against potentially exploitative employers.

The relative success of formal schooling in Arezzo is further proof of the positive feedback mechanisms that linked formality and informality in the town's social life. Arezzo's epistemic patterns became increasingly informal in the postwar decades as a reaction to the formal and proprietary character of Gori & Zucchi's practices. The knowledge "stolen" from Gori & Zucchi was socialized in the informal arenas of family and neighborhood ties. But unlike Valenza Po, Arezzo's informality bore the sign of the larger company's domination. The strategic decisions affecting local economic life, including what kind of knowledge was spread, were taken by one hegemonic actor. Moreover, the local

[71] Alessandro Casini, "Vincoli Ecologici e Innovazione Imprenditoriale," laurea thesis, Facoltà di Economia, University of Siena, 1993–94, 53.

[72] Provincia di Arezzo, *Primo Convegno*, 33.

informal economy was to some extent functional to Gori & Zucchi's strategies. On the one hand, Arezzo's citizens viewed formal technical education as a venue for social promotion and as a step towards more open and democratic arrangements. On the other hand, however, a portion of the knowledge acquired in the public arena was then internalized by Gori & Zucchi, which hired the most promising graduates, thereby creating and extending a cycle that linked formal and informal relations, and proprietary and nonproprietary knowledge.

Throughout this chapter I have steered clear of discussing the relationship between knowledge and politics in terms of social and human capital, even though in the jewelry towns social networks were crucial to the development of local knowledge. Can these networks and skills be examined as forms of capital? And if that is the case, how did these forms of capital develop, and who has gained access to them, and how? My answer to the first question—whether local skills and social networks constitute forms of capital—is a qualified yes. Marx understood the formation of physical and financial capital as thoroughly historical and relational processes rooted in patterns of accumulation and expropriation. As Bourdieu argued many decades later, human and social capital can (and indeed should) be viewed in the same way, despite the methodological individualism that has informed the origin and use of these concepts. Thus, in late-nineteenth-century Valenza Po local skills were produced within networks of political relations whose cement was socialist ideology. Political affiliation could be translated into credit and knowledge for the production of marketable items. The collective nature of these transactions was irreducible to the rationality of single individuals. By the same token, in post–World War II Arezzo the large company tried to build social networks and local skills that were functional to its interests, before the company's privatizing agenda collided with the collective ambitions that the company itself had unwillingly fostered. The main analytical advantage to be gained by the study of these industrial districts lies in their ability to expose the irreducibly collective and relational character of economic action.

If local skills and social networks can be viewed as forms of capital, who gained access to them, and how? While actors in Valenza Po and Arezzo were fully aware of the collective character of local knowledge, this awareness only occasionally led to struggles to make such knowledge truly public—that is, dependent on openly deliberated rules of membership. The divergent attitude of the two towns towards public education is particularly revealing in this regard. After the Fascist era, local knowledge came to be viewed by Valenza Po's artisans as a communal resource to be negotiated vis-à-vis the demands of the state. Therefore, many of the town's residents shunned public education as incompatible with the tacit character of local skills. This attitude was contested for its exclusionary consequences, but it led nonetheless to the preservation of a communitarian form of artisanal economy in which access to knowledge and social connections was made collective (rather than public) within networks of personal relations. In Arezzo, by contrast, the local working class came to view the large company's proprietary knowledge as something to be expropriated and made accessible within the burgeoning "community" through alliances with public authorities and regulatory bodies. As a consequence, public education was embraced as a venue for social promotion. Even in Arezzo, however, these negotiations led to the construction of an increasingly secretive informal economy with its own exclusionary patterns.

In both Valenza Po and Arezzo actors needed to rely on their connections (social capital) in order to gain access to knowledge and skills (human capital). Both forms of capital, as well as the link between them, were an ongoing source of conflict and negotiations among unequal actors. On the basis of their emphasis on the importance of knowledge and network organization, these towns can indeed be viewed as post-Fordist political economies, but their communitarian and exclusionary practices fall short of a truly participatory form of democracy.

Constructing Locality: The Jewelry Towns,
the International Market, and the Italian State

T HE year 1967 was a busy one for the hundreds of thousands of people involved in the production and trade of gold worldwide. The devaluation of the British pound, the increasing deficit in the U.S. balance of payments, and widespread expectations of an impending devaluation of the American dollar drove the demand for gold through the roof. When President Johnson announced that the convertibility of the dollar might soon be repealed, speculators anticipated what would become a reality the following year—the creation of a double market for gold in which private agents would be free to find their own price as central banks kept exchanging the precious metal at the old price of thirty-five dollars per ounce. This would inevitably lead to a sharp rise in the price of gold in the free market. For the first time in many years, the supply of gold, 70 percent of which was mined in South Africa, could not keep up with world demand.[1] The largest Swiss banks were busy raking up all the gold they could find, acting as the main intermediaries between the London market—which until 1968 enjoyed exclusive rights on the commercialization of South African gold—and buyers worldwide. Given the widespread restrictions that many governments imposed on the circulation of gold, much of this metal was refined and recast in Switzerland and then smuggled to all corners of the globe. An astounding share of this illegal trade passed through Italy. According to a smuggler interviewed by the *Corriere della Sera*, the Italian daily, up to half a ton of gold a day illegally crossed the border between Switzerland and Italy in the hottest months of 1967. An unknown but substantial share of this gold also came from the Soviet Union, which had understandably decided to join the fray.[2]

In this context of febrile speculation, the demand for gold jewelry shot up, even though manufactured gold made up only 20 percent of world trade at the time. The Italian jewelry towns hummed with activ-

---

[1] "La febbre dell'oro," *L'Industria Orafa Italiana*, 25 March 1968, 17–24.
[2] See *L'Industria Orafa Italiana*, 25 September 1967, 29.

ity, trying to keep up with the barrage of orders. Jewelry traders, however, could not enjoy this bonanza without a degree of anxiety. The problem was that much of the gold they processed was imported in violation of a state monopoly dating back to the 1930s. Tons of gold were smuggled into the country to evade the steep taxes levied on its exchange. This flagrant illegality could hardly go unnoticed. In the summer of 1967, some of Arezzo's most prominent companies received the visit of the tax police, who demanded to see the invoices for the gold that lay on the premises. Since no documentation could be produced, the officials fined the companies millions of lire. For the first time since the end of the war, despite the exceptionally favorable economic conjuncture, workers had to be laid off. Entrepreneurs immediately turned to Leopoldo Gori, the town's most powerful industrialist, who was simultaneously their foremost supplier and their main competitor. Gori wasted no time and turned to the Chamber of Commerce, the minister of finance, the minister of industry, and a variety of other Christian Democratic members of the government, asking them to turn a blind eye on the jewelry trade's less than pristine practices. Within a few weeks, an agreement was reached. The tax police were instructed to give the Italian jewelry producers a break, while Gori promised the government that the jewelry traders would agree to pay a one-off tax in the near future.

This story shows the ingredients of social capital at work: social networks were mobilized, trust was exchanged, and norms of reciprocity were enacted. The Swiss gold traders relied on the tight ties that bound Arezzo's economic actors to one another, Arezzo's companies knew that they could count on Gori's intermission and sense of community (he did not take advantage of the situation to get rid of his competitors), and Gori could trust the government officials to adapt regulations to the "exceptional" circumstances faced by the jewelry industry. Global networks, local solidarity, and party affiliations all played a role in guaranteeing the continuing success of the jewelry towns. Economic competitiveness and political consensus built on each other.

But these relations were a far cry from the kind of open and democratic social capital extolled by Putnam and others. Secrecy and murky negotiations were its hallmarks. Putnam contrasts the morality of sociability with the costly and coercive nature of state control: "The social contract that sustains . . . collaboration in the civic community is not legal but moral."[3] From this perspective, the vibrancy and richness of civil society in northern Italy relegates the state to a very limited role. Consistent with Putnam's argument, the literature on the Italian industrial districts has ignored the role of the state in facilitating the development of small-scale capitalism, contrasting the spontaneous growth of the Third Italy with the government-supported industrialization of the industrial triangle (Turin-Milan-Genoa) and of the south.[4] But, to use Putnam's language, the historical analysis of the jewelry towns' political economy suggests that the legalities of political control and the moralities of civic interaction cannot be so easily divorced.

In this chapter I will move from the ties of locality to other social and geographical spaces, namely the economic sector at the national level and its international connections. I will examine three interrelated processes: the impact of the global gold trade on the Italian jewelry industry; the development of an extensive informal economy based on gold smuggling and tax evasion; and the political negotiations surrounding gold fineness standards. The general argument of this chapter is that state control, with its multiple rationalities, actively reproduced and sustained the ties of locality on which industrial districts relied. Key actors in each jewelry district were often able to use formal regulation to their advantage by establishing ad hoc compromises with the regulators, and such compromises were crucial to the cohesion and success of local societies. The coexistence of formal and informal relations, a hallmark of the social life of the jewelry towns, was reproduced at the level of national institutions. The successful manipulation of state regulation by key local actors provided the jewelry districts with powerful competitive advantages vis-à-vis their domestic and international rivals. Gold smuggling and tax evasion, which were two sides of the same largely tolerated strategy, were translated into low costs and prices both in the domestic and in the international markets. The evidence suggests that powerful international traders, such as the Swiss banks, chose the Italian districts as their favorite customers also on account of this opportunity. The ability to work out compromises with the state also prevented local fractures from escalating into open conflict.

---

[3] Putnam, *Making Democracy Work*, 183.

[4] See, for example, Franco Amatori and Andrea Colli, *Impresa e Industria in Italia* (Venice, 1999), 281–91. For a review of the literature on the contrast between spontaneous and state-supported development in Italy, see Alaimo, *Un'Altra Industria?* 71–76.

Although these features are in many ways peculiar to the character of the Italian state, these cases raise some general questions concerning the nature of state regulation in modern societies. This chapter attempts to show that—contrary to the assumptions of most scholars of bureaucracy—rules of fiscal conduct, as well as consumption and production standards, are inherently ambiguous. In order to be effective, these seemingly impartial institutions must serve diverse and often contradictory purposes. For example, tax policies have to uphold the prestige and material needs of the state and also allow for the viability of local economic prosperity. Similarly, standards are meant to promote the use of technical routines to settle controversies despite the inherently conventional and consensual nature of the routines themselves. These ambiguities can lead to compromises that often sanction complexity and diversity rather than restrict them. It is this ritualistic character of standards, so evident in the Italian case, that makes state regulation a problematic and yet successful sign of modernity.

"We Are All Criminals": The Jewelry Towns, the State, and the International Gold Market

In January 1955, Vicenza's main newspaper, *Il Giornale di Vicenza*, ran a front-page article whose title read "Even our wedding bands are illegal." The journalist reported on the plight of the city's jewelry manufacturers and explained that the bulk of the gold processed by the city's 160 jewelry firms was smuggled. He argued that this widespread illegality was attributable to the state monopoly on the importation of gold, an anachronistic measure that had survived the fall of Fascism. After analyzing the implications of this measure for the jewelry trade, the less than impartial journalist declared that this was a "corrupting law in and of itself," and that "either the state works seriously toward normalization or it bans gold jewelry production altogether."[5]

Two years later, Luigi Illario, Valenza Po's manufacturer of high-quality jewelry and the town's foremost Catholic politician, spoke similar words in front of the highest representatives of Italy's economic power. In March 1957, at the beginning of the export boom that was about to turn the Italian jewelry industry into an international success,

---

[5] "Anche le nostre fedi matrimoniali sono illegittime," *Il Giornale di Vicenza*, 21 January 1955.

Illario addressed the general conference of the Italian industrialists in Milan. It was the first time that a jewelry maker was given this opportunity, and the stakes for the trade were high. But instead of focusing on the achievements of his colleagues, Illario began his speech with these words: "Personally, I have been breaking the law for twenty years. I am a criminal on parole."[6] The law in question was again the state monopoly on the importation of raw gold. Not only did he buy smuggled gold, Illario argued, he also had to forge invoices to justify the metal he processed. These words resonated with the opinions of Guido Invernizzi, the president of the national association of jewelry makers, who in 1956 informed the public authorities that the state monopoly forced the Italian jewelers to deal with "individuals with whom they'd rather have nothing to do."[7]

The state monopoly had been established by the Fascist government in 1935, at the height of the Ethiopian crisis and the regime's drive towards autarchy.[8] The rationale for the monopoly was to provide state authorities with virtually total control over crucial international transactions and monetary policy. In particular, the measure was viewed as a stepping-stone towards war mobilization and state control over the supply of imported raw materials.[9] Like other Fascist initiatives, this law was preserved long after the fall of the regime, with the rationale that it was necessary to save hard currencies for the importation of goods more important than gold to the reconstruction effort. Until 1968, only the Bank of Italy could import raw gold through the Italian Exchange Office (Ufficio Italiano Cambi) and, except for ad hoc initiatives, private agents had no access to this legally imported metal, which served the purposes of monetary regulation. The legal venues for the supply of gold to manufacturers included coins, whose importation was permitted; recycled metal and residues from domestic production; and semifinished or finished gold products, whose importation required a special license. The temporary importation of gold was

[6] "L'intervento del Rag. Luigi Illario all'assemblea generale confederale," *Informatore Settimanale della Provincia di Alessandria*, 8 March 1957.

[7] Archivio della Camera di Commercio di Arezzo, vol. XIII-8-1/2, Industria Meccanica Orafa, fascicolo Industria Orafa, report of the Federazione Nazionale Orefici Fabbricanti, dated April 1956.

[8] This measure was introduced with Royal Decree number 1935, issued on November 14, 1935 and later converted into law.

[9] For more details, see Giuseppe Di Nunzio, *Oro Come Oro* (Rome, 1986), chaps. 1 and 2.

also allowed, but the whole amount of the metal, short of the manufacturing-related wear and tear, had to be reexported without ownership changes. These restrictions flew in the face of an extremely agile and increasingly global black market, which began to channel hundreds of tons of gold into Italy after the early 1950s. Another widespread practice was for foreign traders to cross the border into Italy with an often substantial amount of gold, hand it over to an Italian jewelry producer for processing, and finally place the merchandise abroad—all in violation of Italian commercial and fiscal laws.

The state monopoly set Italy apart from other major producers of jewelry such as France and West Germany, where restrictions on gold trade were dropped or significantly eased after the end of the war. Yet the international position of Italy vis-à-vis its competitors improved enormously from the late 1950s on, when much of Europe began to be flooded with Italian jewelry. Not only was illegal gold widely available for the domestic market; it also managed to cross the Italian borders twice, first as raw metal and second as manufactured goods. The officially reported export of gold jewelry, which woefully underestimated the actual trade, rose from 4.6 billion lire in 1957 to 55.8 billion lire ten years later—a twelvefold increase. The achievement of international competitiveness in the presence of such severe restrictions is a conundrum whose explanation lies just across the Italian border, in the orderly and sedate towns of Canton Ticino, Switzerland. It was here that the main Swiss banks located some of the world's largest gold refineries, and it was from these refineries that the metal found its way to the Italian jewelry manufacturers.

The privileged relationship between the Swiss banks and the Italian jewelry industry dates back to the early 1950s. The London gold market, the world's main venue for gold trading since the early eighteenth century, shut down from 1939 to 1954 on account of the war. This allowed the Swiss to dramatically expand a trading role that they had been nurturing since the early part of the century. Because of their size and reputation, three banks became especially involved in the gold business: Swiss Bank Corporation, Swiss Credit, and Union Bank of Switzerland. In addition to acting as brokers in the booming markets of East Asia and the Middle East, these banks began to refine South African gold, taking advantage of London's temporary inactivity. It was at this juncture that in 1951 Union Bank of Switzerland (UBS) established a partnership with some local entrepreneurs to found Argor, a refinery of precious metals at Chiasso, a stone's throw from the border with Italy. Argor's main function was to handle the South African ingots, which UBS bought directly or (after 1954) in the London market, and bring their content of pure gold from 916 to at least 995 millesimals. Argor also recast the standard ingots into bars of different sizes for industrial or investment purposes. By the mid-1960s, the company refined more than 250 tons of gold a year, a full quarter of the world production. The national origins of Argor's personnel testify to the strong links between the company and the Italian market: in 1967, twenty-five of the forty workers were Italian citizens, as was the company's director.[10]

Argor's success inspired other local entrepreneurs. After working at UBS's gold trade office in Zurich for several years, Emilio Camponovo returned to his native Chiasso in the mid-1960s and founded Valcambi, another company specialized in the refining of precious metals. In 1967, in the wake of the exceptional surge in demand for gold, Swiss Credit decided to establish a partnership with Camponovo and purchased a large share in Valcambi, eventually taking over the company in 1980. With the crucial contribution of the powerful bank, Valcambi soon became a major player in the gold business, employing up to 350 workers and eventually capturing 40 percent of the Italian market for raw gold. Of course it was no coincidence that two of the three largest Swiss banks chose to locate their gold refineries in the Chiasso area.[11] Easy access to the booming Italian jewelry industry was crucial to the success of these initiatives. With the more recent addition of PAMP, founded by some of Valcambi's former employees near Chiasso, the Swiss town has come to assume some of the characteristics of a specialized industrial district, with constant circulation of personnel and information, an efficient technical and financial infrastructure, and a high level of social control exercised over the people involved in the business. As Camponovo told me in an interview, a refinery worker could not spend hundreds of francs at a night club without being immediately spotted and questioned.[12]

This kind of tight control extended to the Italian entrepreneurs who transformed the refineries' gold into jewelry, often on commission. The link between the Swiss banks and the Italian jewelry industry cut both

---

[10] *L'Industria Orafa Italiana*, 25 November 1967, 54.

[11] The third bank, Swiss Bank Corporation, established Metalor, a refinery near Neuchâtel that catered to the needs of the local watchmakers.

[12] Interview by author, June 2002.

ways. The size of the Italian market was crucial to the banks' localization decisions, and the easy access to Swiss gold greatly reinforced the geographical pattern of the Italian jewelry industry. Actors in the three jewelry towns developed personal contacts with the Swiss agents, establishing a symbiotic relationship from which both parties benefited. In other words, the international gold market, a global business par excellence, generated social and geographical nodes bound by the ties of locality.

In contrast with Italy, gold trade in Switzerland was completely unrestricted. Until 1980, when a tax was levied on the purchasing of gold not destined to be exported, anybody could easily sell and buy any amount of precious metal tax-free. This disparity attracted to Canton Ticino and other regions of Switzerland a veritable army of smugglers, who crossed the borders into Italy, France, and West Germany on a regular basis, hiding gold bars in their cars or under their clothes. For large quantities of metal, smugglers devised all kinds of tricks, including the replacement of entire parts of their cars (the spare tire, the fenders, and so on) with solid gold casts.[13] In the Italian case, many of these smugglers were Swiss or Italian agents specialized in this kind of trade and often connected to the Milanese underworld. In addition to supplying the Italian gold jewelry industry, smuggled gold traveled through the peninsula on its way to India and the Middle East. While Switzerland grew into the world supermarket for gold, Italy became the place where gold could vanish for a while to reappear as stylish jewelry or discretely pass through to replenish the hoarders' stashes in all corners of the globe. While the Swiss banks did not need to get directly involved with these dealings, they did nothing to hinder them.

The Italian government was perfectly aware of the fact that the peninsula was becoming the international crossroads for gold smuggling. The most prominent jewelry manufacturers never tired of complaining to government officials about the situation, which exposed them both to irresistible temptations and unpredictable risks. The large availability of cheap smuggled gold cannot be overestimated as an enabling factor in the jewelry production boom and as an international competitive advantage that Italian manufacturers were eager to exploit. But the same manufacturers had to constantly negotiate with the government to find viable compromises. As we have seen, pleas for regular-

---

[13] See, for example, "Argomenti e Problemi," *L'Industria Orafa Italiana*, 15 Feburary 1957, 5–12.

ization by jewelry producers and traders were very common, while state officials were caught in a dilemma that seemed to have no solution. The main goal of the state monopoly was to avoid a hemorrhage of hard currencies, but since much of the illegal gold trade took place in American dollars, they could neither repeal the monopoly and condone a potentially damaging activity nor face the social and political consequences of a major crackdown. Therefore, starting in the mid-1950s they took steps to at least reduce the phenomenon through ad hoc initiatives that accorded them a degree of control.

In 1957 the Department of Foreign Commerce yielded to the jewelry trade's pressures and decided to allocate 4.3 extra tons of pure gold for industrial use in order to reduce the dearth of precious metal and the producers' need to resort to the black market. The national goldsmiths' association, Confedorafi, was given the task of supervising the distribution of the metal, with the explicit promise that this was only the first deal in what it hoped would be a fruitful relationship between the government and the trade's representatives. The problem was that the price of this legal gold, taking account of several taxes as well as insurance and transportation costs, was four thousand lire higher per kilogram than the metal available in the black market. Moreover, producers were supposed to pay in American dollars, which needed to be wired to one of the Italian Exchange Office branches abroad.[14] When Confedorafi began to collect the orders for the metal, it became painfully clear that only explicit pressures by the association on its members could avoid an embarrassing fiasco. The association had to lobby extensively to convince its members to place orders for the legal gold made available, while specialized traders strongly resented the association's interference.[15] On the one hand, this episode revealed the extent of gold smuggling and its advantages for the jewelry trade. On the other hand, the association's mobilization demonstrated that it was possible to achieve a *modus vivendi* with the state and its monopoly. Aware of the political connections made possible by this bureaucratic structure, the periodical of Confedorafi asked rhetorically in 1966: "Who guarantees that gold imports are allocated exclusively to the trade agents and not to unknown speculators who can then channel the metal to uses that have nothing to do with us, including

[14] See *L'Industria Orafa Italiana*, 15 August 1957, 20–22.

[15] *Atti del IV Convegno Nazionale Orafi e Argentieri, Vicenza, 13 settembre 1957* (Vicenza, 1958), especially Guido Invernizzi's statements.

hoarding?"[16] In other words, Confedorafi suggested that strict regulations prevented gold from ending up in the "wrong" hands. Moreover, personal relations and off-the-book agreements between trade representatives and state officials made possible ad hoc adjustments of the supply of gold.

The Italian government took another step towards the liberalization of the gold market in 1968, in the early stages of the general upheaval that shook the international monetary system and led to the end of the Bretton Woods regulatory arrangements in 1971.[17] The price of gold had been pegged by Roosevelt in 1934 at approximately thirty-five dollars per ounce, and this level remained the cornerstone of the monetary system after the end of the war, since it was at this price that the Federal Reserve pledged to convert U.S. dollars into gold upon request and at any time. In 1961, as world demand for gold escalated, the central banks of the largest Western economies, including Italy, established a "pool" to coordinate their efforts to hold the price of gold steady. This goal became increasingly unrealistic after 1966, when the growing deficit of the U.S. balance of payments raised the pressure on the dollar to unprecedented levels and forced the Federal Reserve to sell ever-growing quantities of precious metal to sustain the currency. By March 1968 it became clear that the old system was no longer sustainable, and the governments of the gold pool, in a last-ditch effort to save the convertibility of the U.S. dollar, agreed to create a two-tier market by which exchanges between the central banks still took place at the old price, while private agents were free to negotiate new price levels. This agreement lasted until 1971, when Nixon finally decided to suspend convertibility once and for all, thereby demonetizing gold and reducing it to the rank of any other commodity.

The 1968 agreement made it impossible for the Bank of Italy to continue its role as direct supplier of gold to the jewelry manufacturers, which the central bank had assumed in the late 1950s. Therefore, a new system was devised according to which the main Italian banks became intermediaries between the government, which did not repeal its monopoly, and the jewelry producers. This meant that jewelry companies needed to apply to the Italian Exchange Office for the allotment of gold batches and indicate what bank they intended to deal with. The metal

---

[16] *L'Orafo Italiano*, 10 October 1966, 18.

[17] For a useful review of the gold trade by an expert in the field, see Timothy Green, *The New World of Gold* (New York, 1981).

was then sent to the intermediary bank and sold at the current market price plus transaction and transportation costs. The jewelry company was also responsible for keeping track of the metal, documenting the transactions it went through, and paying the corresponding taxes.[18] Its higher price and the need to carefully document it made sure that legal gold remained less competitive than smuggled gold, but the new system eased some of the pressure on the most prominent and visible jewelry manufacturers, who could finally justify at least some of the metal they processed. The new system also wove tight ties between the jewelry producers and the banks, which for the first time regarded the jewelry industry as an opportunity for steady profits. In addition to the major national banks, such as Credito Italiano and Banca Commerciale Italiana, the smaller banks located in the jewelry towns became regular suppliers of gold for the jewelry manufacturers. Such was the role played by Cassa di Risparmio di Alessandria in Valenza Po, Banca Popolare Vicentina in Vicenza, and Banca Popolare del Lazio e dell' Etruria in Arezzo.

The 1968 reform of the gold market did not lead to the end of the informal practices that had made the fortune of the Italian gold jewelry industry in the postwar decades. Smuggling continued unabated, mostly because the use of smuggled gold allowed the jewelry producers and traders to evade the steep taxes levied by the government. If anything, the transactions between the jewelry industry and the global gold market tended to assume even shadier overtones in the 1980s and 1990s. The jewelry towns (especially Vicenza and Arezzo) found themselves repeatedly at the epicenter of international police investigations linking Swiss brokers, the Colombian and Peruvian drug traffickers, and a group of international traders based in Panama and specialized in money laundering. This seems to explain why Panama was the second importer of Italian gold jewelry after the United States for much of the 1990s.[19] However extreme, this is a particularly revealing exam-

---

[18] For these reasons, the new system received a lukewarm response from the Italian jewelers' association. See "Per un commercio regolare dell'oro si impone l'abolizione del monopolio," *L'Orafo Italiano*, September 1968, 34–36.

[19] David E. Kaplan, "The Golden Age of Crime: Why International Drug Traffickers Are Invading the Global Gold Trade," *US News and World Report*, November 29, 1999. This mechanism is well known to the U.S. State Department as well: "Gold serves as both a commodity and, to a lesser extent, a medium of exchange in money laundering conducted in Latin America, the United States, Europe and Asia. In this cycle, for example, gold bullion makes its way to Italy via Swiss brokers. There it is made into jewelry,

ple of the ways in which the Italian industrial districts turned the ties of locality, of which trust is a crucial but problematic component, into a source of competitive advantage in the age of globalization. In the face of ongoing illegality, in 2000 the Italian government finally repealed the state monopoly on the importation of gold.[20] While the metal imported for manufacturing remained subject to taxation, Italian agents could now import gold for investment purposes tax-free. Since it is nearly impossible for the government to make sure that the tax-free gold is not channeled to the jewelry manufacturers, the new regulatory regime has effectively liberalized the market. As far as raw gold is concerned, the game of cat and mouse that the Italian jewelers played with the state for decades has ended with the substantial victory of the industry's representatives.

The Jewelry Towns, the State, and Tax Evasion

One of the problems (and opportunities) faced by the jewelry producers was that smuggled gold was not only cheaper and more readily available than legal gold but also that it allowed producers and traders to hide their activities from the state and dodge taxes. Until 1955, the purchase of raw gold and gold coins was subjected to a steep 8 percent tax, since gold for industrial use was regarded as a raw material for the production of consumer goods. After seven years of extensive lobbying by jewelry and gold traders, the government repealed the tax both on the importation of coins and on the purchasing of raw gold within the Italian borders, while the importation of raw gold remained the prerogative of the state. This measure was hailed by the trade representatives as a major victory.[21] The government seemed to have finally embraced three of the arguments espoused by the jewelers: first,

---

much of which is then shipped to Latin America. In Latin America, this jewelry (or the raw gold from which it was made) then becomes one, if not the most important, of the commodities in the black market peso," http://www.state.gov/p/inl/rls/nrcrpt/1999/928.htm, accessed on 29 January 2006. These should be regarded only as well-documented allegations. To my knowledge no one in the jewelry towns has been convicted for these kinds of crimes.

[20] Law number 7/2000, issued in February 2000. This law was also approved under pressure from the European Union, since the Italian state monopoly contrasted with the spirit of the Maastricht agreement, advocating the free circulation of goods.

[21] See "Esenzione IGE," *L'Orafo Italiano*, November 1955, 22–24.

gold jewelry could not be considered a consumer good but rather a form of savings; second, the state had an obvious interest in fostering the inflow of precious metals; and third, the tax created an irresistible incentive for the manufacturers and traders to engage in gold smuggling.[22] This was only the first of a long series of episodes in which the traders took advantage of the ambiguous status of gold jewelry, which could be seen alternatively as a consumption good or as a form of family savings, and as the luxury item par excellence or as a widely popular product linked to a variety of mass rituals.[23]

Despite the lofty aspiration of the trade leaders, the repeal of the sales tax on raw gold and the increased availability of "official" metal after the mid-1950s failed to regularize the jewelry trade. Jewelers did not buy smuggled gold simply because of its lower price. The black market for gold allowed producers and traders to evade the 8 percent tax on the sale of gold jewelry (the infamous IGE), which in theory had to be applied at every passage of the merchandise, from the producer through the wholesaler to the retailer. Widespread tax evasion mandated a high degree of coordination between the components of the jewelry trade. Gold sold under the table at one point could not come to the surface at a later phase of the production and commercialization processes. Moreover, secrecy forged ties of complicity between all sectors of the trade. The unofficial gold that passed through the specialized gold traders (*banchi metalli*), for example, was registered in the companies' books as metal "sold over the counter" so as to conceal the name of the buyer. This applied even to transactions involving many kilograms of gold.[24] The rationale for this practice was to make the tax police's job as hard as possible in case of an enforcement drive. Through these dealings, as we have seen in the case of Valenza Po, gold suppliers and jewelry manufacturers established trust-informed relationships that could be extended to the level of credit.

[22] This tax was repealed with law number 481 issued on 12 June 1955. See Giorgio Quercia, *Attuali Aspetti dell'Imposizione tributaria nel Settore Orafo-Argentiero e degli Oggetti Preziosi*, report to the national conference on the problems of the jewelry industry held in Florence on 16–17 November 1974, 6–7, preserved at the Archivio della Camera di Commercio di Arezzo, vol. XIII-8-1/2, folder Nominativi ditte orafe.

[23] Ing. Beretta, "Approvvigionamento dell'oro: Relazione alla tavola rotonda di Vicenza," *L'Orafo Italiano*, September 1964, 36.

[24] Archivio della Camera di Commercio di Arezzo, vol. 13, Oreficeria Varie, IGE 4, untitled folder, relazione del Presidente Confedorafi Comm. Amirante al Convegno Orafi di Vicenza, dated 11 September 1970, 8.

The 8 percent sales tax was much higher than the average level of taxation, since gold jewelry was regarded as a luxury. Throughout the 1950s and early 1960s, the representatives of the trade lobbied heavily with the government to have this measure changed. They appealed to two main characteristics of their production in their efforts to change its status. First, gold jewelry could not be regarded as a luxury because it played a key role in the social life of the majority of Italians, from baptism gifts to wedding rings. Its symbolic value distinguished jewelry from furs and expensive cars and made it almost necessary to all social classes. As the president of the jewelry manufacturers' association argued in 1956, gold jewelry "cultivates the sense of beauty and art, it promotes familial affection and religiosity, and it also allows the least privileged to accumulate a small patrimony."[25]

Second, the jewelers argued, tax officials should not take the high value of their production as an indication of high levels of value added or profits. Leopoldo Gori and other leading manufacturers engaged in a campaign devoted to convincing the government of the narrowness of their profit margins. In a detailed report sent to several national politicians and members of government in 1960, Gori estimated the manufacturing costs of a gram of mass-produced jewelry (for example, a simple chain or a wedding ring) at 40 lire. Since the value of 18-carat gold was approximately 530 lire, the 8 percent sales tax amounted to 45.6 lire, more than the cost of manufacturing itself. In practice, Gori argued, the payment of the tax even at only the final passage from retailer to consumer forced jewelry producers to work at a loss. The situation for the manufacturers of more elaborate jewelry was even worse, given the high taxes on precious stones.[26]

The jewelers' campaign was successful. In 1963, the government reduced the IGE on gold jewelry from 8 percent to 4.5 percent. Government officials admitted that "tax pressure is so high that economic agents in the industry are often induced to evade the tax, which in many cases damages their activities to the point of paralysis."[27] On the one hand, this was an implicit admission of the importance of tax eva-

[25] Archivio della Camera di Commercio di Arezzo, vol. XIII-8-1/2, Industria Meccanica Orafa, folder Industria Orafa, Guido Invernizzi's typed report in April 1956, 1.

[26] Archivio della Camera di Commercio di Arezzo, vol. 13, Oreficeria Varie, IGE 4, untitled folder, Le Conseguenze Passate, Presenti e Future di Leggi Inappropriate con Inadeguati Istituti per la Loro Applicazione e la Repressione degli Abusi, dated 20 October 1960, 19–20.

[27] Law number 190 issued on 13 February 1963.

sion in promoting the economic "miracle" of the previous years. On the other hand, the tax reduction exposed the main strategy pursued by the state until that moment. The state tried to compensate for high levels of tax evasion with extremely steep taxes, thereby triggering a vicious circle of which the state itself was as much the victim as the promoter. In 1963, government officials hoped to regularize the industry by easing the general fiscal pressure on producers and traders. It was preferable to get less from every agent than virtually nothing at all from anyone.

The 1963 tax reduction was also part of a strategy carried out by public officials and aimed at discriminating between legal and illegal agents as sharply as possible. In pursuing this strategy, tax officials responded to the jewelers' ongoing pleas for the necessity to battle "unfair" competition. The trade representatives and the leading industrialists employed a rhetorical repertoire whose main purpose was to contrast their attempts to play by the rules with the unscrupulous behavior of the *clandestini*, a rather vague category that served an essentially rhetorical purpose. In the jewelers' reports to the public authorities, these agents embodied all the evils of the trade. As Gori put it, "This is not healthy competition that, if carried out by legal and loyal means, is a source of prosperity. In the gold jewelry industry, the unscrupulous agents and the *clandestini* resort to all forms of abuse and illegal behavior, including the breech of labor contracts and standards, the production of fraudulent jewelry, and the total neglect of tax laws."[28] The vague identity attributed to these agents, however, exposed the problematic nature of these remarks. The mysterious *clandestini* could be depicted as all-powerful "foreigners and stateless traders" whose practices included gold smuggling and shady dealings with organized crime,[29] or they might be identified as "retired civil servants who travel abroad and in Italy on behalf of small-scale producers to round out their pension."[30] In other reports, the trade representatives

[28] Archivio della Camera di Commercio di Arezzo, vol. 13, Oreficeria, IGE, Anni 1960–66, folder 14, Le Conseguenze Passate, Presenti e Future di leggi inappropriate con Inadeguati Istituti per la Loro Applicazione e la Repressione degli Abusi, undated memo, 10.

[29] Archivio della Camera di Commercio di Arezzo, vol. 13, Oreficeria Varie, IGE 4, folder IGE Atti più importanti, sottofascicolo Appello della Gori & Zucchi Aprile 1969, Ancora un Provvedimento Amministrativo per gli Orafi non in Regola con l'IGE, 12. Of course "stateless" (*apolide*) was often a euphemism for Jewish.

[30] *Atti del VI Convegno Nazionale Orafi e Argentieri, Vicenza, 14 settembre 1959* (Vicenza, 1960), 45.

defined the *clandestini*, who were "nothing but parasites," as at least as numerous as official agents, thereby implying that most family businesses fell in this category.[31] The ill-defined identity of these agents betrayed the fuzziness of the boundaries between the formal and the informal economies at the local level. In fact, all agents, including the largest manufacturers and Gori himself, engaged in the practices attributed to the *clandestini* and actively supported them. As we have seen, even the leading representatives of the trade openly admitted their "wrongdoing" when such admissions served their cause.

Most importantly, the ill-defined identity of the *clandestini* was the result of the contradictory and paradoxical attitude of the jewelers (both manufacturers and traders) towards state authority. Although the jewelers called on the state to regulate their trade more effectively, the boundaries between "fair" and "unfair" competition were extremely blurred, both in theory and in practice. The jewelers' campaigns were predicated on the coexistence of at least two very different and largely incompatible notions of fairness. The first notion, based on what we might call the morality of the ideal market, saw the state as an impartial institution whose main purpose was to set clear and enforceable rules of conduct in order to distinguish sharply between the law-abiding agents and the unscrupulous traders who populated the informal economy. In this scenario, competition was limited to costs, prices, and product quality. "Official" actors had a vested interest in upholding the normative structure of the trade to the point of denouncing the deviants as swiftly and ruthlessly as possible. Davide Ventrella, the president of Confedorafi in the early 1960s, noted that the public authorities repeatedly urged the jewelers to expose their unscrupulous colleagues to the tax police. But he could not think of any instance in which this recommendation had been followed.[32]

The second notion of fairness that informed the jewelers' ideology explains their reluctance to "collaborate" with the tax police and other enforcement authorities. Rather than on the impersonal and inflexible sanction of the state, this model of fairness was based on reciprocity. Protracted relations and negotiations between economic agents and state officials created expectations that were to be fulfilled. The moral

---

[31] Archivio della Camera di Commercio di Arezzo, vol. XIII-8-1/2, Industria Meccanica Orafa, folder Industria Orafa, report of the Federazione Nazionale Orefici Fabbricanti, dated April 1956.

[32] *Atti dell'VIII Convegno Nazionale Orafi e Argentieri, Vicenza, 9 settembre 1961* (Vicenza, 1962), 63.

principle underlying this notion was the morality of social exchange, and the act differentiating between fair and unfair competitors was the keeping of a promise, rather than the impartial sanction of the state. As we have seen, tax laws were not set in stone, and economic agents tried to manipulate this flexibility to their advantage by forging alliances with key public officials.

A revealing example of the paradoxes engendered by this notion was the condition of those manufacturers and traders who declared only a portion of their revenue, that is, the vast majority of the Italian jewelers. Partial evasion had the unwelcome consequence of making firms visible, which in turn increased the likelihood of fiscal controls. But such controls, as Gori and others argued, only favored total dodgers.[33] Gori went as far as to define the practices followed by the jewelers as courageous. Jewelry producers kept promoting economic development in the face of risks of all sorts: "Even Garibaldi did not follow the norms of his day, but once he achieved his successes *by the means at his disposal*, he did not hesitate to offer them to the cause of national unity."[34] It was not "fair" for state authorities to punish companies like Gori's for their bravery and visibility. Therefore it was necessary to work out specific agreements. Negotiations could be quite straightforward. At the beginning of 1967, for example, Gori met with the president of Confedorafi and two high-ranking officials from the Finance Ministry. The outcome of the meeting was the decision that "in this period . . . the tax police will be given instructions not to intervene in our industry with controls that raise the serious danger of undermining or even shutting down the activities of our firms."[35] Tax amnesties were another widely adopted strategy. Some of them, like the amnesty granted in July 1963, cancelled the whole amount of taxes due for the previous year of activity.

These personal agreements between Gori & Zucchi and the highest tax authorities had powerful effects on the rest of the jewelry trade. Norms of reciprocity exerted their influence on the actors "lower" in

[33] Archivio della Camera di Commercio di Arezzo, vol. XIII-8-1/2, Industria Meccanica Orafa, folder Gori e Zucchi, letter of Leopoldo Gori to Davide Ventrella dated 15 July 1965.

[34] Archivio della Camera di Commercio di Arezzo, vol. 13, Varie, IGE 4, folder IGE Atti più importanti; Oreficeria, Varie 2, folder 1, Etica Orafa ("Goldsmithing Ethics").

[35] Archivio della Camera di Commercio di Arezzo, vol. 13, Oreficeria Varie 2, folder 1, letter of Davide Ventrella to the general director of revenue at the Ministry of Finances dated 18 February 1967.

the economic hierarchy, who wanted the "special" treatment granted to Gori & Zucchi to be extended as much as possible. An exposé by the jewelry wholesalers' association, penned in 1970, reveals on the one hand the economic culture predominant in the trade, and on the other the mechanisms implemented by the leading trade representatives to regulate competition effectively. The exposé was a response to the first major downturn in market demand since World War II. The wholesalers' starting point was the observation that the market crisis mandated "not only the normalization of the trade in terms of fiscal conduct but . . . also the moralization of the industry's commercial practices."[36] The wholesalers proceeded to point out that it was Gori & Zucchi's responsibility, as the largest company in the industry, to set the standards of conduct for the whole trade. Revealingly, this did not mean so much refraining from gold smuggling and tax evasion—although the wholesalers paid lip service to this principle—as making sure that Gori & Zucchi and the wholesalers who worked exclusively for them did not take "unfair" advantage of the preferential treatment accorded to them by the public authorities. In practice, this meant that it was necessary for the prosperity of the trade to prompt Gori & Zucchi to follow well-defined price-fixing practices. The document thus proceeded to list the minimum wholesale prices for different kinds of gold jewelry and the interest rates for delayed payments by the retailers. According to the author of the exposé, the outraged wholesalers who had been complaining about Gori & Zucchi's "shameful" competition could take comfort from the fact that Gori had personally committed himself to respecting the new agreements.[37] The logic of reciprocity had once again prevailed.

The delicate balance between formal standards of conduct and personal agreements such as price-fixing was upset again in the fall of 1972, when the government restructured the fiscal regime by switching from a system based on sales taxes (IGE) to one based on a general tax on value added (IVA).[38] Many leading representatives of the jewelry trade, including Gori, expressed their hopes that this reform would lead to a fresh start for the industry and promote more formal rules of conduct. Under the new system, which is still in place, every business

[36] Archivio della Camera di Commercio di Arezzo, vol. 13, Oreficeria Varie, IGE 4, untitled folder, pamphlet entitled "Primo Congresso dei Grossisti Orafi-Gioiellieri. Napoli 9-10-11 ottobre 1970," 7.

[37] Ibid., 11–12.

[38] The IVA system was introduced by the decree D.P.R. 633, 26 October 1972.

was required to keep detailed records of the value added to products and of the amount of tax paid for raw materials and semifinished products that had to be credited or rebated.[39] This complex system was supposed to build on the chain of relations that linked the different components of the trade (gold banks, manufacturers, wholesalers, retailers, etc.) to the final consumer, who paid a price inclusive of the entire tax. At least in theory, the personal relations of complicity established between economic actors in order to cover up widespread tax evasion could now be manipulated by the state to enforce tax collection. But such an integrated system, in which economic actors at every stage of production and commercialization had to keep track of each other's expenses, was also very fragile. Reiterated defection at one stage of the process might lead to the collapse of the whole structure.

This is precisely what happened in the months that followed the introduction of the tax reform in 1972 and 1973. The weakest link in the chain turned out to be the retailers. Hard hit by the market crisis and reluctant to discontinue a long-standing practice of tax dodging, many jewelry stores kept favoring the wholesalers and manufacturers who were willing to break—or at least bend—the law over those who refused to compromise. These opportunistic behaviors revealed how difficult it was to enforce competitive "fairness" through formal rules, especially when the domino effect triggered by these instances of defection reached the higher levels of the trade. As soon as Gori realized that the tax reform had failed to change the norms of the industry, he resorted to the old norms of reciprocity and political exchange, which bound him to the public authorities on the one hand and the rest of the industry on the other. To ensure that his company would not be penalized because of its size and visibility, in October 1973 Gori sent an exposé to Christian Democratic senator Bartolomei, foremost patron of Arezzo's jewelers with the national government, and called for either stricter and more widespread controls or an indiscriminately lenient attitude towards the jewelry businesses. Gori attached some reports from the company's commercial branches in Milan, Naples, and Vicenza. The Vicenza branch, for example, complained in a familiar language, "The few who keep working by the books are opposed by a multitude of improvised agents, who offer hundreds of kilos of mer-

---

[39] For a more technical and comparative discussion about the difference between sales taxes and value added taxes, see B. Guy Peters, *The Politics of Taxation: A Comparative Perspective* (Cambridge, 1991), 35–37.

chandise of shady origin without invoice, an irresistible temptation for the greedy, who constitute the majority of the wholesalers and —even more— of the retailers."[40] Thus Gori exploited the pressures arising from the "bottom" of the economic hierarchy (the retailers) in his political negotiations with the state, and then went on to share the "benefits" of these negotiations with the rest of the industry.

Unsurprisingly, these clientelistic practices effected a return to the status quo before the tax reform. The combination of sporadic fiscal controls, intricate rules, and ad hoc personal agreements created a network of economic and political relations that, despite its ambiguities, managed to ease the contradiction between regulation and flexibility. The "failure" of the 1972 tax reform was the final stage of a process begun shortly after the end of the war. In the crucial years of the economic miracle, the elites of the gold towns turned state regulation into a flexible tool for their advancement, reinforcing the ties of trust and complicity that linked them to less powerful agents. While the tax on value added was implemented to align the Italian fiscal system to the standards mandated by the European Economic Community, its effects on Italy's industrial structure amplified the already established trend towards economic fragmentation. Subcontracting practices received a boost by a tax regime in which fiscal pressure did not rise with the number of passages a good went through during the manufacturing cycle. At the same time, the increased sophistication of the accounting procedures favored the concentration of crucial consulting services in a few expert hands. The upshot of this system was the creation of local hierarchies of economic agents in which the smaller firms depended on leading companies for legal and financial services as well as for protection from the government's erratic control.[41]

The state's failure to impose strict standards of conduct even in the crucial field of fiscal policy reveals the strength of local societies vis-à-vis the national government. The weakness of state authorities certainly favored this process of co-optation. But this is only part of the story. The manipulation of regulation flourished on the ambiguities that characterized the notion of fairness: fairness as rule-making, and fairness as promise-keeping. Although the local patrons benefited from their

---

[40] Archivio della Camera di Commercio di Arezzo, vol. 13, Oreficeria Varie 2, folder 2, Problemi fiscali del settore orafo, exposé dated October 5, 1973.

[41] See Centro Studi Federlibro, FIM, SISM-CISL, *Piccola Azienda Grande Sfruttamento: Note sul Decentramento Produttivo* (Verona, 1974), 67–70.

power to mobilize the public authorities and reap the rewards of the informal economy, tax evasion also worked as an effective aid to social mobility for an increasing number of small-scale entrepreneurs. The interplay of the informal and the formal economies did not lead to purely exploitative and overcompetitive conditions. After all, tax dodging benefited start-up firms even more than well-established companies. By building extensive networks of complicity, tax evasion became a source of social integration at the local level, rather than a source of cutthroat competition. The compromised nature of fiscal regulation managed to turn internal competition into international competitiveness.

Of course the subtlety of the negotiations taking place among social actors in the industrial districts and between trade representatives and government officials does not detract from the fundamental lack of fairness of these compromises at the level of society as a whole. Since the years of the economic miracle, tax evasion has evolved into one of Italy's most intractable political problems.[42] Widespread dodging by the self-employed, including the army of small-scale entrepreneurs located in the country's countless industrial districts, sorely contrasts with the high fiscal pressure exerted on salary and wage earners. As a very problematic testament to the power of social networks, the ties that bind these two groups both structurally and culturally have prevented this potentially explosive tension from escalating into overt conflict. Despite relying on salaries and wages, many Italian families have a shopkeeper or a small-scale manufacturer among their members and neighbors, and tax evasion is often condoned as the gateway to the goal of "independence" in the face of a rapacious state. It would be hard to imagine a more powerful reminder of the fact that trust, networks, and reciprocity (the components of social capital) do not necessarily lead to justice and political legitimacy.

NEGOTIATING THE "GOLD STANDARD": THE POLITICS OF GOLD FINENESS

At least at first sight, tax evasion damaged the prestige and credibility of the state, even though personal agreements enhanced the discretionary power of the state authorities vis-à-vis local societies. By contrast,

---

[42] See the passionate analysis by Paul Ginsborg, *Italy and Its Discontents: Family, Civil Society, State: 1980–2000* (New York, 2003), especially chaps. 1 and 2.

the violation of production and consumption standards, especially in terms of gold fineness, threatened to destroy the reputation of specific firms and of the industry as a whole. Publicly sanctioned consumption standards are distinctive signs of modernity, embodying many of its ambiguities and paradoxes.[43] The relationship between consumption standards, social welfare, and political status lies at the core of our idea of the polity. The individuation of the citizen-as-consumer and her protection is one of the main strategies for the legitimation of state power.[44] Standards are supposed to regulate competition between producers and protect the health or the good faith of consumers. In this process, however, public authorities become the target for ongoing mobilization efforts by private actors, who attempt to rally as many forces as possible under the banner of "fairness," "precision," "purity," "novelty," and so on. The contestable—and indeed contested—nature of these ideals exposes fractures between social actors that could otherwise remain undetected. Standards are conceived to stem conflict and promote trust between social actors by providing measurable, rulebound procedures of control. Yet they often become the focus of litigation and political negotiations.

Gold fineness standards were no exception to this pattern. Because of its symbolic connotations, gold fineness may be regarded as the consumption standard par excellence. No one wants his or her faith in the virtues of marriage represented by a wedding band whose fineness is illegally low. Yet it is costly and difficult to assay gold jewelry, and therefore consumers must rely on the say-so of the retailer, who in turn must rely on the reputation of the wholesaler, and so on. In this way, a chain of trust binds the final consumer to the retailer, the wholesaler, and the producer.

The grade of jewelry is usually measured in carats. Pure gold is denoted as 24 carats, while 18 carats denote an alloy that has three parts

---

[43] By consumption standard I mean a quantifiable and verifiable set of rules that are supposed to protect the health or good faith of consumers. Of course consumption standards are always production standards as well, but the political relevance of the standards imposed on consumer goods is more direct, since it involves a nonmediated "contract" between the producer, the state, and the consumer. According to this definition, production standards *strictu senso* affect processes, whereas consumption standards affect the products sold in the final market.

[44] The relationships between consumption and cultural and political identities are explored Victoria De Grazia, ed., *The Sex of Things: Gender and Consumption in Historical Perspective* (Berkeley, 1996).

of gold out of four, and so on. In the metric system, used in most official cases in continental Europe, the grade of gold jewelry is expressed in millesimals. An alloy that has three parts of gold out of four is said to be 750-millesimal gold, which corresponds to 18 carats. There are many reasons to alloy gold, of course. Considerations of cost, durability, and aesthetics all play a role. No degree of fineness is ideal. All the consumer can hope for is to be reasonably well informed about the content of her purchase. And this is one of the functions that modern consumption standards are supposed to fulfill. But standards have different meanings for different social actors, and these meanings are historically contingent and negotiated. The seemingly unproblematic character of standards (their invisibility) is the product of layers of often contradictory claims. The same standards can draw their authority from expert judgment in one network (communities of specialized engineers, for example) and exactitude in others (the final markets for a given product, for instance).[45] By the same token, negotiations over a certain process of standardization can take place through clientelistic and informal relations at one nexus (for example between the government and powerful local actors) and through bureaucratic control at another (say, between the government and less well-connected actors).[46] Finally, at the receiving end of the deal, the same standard can be interpreted as an instance of moral rigor by one group and as a product of self-interest or abuse of power by another.[47]

[45] See, for example, Geoffrey Bowker, *Science on the Run: Information Management and Industrial Geophysics at Schlumberger, 1920–1940* (Cambridge, Mass., 1994); and Amy Slaton, *Reinforced Concrete and the Modernization of American Buildings* (Baltimore, 2001). The problematic importance of quantification in political and economic life is stressed—even at the expense of other modes of negotiation—by Theodore Porter, *Trust in Numbers: The Pursuit of Objectivity in Science and Public Life* (Princeton, 1995).

[46] The multiple nature of state control has been a major focus of politological and sociological studies aimed at criticizing modernization theories and simplistic interpretations of Weber's theory of bureaucratic rationality, although in many of these studies the relationship between patronage and standardization is more implied than examined.

[47] The notion that economic and technological regimes embody contested moral values (e.g., precision and uniformity) is a central theme of much recent and not so recent social history of industrialization. A moral understanding of techno-economic change is consistent with the historicist attempt to take the worldviews of historical actors seriously and therefore with antiteleological interpretations of industrialization and modernization. For two influential works in this field, see Michael Sonenscher, *The Hatter of Eighteenth-Century France* (Berkeley, 1987); and Ken Alder, *Engineering the Revolution: Arms and Enlightenment in France, 1763–1815* (Princeton, 1997). See also M. Norton Wise, ed., *The Values of Precision* (Princeton, 1995).

In the Italian context, the early history of gold fineness standards was quite tortuous. After the abolition of the guilds during the Napoleonic era, some Italian states opted for the enactment of mandatory standards, expressed in the new rational language provided by the metric system. For example, the Kingdom of Sardinia, which included Piedmont, issued a law in 1824 for the strict regulation of the gold jewelry trade. The law permitted only two degrees of fineness and imposed the identification mark of the producer on all gold jewelry items. Ironically, the first governments of unified Italy saw these standards as corporatist relics and as an impediment to the uninhibited growth of the industry. In 1872, the national government deregulated the production of gold jewelry and made identification marks optional. The producer could still obtain the sanction of the state, but the service was provided at a fee. On the other hand, the law established a system of assaying laboratories in every province of the kingdom by relying on the network of the chambers of commerce. This measure, however, ran against the imperatives of tight public budgets, and these labs remained remarkably understaffed for decades.

The consequences of this deregulation were problematic. Some producers continued to advertise the fineness of their jewelry even though the actual content of gold was much lower than the one declared. In 1879, the assaying lab of Alessandria, the capital of the province where Valenza Po is located, felt compelled to remind the public that buyers could have their jewelry assayed at a public lab and that frauds could be prosecuted.[48] Moreover, some jewelry manufacturers saw the absence of regulation as an insurmountable obstacle to exports, which in fact were extremely limited in this period, and even as a competitive disadvantage within the Italian domestic market vis-à-vis the French and German producers, who sold increasing quantities of jewelry in Italy. Consequently, they campaigned for the reintroduction of mandatory standards and marks.[49] Other manufacturers, however, saw mandatory measures as "contrary to all the principles of freedom of economic activity."[50] Confronted with these fractures, in 1892 Parliament rejected a law proposal for the implementation of compulsory stan-

[48] Archivio Storico della Città di Valenza, vol. 846, folder 444, circolare dell'Ufficio Metrico e dei Saggi di Alessandria.

[49] See, for example, the letter of Gastaldo Emanuelli, a goldsmith from Turin, in *Oreficeria Italiana*, January 1917, 8–13.

[50] Archivio Storico della Città di Valenza, vol. 846, folder 448, letter of the Società di Mutuo Soccorso Orefici di Roma, dated 1898.

dards. Even as late as the 1920s, some representatives of the jewelry trade maintained that state regulation was unnecessary or even harmful. In 1925 Emilio Boselli argued in his widely read technical textbook for jewelers that "industries must be free and respect only the consumer's laws."[51] All controls should be abolished, as in Great Britain, Boselli maintained, and impersonal mechanisms should be replaced by the exclusive and complete "responsibility" of the jewelry maker.

It was the Fascist government that decided to override the debates within the trade and impose compulsory gold fineness standards in 1934,[52] shortly before the establishment of the state monopoly on commerce in raw gold in 1935. The 1934 law set four degrees of gold fineness as the only permissible ones, and at the same time made compulsory the printing of the producer's hallmark. Of the four permissible degrees of fineness, the 18-carat standard soon became the sole grade in use in the Italian market, thereby replacing the undisciplined coexistence of low- and high-grade gold jewelry. The law was supposed to tighten the chain of trust that bound producers, traders, and consumers. By simplifying the producers' and traders' practices, and by facilitating the consumers' ability to read the signs of fineness, this standard was meant to become a sort of lubricant for economic transactions.[53] The combination of the 18-carat standard and the printing of the producer's identification mark allowed buyers to know what they were buying and from whom. Yet, as is often the case, this standard also became the focus of litigation and conflict. In the 1950s and 1960s, when Italy developed into the largest producer and exporter of gold jewelry in the world, producers began accusing each other of cheating domestic and international customers by selling jewelry of a grade lower than the one declared. The fineness standard then became the main marker discriminating between "moral" and "immoral" agents, and between those who were genuinely interested in the destiny of the industry and the unscrupulous parvenus who wanted to reap short-term profits at any risk.[54]

---

[51] E. Boselli, *Manuale per l'Orefice* (Milan, 1925), 387.

[52] Law number 305, issued on 5 February 1934.

[53] The notion of trust-promoting institutions as means of "lubricating" economic transactions belongs to Williamson, *Markets and Hierarchies*.

[54] See Leopoldo Gori, *Etica Orafa* ("Goldsmithing Ethics"), pamphlet preserved at the Archivio della Camera di Commercio di Arezzo, vol. 13, Oreficeria Varie, IGE 4, folder IGE Atti più importanti.

The controversies over the fineness standards exposed the complex fractures dividing social actors within and between the three main Italian jewelry districts. These fractures were economic (between larger and smaller firms and networks of firms), technological (between the supporters of mechanization and the defenders of artisanal traditions), and political (between socialists and communists on one side and Catholics on the other). The main divide, however, ran across geographical boundaries, technical specializations, even political orientations. The tension that characterized all three districts was that between formal and informal relations. The case of Arezzo's Gori & Zucchi illustrates this point clearly. As we have seen in chapter 4, the company—which by the mid-1960s was the largest producer of gold jewelry in the world—had built much of its reputation on the "purity" and reliability of its production. The company's main marketing strategy was to promote the identification of its hallmark, 1-AR, or Uno-A-Erre, with the legal standard of fineness *tout court*. This was the company's rationale for using its hallmark as a heavily advertised brand name.[55] At the same time, however, Gori & Zucchi tolerated and encouraged the proliferation of a network of small firms in the Arezzo area, some of whom soon turned into unwelcome competitors. The large company was unable to beat this competition on the level of costs and prices, since the smaller firms could reap all the benefits of the informal economy. In fact, Gori & Zucchi needed this network of subcontractors to keep its own prices down. As a consequence of this contradictory situation, gold fineness became even more important for Gori & Zucchi, both as a competitive advantage and as a defense of its leadership. Therefore, the tensions between Arezzo's formal and informal economies found in the fineness standards a catalyst for conflict.

In pursuing this strategy, Gori & Zucchi was not alone. Other large manufacturers (for example Balestra in Bassano, near Vicenza) and trading companies viewed the stricter enforcement of the fineness standard as a way of strengthening their leadership, cracking down on the gray-market activities from which they had till then profited, and upholding their reputation vis-à-vis the international buyers. If the target of this campaign was local (the increasing number of unruly

---

[55] As he proclaimed in front of five hundred jewelry retailers in June 1964, Gori's notion of quality was based on "highly pure alloys; easily readable hallmarks; content of gold not lower than the one declared regardless of legally admitted tolerances," and other such attributes. Archivio della Camera di Commercio di Arezzo, vol. XIII-8-1/2, Premio G. Z., folder Primo Convegno Orafi Dettaglianti 25.6.1964.

small entrepreneurs), its audience was international. Exporting companies thought that a signal had to be sent to the Swiss, French, and German custom officials, who assayed Italian jewelry and found a high percentage of merchandise at fault. Assaying techniques involved the removal of parts of the objects, which were then shipped back to the sender with the rest of the deficient lot.[56] Another problem was raised by the so-called "invisible exports," that is, gold jewelry that tourists bought in Italy and took to their home countries without declaring it to customs officials. The amount of jewelry that left the country this way was remarkable. Tourism was one of the main venues for the internationalization of Italian consumers goods, including gold jewelry. Research carried out in the early 1970s estimated the importance of invisible exports at 14 percent of Italian production and 28 percent of total gold jewelry exports.[57] Once home, some tourists had their jewelry assayed by nondestructive and therefore highly inaccurate means. The extent of the gap between the actual content of gold and the declared fineness was such that even these crude procedures were sometimes sufficient to reveal the fraud. The necessity of protecting these tourists' good faith became another leitmotif of the debate.[58]

The costs of these incidents for the Italian producers and traders in terms of money and reputation were remarkable. Who was the real culprit? The myriad small firms that had mushroomed in recent years, or the more established companies that used these firms to cut labor and overhead costs, and share the benefits and the risks of the informal economy? The 18-carat standard and its violations embodied the contradictions of Italy's small-scale industrialization. Therefore, this standard became the object of controversy at a pivotal moment in the history of the trade.

[56] Archivio della Camera di Commercio di Arezzo, vol. xiii-8-1/2, Industria Meccanica Orafa, folder Gori & Zucchi, letter to the Ministry of Finance dated 7 November 1968.

[57] In monetary terms, invisible exports represented a 63-billion lire business in 1973. Paper written by Mario Giannoni entitled "Le Esportazioni Invisibili di Preziosi," preserved at the Archivio della Camera di Commercio di Arezzo, vol. 13, Oreficeria Varie 2, folder Incontro col Segretario Pandolfi al Ministero delle Finanze.

[58] See Gori's report to the manufacturers' association of Arezzo in June 1664 entitled *Promemoria Progetto Legge per Eliminazione Titoli Metalli Preziosi*, preserved at Archivio della Camera di Commercio di Arezzo, vol. 13, Oreficeria, IGE, Anni 1960–66, folder 10 Problemi delle Industrie d'Oreficeria.

The main problem faced by the leading Italian producers and traders in the early 1960s was how to persuade international buyers and custom officials of their good faith. This was not an easy task. After all, a law regulating fineness standards was already in place, and little could be done to monitor the hundreds of producers and traders who dealt with the international market. Well connected to the highest spheres of Roman politics, the leading jewelers decided to try to redirect the attention of international agents away from the industry's structural problems, such as the uneasy coexistence of highly visible and completely undocumented firms. The 18-carat (or 750 per thousand) standard seemed to serve this purpose beautifully. The 1934 law had allowed for relatively wide tolerances. An alloy whose gold content was 748 (or—in theory—752) per thousand could still be marked and sold as 750-millesimal (or 18-carat) gold. Wider tolerances, up to twenty millesimals, were admitted for soldered items, given the difficulty of reaching a high level of accuracy in the brazing alloys. The 1934 law implicitly espoused the view that standards are statistical variables rather than exact measures. Thirty years later, the leading jewelers decided to challenge this functional perspective and fight for absolute precision as a statement of the purity and honesty of their trade. Throughout the late 1950s and early 1960s they carried out a campaign for the abolition of all tolerances—tolerances that they now portrayed as the loopholes that allowed the shady practitioners to plague the industry.[59]

There is little doubt that the campaign against tolerances was staged with a degree of disingenuousness. But as a rhetorical move it had a sharp edge. First of all, it met and surpassed the standards imposed by countries like France, which allowed tolerances for domestic production but admitted no deviation for imported jewelry. This badly disguised form of French protectionism could only be counteracted by a bold statement, such as a claim of absolute precision. But second—and ironically—the campaign against tolerances exposed the conventional nature of consumption standards. If such standards were tools of persuasion, what could be more convincing than a claim of absolute precision? And conversely, what arguments could the supporters of the status quo put forward without being immediately suspected of

[59] The best source for the reconstruction of this campaign is *L'Orafo Italiano*, the periodical of the Italian association of jewelry manufacturers and traders. See for example the December issue of 1964 and the February issue of 1966.

defending fraudulent or sloppy practices? The supporters of the status quo were indeed at a loss. In the countless meetings involving all the trade's components (large-scale manufacturers, artisans, commercial agents, retailers, etc.) very few people dared to speak against the abolition of tolerances.[60]

This does not mean that the campaign convinced everybody. Artisans were quick to realize that it was a campaign waged primarily by the kinds of large-scale industrial and commercial concerns that could absorb the additional costs incurred by a small increase in the grade of their jewelry through minor revisions of their production and marketing practices. Moreover, only the larger concerns had access to the measuring instruments necessary to assess (or claim to assess) gold fineness with a relatively high degree of precision. The political divide between the artisans, who generally leaned towards the left, and the large-scale manufacturers and traders, most of whom were Christian Democrats, raised the stakes of the confrontation even further. Two distinct law proposals, one supported by the Christian Democrats and calling for the repeal of the tolerances, and the other backed by the Communist Party and arguing for their preservation, remained for years in the Parliament's agenda. The left-wing artisans came to see the campaign against the tolerances as part of a "monopolistic" strategy aimed at squeezing them out of the market.

The debate about gold fineness standards also transformed the political and economic configuration of the trade. The controversy created an arena in which social actors could develop and reshape their political identities. Some jewelry manufacturers and artisans began to conceive of themselves as representatives of their hometowns, regardless of local fractures. Gori and his collaborators immediately couched the conflict between Valenza Po's artisans and Arezzo's Gori & Zucchi in terms of a clash between localities. For example, when Valenza Po's producers gained exclusive access to the Nations' Building at the 1964 International Fair in Milan, Gori replied angrily that a model of his company's assaying labs should be displayed and advertised widely at the fair's Arezzo pavilion, implying that fineness accuracy was Arezzo's strength and Valenza Po's weakness (as if Arezzo did not harbor many small-scale firms, many of these closely allied with Gori and

---

[60] See, for example, *Atti dell'VIII Convegno Nazionale Orafi ed Argentieri* (Vicenza, 1962).

yet prone to shave off standards).[61] In response to this, Luigi Illario, Valenza Po's manufacturer of high-quality jewelry and prominent Christian Democratic patron, took the opposite tack and converted to the cause of his hometown's left-wing artisans. In the early 1960s, Illario had been a vocal supporter of the abolition of the tolerances.[62] Later in the decade, he was convinced by his fellow citizens that the status of Valenza Po as an artisanal center was at stake. Thus, he set aside his national political and economic affiliations and instead acted as Valenza Po's patron, campaigning with the left-wing artisans. From that moment on, Valenza Po presented itself as a unified front.

Despite these efforts, however, Parliament issued a new law in January 1968 that repealed all tolerances and embraced the larger companies' point of view.[63] At this stage, the artisans decided to counterattack. In order to become operative, the law needed specific regulations of application. The left-wing artisans saw this final regulatory step as the last opportunity to voice their concerns.[64] The problem was that they lacked an argument sharp enough to persuade the parliamentary committee to reintroduce the tolerances without raising suspicions of bad faith. Fortunately for the artisans, their foremost political patron was more than fit for the challenge. Luciano Lenti, elected national deputy for the Communist Party in the Valenza Po district in 1966, was not just a former wartime partisan, a gold refiner, and Valenza Po's former mayor for two terms. Crucially, he also held a university degree in chemistry.

Luciano Lenti and the left-wing artisans enacted a cumulative three-step strategy. First, they had to convince the public authorities and Parliament that they represented Italy's "authentic" jewelry tradition, and that they had been key to the industry's international success. This was an easy task. As we have seen in chapter 5, even the large-scale manufacturers—some of whom had more than a thousand employees—were wont to use the language of artisanal tradition. Typical in this

[61] Archivio della Camera di Commercio di Arezzo, vol. 13–8–2, Premio G. Z., folder Primo Convegno Orafi Dettaglianti 25.6.1964, letter of Gori & Zucchi's commercial branch in Naples dated 19 November 1964.

[62] See his speech at the seventh meeting of the national goldsmiths' association, in which he doubts the good faith of the "abolitionists." See *VII Convegno Nazionale Orafi e Argentieri, Vicenza 17.9.1960* (Vicenza, 1961), 36.

[63] Law number 46 issued on 30 January 1968.

[64] See the periodical of the jewelry manufacturers of Valenza Po, *L'Orafo Valenzano*, January 1969 and February 1969.

regard was Gori & Zucchi, which tapped into Arezzo's Etruscan and Renaissance past as a (somewhat clumsy) promotional strategy and as a source of cultural legitimation.[65] The ambiguities of the notion of craftsmanship were fully exploited by a variety of social actors. The term *artisan* could apply both to the family businesses that reproduced Gori & Zucchi's production practices on a much smaller case (these were the businesses Gori denounced as "unfair" competitors), and it could also apply to the manufacturers who processed precious metals and stones to produce high-quality jewelry, although some of them— like Illario—employed a few hundred workers. Second, the left-wing artisans focused on a particular technique, microfusion, as their distinctive domain. This process had been recently perfected so as to allow the production of a limited series of relatively elaborate objects such as rings or brooches. The artisans chose this process as the technical divide between craftsmanship and industry, although many industrialists adopted microfusion and many artisans did not. Third —and this is where Lenti's intervention proved crucial— microfusion provided the artisans with a "scientifically" based argument against the abolition of tolerances.

Microfusion had been invented in the 1930s by Detroit-based Kerr Manufacturing, a company specializing in the production of dental prostheses, and it was applied to jewelry shortly before the war.[66] Its main innovation consisted in the vulcanization of a mold of rubber from a pattern made of base metal. The mold was then filled with liquid wax. This operation could be repeated several times, thereby producing multiple casts (for instance several brooch bases). The casts were mounted on a round frame, called a tree, and covered with quick setting plaster. The wax melted in a low-heat furnace, after which the gold alloy was injected into the frame as the whole structure whirled in a centrifuge, ensuring that the metal reached all sections of the molds. A different "tree" had to be built for each part of the object, after which the components were soldered into the final piece of jewelry.

It was somewhat ironic for the artisans to choose this process as their technical symbol, since microfusion transformed the prime goldsmithing artisanal technique, lost-wax casting, used since classic times to produce unique items, into a modern (and American) process founded on the principle of serial production. Microfusion had one ad-

[65] See Gori & Zucchi's self-celebratory pamphlet *Viaggio nel Pianeta dell'Arte Orafa.*
[66] Lenti, *Gioielli e Gioiellieri*, 197–98.

vantage, however: it involved centrifugal force. Backed by his expertise as a chemist, Lenti explained to the parliamentary committee that
18-carat gold was inevitably an "impure" cocktail of different metals
(gold, silver, copper, nickel, etc.), each with its specific weight. When
they were subjected to centrifugal force, the different elements dispersed in a heterogeneous way, with the "heavier" metals more likely
to be propelled to the external sections of the molds. But because custom officials removed and assayed a part of the object at random, it
was entirely possible for them to choose a low-grade section, although
the object as a whole was perfectly legal.

Lenti's argument worked. The regulations of application of the 1968
law made an exception for jewelry produced by microfusion, for which
the old tolerances remained valid, even though the pivot now became
753 rather than 750 millesimals. And because there was no way for
custom officials—or consumers, for that matter—to establish with cer-
tainty whether any piece of jewelry had been produced by microfusion, the practical upshot was a return to the old system (plus 3 millesimals, so to speak). But the brilliance of this argument was that it
represented was a two-way victory: industrialists could still maintain
that tolerances had been officially repealed. Thus, an economist hired
by the manufacturers to assess the consequences of the new law argued in 1974 that "the abolition of the tolerances has qualified our production, which now ranks first in the world."[67] The perfunctory character of the law is revealed by those clauses that regulated inspection
procedures. Despite the enormous expansion of Italy's gold jewelry
production in the previous two decades, the 1968 law established the
number of public inspectors at 215, 21 fewer than those recommended
by the 1872 law! The tolerances had been formally abolished, but only
for some products, and without the possibility of systematic controls.
The coexistence of formal and informal arrangements was once again
established, even at the level of national law.

Even though Luciano Lenti told me that "the abolition of the fineness tolerances challenged a scientific principle . . . and that is why my
argument became irrefutable,"[68] the significance of this story lies in the

---

[67] Franco Cantile, Pratica Applicazione della Legge 30 Gennaio 1968, N. 46 sulla Dis-
ciplina dei Titoli e dei Marchi di Identificazione dei Metalli Preziosi, Florence, 16–17 November 1974, memo preserved at the Archivio della Camera di Commercio di Arezzo,
vol. 13, Oreficeria Varie 3, folder Convegno Nazionale sui Problemi dell'Oreficeria e
dell'Argenteria.

[68] Interview by author, October 1996.

way that the artisans successfully countered the industrialists' masquerade of absolute precision with their own masquerade of science-based inaccuracy. Unsurprisingly, the outcome of the controversy was a compromise that exposed the inherently contestable nature of the fineness standard. Although this was a battle in which rhetorical skills and strategies of persuasion were key, the upshot had a very material consequence. The compromise reconsolidated the two main components of the jewelry trade (the formal and informal sectors) and reunited them through the very ties of loyalty and complicity that the fineness controversy had threatened to sever. There is little doubt that the persistence of these ties proved crucial to the continuing success of the Italian jewelry industry.

If all the producers got their share of victory, what about the consumers? In early-1970s Italy there was one jewelry store per approximately every three thousand people.[69] Arguably, the face-to-face relationship with the neighborhood jeweler provided the guarantees that no legal standard could provide. As to the international market, Italian jewelry continued to expand its world share, despite the ongoing diffidence of customs officials. Official exports, which did not include "invisible" and clandestine purchases by foreign agents, tripled in the years after the enactment of the new law, reaching 150 billion lire in 1973. Overall, the low prices and flashy style of Italian jewelry more than compensated for its less than pristine reputation in terms of gold fineness. It can actually be argued that Italian producers managed to transform their jewelry, like other fashion goods, into the stylistic standard for a large part of the world, regardless of other less visible properties.

The construction of the gold fineness standard in post–World War II Italy can be seen alternatively as a case of failed standardization or as a paradigmatic example of how standards work in practice. I propose to take the actors' words seriously and espouse the latter interpretation. The development of the Italian gold jewelry industry during the economic "miracle" challenges a series of assumptions about local identities, state control, and market rationality. The construction of the fineness standards shows that the ties of locality were not the unprob-

---

[69] Uberto Breganze, Il Settore Orafo Italiano in Cifre: Attualità e Prospettive, Florence, 16–17 November 1974, memo preserved at the Archivio della Camera di Commercio di Arezzo, vol. 13, Oreficeria Varie 3, folder Convegno Nazionale sui Problemi dell'Oreficeria e dell'Argenteria.

lematic outcome of tradition, defined in opposition to the state and to economic globalization. What it meant to be a Valenza Po artisan changed in response to local and global pressures. Local norms creatively enrolled state regulations in order to enhance their strength and credibility, while local identities were forged in ongoing negotiations with the government and global traders. Paradoxically, a universalizing language (chemistry) and a global technology (microfusion) combined to define what a bona fide local artisan ought to be. By the same token, government regulation combined clientelistic ties to key local actors with bureaucratic control. Clientelistic ties were crucial to the survival of thriving informal economies (as well as to political consensus), while formal rules constituted a resource that weaker actors could tap in order to protect themselves from perceived abuse. Gori & Zucchi's connections in Rome did not prevent Luciano Lenti from winning a crucial argument based on formal procedures. Finally, global traders and gold suppliers had to strike a balance between the protection of the local informal economies that they had contributed to creating and their need for accountable procedures capable of crossing geographical and cultural boundaries. As tourism blurred the distinction between domestic and international markets, global traders came to accept the messy outcome of the fineness controversy.

Between Development and Decline:
Jewelry Work from an International Perspective

As social spaces simultaneously bounded by the ties of locality and connected to global networks, the Italian jewelry towns tell a story shared by countless other areas around the world. The increasing interconnectedness of contemporary capitalism has not erased local differences, which both entrench themselves in defiance of threats of homogenization and (somewhat ironically) fuel the very diversity that makes global interconnections profitable. From this perspective, gold truly constitutes the archetypal global commodity. Imagine that we could follow a gram of gold around the world. Mined in South Africa; traded in the City of London; stored in an international bank in Zurich; refined in a factory in Canton Ticino, Switzerland; manufactured into a little chain in Arezzo; sold in the "free trade" area of Panama; melted again somewhere in South America; and shipped back to Switzerland, a gram of gold relies on the almost unique distinctiveness of many places, each with its networks of knowledge and practice, to travel its global journey.

Nevertheless, for all its symbolic power, gold is far from unique in its ability to weave distinctive localities into a global pattern, nor are the Italian jewelry towns unique in having negotiated over time distinctive ways of reproducing their differences and relating themselves to the wider world. I chose to focus on gold jewelry to illustrate the history of Italy's small-scale industrialization because I sensed that, for all its peculiarities, this industry exposed the opportunities and contradictions of the country's recent economic change in a particularly salient way. The jewelry towns held the potential to show how locality, especially the type of locality that constitutes an "industrial district," is constructed over time, how the Italian state engaged in complex and often contradictory negotiations with localities, and how global markets took advantage of and reshaped the bewildering diversity of the Italian economic landscape, especially after World War II.

The ability of gold to weave ties of trust and secrecy at the local, national, and global levels makes the jewelry towns paradigmatic of larger processes, in spite of their distinctive (even atypical) features. Even though materials transformed into other "made in Italy" goods were not smuggled into the country in overt defiance of state authority, as gold was until 2000, those materials also contributed to defining bounded communities of knowledge and practice where trust and secrecy (as well as tax evasion and the bending of labor regulations) built extensive informal economies. The history of the shoe-making towns of the Marche, studied by Michael Blim and others, for example, demonstrates very clearly the link between the construction of locality, the creation of international ties, and the expansion of informal relations.[1] Likewise, the hybridization of familial, political, and business bonds characteristic of firms and other institutions in the jewelry towns resembles quite closely similar processes described for the silk region of Lombardy by Sylvia Yanagisako, Anna Cento Bull and Paul Corner, and others.[2] In other words, actors in the jewelry towns forged patterns of relations shared by many other areas in northern and central Italy, even though these patterns were colored in countless ways in different places and at different historical junctures.

In this chapter I will cross the Italian borders and relate the experiences of the Italian jewelry towns to other places, especially to Providence, Rhode Island, home to the largest jewelry district in the Unites States. In the last few decades historians have been particularly active in pluralizing and decentering the older narratives of industrialization and modernization that aimed at capturing the essential traits of each "national case." A new awareness of the complex and contingent interplay of local, national, and global geographies has made these nation-centered narratives seem hopelessly simplistic. In the Italian case, this has led to a new appreciation for local change, viewed as a partially autonomous process rather than as a derivative dimension dependent on "larger" forces. Notions of flexible specialization, industrial districts, embeddedness, and even social capital have all contributed to complicating older narratives of development and backwardness, to the point of turning small-scale industrialization and the social construction of the market into the new analytical paradigms for the study of Italy's recent economic change. At least in this sense, the Italian case

---

[1] Blim, *Made in Italy*. See also Patrizia Sabbatucci Severini, "Il distretto calzaturiero marchigiano (1910–1960): Alle origini di una grande affermazione," in Amatori and Colli, *Comunità di Imprese*, 361–412.

[2] Yanagisako, *Producing Culture and Capital*; Cento-Bull and Corner, *From Peasants and Entrepreneurs*.

can be viewed as emblematic of the direction taken by studies of economic change more generally. Students of Italy moved away from nation-centered narratives earlier and more decisively than scholars dealing with other parts of the world.[3]

But this rediscovery of the local, with its important theoretical and methodological implications, has not even spared the areas that used to provide the paradigmatic examples of industrial modernity—Britain and the United States. Recent works on British industrialization have challenged older narratives centered on a simple two-stage process, starting with Britain's pioneering role in ushering in the age of mass production during the Industrial Revolution, followed by the inability of British manufacturers and traders to maintain their leadership and successfully imitate America's organizational and technological innovations. Francesca Carnevali, for example, has shown how the jewelry district of Birmingham, made up of predominantly small and medium-size firms, long survived its putative decline in the late nineteenth century and thrived for much of the following century, employing tens of thousand of workers and catering to a bewildering variety of tastes and international markets.[4] Even in the British context, shifts in perspective and emphasis have led to the reappraisal of long-neglected experiences that can only be regarded as marginal or peripheral by positing the exclusive relevance of a single "national" narrative.

In a similar vein, Philip Scranton has reexamined the history of American industrialization, long regarded as the stage for the final triumph of mass production and the multidivisional corporation, by "rediscovering" a wide variety of historical experiences that defy the dominant narrative of industrial modernity and yet proved vital and even quantitatively very significant. As his research shows, "There were more critical players in industrialization than we may have realized. Many of those once thought peripheral constructed winning strategies in challenging markets and were far more central to building the nation's industrial base than one realized. If the old teleological and reductionist accounts are no longer tenable, building a new, inclu-

---

[3] It is worth noting here that to challenge nation-centered narratives of economic change does not mean to dismiss the role of the state as a historical actor.

[4] Francesca Carnevali, "Golden Opportunities: Jewelry Making in Birmingham between Mass Production and Specialty," *Enterprise and Society* 4 (2003): 272–92; see also the essays in John Wilson and Andrew Popp, eds., *Regions and Networks: The Dynamics of Industrial Clustering in England* (Aldershot, 2002).

sive narrative of American industrialization is now conceivable."[5] As we will see later, Scranton has included the jewelry district of Providence among his case studies, although this example plays a somewhat negative role in his general scheme.

From a methodological standpoint, these studies confront a variety of narratives, above all but not exclusively about mass and specialty production, without privileging one of them or even arranging them in a hierarchy. Economic and political diversity is not only what needs to be explained but also the basis for any possible explanation. Narratives are emplaced, and these studies refuse to rely on the traditional geographies centered on the nation-state and founded on unproblematic distinctions between center and periphery. The relative autonomy of the local as an analytical unit and as the basis for experience is the most visible outcome of this methodological shift. But of course narratives are also about temporality, and new studies about industrialization also acknowledge the multiple ways in which economic change is told and experienced over time. In other words, they acknowledge the existence of multiple economic temporalities. For example, until the 1970s the traditional binary opposition between the large-scale industrialization of the Italian "industrial triangle" and the underdevelopment of the Mezzogiorno prevented scholars and policymakers from appreciating what was taking place in the rest of the country, where notions of "tradition" and "modernity" could not be as easily deployed. Similarly, the epic of American industrialization, founded on a steady progression from self-reliance to wage work, from small to large companies, from craft to mass production, from local to global ties, from ethnic to national loyalties, and so on, ignored the countless experiences that did not "progress" in the same direction and at the same pace, or treated them as exceptions.

These spatial and temporal dissonances between different narratives are not limited to the realm of scholarly analyses; historical actors are themselves often immersed in (and aware of) them. Economic life is not only embedded in networks of social relations but also in multiple understandings of the economy. Small-scale industrialization, for example, can assume radically different meanings in different geographical and temporal contexts, depending on the role it plays in intersecting local, national, and global narratives of development and backwardness. In this chapter I will focus on the jewelry district of

[5] Scranton, *Endless Novelty*, 355.

Providence, one of the many "side stories" removed from the mainstream of American industrialization, an instance of economic change profoundly embedded not only in its territory but also in contested narratives of decline and deindustrialization.

As we shall see, the Italian jewelry districts shared many "structural" similarities with Providence, including the hybridization of economic, familial, and political life; the coexistence of institutions of trust and a secretive informal economy; the availability of patronage- and class-based political action; and strongly gendered understandings of entrepreneurship. But despite these similarities, which defy familiar dichotomies of Italian "tradition" and American "modernity," small-scale industrialization meant something radically different in Providence. Jewelry work, despite being one of the largest sources of income for Providence families from the 1930s to the 1960s, came to be seen as the most visible symptom of the city's decay.

In order to understand this divergent outcome, it is necessary first of all to set the development of the jewelry industry in the economic history of Providence and southern New England more generally. Second, we must measure the distance between jewelry work and the normative visions of economic development prevalent in the central decades of the twentieth century, at both the local and the national levels. Finally, we must relate the experiences of local actors to the policies carried out by state officials, themselves the carriers of strong prescriptions for development, and to the particular niche that the jewelry district came to occupy in an increasingly interconnected global market.

The Providence Political Economy between the Two World Wars

Providence and Rhode Island were the cradle of the Industrial Revolution in North America. By the early twentieth century, the Ocean State and its capital could proudly point to their pioneering role in a variety of industrial sectors. Guidebooks invited visitors to contemplate Providence's "Five Industrial Wonders of the World": Corliss, which produced the most powerful steam engines in the world; Browne & Sharpe, the largest precision tool company in the United States; Nicholson File, the largest file factory; Gorham Silver, whose elegant artifacts embellished the kitchens and living rooms of middle-class homes across the country and beyond; and even American Screw, the largest

283

screw factory ever built. None of these wonders, however, could compete with the textile industry in terms of the size of its workforce, largely made up of immigrants from Ireland and French Canada first and then from Italy and eastern Europe. The Providence area had long been a major hub for cotton textiles (it was here that Samuel Slater had established the first functioning automatic loom on American soil in the 1790s, and it was in Providence that Fruit of the Loom had its origins), but the woolen industry was also well represented. At its height in the aftermath of World War I, the Rhode Island textile industries employed 75,000 workers, or 53 percent of all wage earners in the state. Thanks to this strong industrial base, which attracted immigrants both from overseas and from the rest of New England, the population of Rhode Island increased from 83,000 in 1820 to more than 600,000 a century later. The city of Providence alone grew from a population of 50,000 in 1860 to 225,000 in 1910. In that year, a full third of Rhode Islanders were foreign born and more than two-thirds were of "foreign stock" (meaning that at least one of their parents was born abroad).[6]

Each of Rhode Island's main industries had its good founding father to revere and celebrate: Samuel Slater, George Corliss, Lucien Sharpe and Joseph Brown, and so forth. The jewelry industry was no exception. The origins of the industrial manufacturing of jewelry in Providence date back to the 1790s, when Nehemiah Dodge invented a process for plating a thin leaf of gold and silver onto a base-metal basis. Rolled gold, as the product was called, made the veneer of luxury accessible to ever larger population strata, thereby becoming one of the core specialties of the steadily growing jewelry district in the next century and a half. One of Dodge's apprentices, Jabez Gorham, used his expertise as a jewelry maker to found his silverware empire in 1831. By the 1870s, Providence was already the leading American center in the production of costume jewelry, while New York City specialized in the upper end of the market. The number of firms specialized in jewelry making in the state rose from 133 in 1875 to 214 in 1900, while workers increased from 2,617 to 7,200 in the same period.[7] In Providence, mechanization did not lead to vertical integration and the creation of large factories, but to the increasing specialization of tasks car-

---

[6] Data from Kurt Meyer and Sidney Goldstein, *Migration and Economic Development in Rhode Island* (Providence, 1958).

[7] George Frankovich, "History of the Rhode Island Jewelry and Silverware Industry," in *Rhode Island Yearbook* (Providence, 1971), 83–88.

ried out by small and medium-size companies clustered in a well-defined urban area south of City Hall. By the turn of the twentieth century the Providence jewelry industry had assumed the characters of a classic Marshallian industrial district.

The jewelry firms of Providence produced a wide variety of items, but they tended to concentrate on the medium- to low-end segments of the market. From the 1940s to the 1980s, the censuses of manufactures classified approximately half of the firms in the area as producers of fine jewelry, employing precious metals, and the rest as manufacturers of costume (nonprecious) jewelry, with relatively small changes over time. The boundaries between the two tiers of the industry, however, were never clear cut. Overall, the Providence jewelry districts encompassed products as diverse as low-grade gold and silver jewelry on the one hand and imitation pearls on the other. These activities share very low capital requirements, a high intensity of labor, and therefore a tendency to create very competitive networks of firms. The attainment of small-scale proprietorship was made even easier after the 1890s, when increasing mechanization made possible the mass production of castings of jewelry parts ("findings," in the trade's jargon). Enterprising skilled and semiskilled workers could establish connections with the suppliers of findings and other services and proceed to start their own shops.

The end of the nineteenth century also saw the growth of industrial homework, from which small-scale entrepreneurship was often hardly distinguishable. According to one source, the first promoters of homework were "journeymen who, reverting to the status of independent artisans, bought up and took home jewelers' findings to work after hours." These journeymen would first employ their family members and then their neighbors, and were routinely accused of "depressing prices and workers' conditions alike."[8] Therefore, homework was a consequence of industrialization and modernization, rather than a vestigial trait. The lure of proprietorship, which made the jewelry industry the most "democratic of private enterprises,"[9] was only one of the reasons for the spread of homework. Costume jewelry, like its more ex-

[8] Providence Community Center, *Preliminary Report on the Jewelry Manufacturing and Silverware Industries in Rhode Island* (Providence, 1938), 5.

[9] Bruce Butterfield, *Working in Jewelry Series, Providence Journal Bulletin*, 21–27 June 1981, quoted in Nina Shapiro-Perl, "Labor Process and Class Relations in the Costume Jewelry Industry: A Case in Women's Work," (Ph.D. diss., University of Connecticut, 1983, 55.

pensive cousin, was (and is) a highly seasonal industry whose demand reached a major peak in the fall and a lower one in the spring. Employment needed to expand and contract accordingly, and the use of homework provided the kind of flexibility that could only be attained in traditional factories by hiring and firing workers every few months— a practice far from unknown in Providence but whose social and economic costs were apparent. On these bases, the growth of the industry continued unabated, reaching 12,500 official wage earners in 1919.

In his wide-ranging revision of America's industrial past, Philip Scranton has recently taken the Providence jewelers as examples of "networked specialists," interconnected actors who simultaneously compete and cooperate in a well-defined geographical area, such as a neighborhood, a town, or a region. Scranton also follows the trajectory of the Providence jewelry district from what he calls the relatively prosperous 1890s and 1900s to the troubled 1910s and 1920s, when the industry fell prey to "opportunism, design copying, interfirm suspicion, and price shaving under seasonal time pressures, defenseless against the flow of worker-entrepreneurs who fueled these abuses."[10] Scranton gives a technical and economic explanation of this pattern of spiraling competition: "The 'evils of overcompetition' derived from the jewelry sector's own structure and technical capacities,"[11] namely the very low barriers to entry into the industry and the industry leaders' inability to devise marketing strategies capable of withstanding the pressure exerted by New York–based wholesalers, eager to play one manufacturer off against another in their quest for ever-lower prices. While this interpretation captures some important trends in the district's history, the sheer longevity of jewelry making in the Providence area warrants a degree of caution. The jewelry industry's troubles—much like those of Providence as a whole—were to last for at least another half century, a period through which jewelry manufacturing kept growing in size and scope. The industry employed more than fifteen thousand workers from the late 1940s onwards, roughly doubling its size from its low point in the midst of the Great Depression—hardly the hallmark of a troubled sector bound to unqualified failure (see table 8).

[10] Scranton, *Endless Novelty,* 326.
[11] Ibid., 244.

TABLE 8
Jewelry Firms in Rhode Island

Year	Firms	Employees	Employee/Firm
1927	188	9,272	49.3
1935	141	7,180	50.9
1947	477	17,463	36.6
1963	557	14,900	26.7
1972	469	15,100	32.2
1987	545	16,000	29.3

Source: U.S. Bureau of Census, Censuses of Manufactures.

Rather than seeing the jewelry industry as a self-contained system with its own technological and economic logic, it is fruitful to set its development in the larger context of Providence's changing political economy. Two major structural trends informed the coexistence of growth and self-perceived crisis after World War I: the collapse of the textile industry, and the rise of immigrant (and to an extent ethnic) entrepreneurship. These trends coincided with the radical restructuring of local politics and the growth of an urban-based political machine that empowered previously disenfranchised groups of first- and second-generation immigrants, colliding with the development of increasingly active regulatory bodies.

Dominated by relatively large corporations whose scope extended throughout the country and beyond, in the early 1920s the cotton industry began to relocate to the South. This process, compounded by the proliferation of locally grown southern companies, constituted the first instance of deindustrialization in Rhode Island history. Accelerated by the depression after 1929, the migration of the textile industry to the southern states led to the loss of some seventeen thousand manufacturing jobs statewide between 1919 and 1939. Over the same period, approximately fifteen thousand more jobs were lost in the other industrial sectors, with the only exception of the jewelry industry, whose official employment—after declining in the early 1930s—reverted to its previous level of approximately twelve thousand by

1939.[12] This massive process of deindustrialization led to the creation of an army of underemployed and unemployed workers. Since by World War I Rhode Island had one of the largest female employment rates in the country and the textile industry was the largest employer of women in the state, deindustrialization and the depression meant that thousands of previously employed women had to look for alternative sources of support for themselves and their families.

As this occupational crisis unfolded, the ethnic makeup of the jewelry industry changed radically. The 1895 state census reported that 83 percent of the jewelry workers were born either in the United States or in England. Already in 1915, according to one local source, almost one-fourth of jewelry workers were of Italian origin and 9 percent were eastern European Jews. Soon enough, this kind of ethnic specialization crossed the blurred boundary between wage work and small-scale entrepreneurship. The main employers' organization, the New England Manufacturing Jewelers' Association (NEMJA), had been founded in 1879 after a baseball match between Providence manufacturers and New York City wholesalers, and it long remained an example of the hierarchical and secretive way in which things were run in Providence. The association functioned mostly as a venue where the relatively homogenous elite of Yankee industrialists could socialize and network in a relaxed and informal atmosphere. At the turn of the century only forty-nine of the more than two hundred companies even bothered to apply for formal membership.[13] Even though NEMJA's size and scope expanded in the first two decades of the twentieth century, the leadership of the association remained in the hands of a tightly knit network of established manufacturing families of Anglo-Saxon stock.

In the meantime, at the periphery of this old boys' club, different kinds of networks developed in the city's ethnic neighborhoods—networks that proved crucial to the promotion of their members' social mobility. Beginning in the 1920s, a strong tie developed between the Italian community and jewelry work, with an increasing presence of Italian-American entrepreneurs.[14] Seventeen of the twenty-six manufacturers mentioned in Ubaldo Pesaturo's 1936 list of prominent Ital-

---

[12] Data from Kurt Meyer, *Economic Development and Population Growth in Rhode Island* (Providence, 1953).

[13] For a history of the association, see http://www.mjsainc.com/about/centennial/timeline.php, accessed on 29 January 2006.

[14] On the early history of the Providence Italian-American community, see "The Italian Colony," *Providence Board of Trade Journal*, April 1910, 152–61. See also Judith Smith,

ians of Rhode Island were involved in the jewelry business.[15] The physical makeup of the district itself was reshaped in the 1930s and 1940s by the increasing Italian presence. Until the early 1920s, Providence jewelry firms clustered in a well-defined area south of City Hall. After that date, an increasing number of jewelry establishments migrated to Federal Hill, the Italian neighborhood west of the downtown area. Streets such as Federal and Atwells became the site of a multitude of specialized jewelry businesses of all sizes.[16] Relatively large establishments advertising the entrepreneurial success of their founders coexisted with undocumented sweatshops working only for a few months a year.

The career of Vincent Sorrentino, "a poor Italian immigrant who went on to found the world's largest ring manufacturing company," highlights the close relationships between social, political, and economic achievement in the Italian-American community.[17] Born near Naples in 1891, Vincent came to Providence in 1906. After working as an apprentice for a plumber, he switched to jewelry, married into a Jewish family, and in 1912 opened up his business, Uncas Company, in the heart of Federal Hill. The next twenty years proved to be extremely profitable. Economic success went hand in hand with his political involvement with the Republican Party, the local Masonic lodge, and a variety of charitable organizations. In the early 1930s Vincent also became the president of the Board of Directors of the Columbus National Bank, the main financial institution of the state's Italian-American community. In 1939, Governor William Vanderbilt rewarded his profitable connections with the directorship of the Department of Social Welfare. Sorrentino's appointment, however, outraged the local Democrats, and he had to resign two years later. After World War II he kept a lower profile, concentrating on the management of his rapidly

Family Connections: A History of Italian and Jewish Lives in Providence, Rhode Island, 1900–1940 (Albany, 1985).

[15] Umberto Pesaturo, *Italo-Americans of Rhode Island: Their Contributions and Achievements* (Providence, 1936).

[16] A survey carried out in 1936 reported that 91 percent of the Rhode Island jewelry plants and 90 percent of the workers were located within a 1.5-mile range south and west of Providence's City Hall. State of Rhode Island. Department of Public Health, *A Survey of Industrial Hygiene Conditions in the Jewelry Industry of Rhode Island* (Providence, 1938), 9–10.

[17] "Vincent Sorrentino Dies; Lived American Dream," *Providence Journal*, 4 February 1976, B2. See also Pesaturo, *Italo-Americans of Rhode Island*, 138–40.

growing company. Nonetheless, he remained a highly respected political and economic patron for the Italian-American community throughout his life. His position as a jewelry manufacturer, a banker, and a well-connected politician enabled Sorrentino (and other local "bosses" like him) to distribute favors and opportunities.

Sorrentino's multiple memberships and affiliations were far from uncommon in the ethnic enclaves of Providence. Italian immigrants forged extensive networks of associations in Rhode Island. Following a pattern similar to other ethnic groups in industrial America, the Italians of Providence established mutual aid societies (*società di mutuo soccorso*) devoted to providing their members with sick and death benefits, in addition to constituting the backbone of neighborhood social life. In the first two decades of the twentieth century, membership in many of these associations was restricted to *paesani*, immigrants from a specific locality in the Old Country bound to shared dialects and traditions, but in the course of the 1920s—especially after the establishment of immigration quotas in 1924—such restrictions were lifted in an attempt to stem incipient decline. At the height of their success in the late 1910s, Providence boasted one hundred Italian societies with several thousand members; their names celebrated Verdi and Rossini as well as Garibaldi and Carlo Marx.[18] The ability of these southern Italians to promote such a vibrant associational life in North America highlights the historical and methodological limitations of Putnam's contrast between northern and southern Italy. If social capital is to be measured in terms of the readiness to participate in voluntary associations, southern Italians had social capital to spare. The norms of reciprocity and the practices of mutual help nurtured by these associational networks proved crucial to the social and economic promotion of some of their members. But, as we will see, they also exerted kinds of social control that combined loyalty and coercion, thereby enforcing inequalities as well as participation.

The crisis in membership that most mutual aid societies experienced after the mid-1920s was not only related to the decline in the numbers of new immigrants. Equally important was the restructuring of local politics. In 1928, property qualifications were dropped for the election of city councilors, enabling poor immigrants to participate more actively in the institutionalized political life of the city. Together with the election of Theodore Francis Green as the first Democratic governor of

---

[18] See Smith, *Family Connections*, 4.

the state in 1934 and his takeover of the state senate in 1935 (the so-called Green coup), the 1928 extension of the suffrage led to the end of the long-standing rural-based Republican machine and its replacement with an urban-controlled system dominated by the Democratic Party and destined to survive almost unchanged into the 1970s.[19] The Italians were not the group that benefited most from these changes: thanks to their higher levels of political mobilization and economic clout, the Irish came to dominate the new machine. All Providence mayors from 1907 to 1974 were of Irish descent, as was the majority of the city council members.[20] The competition between Irish and Italians, the two largest ethnic groups in Providence, for political posts translated into fierce competition between Democrats and Republicans for the votes of the Italian community, which remained heavily but never overwhelmingly Democratic and proved willing to support charismatic Republican candidates of Italian descent (most famously with the election of Cianci, a Republican, as the first Italian-American mayor of Providence in 1974). Though struck by ongoing scandals and investigations, the Providence political machine proved to be extremely resilient, leading to the creation of vertical ties of patronage in which favors were exchanged for protection. These ties informed the ways in which the New Deal legislation would be applied at the local level in the wake of the Great Depression, both channeling the resources provided by the public authorities and hindering the regulatory zeal of the most ambitious of their representatives.

The jewelry industry represents an ideal vantage point from which to appreciate the interaction among these different processes: the beginning of deindustrialization and the consequences of the Great Depression, especially on women's employment conditions; the rise of economic and political entrepreneurship among the city's ethnic groups, with the concomitant increase in informal practices; and the simultaneous development of a city-based political machine and of an increasingly interventionist state. Due to its embeddedness in local society and its ability to blur distinctions and boundaries that the reformers held sacred, jewelry work rapidly became a terrain of political con-

[19] See Richard Gabriel, *The Political Machine of Rhode Island* (Kingston, R.I., 1970).

[20] Richard Gabriel, *Ethnic Voting in Primary Elections: The Irish and Italians of Providence, Rhode Island* (Kingston, R.I., 1969). See also Elmer Cornwell, "Party Absorption of Ethnic Groups: The Case of Providence, Rhode Island," *Social Forces* 38 (March 1960): 205–10.

frontation between different segments of society and the very symbol of an intractable local political economy.

The depression reduced employment in the jewelry industry by 40 percent between 1929 and 1933, and the smaller firms were disproportionately penalized by the simultaneous collapse of demand and credit. Such a drastic selection constituted an unprecedented opportunity for the local manufacturing elite to restructure the industry and impose a workable level of order and predictability. This opportunity seemed to materialize in 1933, when President Roosevelt created the National Recovery Administration (NRA), which called for the drafting of fair competition codes for each economic sector in the country, regulating hours of work, setting wage rates, and allowing the fixing of prices. In the case of low-grade jewelry, the task fell to the NEJMA, which responded enthusiastically. Edward Otis, the secretary of the association, convened its members and set up the Council for Jewelry and Allied Industries, a body in charge of policing all jewelry establishments in the Providence area. Among other provisions, the code called for an average work week of forty hours (allowing companies to demand forty-eight hours of their employees during rush periods), imposed a minimum wage of 32.5 cents an hour, and banned homework for all but specific categories of disabled workers.[21] Although NEJMA had grown considerably since the beginning of the century, it still only represented the more "respectable" portion of the industry, and it excluded the army of jobbers and cottage workers who populated the city's back alleys. These small-time entrepreneurs were useful to the more established companies in periods of expansion, but in the early 1930s they represented a liability and a source of embarrassment. The suspicion arose that the manufacturing elite could manipulate the NRA code to weather the crisis by sustaining profits and prices, with only marginal benefits in terms of employment.

In Providence, the debate over the NRA explicitly articulated the contradictions between small-scale capitalism—viewed by many as a form of economic democracy—and the regulation of civil society by the state—viewed as necessary to the protection of the polity in the name of the common good. In a correspondence carried out in 1935, Zacharias Chafee, Providence-born professor of law at Harvard, expressed his concerns with regulation to Lewis Walling, the young di-

---

[21] State of Rhode Island, Department of Labor, *Annual Report for the Year 1935* (Providence, 1936), 115.

rector of the newly established Rhode Island Department of Labor. Chafee's objections to the NRA fell in two categories. First, he viewed the NRA as an example of government by appointed boards, rather than by elected officials, and therefore as an initiative incompatible with the American democratic tradition. Second, the NRA codes threatened to favor more powerful and better-connected companies to the detriment of the individual entrepreneur—another pillar of American society: "Regulations make against flexibility in production and are particularly hard upon 'little' people who must act quickly to serve their customers or they will lose their businesses."

To Chafee's second objection, Walling replied that successful regulation must strike a delicate balance between the protection of competition and techno-economic imperatives: "We still want to give enough reward to the small fellow so that he can give lusty competition to the big fellow and keep the latter on his toes, but we must recognize that many of the difficulties which the little fellow now confronts are the result of the economic tendency of the times, which seems to favor concentration of industry."[22] As to the first objection, Walling argued that formal regulation had primarily a pedagogic and temporary function. In a polity fully versed in the principles of fairness and aware of the common interest, informal relations would suffice to guarantee stability and prosperity: "It does seem to me that public opinion is the ultimate sanction, but for the immediate need we have to rely on some kind of more stringent law enforcement to act more quickly in the social interest."[23] Especially in Providence, where an extensive political machine was taking hold, local civil society could not be trusted to set its own standards through the democratic process. Only a few weeks after this exchange, the U.S. Supreme Court declared the NRA unconstitutional on the basis of an argument similar to Chafee's: the codes unduly extended the powers of the executive in fields whose jurisdiction should be reserved to elected legislative bodies.

The gender dimension of this debate should not be overlooked. The "little fellow" on whom Chafee and Walling focused their intellectual energy was above all the recent male immigrant who struggled to negotiate the rights and duties of American citizenship in an increasingly challenging environment. In the face of mounting economic difficul-

[22] Archive of the Rhode Island Historical Society, Lewis M. Walling Papers, box 7, folder Correspondence 1935, letter dated 11 April 1935.
[23] Ibid.

ties, the pedagogic function of state intervention became a central element of a more general process of assimilation of disparate ethnic groups into a more orderly polity. After the NRA was declared unconstitutional, the Providence reformers shifted their attention from the construction of male citizenship through monitored self-regulation to the protection of women and children, viewed as the main victims both of the economic crisis and of an unscrupulous civil society. Margaret Ackroyd, one of leaders of the Division of Women and Children at the Rhode Island Department of Labor and longtime activist, looked back in 1953 to the pioneering initiatives of the 1930s. According to her, protective laws were "based upon the biological function of women and their responsibility as homemakers and wage earners. They are not only for the protection of the women themselves but for the health and welfare of the national population. It is well established that women workers, as a class, are more susceptible to exploitation than men."[24] Women's vulnerability called for a concerted effort of protection, based above all on the establishment of minimum wage levels and on the prohibition of industrial homework.

In the late 1930s, as most industries kept losing jobs, jewelry began to show signs of recovery. Undoubtedly, the rebound was connected to the increasing availability of low-wage labor. As alternatives dwindled, many women took up jewelry work—in the shops, at home, or often both. Therefore, the jewelry industry became the main testing ground for the Rhode Island reformers. In August 1937, jewelry making became the first industry in the state to be subjected to a mandatory minimum-wage order. This measure only affected women and minors, who made up between 50 and 60 percent of the workers. Given the wide wage differential between men and women (the median hourly wage was 47.50 cents for the former and 33 cents for the latter), the order had the potential to radically change the local labor market.

The experimental nature of the minimum-wage order for the jewelry industry exposed many of the assumptions shared by the reformers, and set a precedent for later interventions. The board organized by the Department of Labor to discuss the details of the act included economists, union representatives, and the leading representatives of the

---

[24] Archive of the Rhode Island Historical Society, Margaret Ackroyd Papers, folder Work-Related Papers, speech delivered to the American Association of American Women in Minneapolis on 24 June 1953.

manufacturers' association.[25] The debate took place on the basis of a detailed survey of the industry carried out a year before and covering a large sample of the more than two hundred firms in the state.[26] Almost immediately the discussion focused on the goals and meanings of a protective minimum wage for women: did such a wage have to be a living wage as well? The answer to this question ensured that the new standard would fail to promote a radical transformation of the industry.

The union representative proposed at first a minimum pay of 40 cents an hour, calculated as the lowest possible wage for an *independent* woman to live on. But this did not reflect the actual conditions of the majority of the female jewelry workers, most of whom fell in two categories: single women in their late teens or early twenties who worked in factories and still lived with their parents, and married women who linked, polished, and packaged jewelry at home.[27] The notion that a minimum wage for women should be based on their potential status as breadwinners was never taken seriously. Moreover, the extreme seasonal swings typical of the jewelry market made the prospect of providing all workers with a living wage all year round particularly unpalatable to the employers on the panel.[28] On account of their interpretation of the industry's demographic and economic structure, the manufacturers started the bargaining process by proposing a 20-cent limit. The final compromise was 30 cents, two and a half cents lower than the level set up by the NRA four years earlier. But since one-third of the jewelry workers were paid less than 30 cents an hour in 1936, the new standard was hailed as a major step in the right direc-

[25] Archive of the Rhode Island Historical Society, Lewis M. Walling Papers, box 7, folder Minimum Wage Board, Jewelry industry, Meetings.

[26] State of Rhode Island, Department of Labor, *Survey of Hours, Wages, and Other Conditions of Employment in the Jewelry Industry in the State of Rhode Island* (Providence, 1936).

[27] This was a long-standing trait of the industry. In 1922, 84 percent of the women working in the jewelry industry were single, and 89 percent were living with relatives rather than boarding. See U.S. Department of Labor, Women's Bureau, *Women in Rhode Island Industry* (Washington, D.C., 1922), 68. In 1930, the percentage of single women in the industry was 78 percent, as opposed to 66 percent in all manufacturing industries combined. Moreover, 41.5 percent of the women workers were younger than twenty, as opposed to 19.2 percent of the men. See Providence Community Center, *Preliminary Report*.

[28] Employment fluctuated widely over the year. In the late 1930s, employment levels in December were approximately one-third higher than in April. As expected, the difference was highly gendered. Male employment was only 20 percent higher in December than in April. By contrast, female employment was almost 40 percent higher. These data, moreover, take only official employment into account.

tion. Moreover, the Rhode Island standard exceeded by 5 cents (or 16.7 percent) the minimum wage established in 1938 at the federal level by the Fair Labor Standard Act, irrespective of gender.

The Department of Labor strongly argued that the minimum-wage order could be enforced only if the labor practices of the industry changed radically. In particular, homework had to be eradicated. Industrial homework had been outlawed by the NRA code, but immediately after its repeal in 1935 the state Department of Labor lamented, "There is abundant evidence that home work is rapidly returning to Rhode Island industry."[29] In fact, there was abundant evidence that the NRA code had hardly been applied in the first place. In the next few years it became apparent that the struggle against homework was the most difficult part of the reform, since the boundaries between homework and small-scale entrepreneurship, as well as between households and local communities, were ill defined at best. The state passed a Homework Law in 1936, even before the enactment of the minimum-wage standard, banning the practice for all but a few categories of workers. Exceptions had to be evaluated case by case, and employers found it increasingly hard to obtain a license after 1936. In 1938, for example, the Department of Labor allowed the employment of only fifty-six home workers. In its essence, this measure was confirmed by the 1938 Fair Labor Standards Act.

Because of its embeddedness in local society, homework was experienced and interpreted in a wide variety of ways. The reformers saw it as a retrograde and exploitative practice that violated the separation of the private and public spheres, and as a major threat to normative family relations (above all the tie between mothers and children). In 1935 the Women's Bureau of the U.S. Department of Labor carried out a survey of homework nationwide and chose to open the publication of its results with a vignette depicting an infant's dress menacingly looming over the skyline of a modern city. In the foreground slum dwellers were sketched busy at needlework, oblivious to their children, depicted as they roamed the filthy streets in the company of chickens. The caption read: "In the shadow of beautiful buildings the industrial home workers embroider lovely infants' garments in miserable homes."[30] Homework not only provided extremely low wages; it

---

[29] Rhode Island Department of Labor, *Annual Report 1935*, 115.

[30] U.S. Department of Labor, Women's Bureau, *The Commercialization of the Home through Industrial Home Work* (Washington, D.C., 1935).

also prevented poor women from fulfilling their maternal duties. Even worse, the image suggested, was the fact that poor women's neglect of their children allowed richer women to buy their kids lovely and cheap clothes. In other words, homework disrupted the natural unity of womanhood. The 1936 Rhode Island law mandated that the few officially recognized home workers receive the same wages as their colleagues in the shops. But it was clear that the reformers' goal was not the improvement of the home workers' conditions but rather the complete elimination of homework. As Ackroyd put it, women's responsibilities included homemaking and wage work—the former falling outside of public regulation and the latter fully open to the monitoring gaze of state officials. There was no place for homework in this scheme.

Organized labor held similar positions, even though in this case the main problem with homework was the blurring of the distinction between employer and employee. In the late 1930s, the International Jewelry Union, founded in 1916, organized only a handful of companies and less than 5 percent of the workers. During the public hearing that led up to the minimum wage order, Samuel Beardsley, the union representative, stressed the seriousness of the challenges that the growing informal economy could raise for organized labor: "There is no other trade in the U.S. cursed by home work as the jewelry trade. . . . Everyone [sic] of our strikers is potentially a manager the minute a strike is declared, and instead of picketing the shops, the homes should have to be picketed."[31] In other words, homework not only undermined class unity by replacing solidarity with cutthroat competition for ever-lower wages; it also encouraged the creation of a hybrid class of economic agents who combined wage work with self- and family employment. It is worth noting that organized labor interpreted industrial homework in no less gendered terms than state officials, but it focused its attention on male workers—its natural constituency. In this context, homework was a synonym of male self-exploitation as much as a practice that victimized women and children.

Manufacturers showed a more conflicted attitude towards homework. On the one hand, they actively participated in the drafting of the 1936 law and never tired of depicting homework as one of the main problems that plagued the jewelry industry. Homework was tantamount to unfair competition, which drove down prices and quality,

[31] Archive of the Rhode Island Historical Society, Lewis M. Walling Papers, box 7, folder Minimum Wage Law, Public Hearing, 25 January 1937, 38–39.

spelling ruin for the entire sector. It was necessary to ban homework in order to draw a clear boundary between the well-established and progressive majority of the companies in the district and the unscrupulous small-time bosses who took advantage of cheap labor and were on a constant hunt for a quick buck. Here was the main obstacle to healthy cooperation among producers. On the other hand, established manufacturers relied heavily on the contractor system, through which they entrusted jobbers and small-scale entrepreneurs with specific phases of the manufacturing process. If homework and the disrespect of labor standards led to lower costs, the savings were enjoyed by the larger concerns as much as by the much maligned intermediaries. As we will see, regulation drives made the activities of these intermediaries all the more precious to the manufacturers, who used them to shield themselves from prosecution. It would be inaccurate to argue that the industrialists put on a facade of compliance and cooperation with the authorities to hide their real interests. Homework and the informal economy in general represented both a genuine threat and an irresistible opportunity. Caught in this quandary, the larger companies simultaneously supported and hindered the public authorities' regulation drives.

Missing from these debates were the perspectives of the home workers themselves. The evidence suggests that their attitude towards the practice was no less conflicted than that of the manufacturers. On the eve of the regulatory drive of 1936–38, the Department of Labor became the addressee of an increasing number of usually anonymous exposés. The language of these letters and their demands show how deeply supported the regulatory drive was among sections of the local working class. A typical letter, received by the Department in the fall of 1936 (that is, during the peak season) read:

> It has been brought to my attention that [names omitted] have been working their girls outrageously. For the past two months they have worked between 58 and 62 hours a week, besides taking work home. The employees that take their work home are also helped by school children. That is a true fact. When any men are sent to investigate they have a set of cards that show no overtime which they show the investigators. The girls very often work in their lunch hours also.[32]

---

[32] State of Rhode Island, Department of Labor, *Results of the Minimum Wage Order in the Jewelry Industry* (Providence, 1938), 2.

However, in this and other letters it was not homework per se that was the object of resentment and outrage but the fact that some employers broke the rules of the game by forcing women to work at home after hours.

Women's and labor historians have collected much evidence showing that homework was a crucial element in the survival strategies of working-class families. In her study of homework in Rhode Island before World War II, Susan Porter Benson synthesizes her findings by arguing, "The homeworkers were involved in a wide variety of reciprocal relationships with one another and with other women, exchanging money and services. . . . Homework fit nicely into the exchange networks among women: it was adaptable to family demands, it was easily integrated into the sharing of services, and it provided cash income which could circulate to those in special need."[33] Judith Smith has shown that jewelry homework was remembered by Providence women as part of complex family rituals. The recollections of a Providence-born Italian woman meshed jewelry homework and family cohesion in a seamless narrative:

> I was about . . . thirteen years old. And then my mother would send me to the Uptown Theatre, in the afternoon, after school, and I would watch the movie. And then, at night, when we would sit down and do the work, I would tell my brothers and sisters about the movie I saw. . . . I would tell them the whole movie. And that kept us busy doing the work. We used to stop and have our milk and cocoa, some pastry; my mother would bake during the day.[34]

Homework was so embedded in neighborhood life that the linking of jewelry could be used to combine work and leisure during visits. Nina Shapiro-Perl tells of a Providence woman who slipped her pliers into her pocket on her way to some neighbors' place for a card game with her husband. When she became tired of playing cards, she took out her pliers and helped her hostess link chains for a while.[35]

The strident contrast between these private recollections and the public discourse around homework exposes the complex and multifac-

[33] Susan Porter Benson, "Women, Work, and the Family Economy: Industrial Homework in Rhode Island in 1934," in Eileen Boris and Cynthia Daniels, eds., *Homework: Historical and Contemporary Perspectives on Paid Labor at Home* (Champaign, 1989), 63.

[34] Smith, *Family Connections*, 56.

[35] Shapiro-Perl, *Labor Process and Class Relations*, 100.

eted character of sociability. As we will see in more detail later, it was not the home workers' isolation that hindered the reform of the Providence jewelry industry but their connectedness in multifunctional networks of relations that straddled the private sphere of family life and the public sphere of neighborhood and political ties. From the perspective of the reformers and organized labor, the "social capital" of these workers enabled their exploitation. From the perspective of the home workers themselves, their social relations allowed them to survive in a challenging economic environment.

In stark contrast with the Italian towns, the notion of family business was never used to describe the activities of Providence households, even though the two contexts shared many characteristics—including a strongly gendered understanding of work and a socially embedded informal economy. The meshing of familial and economic relations, so crucial to the Italian economic boom, was not experienced as a sign of entrepreneurial vitality but as a symptom of disorder and decadence. In Providence, only formal regulation seemed to provide hope.

In the late 1930s, the state Department of Labor projected an image of unqualified optimism. Thomas McMahon, the new director, stressed the progressive dimension of the new regulations in a 1937 radio address: "I request the Department of Labor to enforce the splendid laws enacted by the last legislature, because this should result in driving sweat-shops out of this state; in the protection of women and children; and in the definitive abolition of child labor."[36] This optimism contrasted with the doubts expressed by economist Brown in front of the state congress in January 1937. Brown pointed at the fluidity of social roles as a hindrance to strict regulation. In particular, subcontracting relations were very hard to monitor. Yet without their strict policing, "There would clearly be a means available for the evasion of the minimum-wage order through the growth of the contractor system."[37] This is exactly what happened after World War II.

---

[36] Archive of the Rhode Island Historical Society, Lewis M. Walling Papers, box 7, folder Minimum Wage Board, Jewelry Industry, Notes.

[37] Archive of the Rhode Island Historical Society, Lewis M. Walling Papers, box 7, folder Minimum Wage Law, radio address of February 16, 1937, public hearing 25 January 1937, 23.

EXPANSION OF THE INFORMAL ECONOMY AFTER WORLD WAR II

After 1945 Providence and the rest of New England witnessed the intensification of the social and economic trends that had been set in motion in the 1920s. Deindustrialization continued unabated, now compounded by the relocation of former city dwellers to the suburbs. By the 1950s many blamed Providence's industrial legacy itself for its economic decline. In 1958 demographers Kurt Meyer and Sidney Goldstein saw the entire period since the 1910s as a downward slope for Rhode Island: "After 1910 ... the impetus of economic growth began to slacken markedly because the state continued to depend almost exclusively upon the same long-established industries—textiles, metals and machinery, jewelry, and rubber goods—which had been the backbone of its economy in the nineteenth century."[38]

As we will see, unlike the other sectors mentioned by Meyer and Goldstein, the jewelry industry grew by leaps and bounds in the late 1940s. But the general assessment of the sector's health was far from positive. Already in 1939 the local public authorities depicted the history of Providence jewelry as a descending parable on account of "the gradual but inexorable obsolescence of craft skills, including of course the 'all-around jeweler,' and the steady retreat of gold and silver before alloys and substitutes."[39] Like the rest of manufacturing in the state, the jewelry industry was increasingly feminized. The percentage of women in the official workforce rose from 37 percent in 1909 through 56 percent in 1936 to 61 percent in 1961. If the state economy had been struck by disease, jewelry was its most painful symptom. Drawing on their experiences from the late 1930s, state administrators, manufacturers, and organized labor focused their reforming energies on this industry, trying to devise a cure, which kept eluding them.

The pent-up demand created by the war led to an unprecedented rise in the quantity of orders for jewelry. The number of official firms in the district increased from 167 in October 1945 to 333 a year later. Employment rose by 36 percent over the same period, and it continued for some years afterwards (see table 8). Many observers viewed this increase in start-ups as temporary: "Old established firms have been

---

[38] Meyer and Goldstein, *Migration and Economic Development*, 16.
[39] Providence Community Center, *Preliminary Report*, 2.

held down on production by material allotments and have not been able to meet fully demands for their products. The business they have been unable to handle has fallen to other firms. But the large firms will be back."[40] This prediction was only partially realized. Although some large firms never lost their hold on the local economy, start-up proliferation remained a common trait of the industry in the following years. The contractor system, the archenemy of the reformers, grew in size and scope. Even more than in the prewar period, chains of subcontracting relations created networks of firms and other actors, making surveys and controls extremely difficult. The Department of Labor lamented that, "materials distributed by one manufacturer to be returned to him may pass through the hands of several persons, contractors and sub-contractors, before it [sic] is delivered to the homeworkers who actually perform the work."[41] As labor practices became increasingly fluid, the attitude of the public authorities grew more uncompromising, while many of the leading industrialists became experts at double dealing, on the one hand calling for stricter regulation, and on the other taking advantage of the growing informal economy through the promotion of subcontracting relations. In the long run, by restricting the realm of legitimate practices, the ongoing enforcement drives of the regulators only managed to expand the size of the informal economy.

The Department of Labor did not spare its energies in enforcing the regulations. In 1946 alone, the Division of Women and Children paid almost 1,200 visits to 742 jewelry firms. Despite the extent of this enforcement drive, violations remained widespread. An even more comprehensive antihomework campaign took place in 1948 under the auspices of the state and federal departments of labor, and with the formal support of both the industrialists' association and the union.[42] By this time, it had become apparent that the bureaucratic structure and the routine controls of the state Department of Labor were insufficient to "moralize" the industry. Attitudes towards work and state regulation needed to change, and the local press felt compelled to join the effort.

The *Providence Journal* carried out its own survey in the neighborhoods of Providence where illegal jewelry homework extended its

[40] "State's Jewelry Industry Booms," *Providence Journal*, 24 November 1946, 1.

[41] State of Rhode Island, Department of Labor, *Annual Report for the Year 1948* (Providence, 1948), 55.

[42] "Jewelry Problem to Be Discussed," *Providence Journal*, 29 January 1948, 9.

"shadowy roots," that is, Federal Hill, home to the Italian-American community, Fox Point, populated mostly by Portuguese, and South Providence. In a series of articles, the daily depicted a scenario of pervasive illegality. Homework was largely done at night, and specialized jobbers were the key actors. Typically, the jobber got in touch with the home worker—usually a housewife—in the afternoon with an order he could not complete in his shop. He would tell her to finish the work by the next day at noon. Since the assignment tended to be unrealistically heavy for one person, the housewife would call her relatives and neighbors—including children—for help.

The ties between jobbers and workers, however, were not simply exploitative. Many of the jobbers were small-time bosses well connected to the neighborhoods: "The illicit jobber is mightily careful to whom he farms out homework. The applicant must have 'trustworthy' references. Sometimes the boss will insist that she work in his shop first to make sure that she doesn't have a 'big mouth.' "[43] Although most of these women worked to support the family income, rates could be as low as fifteen cents an hour (though on occasion they surpassed eighty cents an hour). Moreover, some women used to sublet their work to other women at even lower rates. Finally, the jobber took a flat 20 percent out of the weekly wage as a kind of "trust fund" in case the labor inspectors caught him.

The enactment of a new state law closely followed the inspections in 1948. The law greatly increased the Department of Labor's power to control industrial homework and the informal economy in general. The inspectors could investigate, administer oaths, take affidavits and deposition of witnesses, and issue subpoenas for witnesses, records, and other evidence. Fines were raised from one hundred to three hundred dollars for each offense. Finally, the category of homework was extended to the cases in which the person who lived in the dwelling owned the materials he or she processed. This measure was meant to eradicate the so-called tenement shops, in which the home workers bought semifinished jewelry from the jobber, processed it, and then sold the manufactured items back to him. Again, in stark contrast with the Italian context, this practice was viewed as a mere expedient meant to dodge the increasingly strict regulations, rather than as an entrepre-

[43] "Wages in Jewelry-at-Home Trade Run as Low as 15 Cents an Hour," *Providence Journal*, 1 February 1948, 1.

neurial transaction.[44] The new director of the Department of Labor, Joseph Cahir, went as far as to urge anyone aware of people doing homework in the industry to submit names and addresses to the regulators. As we will see, evidence suggests that few people responded, both out of fear of reprisals from the jobbers and out of concern for the workers involved, some of whom were women who worked in shops and distributed homework to their colleagues and neighbors.[45]

The scenario portrayed by the *Providence Journal* certainly captured part of the problem. The evidence shows that some firms were indeed exploitative and engaged in outright illegal practices. Even these actors, however, did not operate in a social vacuum. The case of Leonard Jewelry Company, a mostly seasonal establishment specializing in bead and pearl stringing on a contract basis, clearly illustrates this point. Like many similar firms, labor turnover was extremely high at Leonard. When the inspectors started their investigation in 1948, they discovered that more than 120 workers had been on the firm's payroll in the previous year, although the average employment was 7.5 workers. According to the federal inspectors, most of these workers were "high-school students and young mothers all of whom, motivated by their necessity to supplement the family income, have accepted . . . the sub-standard conditions prevalent in this particular plant."[46] The use of homework and violations of the minimum-wage law were apparent. Despite its marginal status and the "very poor reputation" enjoyed by its proprietor, William Lo Nardo (anglicized as Leonard), the company did most of its work for Arden, one of the oldest and largest companies in town. Arden's power over Leonard made the inspectors argue that "although this and other businesses of this type are independent entities operated by their owners, the power of economic life and death rests with the principal suppliers."[47] Rates could change arbitrarily, and

[44] "New England Jewelry Group Favors Banning of Tenement Shops," *Providence Journal*, 4 April 1948, S, 7. The industrialists supported the law hoping that it "would do away with unfair competition in the trade and work to the betterment of the legitimate manufacturers and therefore of the industry."

[45] Typical was the case of Idelia P., an operator at H&D Jewelry in Pawtucket, who distributed homework to thirty of her colleagues with the collaboration of neighbor William S. The two were fined nine hundred dollars in 1955 for employing home workers and violating the minimum wage law, including wage restitutions. See "Two Fined $900 in Wage Case," *Providence Journal*, 20 October 1955.

[46] National Archives, Northeast Region, RG155, Wage and Hour Division, General Records, Selected Inspection Case Files, box 50720, folder 18081, Leonard Jewelry Co.

[47] Ibid.

if the smaller company refused the offer, another start-up firm was ready to step in. Therefore, the inspectors argued, Arden and similar companies were guilty of cutting prices and of encouraging their contractors to engage in homework and other illegal practices.

These informal ties between entrepreneurs were matched by the informal relations between workers. Despite the anonymous complaints that had initiated the investigation, the inspectors could not convince any of Leonard's suspected home workers to testify in court. When the inspectors showed up at one of the suspected home workers' place, located in Federal Hill, they discovered that she had moved. The neighbors were reluctant to talk about her and disclaimed any knowledge of her whereabouts. This reluctance to collaborate with the authorities was commonplace. As was the case with the relations between firms of unequal power, trust-informed obligations and outright coercion coexisted, even to the point that participants condoned the use of child labor. After receiving an anonymous complaint, state inspectors knocked on the door of Rim Jewelry, a costume jewelry firm employing seventy-six workers. There they discovered that a French-Canadian boy had been working sixty-seven hours a week, nights included, on a piecework basis. One of the proprietors, Pasquale M., allegedly threatened the boy soon after being notified of the investigation. The inspectors reported dryly, "The family took [the boy] out of work because they were afraid that an accident might happen to him."[48] Rim's case was not extreme or uncommon. The forelady at Park Jewelry in Cranston, home to the second-largest Italian-American community in the Providence area, went into hiding in order not to have to talk to the inspectors. Threatened by her boss, she eluded the inspectors for weeks. When they finally reached her, she begged them not to get her "into trouble."[49] Even in this case, however, the inspectors had to face the hostility of most of the employees. Unmoved by the coercive attitude of their boss, some of the workers took advantage of the lax labor practices to supplement their income. One of Rim's workers even took work home behind her boss's back: "I'd take the work that I did at night and report it on my following morning's work by making believe that I'd do work on that rack the first thing in the morning."[50]

---

[48] Ibid., box 44953, folder 1106, Rim Jewelry Co.
[49] Ibid., box 50726, folder 20344, Park Jewelry Co.
[50] Ibid., box 44953, folder 1106, Rim Jewelry Co.

The regulators, however, used a very inclusive notion of homework, which denoted not only the work performed by poor women and children in their homes, but also the activities of skilled male workers starting up their own shops. When the inspectors visited Barklay Company, a firm employing 150 workers and specializing in gold-filled jewelry, they discovered that four regularly hired male solderers had solicited homework from their superintendent. The latter told them that they had to be listed at City Hall as having a regular place of business, which the workers promptly did. There is little doubt that the four viewed the request as an entrepreneurial move: "The homework operations were carried out in the cellar or kitchen of the homes involved. ... The four workers all worked exclusively for the subject company at piecework rates which it fixed. The prices paid for homework enabled them to earn more than for similar work at the plant."[51] The inspectors calculated that the hourly earnings of these skilled workers were as high as $2.50. Since the inspection took place before the enactment of the 1948 law, this particular form of homework could not be prosecuted. But under the new law the solderers would not have qualified as independent firms, since they only worked for one subcontracting agent. Again, the contrast with the Italian context is striking: in Arezzo and Valenza Po the four workers would have been viewed as entrepreneurs rather than as home workers. Despite the regulators' attempts, what constituted an independent (and therefore legitimate) business remained very unclear even after 1948.

The prosecution of these irregularities was a daunting task for the public authorities. First of all, as we have seen, workers, their families, and their neighbors were reluctant to collaborate with the authorities for a variety of reasons, ranging from Mafia-like intimidation through convenience to complicity. Second, a network of somewhat shady connections linked many firms to local politics and offered them a degree of protection. Machine politics was deeply rooted in the Providence neighborhoods, and one of the patrons' prerogatives was the protection of their clients from unwelcome regulation by the state. In February 1949, for example, one of the Department of Labor inspectors received a phone call from Joseph Veneziale, federal attorney in Providence, about the case of the Asprinio brothers, owners of Tesoro Manufacturing, suspected of not paying overtime and employing home workers: "He said that he hoped the case would be given no

---

[51] Ibid., box 44951, folder 720, Barklay Co.

undue publicity because of a close relationship between the boys and the Governor of the State. . . . Mr. Veneziale said that he felt any monetary adjustment would be made upon our request."[52] The charges were eventually dropped.

In some cases, protection seems to have been directly incorporated into the companies' daily management. Several establishments had on their payroll an elected politician who also acted as an "accountant." Typically the inspectors had to deal with these characters as soon as they started their investigation. Some local jobbers were obviously very well connected. During the enforcement drive of 1955 the federal Department of Labor received a phone call from Michael Sepe, an elected representative to the Rhode Island state legislature and an "accountant" for Bell-I-Jewelry, a firm in Federal Hill heavily suspected of illegal labor practices. When Sepe found out that the inspector was not available, he "became very profane and abusive. . . . He said that he would take the floor of the House and denounce all concerned. He said we [the Department of Labor] also had a couple of guys out in Cranston bothering his clients."[53] Given this social and political climate, it is not surprising that few criminal charges were filed against the Providence "sweaters." Usually a fine settled the issue.

A third and most damaging difficulty for the reformers lay in the fact that public opinion, Walling's ultimate sanction, failed to deter illegal behaviors with any degree of consistency. The case of Leonard Jewelry is once again instructive. After being fined in the late 1940s for his practices, "Uncle Bill," as Lo Nardo was known in the Italian neighborhoods, incurred the wrath of the Department of Labor at least two more times in the 1950s. By 1952 the entrepreneur had a much larger clientele than in 1946–48. He had diversified his activities into the stringing and sale of beads and pearls, and he was trying to "induce plants to close their stringing departments and to contract with him to do this work."[54] Far from having been ostracized for his practices, Uncle Bill was even more connected than before to the social and economic life of the neighborhood. The inspectors discovered that an even more far-reaching network of informal relations linked Leonard to Genser, a medium-size firm, and finally to Coro, the largest jewelry firm in town, employing more than two thousand workers. The inspec-

---

[52] Ibid., box 50725, folder 20892, Tesoro Mfg.

[53] Ibid.

[54] Ibid., box 50720, folder 18081, Leonard Jewelry Co.

tors conferred with the management of these larger companies to assess their responsibilities, but their legal tools were quite inadequate to disentangle the web of complicity that tied actors at different levels of the social and economic hierarchy. Once again, Uncle Bill bore the brunt of the public authorities alone. The sanctions, however, did not keep him from carrying out his business as usual. In 1956 he was subjected to yet another series of inspections. At that point, probably a comfortable man, he decided to desist.

This example shows that unfair competition was not the exclusive domain of small start-up companies. But, as the critics of the regulatory system had predicted in the 1930s, the smaller firms came to be disproportionately targeted by investigators. Suspicion grew that the larger companies had the best of both worlds: they were able to cut costs and prices by profiting from the informal economy, and they could lay the blame on their subcontractors whenever the informal economy came under attack. Some regulators were aware of this arguably unfair situation, but they were unwilling or unable to act against the larger firms in the area. The proprietor of Doreve Jewelry, a jobbing shop located in Cranston, violated labor laws routinely. Her company worked mostly for Coro, the largest and most powerful establishment in Providence. The regional attorney, frustrated with the proceedings of the investigation, addressed Doreve's proprietor directly in June 1955: "Coro, Inc. intentionally, regularly, and knowingly benefited from these illegal practices. . . . I do not blame you wholly, as the manufacturer [i.e., Coro] is equally guilty."[55] Yet in this and in many other cases Coro deftly got off the hook. Therefore, in most cases small-scale entrepreneurs could not resort to the Department of Labor for help and protection. Only the informal relations of local politics and neighborhood life could shelter them from the double pressure applied by the regulators and the larger manufacturers.

Regulators faced an uphill battle trying to disentangle the web of ties linking larger and smaller firms—ties that combined coercion and loyalty as well as opportunism and trust. But their relationship with the lower echelons of the local working class were no less problematic. For the poorest citizens of post–World War II Providence, jewelry homework became a way of augmenting the meager income they drew from public relief and unemployment benefits, which were set at a level lower than what an unskilled worker could earn in the lowest-

[55] Ibid., box 50725, folder 20302, Doreve Jewelry Co.

paying job in each industry (for example, thirty dollars a week vis-à-vis thirty-seven dollars in the case of jewelry in the late 1950s). Again, this practice was highly gendered. The high labor turnover predominant in the industry affected a disproportionate number of women, who were almost twice as likely as men to be laid off in the slack season, though they were often hired back by the same companies. In March 1958, 30 percent of the 26,267 workers drawing unemployment benefits in the state were former jewelry workers, and 71 percent of those were women. The *Providence Journal* did not hesitate to argue that the large presence of women on the dole was "the dominant feature of employment security experience in Rhode Island," only to add almost in the same breath that the difference between employment benefits and pay was so small that workers were induced to "loafing at the expense of the jobless insurance system."[56] In the late 1950s, the jewelry industry was repeatedly accused of using the welfare funds of the Department of Employment Security as a safety net in the off-season. In other words, society as a whole had to pay for the erratic course of jewelry production.[57] The local press also claimed that many seasonal workers, especially those who worked at home illegally, managed to remain on some form of welfare all year round.[58]

The *Providence Journal*, ever ready to denote homework as a social evil and a disgrace, showed little sympathy for the home workers themselves. But for many—women as well as men—homework still constituted a long-term strategy for family survival, as it had during the depression. In the course of their 1952 investigation of Leonard's activities, the inspectors knocked on the door of a "crippled" man who lived in a "railroad flat" near downtown Providence. He had a wife and two kids and had been doing jewelry work at home for two years while on public assistance. With the help of his wife, he managed to make fourteen dollars a week stringing beads for Lo Nardo, whom he knew well enough to have borrowed money from. A few days later the inspectors visited a woman who could barely speak English and was, they argued, "too old for factory work." She also had been on and off public assistance and relied on the money her sons

---

[56] The data were collected by the Department of Employment Security. See "Jewelry, Textile Workers Top Jobless List," *Providence Journal, Evening Bulletin*, 26 June 1958, 4.

[57] The cost of this practice was estimated at $500,000 annually. "Jewelry Labor Turnover Costs $500,000 annually," *Providence Journal*, 15 October 1959, 27.

[58] "The Jewelry Industry Should Revise Its Hiring Practices," *Providence Journal*, 12 September 1959, 13.

occasionally sent her. One can only imagine the fear these workers must have felt at the prospect of being deprived of welfare, home-work, or indeed both.

The crisis of the ethnically based mutual aid associations and the rise of public welfare did not lead to the complete demise of neighbor-hood and family ties. Poor workers tried their best to integrate public assistance and other forms of support. Some evidence suggests that in Providence ethnic and neighborhood ties did not die out with subur-banization and the relocation of thousands of families from the old en-claves to newly developed areas in the course of the 1940s and 1950s. Some ethnic communities tended to relocate together. In the 1950s, for example, Federal Hill, where 15,500 people lived in one-third of a square mile in 1950, depopulated at a higher rate than any other sec-tion of the city. Approximately 6,000 people (corresponding to 38.7 per-cent of the population) moved out of the Italian neighborhood between 1950 and 1960. But the vast majority of these families relocated to spe-cific areas in the westernmost part of the city and in the neighboring suburbs of Johnston and Cranston, whose combined population grew by 23.8 percent in the same period.[59] With them moved many jewelry firms and the social context in which the firms were embedded. Never-theless, these population movements tended to leave behind a heavy concentration of older and lower-income people in the inner city. By 1960, 49 percent of the population of Providence could be classified as "lower blue collar," and 22 percent earned less than three thousand dollars a year.[60]

At least until the 1960s, the attitude of organized labor towards these complex and rapidly changing webs of social relations remained am-biguous at best. The highly skilled tool-and-die workers came to be organized by the International Association of Machinists and gained several victories in the late 1940s in terms of both pay and working conditions. They also successfully collaborated with the management of the forty largest companies in the district to regulate apprenticeship programs.[61] Through the 1950s, however, unions in Providence hesi-tated to reach out beyond male skilled workers and the larger firms,

[59] All data from Sidney Goldstein and Kurt Meyer, *Metropolitanization and Population Change in Rhode Island* (Providence, 1962).

[60] Gabriel, *Political Machine*, 10.

[61] See "Pay Boost Given to Jewelry Workers," *Providence Journal*, 16 November 1946, 1; and "Long-Term Plan Designed to Fill R.I. Demand for Jewelry Craftsmen," *Providence Journal*, 20 August 1948, 1.

and in many cases they even failed to represent their members in Providence's few unionized companies with any degree of credibility. As a harbinger of worse things to come, in 1947 the International Jewelry Workers Union—AFL (IJWU) decided to expel all "reds" from its ranks, receiving the congratulations of the Rhode Island Department of Labor.[62] Barely a year later, Josef Morris, the union's president, became one of the promoters of the 1948 regulation drive, and after that he never tired of depicting homework and the informal economy as the archenemies of labor rights.

Some large companies were highly unionized in the late 1940s: a full half of Coro's 2,200 workers were members of the IJWU, for example. But even in large companies the union's behavior repeatedly came under attack from the workers themselves. When a spontaneous wildcat strike broke out at Coro in October 1949, the workers openly criticized the accommodating attitude of Morris and the IJWU leadership towards management strategies. In fact, the union's contract with Coro even included a no-strike clause. Morris immediately tried to convince the strikers to go back to work, and in the face of their refusal he organized a labor-management commission where workers could air their grievances. The strike did end, but the workers' requests went unfulfilled.[63]

Unfortunately for the workers, lack of nerve was the least of the union's problems. In the course of the 1950s suspicion grew of the union's corruption and its connivance with the employers and the Mob. A full-blown scandal broke out in 1959 in the wake of a campaign carried out by the Senate Rackets Investigating Committee. Morris was forced to resign. On his way out of a national conference in Washington, he remarked angrily that "if they want to turn the union over to the Commies, why that's their business."[64] Several locales seceded, and national membership plummeted from twenty-eight thousand to thirteen thousand in less than a year. Even though the scandal hit the New York and New Jersey locales harder than those of southern New England, the union's credibility in Providence was never fully restored.

---

[62] "Jewelry Workers Ban All Reds from Holding Any Union Office," *Providence Journal*, 16 May 1947, 1.

[63] " Coro's Employees in Wildcat Strike Tieup," *Providence Journal*, 8 October 1949, 20; "Powell Will Meet Strikers at Coro," *Providence Journal*, 9 October 1949, 24; "Coro Strike Ends, Grievances Aired," *Providence Journal*, 12 October 1949, 19.

[64] "Jewelry Union Breakup Seen," *Providence Journal*, 4 May 1959, 16. See also "Fusion Ticket Formed by Jewelry Workers," *Providence Journal*, 15 May 1959, 13.

In the face of this kind of incident, jewelry workers continued to view the local informal economy as a venue for protection and social promotion, despite its highly problematic features. The *Providence Journal* repeatedly depicted homework and the contractor system as a "racket" with "shadowy roots" but—unlike the racket that linked union leaders, employers, and mobsters—the practices of the informal economy were at least embedded in the multifunctional networks of family and neighborhood. They might have been "shadowy" from the perspective of the state, but they wore faces familiar to many workers.

In the course of the 1960s, the union tried to recover its lost credibility by waging a rearguard battle against homework and the contractor system, and by organizing membership campaigns in the smaller companies. In 1962, for example, the IJWU reached an agreement with Coro that attempted to patch up the porous boundaries of the firm: it was established that if a foreman or department head (or a member of his family) had a financial interest in a subcontractor company, he would not distribute work to that company in periods when Coro had any regular employees on layoff. Moreover, a committee was formed to devise ways of reducing subcontracting as a whole.[65] But these kinds of agreements demonstrated above all the difficulties the union faced in enforcing the distinction between wage work and self- (or family) employment, as well as in monitoring the boundaries between firm, family, and neighborhood.

When it came to membership drives at smaller companies, the union had to face the overt hostility of the entrepreneurs. Some bosses used both the stick (the threat of unemployment) and the carrot (for example the increase in paid holidays at the height of the drives) to discourage unionization.[66] These kinds of dealings, however, cut both ways: sometimes workers signed the union membership cards only to vote down the union in formal elections, thereby using the threat of unionization to gain minor concessions from their bosses. The union had more success at employing the civil rights legislation to tackle some of the most entrenched practices in the industry, such as the laying off of women during the slack season. For example, despite a recent successful membership drive at Vacuum Plating, a firm with thirty workers,

[65] Archive of the Rhode Island Historical Society, International Jewelry Workers Union, Local 18, box 1, folder Miscellaneous.

[66] This was the case at Union Tool, a firm with forty-nine workers specialized in the production of jewelry findings, in 1964. See ibid., folder Union Tool.

the owner decided to lay off twelve workers in January 1965, at the beginning of the slack season. Eleven of the workers were women and one was an African-American man—all recent union members. The union filed a suit with the National Labor Review Board (NLRB) for antiunion activities and gender and race discrimination. Whereas the women kept a low profile during the case, the man overtly accused his boss during the court hearing. In the meantime, the owner had replaced him with his former aid, an Italian-American man who had just returned from Vietnam with a letter from the Veterans Office recommending his reinstatement. The owner tried to play the patriotic card with the NLRB, but to no avail. He had to hire back the workers and sign a pledge promising that he would no longer use a normal economic slowdown as a reprisal for union activity and as an excuse to engage in discrimination.[67]

Despite these sporadic successes, however, unionization remained very low. As late as 1978, only 16 percent of the more than fifteen thousand jewelry workers in the district were unionized, with a marked concentration in the larger firms and among more skilled workers. By then, the link between "powerlessness and inadequacy" on the one hand and the feminization of the workforce on the other had assumed the status of a self-evident explanation: "Because of the large number of women and minorities working in jewelry shops there are cultural and linguistic differences and problems of home management and child care which tend to make the workers less cohesive."[68] In an interview carried out in 1979 by Nina Shapiro-Perl, a Department of Labor official went as far as to liken the relationship between manufacturers, jobbers, and home workers to pimping.[69]

For the industry leaders it was customary to justify the ever growing role of the informal economy by bemoaning increasing competitive pressures from other areas. In the 1930s and 1940s, the representatives of the Providence manufacturers routinely complained about the unfair competition of substandard companies located in New York City, which struck deals with chain stores and undercut the supposedly more scrupulous producers in Rhode Island.[70] Starting in the mid-

---

[67] Ibid., folder Vacuum Plating.

[68] "Jewelry Workers Hope to Overcome Record of Defeats," *Providence Journal*, 26 February 1978, B5.

[69] Shapiro-Perl, *Labor Process and Class Relations*, 135.

[70] See, for example, "R.I. Jewelers Make Complaint: Declare 'homework' Competition in NY Injures Trade," *Providence Journal*, 6 March 1940, 22.

1950s, Japan and Hong Kong became the prime targets of the manufacturers' complaints. Both industrialists and union leaders waged ongoing campaigns for higher tariff protection from what they called the "alarming cancer" of foreign competition.[71] The explanation they proposed for competitiveness of Japanese products was somewhat ironic. One of the union leaders declared in 1956, "We prohibit homework and child labor in this country, but by allowing imports from countries that exploit workers we are encouraging sub-standard conditions abroad."[72] The other sin committed by the Japanese was plagiarism of styles and design. Frankovich, the secretary of the manufacturers' association, denounced that some branches of the industry had been completely routed by foreign competition. The workers employed by firms making imitation pearls, for example, had dropped from five thousand in 1945 to five hundred in 1954. The quality of Asian products, Frankovich argued, had improved dramatically "by a very simple device—poll-parroting the latest designs of American manufacturers."[73] Minor victories were achieved in protecting some products in specific commercial treaties, but overall the United States began to run a trade deficit in all branches of jewelry both with East Asia and western Europe (including, of course, Italy).

As the Providence jewelry industry lost ground vis-à-vis its foreign competitors, the local authorities grew increasingly more impatient with the social consequences of *local* competition between manufacturers. Under the pressure of a mounting press campaign accusing jewelry companies of taking advantage of the welfare system during the slack season, the jewelry manufacturers attempted to level off the peaks and valleys of their business by urging the wholesalers to place their orders well in advance. After experimenting with occasional fairs, in 1959 the leaders of the manufacturing association set up a semiannual jewelry show for domestic and foreign buyers. According to most manufacturers, this was a long-overdue initiative. The double attack of foreign competition and part of local public opinion made the decision to resort to collective action no longer deferrable. Strict rules regulated access to the show, open only to the wholesalers. But when the show opened in early November 1959, it became painfully clear that many exhibitors were "jumping the gun." In order to beat the competi-

---

[71] "Jewelry Drop Laid to Competition," *Providence Journal*, 10 February 1958, 1.

[72] "Jewelry Union Studies Imports," *Providence Journal*, 6 December 1956, 36.

[73] "Imports Worry Jewelry Plants," *Providence Journal*, 26 November 1956, 1.

tion, some producers held "their own show in advance of the united show. . . . [This was] based on an old philosophy of 'get mine first, and the devil take the hindmost.'"[74] The consequences of these private preshows, attended not only by wholesalers but also by retailers and other manufacturers, were potentially dire. Plagiarism, for example, was a constant temptation. Moreover, preshows gave wholesalers additional leverage in negotiations over prices.[75] The organizers of the show still complained about the same kind of opportunistic behaviors twelve years later: "If you would keep out those who presold, you would keep out 50 percent of the people."[76] The show provided some exposure for small and medium-size companies, who could not afford the commercial infrastructure necessary to sell direct to retailers, but it failed in its original goal—to distribute demand more evenly over the year.

Arguably the only truly celebrated example of successful cooperation among manufacturers effected a similar result: the strengthening of an uneasy pact between the established companies and the more efficient and "reputable" smaller firms in the area. In 1956, the jewelry manufacturers' association established a shipping service that was incorporated in 1962 as a cooperative called the Jewelers' Shipping Association. Member companies of all sizes could achieve economies of scale by pooling their shipping costs, which were cut in half.[77] However important to the survival of smaller firms, these kinds of initiatives did little to change the relationship between the industry and the city. Neither the enforcement drives of the state authorities nor the institutionalized self-regulation of the manufacturing community was able to solve the contradictions of an industry that was both deeply embedded in the social life of the city and thoroughly at odds with its aspirations.

In this chapter I have attempted to reconstruct some of the salient features of Providence's political economy without privileging the perspective of any single actor and without superimposing an overarch-

---

[74] "Jewelry Industry Mavericks Threaten Welfare in Rhode Island," *Evening Bulletin*, 10 November 1959, 17.

[75] "Jewelry Showing Sidestepping Original Goals," *Providence Journal*, 8 November 1959.

[76] "The United Jewelry Show: Despite Complaints, It's Vital to the Industry," *Providence Journal*, 5 December 1971, I16.

[77] Douglas Johnson, "The Rhode Island Jewelry Industry: Perspectives on Development and Reform," Ph.D. diss., Massachusetts Institute of Technology, 1976, 15–16.

ing narrative on a complex historical record. The reason for this methodological choice is first of all empirical: local society rarely—if ever—spoke with a single voice, and no single voice in local society spoke with unchallenged authority. A theoretical argument emerges from this multiplicity of perspectives: if historians are to take seriously the notion that economic action is embedded in social and political relations, attention must be paid not only to the structural context in which economic behaviors unfold but also to the often conflicting meanings that these behaviors assume over time. This realization closes a loop between structure (the constraints facing historical actors), action (the ways in which actors creatively deal with and transform such constraints), and culture (the flexible and multiple ways in which structure and action are interpreted by the actors themselves).

We can begin to apply these insights to a comparison between Providence and the Italian jewelry towns by problematizing the distinction between success and failure. Was the Providence jewelry industry an example of failed economic development, as Scranton and many other commentators have argued? The fact that jewelry making remained the main industry in Providence for much of the twentieth century strongly militates against viewing its history in terms of failure. This industry survived (and adapted to) the changing conditions brought about by deindustrialization, the Great Depression, World War II, and suburban flight. Therefore, it is the industry's flexibility and resilience that demand an explanation, rather than its alleged failure. This resilience has a lot to do with the embeddedness of jewelry making in the social fabric of the city: no single actor or group of actors, for example, had the power to relocate the industry to a different region, and, despite the general assumption that costume jewelry making was a low-skill activity, the location advantages provided by the clustering of firms, workers, institutions, and forms of knowledge were clearly sufficient to firmly root this activity in Providence for almost two centuries. This holds true for the Italian jewelry towns as well: in both contexts networks of heterogeneous actors generated, reproduced, and put to value unique ties of locality.

It would be simplistic to build a comparison between Providence and the Italian towns around the dichotomies of opportunism and trust. As was the case in Italy, trust in Providence assumed multiple forms and meanings: trust could be linked to mutual respect, as was the case with the working-class families who shared the burdens of work and child rearing by doing jewelry homework together; trust could be linked to loyalty, as was the case with the home workers who refrained from turning in their suppliers; trust could be linked to complicity, as was the case with the jobbers who struck deals with the large firms to protect their activities from state regulation; and trust could be linked to political and ethnic affiliations, as was the case with the industry's reliance on the political machine.

There was plenty of "community" and associational life in Providence, and even the general flight to the suburbs did not break social ties overnight. All these ties combined trust and coercion, and they extended from City Hall to the relations between family members. There is no need to resort to techno-economic determinism or to cultural essentialism to explain the striking similarities between the local economies of Rhode Island and northern Italy. In both contexts, the blurring of these dichotomies was the main product of embeddedness. The survival of the jewelry industry relied on multifunctional ties that were simultaneously economic, political, cultural, and even emotional, as was the case between family members and neighbors.

By the same token, the differences between Providence and the Italian jewelry towns were neither narrowly technical and economic nor rooted in unproblematic and fixed cultural attitudes. Rather, these differences were broadly contextual. To begin with, in Providence jewelry making reached its apex in a context of economic crisis and deindustrialization, whereas in the Italian towns it constituted a venue for the modernization of previously rural areas. The Providence jewelry industry expanded by relying on labor expelled from other sectors (above all textiles and machinery), whereas in Italy former sharecroppers and rural laborers willingly left their farms to work in jewelry shops, often aspiring to start their own businesses. Relatively low wages provided a competitive advantage in both contexts, but workers experienced their economic conditions in radically different ways. In Providence jewelry work became increasingly feminized, first of all at a structural level (the percentage of women in the workforce increased from the 1930s onwards), but also in the way the industry was perceived and understood by government officials, union leaders, the local press, and ultimately society at large. The memory of a glorious manufacturing past replete with founding fathers and pioneering figures was constantly contrasted with a present populated by anonymous, disorderly, and strongly gendered exploitation.

A comparison between Providence and Arezzo is quite fitting with respect to the gendering of work. Women also made up the majority of Arezzo's jewelry workers after World War II, and in Arezzo, too, local society perceived this process of feminization as a problem. But in Arezzo a fragile pact among local government, organized labor, and the town's leading company led to the masculinization of the industry through the promotion of small-scale entrepreneurship. Again, this was not only—or even primarily—a structural process. Women remained a numerically important component of Arezzo's jewelry industry. What changed was the political role that working women played in local society: the proliferation of family businesses led to the decreasing visibility and growing "naturalization" of female work. In Providence, by contrast, the blurring of the boundaries between family and work, and between wage work and self-employment, was experienced by the local elites as a retrenchment from a kind of industrial modernity that the city had done so much to define in previous decades and that was now slipping away.

The contrasting attitude towards female and family work in Rhode Island and Italy suggests another theoretical argument about the relationships between sociability and economic action. Relations in civil society do not produce value in isolation from the political and cultural context in which they are embedded. In Providence, a whole legal and bureaucratic apparatus was established to separate the ties of family and locality from economic behavior. From the 1930s onwards, government officials declared a war on the "commercialization of the home." In the Italian towns, by contrast, the notion that family and neighborhood ties could be effectively put to value in an expanding marketplace lay at the very core of the postwar economic miracle, to the point of naturalizing the compenetration of household and work through the construction of problematic myths of origin that connected small-scale industrialization to a reinterpretation of the rural past. Italian labor unions and local governments, strongly influenced by the Catholic and Marxist parties, in many cases promoted (or at least condoned) the proliferation of family businesses. In Providence, by contrast, the traditional factory remained the site of a normative development that proved increasingly elusive. The contractor system, with its intractable mix of "democratic" and coercive practices, was openly encouraged in the Italian towns and (at least formally) opposed in Rhode Island.

These different attitudes toward the informal economy produced contradictions in both contexts, albeit of a different kind. In Providence, a general consensus on the necessity of increasingly strict state regulation had the unwelcome consequence of pushing to the margins of illegality social and economic relations that were crucial to the survival of the most vulnerable members of local society. The paradoxical outcome of this process was the disempowerment of a large section of the working class, who experienced an increasing disconnect between their immediate needs and the vision of an orderly and fair future envisaged by the state. This disconnect was exacerbated by the duplicities of political life in a city where a political machine distributed protection and opportunities, and where union leaders simultaneously railed against the informal economy, accepted kickbacks from the manufacturers, and shared their illegal earnings with the mobsters. In the process, the jewelry industry became something of a residual sector and an activity that took place in the interstices of society, largely carried out by overworked women in their spare time and by people trying to juggle work and welfare. In the mid-1970s, jewelry manufacturers complained about the difficulty of finding workers at a time when the unemployment rate in the city was close to 12 percent.

In the Italian towns, by contrast, informal relations remained at the center of the local political economy, despite erratic attempts to curb widespread illegality. Small-scale companies did not emerge naturally from the life forms of civil society; they were rather cultivated and promoted by a variety of political forces (including the state) both as a response to increasing market opportunities and as a project for modernization. This process empowered an emerging class of actors straddling wage work and self- (and family) employment, but it also led to the entrenchment of new forms of inequality and to a deepening dichotomy between civil society (the so-called "real Italy") and the state (the so-called "official Italy") at the level of political culture and social practice.

The comparison between the Italian jewelry towns and Providence shows the limitations of nation-centered narratives of industrialization and modernization. "America" looks somewhat unusual from the vantage point of Providence's back alleys, even though most of the processes discussed in this chapter (immigration, assimilation, deindustrialization, suburbanization, etc.) constitute the building blocks of familiar narratives. Similarly, the "Italian path to modernity" assumes very different connotations depending on whether we spin our narrative from Milan or from a town like Valenza Po. The main lesson of the microhistorical approach is that choices of scale are anything but neutral. The nation is not simply a collection of localities, and the master narratives of national development do not emerge naturally from syntheses of more localized experiences.

The neglect of this fundamental methodological distinction has marred the interpretations of generations of American social scientists, from Banfield to Putman, interested in Italy and in what the Italian context can teach about social change more generally. Judging from its thriving networks of associations and the embeddedness of its economy, Providence had as much "social capital" as any of the Italian jewelry towns, and it would be easy to interpret some social relations in both contexts in terms of "amoral familism" (Banfield's theoretical claim to fame). But the Italian jewelry towns came to be seen as examples of the burgeoning national narrative of economic development, founded on family businesses and design. By contrast, jewelry work in Providence, in spite of its size, came to be viewed as a marginal activity at odds with American modernity. In both cases, however, success and failure were constructed in the political arena. There are signs that the current crisis of most Italian industrial districts is rapidly spawning new narratives of decline, which might affect towns like Valenza Po and Arezzo as powerfully as they did Providence in the central decades of the last century.

During my interviews I was impressed with my informants' ability to conceive of themselves simultaneously as actors deeply immersed in the lives of their communities and as detached and ironic observers of their social context. Aldo Annaratone, one of my interview partners in Valenza Po, provided a telling example of this attitude. Our conversation touched on the relationships between jewelry manufacturers and the local dealers of precious stones, who traveled back and forth from Paris, Amsterdam, and Antwerp smuggling their merchandise into the country. These traders were prime targets for the tax police. But whenever news spread of an impending enforcement drive, the stone dealers rushed to the homes of their customers (typically small-scale manufacturers) and hid thousands of dollars' worth of stones in their safes. "The person entrusted with the stones suffered even more than the trader who left them there, because the trader trusted him," Annaratone argued. "I say jokingly," he continued, "that this is a reversed Mafia (*mafia alla rovescia*). . . . If someone slips up, he's out; he has to change trade. I met a few people who had to go from goldsmith to ironsmith because of that."

Annaratone's remarks brilliantly capture the complexity of social relations in Valenza Po and the other jewelry towns. He spoke both as an informant and an ethnographer, as a participant and an observer. But what did he mean by "reversed Mafia"? The secretive and informal character of many social relations in Valenza Po, their being bound by a code of honor, might have reminded him of the rituals of organized crime. Also, as with the Mafia, relations in Valenza Po were not symmetrical. The stone dealers kept score of the manufacturers who slipped up and made sure that whoever stepped out of line would be ostracized and punished. But in what sense was this kind of mafia "reversed"? Annaratone's ability to joke with me is in itself part of the answer. He could see these tight and secretive relationships from a distance and smile at them with a stranger. He could step out of the boundaries of his community and put himself in the shoes of the smugglers, the dealers, the manufacturers or even the tax police. He could see these relations through my eyes, "reverse" them, and find the irony in them.

But I would venture that in conjuring up the image of the Mafia, Annaratone was also gesturing towards narratives of development and backwardness with which all Italians are familiar. The irony in his comment stems from his ability to complicate, if not reverse, the usual contrast between northern and southern Italy. He was telling me: "Look, the difference between 'us' and 'them' is not as large as one might think." In his tale, trust is the wage of secrecy and honor. Despite his overtly leftist politics, he seemed to understand, if not condone, behaviors that deprived the larger community of substantial resources in the form of dodged taxes. But then again, life in Valenza Po was not just about tax evasion, and the same relations that allowed revenue to be hidden from the tax police also produced egalitarian consequences, for example by protecting the activities of the small-scale artisans.

I started this project to respond to a series of studies that linked trust and economic development and addressed the northern Italian industrial districts as a positive example (as in Putnam's case) or a negative one (as is the case with Fukuyama's comparative work). Trust seemed to me an ideal concept to bring politics and culture back into the study of economic change, now the preserve of a radically reductionist approach based on rational choice and methodological individualism. Trust was also tightly linked to notions of embeddedness and social capital, which held the potential to cast a bridge between historical analysis and other disciplines, above all sociology and political theory. Finally, I noticed that trust in these theoretical frameworks was connected to the metaphor of the network, an increasingly popular concept that promised to hold the key to the analysis of a wide range of social phenomena.

In the course of my research, however, it became clear to me that the understandings of trust prevalent in the social sciences could not do justice to the complexity of social life in north-central Italy, some of which transpires in Annaratone's remarks. This book has tried to move beyond both a functionalist notion of trust, viewed as an unproblematic substance capable of lubricating economic transactions, and a communitarian understanding of trust, predicated on the more or less automatic reception of shared cultural codes.[1] Instead, I have argued that

---

[1] Throughout this book, I have asked, "What does trust mean?" rather than, "What function does trust serve?" A functionalist approach is what links conceptions of trust

trust in the jewelry towns was a historical process that assumed a variety of meanings for different actors and at different junctures. Enforced
by special-purpose institutions, embedded in the relations of kin and
neighborhood, or expected as the wage of party affiliations, trust was
the product of political deliberation, and therefore it was always provisional and contested.

Conceptualized as the outcome of a political process and as a commitment for the future, trust cannot be divorced from power. The
definition that emerges from the evidence presented in this book is that
trust is an expectation of reciprocity that stems from the collective delimitation of power. Trust makes one party vulnerable to the other party's power to betray, coerce, or exploit. Therefore, the scope of trust
is conceptually and practically defined by the possibility of coercion.
Crucially, this process of delimitation cuts both ways: it bounds the
scope of power within a context or a network, but it can also create the
possibility of exerting power over other contexts and networks. For
example, a tight network of artisans and traders may build institutions
that encourage the forbearance of coercion among them, but the very
trust-based ties thus established may be employed to prevent female
home workers from stepping out of line. At the same time, as the Providence case shows, the relations between the home workers and the
traders who provide them with work might well be infused with a
complex combination of sentiments, including trust, deference, and the
kind of resentment that might be a prelude to resistance. In sum, trust
is one of the ways in which networks police their boundaries and distinguish between insiders and outsiders. This process of policing is collective, in the sense that it is embedded in collectively deliberated institutions. Therefore, methodological individualism is ill-equipped to
make sense of social trust, beyond the postulation of basic mechanisms
of action and reaction.

This understanding of trust recasts the meaning and scope of some
influential social scientific concepts, such as embeddedness, social
capital, and the informal economy. This study illustrates the fruitful-
ness of the notion of embeddedness, viewed as an alternative both to
reductionist rational-choice approaches and to explanations of economic diversity that rely on cultural determinism. Economic action in

---

as different as that of transaction-cost economics and Niklas Luhmann's. For the latter,
see above all his *Trust and Power* (New York, 1979), where he defines trust as a device
that reduces the complexity of the future.

the jewelry towns was embedded in extensive networks of interpersonal relations, which allowed actors to expect a relatively high degree of reciprocity. These networks of social relations also correlated with economic fragmentation. As predicted by Granovetter's thesis, networks of social relations made transactions between firms a possible alternative to vertical integration and hierarchical governance by large-scale corporations.

The evidence presented in this book, however, suggests that this structural understanding of embeddedness must be refined in at least two ways. First, cultural and political relations must be brought into the picture. Social networks should be viewed not as static structures but as historical processes forged in conflicts and negotiations over the distribution of resources and projects for the future. In the Italian jewelry towns, political understandings of the economy, founded primarily on socialist-inspired critiques of unbridled competition, constructed the networks that made up the local economies and connected them to the larger world. But these political cultures rarely offered the unproblematic repertoire of shared meanings often ascribed to them in the literature on the Marshallian industrial districts; these cultures remained contentious constructs and, especially in periods of economic crisis, they fueled conflict at least as much as they defused it.

Second, structural embeddedness needs to come to terms with historical actors' ability to reflect on their own lives and embed economic action in, or disembed it from, other realms of action. In other words, the boundaries of "economic action" are historically constructed and should not be taken for granted. In the jewelry towns economic calculation coexisted with the affective bonds of familial life, the passions of political struggle, and the attachments of neighborhood and (in the case of Providence) ethnic ties. Actors in these towns devised painstaking rules of conduct, subtle institutional arrangements, and rituals of cooperation to map the treacherous territory defined by these overlapping commitments. Some of these devices deliberately blurred the distinction between economic action and other realms. The institutionalization of "family firms" is a case in point. In other instances, detailed rules made sure that actors would not exploit their multiple ties to gain an undue competitive advantage, thereby singling out economic calculation from other modes of action. The institutional devices aimed to discourage plagiarism by preventing certain categories of people from accessing specific spaces and information fall in this category. But these ways of embedding and disembedding economic action and motives were not always successful. Especially in periods of shrinking opportunities, the existence of multiple commitments easily led to incompatible expectations and thus to conflict and crisis. The chain of bankruptcies in Valenza Po before World War I and the vicissitudes of Vicenza's cooperative in the 1900s clearly illustrate these risks. In sum, detailed historical analysis is necessary to map the contingencies and events that lead to different kinds and degrees of embeddedness, as well as to "positive" or "negative" outcomes.

One of the risks associated with the embeddedness thesis, and especially with its structural version, lies in connecting certain kinds of social networks to specific economic and political outcomes. In other words, the notion of embeddedness can degenerate into a form of social determinism. Throughout this book I have employed the concept of social capital to avoid this risk. My understanding of social capital, however, is quite different from that popularized by Robert Putnam and much closer to the original meaning attributed to it by Pierre Bourdieu. Actors in the jewelry towns turned specific social and political relations into "capital," that is, into sources of economic value, through acts of deliberation. In other words, I conceptualize social capital as the property of individuals or networks, as the product of intentional acts, and therefore as a feature of social relations that does not necessarily lead to harmony and cooperation.

In all the social spaces examined in this book, for example, political affiliations could be used to access credit, materials, skills, and other kinds of resources. Indeed, the social networks that capitalized most effectively on their political affiliations, such as Valenza Po's socialist entrepreneurs at the turn of the twentieth century or the communist workers-turned-subcontractors of Arezzo's large company in the 1960s and 1970s, increased their status and wealth in local society. Nonetheless, social and political ties could also be crucial to the survival of vulnerable actors, as well as to the perpetuation of coercive relations, as was the case with Providence's home workers and the self-exploitation of many family businesses in the Italian jewelry towns. The historical question in this context is not to distinguish towns, regions, or cultures according to the amount of social capital they possess, but to investigate the practices that allow certain groups to "valorize" their relations more effectively than others. In other words, like any other form of capital, social capital is an asset that can be accumulated and protected, and that can be used to gain access to other kinds of resources. Therefore, social capital is often a source of inequality and even of conflict.

If this understanding of social capital is correct, the participatory and egalitarian qualities ascribed to it by Putnam and others, as well as the undeniable differences between the political economies of different parts of Italy, must be due to other kinds of historical processes. The evidence from the jewelry towns suggests that equality and participation were not unintentional consequences of the "life forms" of civil society, for example in the form of voluntary associations, but goals that were deliberately pursued or resisted by different actors and political groups. The sharecroppers' unions of central Italy after World War II, for example, fought for a higher degree of equality and participation. The same can be argued for Vicenza's cooperative movement or for the defenders of civil rights in Rhode Island. Quite often, as soon as members of these groups tried to use the social connections acquired in the political arena to gain economic benefits (that is, when they started acquiring social capital), their participatory and egalitarian élan began to flag. The social order of central Italy's industrial districts, for example, was distinctly less egalitarian and participatory than the world envisaged by the sharecroppers' struggles, although some sharecroppers did indeed turn from peasants into entrepreneurs. In sum, trust, networks, and even norms of cooperation are no substitutes for purposeful social struggle. Under certain circumstances, trust and networks can have highly exclusionary consequences. The Sicilian Mafia is an extreme example of this process, but even the northern Italian districts of small firms were shot through with exclusionary relations, which were sometimes accepted and other times bitterly resisted.

The extent to which actors in the jewelry towns could "valorize" their social relations and accumulate social capital (and thus gain access to and produce a variety of resources) largely depended on the historically grounded connections they entertained with centers of economic and political power, which were usually located outside of their communities. Starting in the 1950s the Italian jewelry towns benefited immensely from their connections to a variety of international actors, who saw these burgeoning centers of production as profitable nodes in an increasingly global network of transactions. The French jewelry *maisons*; the Milanese, German, and American wholesalers; and of course the major Swiss banks all established, for different reasons, ties to specific actors and institutions in Valenza Po, Vicenza, and Arezzo, thereby contributing to the transformation of these towns into economic and stylistic powerhouses. In this book I have showed how contentious the access to these kinds of international relations (or to this kind of social capital) could be at the local level, and that social struggle in these towns largely hinged on how widely the fruits of these connections would be shared. The outcome of these negotiations depended on the contingencies of political struggle among local actors. Indeed, these negotiations greatly contributed to reshaping both the social structures and the political cultures of the Italian jewelry towns.

Another center of power crucial to the valorization of social relations was of course the Italian state. This book has attempted to demonstrate that the extensive informal economies typical of the Italian industrial districts were not the legacy of tradition or backwardness, but rather the outcome of deliberate strategies on the part of both state officials and local actors. In other words, the informal economy was deliberately constructed and nurtured in the political arena. Thus, patronage relations proved crucial to the construction of both the market and the bonds of local society. State officials, both at the local and national levels, established long-lasting ties with traders and producers, who exchanged political consensus for favors and protection from regulation. These exchanges greatly contributed to the production of locality and to the creation of tight networks in which trust, knowledge, and other resources circulated effectively. International traders and suppliers soon realized the potential of these relations in terms of lower costs and social control over the quality of production. These negotiations between local actors, state officials, and international traders explain why a country with western Europe's most stringent restrictions on the importation and exportation of gold became the world leader in the production and trade of gold jewelry.

These strategies of valorization also depended on the particular niche occupied by jewelry work in the narratives of development that constituted these towns' self-understanding. The trajectories followed by the jewelry sectors in each town were "path dependent," in the sense that their histories did not unfold as the unraveling of conditions embedded from the beginning in a resilient social structure or economic rationality. Rather, choices and events shaped the world with which actors had to contend and, at every stage, informed future developments. But jewelry work in these towns was also more broadly "history dependent," in the sense that it was strongly embedded in powerful narratives of change.

In the Italian towns, strategically located actors understood small-scale industrialization, together with the formal and informal institutions that sustained it, as a desirable path to modernity that respected local traditions (however invented) and aspirations (however contentious). After centuries of poverty and relative isolation, and after decades of social conflict and Fascist repression, Valenza Po, Vicenza, and Arezzo found not only economic prosperity but also a fragile collective identity in the manufacturing and selling of gold jewelry. This narrative of progress, shared by the major political parties and endorsed by state officials, hid many stories of persisting conflict and inequality, but it nevertheless contributed to the valorization of local relations by focusing collective efforts and setting goals for the future.

Jewelry work in Providence, by contrast, offers an example of an activity linked to deindustrialization and perceived decline. In spite of striking structural similarities to the Italian industrial districts, including the ability of local actors to embed economic action in multiple relations and institutions, many actors in Providence understood the local jewelry district as a symbol of the city's intractable problems, largely due to the crisis of traditional manufacturing. The perception of jewelry work as a feminized and irreducibly ethnic activity contributed to its relegation to the margins of Providence's political economy and shared identity. Actors in Providence produced and accumulated social capital, too, for example by relying on ethnic, political, and neighborhood ties to gain access to jobs and resources, but they did so in a context of increasing isolation and in stark contrast to the aspirations of state officials and other elite groups, including the larger companies and (at least for a while) the union leaders. This led to something of a self-reinforcing cycle of marginalization and isolation, which made jewelry work simultaneously the largest and least visible industry in town.

The similarities between the Italian jewelry towns and Providence show the limits of viewing Valenza Po, Vicenza, and Arezzo as examples of an essentially Italian (or even north-central Italian) path to modernity. Nevertheless, if any instance of economic change is, as I believe, always also local, in the sense that it is emplaced in specific spaces, embedded in specific social relations, and enacted in specific experiences of temporality, it is equally true that no instance of economic change is understandable outside of its connections to its broader context. Thus, a similar kind of informal economy can have dramatically different consequences in Italy and in the United States, and be positioned in dramatically different ways within narratives of historical change in different national contexts. In other words, the "Italianness" of these experiences does matter, although it should not be essentialized.

If that is the case, what can the jewelry towns tell us about "Italian history" writ large? The history of these towns contributes above all to complicating the usual contrast between northern and southern Italy. This book rejects simplistic arguments about northern prosperity and southern backwardness, especially those based on cultural dispositions such as "amoral familism" or "lack of social capital." Several studies have questioned the alleged "irrationality" of local southern economies.[2] This study carries out a specular operation on the allegedly "rational" northern local economies. Indeed, informality, patronage, and even "corruption" were an integral part of the northern economic miracle. The prosperity achieved by the jewelry towns was due to complex strategies of valorization involving a variety of local and extralocal actors. These strategies were not necessarily "moral" or even democratic, although the presence of combative political networks made sure that the benefits of economic growth would be relatively widely shared. The current crisis affecting many Italian districts of small firms, including the jewelry towns, suggests that the old strategies might no longer be effective in guaranteeing growth within increasingly competitive global scenarios. Again, though, to attribute the current crisis to a loss of community or to social decline would be widely off the mark.

This book also tries to move beyond the usual dichotomies of resistance and co-optation that inform discussions of the relationships between local societies and the nation. Ordinary people in provincial Italy developed strong local identities together with distinctive political economies based on the valorization of locality. These identities were often articulated in universalistic languages of solidarity, especially socialism in the case of the jewelry towns. But these languages were not instances of resistance to state authority and the instrumen-

---

[2] For Calabria, see Marta Petrusewicz, *Latifundium: Moral Economy and Material Life in a European Periphery* (Ann Arbor, 1996). For Palermo and other coastal areas of southern Italy, see Salvatore Lupo, *Il Giardino degli Aranci: Il Mondo degli Agrumi nella Storia del Mezzogiorno* (Venice, 1990). For an insightful review of recent studies on the Italian south, see John Davis, "Casting Off the 'Southern Problem,' or the Peculiarities of the South Reconsidered," in Jane Schneider, ed., *Italy's "Southern Question": Orientalism in One Country* (Oxford, 1998), 205–24.

tality of the market; rather, local political cultures and identities negotiated the meanings of the nation and the market, which were themselves strongly implicated in the construction of locality. This interactive process was not devoid of conflicts and contradictions, especially when it produced inequalities that could be naturalized as features of community and tradition, as was the case with gendered divisions of labor or the opportunities available to recent immigrants. But the mutual construction of locality, state power, and the market went a long way towards legitimizing capitalism and the nation in large portions of central and northern Italy. These processes of legitimization were (and are) extremely vulnerable. Obviously, a state that condones tax evasion as a strategy for development and political consensus builds its power on rather shaky ground. Likewise, local societies that increasingly rely on economic prosperity for their identities and cohesion make themselves vulnerable to decisions made at faraway nodes within interconnected global networks over which they have little or no control.

But for all their distinctiveness and local "color," the Italian jewelry towns were far from unique in their attempts to reconcile capitalist change, social cohesion, and political legitimacy. This book refuses to treat Italy as an exception to models of liberal modernity. Rather, I have tried to show that these Italian experiences offer the opportunity to critically assess the usefulness of those models themselves. The construction of Italian modernity after World War II represents a distinctive (but also highly revealing) example of the necessity to move from the dichotomies of normative liberal thought to the subtler complexities of new interpretative horizons. Over the last half century Italy has both benefited and suffered from the blurring of the boundaries between economic, social, and political relations, as well as from the intertwining of the public and private spheres. The economic boom of the 1950s and 1960s—much like the recent political crisis that led to the ascent of Berlusconi—should be viewed as paradigmatic examples of the difficulties of reconciling economic prosperity, social cohesion, and political legitimacy. An impassioned historical look at the political economy of these areas shows that community and trust never ceased to be highly problematic constructs in Italy's putatively civic-minded industrial districts of small firms.

Dispassionate historical analysis, however, need not lead to political cynicism. I must refrain from discussing whether capitalism (even the small-scale and community-based capitalism of provincial northern

Italy) can reconcile the contradictions between economic power and political legitimacy. What is clear is that northern Italy's local societies have not solved such contradictions. The mobilization of social and political networks—the core of the social capital approach that makes analytical and historical sense—has been crucial to the construction of the Italian economy, but the establishment of a truly just and democratic polity remains as elusive as ever.

Index